THE RETU
GEOPOLITICS I

C000066498

The end of the Cold War demonstrated the historical possibility of peaceful change and seemingly showed the superiority of non-realist approaches in International Relations. Yet in the post-Cold War period many European countries have experienced a resurgence of a distinctively realist tradition: geopolitics. Geopolitics is an approach which emphasizes the relationship between politics and power on the one hand; and territory, location and environment on the other. This comparative study shows how the revival of geopolitics came not despite, but because of, the end of the Cold War. Disoriented in their self-understandings and conception of external roles by the events of 1989, many European foreign policy actors used the determinism of geopolitical thought to find their place in world politics quickly. The book develops a constructivist methodology to study causal mechanisms, and its comparative approach allows for a broad assessment of some of the fundamental dynamics of European security.

STEFANO GUZZINI is Senior Researcher at the Danish Institute for International Studies, Copenhagen and Professor of Government at Uppsala University, Sweden.

CAMBRIDGE STUDIES IN INTERNATIONAL RELATIONS: 124

THE RETURN OF GEOPOLITICS IN EUROPE?

Cambridge Studies in International Relations is a joint initiative of Cambridge University Press and the British International Studies Association (BISA). The series will include a wide range of material, from undergraduate textbooks and surveys to research-based monographs and collaborative volumes. The aim of the series is to publish the best new scholarship in International Studies from Europe, North America and the rest of the world.

CAMBRIDGE STUDIES IN INTERNATIONAL RELATIONS

Series list continues after index

THE RETURN OF GEOPOLITICS IN EUROPE?

Social Mechanisms and Foreign Policy Identity Crises

Edited by

STEFANO GUZZINI

CAMBRIDGE
UNIVERSITY PRESS

CAMBRIDGE UNIVERSITY PRESS
Cambridge, New York, Melbourne, Madrid, Cape Town,
Singapore, São Paulo, Delhi, Mexico City

Cambridge University Press
The Edinburgh Building, Cambridge CB2 8RU, UK

Published in the United States of America by Cambridge University Press, New York

www.cambridge.org
Information on this title: www.cambridge.org/9781107676503

© Cambridge University Press 2012

First published 2012
First paperback edition 2013

A catalogue record for this publication is available from the British Library

Library of Congress Cataloguing in Publication data
The return of geopolitics in Europe? Social mechanisms and foreign policy identity
crises / edited by Stefano Guzzini.
pages cm. – (Cambridge studies in international relations ; 124)
Includes bibliographical references and index.
ISBN 978-1-107-02734-3
1. Europe–Foreign relations–1989– 2. Geopolitics–Europe–History–20th
century. 3. Geopolitics–Europe–History–21st century. I. Guzzini, Stefano.
JZ1570.R48 2013
327.4–dc23
2012018839

ISBN 978-1-107-02734-3 Hardback
ISBN 978-1-107-67650-3 Paperback

CONTENTS

FIGURES AND TABLES

Figures

Tables

CONTRIBUTORS

ALEXANDER ASTROV is Associate Professor in the Department of International Relations and European Studies at the Central European University, Budapest, Hungary.

ANDREAS BEHNKE is Lecturer in Political Theory in the Department of Politics and IR at the University of Reading, UK.

PINAR BILGIN is Associate Professor in the Department of International Relations at Bilkent University in Ankara, Turkey.

ELISABETTA BRIGHI is Teaching Fellow in the Department of Political Science at University College London, UK, and Visiting Lecturer in International Relations at Middlesex University, UK.

PETR DRULÁK is Director of the Institute of International Relations (IIR), Prague, and Associate Professor at Charles University in Prague, Czech Republic.

STEFANO GUZZINI is Senior Researcher at the Danish Institute for International Studies, Copenhagen and Professor of Government at Uppsala University, Sweden.

MERJE KUUS is Associate Professor of Geography at the University of British Columbia in Vancouver, Canada.

NATALIA MOROZOVA is Lecturer in the Faculty of International Relations, Nizhny Novgorod State University, Russia.

FABIO PETITO is Senior Lecturer in International Relations and Director of the Sussex Centre for International Security at the University of Sussex, UK.

ACKNOWLEDGEMENTS

This book has been far too long in the making. Accordingly, from the very start, I need and want to underline how much gratitude I owe to the authors in this volume, who have continued revising their chapters over the years in the light of the evolving research project. They did so even when they could not win any 'brownie points' with a mere book chapter that had no secure publication outlet for much of the time. Having received no major funding, the project could not buy them out of their normal commitments. Luckily, all of them saw their intermediate or related research results published during that process, mainly as journal articles (see the Bibliography for more details).

Having taken so long, the project has incurred many intellectual debts. Its concept paper was presented at the joint ISA–CEEISA conference in Budapest in June 2003, where it received a spirited discussion by Yosef Lapid (thanks again). Country chapters were presented at panels we organised for the ISA convention in Montréal (March 2004), the SGIR conference in The Hague (September 2004), the CEEISA convention in Tartu (June 2006), and the ISA convention in San Francisco (March 2008). Thanks for all the comments and criticisms from the discussants and the audiences at those events.

Two events have been particularly helpful for advancing the project. The project was part of the EU-financed COST Action A24 ('The Evolving Social Construction of Threats'), which paid for a workshop meeting of all the participants on 5–6 June 2006 in Copenhagen at the Danish Institute for International Studies (DIIS). That workshop proved very important, since the first empirical findings, when discussed together, made it possible to reframe the entire project. Then, more personally, I was granted a fellowship at the Hanse Institute for Advanced Studies (HWK) in Delmenhorst, near Bremen, for the academic year 2007–2008. The opportunity to have time off to conduct research in political and critical geography, as well as interpretivist methodology, was fundamental for the present book. The major part of its introductory chapters was written there. My most sincere gratitude to colleagues and staff at the HWK.

Since 2008, I have presented the findings of the general project in lectures at the Hebrew University (Jerusalem) and the universities of St Andrews and Tübingen, as well as at research workshops and seminars at DIIS, Uppsala University, the Instituto de Relações Internacionais (IRI) of the Pontifícia

Universidade Católica do Rio de Janeiro (PUC-Rio), the COST Action A24 final meeting in Brussels (June 2008), the 'Uses of the West' conference organised at SAIS, Bologna (November 2008), and at a PhD workshop at DIIS co-taught with Ned Lebow and Janice Stein on 'Foreign Policy Analysis: Revisiting the Role of Ideas, Psychology and Causality' (2011), which was financed by the Danish Polforsk network. I thank all participants for their insightful comments – which I attempted to address, but was unable to do so in all cases.

Several colleagues and friends have been so kind as to take time off from their own work to read parts, and sometimes all, of my chapters for this volume between late 2008 and 2011. I am sure the following list is not complete, for which I apologise to all those I do not explicitly mention. But I owe at least to try to remember the many over the many years. My thanks go to Emanuel Adler, John Agnew, Marco Antonsich, Eiki Berg, Fredrik Bynander, Simon Dalby, Thomas Diez, Stuart Elden, Carlos Frederico Pereira da Silva Gama, Tine Hanrieder, Jef Huysmans, Piki Ish-Shalom, Peter Katzenstein, Friedrich Kratochwil, Victor Lage, Anna Leander, Ned Lebow, Mikkel Runge Olesen, Nick Onuf, Nick Rengger and PerOla Öberg.

Finally, I wish to thank John Haslam at Cambridge University Press for his support and patience. After the first reports, which asked us to go the extra mile, the referee and revision process took some time, but has been very useful for improving the quality of the book. My thanks go also to Louise Clausen and Njeri Jensen for their assistance at DIIS, Catherine Schwerin for her language editing of the first submission, and John Carville for his thorough editing of my chapters for the final submission (and DIIS for providing financial support for the editing).

Introduction. The argument: geopolitics for fixing the coordinates of foreign policy identity

STEFANO GUZZINI

How is it that, precisely as the Cold War came to an end in a development that demonstrated the historical possibility of peaceful change against all (determinist) odds and seemed to herald the superiority of non-realist approaches in International Relations,[1] many European countries – in both the East and the West – experienced a revival of a distinctively realist tradition, that of geopolitics – a tradition that suddenly dared to say its name?

Most prominent in this context is perhaps the case of Russia, which has witnessed a quite remarkable turnaround. Banned during the Cold War as a mistaken theory, if not ideology, by the Soviet authorities, geopolitics has since acquired an almost dominant place in Russian analysis of world politics.[2] For a while, even a new parliamentarian committee on 'geopolitics' was established in 1995 (lasting until 1999), chaired by Vladimir Zhirinovsky's former right-hand man Aleksey Mitrofanov. Although the actual influence of geopolitical thinking on 'ordinary Russians' is debated,[3] there have been consistent and widespread references back to early twentieth-century geopolitical thought and 'geopolitical necessities', not least by Aleksandr Dugin. The latter is perhaps the best-known representative of this resurgence, both through his *Fundamentals of Geopolitics*, reprinted several times, and through his political activism as party leader, director of a Centre for Geopolitical Expertise (founded late 1999) and adviser to the speaker of the Duma, Gennadii Seleznev.[4] From Marx to Mackinder.[5]

But, the smaller countries in the post-Soviet space have also seen a revival. Although the exact status of geopolitical thought in Estonia continues to be

---

[1] Allan and Goldmann, 1992; Lebow and Risse-Kappen, 1995.
[2] Tyulin, 1997; Sergounin, 2000.
[3] O'Loughlin, 2001.
[4] Dugin, in particular, has attracted the scorn of critics, who have even likened him to a neo-fascist. See Ingram, 2001.
[5] See now also Bassin and Aksenov, 2006.

disputed,[6] the place reserved for Huntington's 'clash of civilizations' thesis in that country has been truly remarkable. Estonia's minister of foreign affairs wrote the foreword to the 1999 Estonian translation of Huntington's *The Clash of Civilizations and the Remaking of World Order*. For the book's launch, Huntington visited Estonia and spoke at a press conference together with Estonia's prime minister and minister of foreign affairs.[7] His book was extensively reviewed in major newspapers and has more generally become part of popular discourse.[8] Nor does the revival stop on the Eastern side of the former Iron Curtain. Quite strikingly perhaps, Italy has also seen a revival of 'geopolitics', with military general and political adviser Carlo Jean as its figurehead[9] and a relatively new journal of geopolitics called *Limes: Rivista Italiana di Geopolitica* (the Italian equivalent to the French *Hérodote*, but with national success on the level of *Foreign Affairs/Foreign Policy*) as its main outlet.[10] In Italy, Jean's books are the most widely read books in international relations written by an Italian. Together with *Limes*, they have accompanied and arguably contributed to the permeation of the discourses of politicians and newspapers by geopolitical vocabulary.[11]

So, why is this? By analysing the relationship between the events of 1989 and the resurgence of geopolitical thought, the present collaborative study aims to contribute to the understanding of the relationship between international events or crises and foreign policy thought (and strategy) – or, more generally, between modes of thought and particular historical contexts in international relations. At the same time, it contributes to constructivist theorising in proposing a way to study shifts in what Alexander Wendt has called the 'cultures of anarchy' in international society. The four central empirical claims it makes are set out below.

First, although we will show a relationship between international events and shifts in foreign policy modes of thought, this cannot be adequately understood in terms of a mere outside-in analysis, whereby an international event causes shifts in foreign policy ideas. In the context of the geopolitical revival after 1989 in Europe, it was apparently not self-evident – as our puzzle shows – that the success of *Ostpolitik* (the international event as seen by the German elite) would put an end to realist geopolitical thought as part of traditional Cold War thinking, in the same way as it did to the Cold War, even if many observers would have expected this to happen (particularly in Germany). Nor, as we will show, was a return to geopolitical thought necessary in the light of the ethnic

---

[6] For an overview, see Aalto, 2000 and 2001.
[7] Kuus, 2002, 307.   [8] Aalto and Berg, 2002, 261–262.
[9] Jean, 1995 and 1997.
[10] Lucarelli and Menotti, 2002c. Dugin participated in the launch (and is a member of the editorial board) of yet another geopolitical journal in 2004, entitled *Eurasia: rivista di studi geopolitici*.
[11] Antonsich, 1996.

wars in the Balkans, as suggested by many realists. In other words, '1989' – our 'event' – caused no necessary shift towards understandings informed by either peace research or geopolitics. Instead, the significance and effect of the event have themselves been a result of the ways in which foreign policy discourses in different countries understood that event. This study claims that we need to understand the role of international events on foreign policy ideas from the inside out – that is, in the way the meanings of such events as '1989' are articulated within national foreign policy discourses.

This leads to our second claim, namely, that the revival of geopolitical thought is best understood in the context of several foreign policy identity crises, a kind of 'ontological insecurity'[12] that foreign policy elites encountered in Europe after 1989. We can distinguish here three types of such potential identity crises – that is, instances where previously established self-understandings and external role conceptions were susceptible to challenge. In some cases, for example in Russia, a country's place in the world was no longer self-evident, as previously established roles and self-understandings no longer seemed valid (post-1989 Russia could neither unproblematically refer back to the Soviet Union nor to Tsarist Russia). Sometimes, a country's role had been previously defined in a passive fashion – as in Italy, where the Cold War divide had done much of the job for Italian foreign policy thought. And, finally, some states would be recreated (as in the case of Estonia) or reunited (as in the case of Germany) as a result of the events of 1989, making it necessary to articulate an updated foreign policy identity. Hence, we have three potential crises: no identity, no longer the previously established identity, and no identity yet. Accordingly, we claim that the effect of the events of 1989 on foreign policy thought are best understood in the context of an identity crisis. Such an identity crisis occurs when a country's general foreign policy or its national-interest discourses face problems in their smooth continuation, because taken-for-granted self-understandings and role positions are openly challenged – and eventually undermined.

Third, we claim that mobilising geopolitical thought seems particularly well suited to respond to such an ontological anxiety or identity crisis. Geopolitical thought provides allegedly objective and material criteria for circumscribing the boundaries (and internal logics) of 'national interest' formulations. Invoking national interests almost inevitably mobilises justifications in terms wider than the interest of the ruler or the government. Such wider justification can be given by ideologies, as in the case of anti-communism and anti-capitalism during the Cold War, or through references to the 'nation', for instance. But, when yesterday's certitudes have gone missing, national interests have to be anchored anew. In such a context, geopolitics in its classical understanding provides 'coordinates' for thinking a country's role in world affairs. Deprived of

---

[12] Agnew, 2003, 115. For the concept of ontological security, see Huysman, 1998, Mitzen, 2006 and Steele, 2005 and 2007.

traditional reference points and with a challenged self-understanding or outside view of its role, spatial logic can quickly fill this ideational void and fix the
place of the state and its national interest within the international system or
society. And geopolitics is particularly well suited to such a role, since it relies
upon environmental determinism from both physical geography (mobilised
often through strategic thinking) and human/cultural geography typical for
discourses essentialising a nation.

Yet, although geopolitical thought fulfils this function handsomely, there
is no necessity that it will be mobilised in national security or foreign policy
discourses. To assume otherwise would be to commit a functional fallacy.
Accordingly, our fourth claim is that whether or not geopolitical thought is
mobilised to fulfil the above-mentioned function is dependent on a series of
process factors: the 'common sense' embedded in the national-interest discourse that predisposes for it, the institutional structure (and political economy) in which foreign policy thought is developed, and the mobilisation of
agents in the national political game.

Besides answering the empirical puzzle of a geopolitical revival after the end
of the Cold War, the present study also aims to adapt methodological and theoretical tools for constructivist analysis. First, it uses a version of 'process tracing'
in an interpretivist manner. The analysis is a version of *process tracing*, since it
does not simply assume that when outside pressures translate into more or less
uniform outcomes, they do so for the causes hypothesised. Without empirically checking the process of how international inputs translate into domestic
responses, it is not possible to control for the risk of equifinality – that is, the
possibility that the same outcome may have been reached by following different processual paths. Moreover, whatever regularity found without checking
the process can be spurious and easily falls prone to the functionalist fallacy
just mentioned.

It is *interpretivist* process tracing because its starting point is in the understanding of international events, not with those events in themselves.[13] The tracing starts with the already diverse national interpretations of the international
event. The 'international' event is therefore no constant and equal input for all
country cases, a constant against which the variance of national process can
explain the differing political responses, as in many research designs around
globalisation and the hypothesised convergence of (economic) politics and
institutions, for instance. The significance of the input – and indeed the input
itself – is endogenous to the process. Moreover, as the conclusion will elaborate,

---

[13] Moreover, it is about the interaction effects of such an interpretation with the events themselves in that the interpretation of what '1989 means for post-1989' interacts with the events
of post-1989. For the concept of 'interaction effects', see Hacking, 1999, 31–32. For the discussion, see Chapter 11 of this volume.

this process tracing is best understood as a multilayered process of parallel dynamics and their interaction, rather than a single linear process.

Finally, the book wishes to contribute to theory development in constructivist IR by providing tools and micro-dynamics for analysing structural change. It does so by defining an analysis of social mechanisms that is consistent with constructivist and post-positivist assumptions, and by specifying two such mechanisms. The first mechanism of foreign policy identity crisis reduction is the core of the analysis. In the context of a foreign policy identity crisis, where self-understandings or outside role recognition have been challenged by the interpretation of events, agents try to remedy the situation in at least four ways: they either deny the existence of any crisis, define it as a misunderstanding and negotiate with the outside about it, adapt to it, or try to mould international society to fit its own identity discourses.

A second mechanism relates to the underlying 'culture of anarchy', to use Wendt's expression. If 'anarchy is what states make of it', and if that making happens through and within the lifeworld of different 'cultures of anarchy', then the proposed analysis probes into the dynamics of such cultures, since these cultures are also what states make of them. It suggests that the evolution of the culture of anarchy in Europe after 1989 is fruitfully analysed through the way the interpretations of major events are driven and interact with different national foreign policy discourses, and how those in turn interact with each other in the reproduction of the more general culture. For this, the book proposes a mechanism called a 'vicious circle of essentialisation'. This forms part of a structural but bottom-up analysis in which the meaning given to the events of 1989 – an event that, to use the categories of the English School and Wendt, should have heralded and reinforced a dynamic from a Lockean to a Kantian culture in Europe – paradoxically also produced a movement in the opposite direction. For if the theoretical parameters of geopolitical analysis were taken seriously on both the national and the international levels, its dynamics of essentialising physical and cultural geography would produce an environment more akin to a Hobbesian culture.

In other words, where geopolitics has been used to resolve foreign policy identity crises, the very success of the 'desecuritisation' that occurred at the end of the Cold War might contribute to ushering in a 'resecuritisation'. Or, put differently, under certain conditions Kant makes Hobbes possible again. Now, through our understanding of the concatenation of the two mechanisms at work, we are able to see that a movement to a more Hobbesian culture happened not *despite* the end of the Cold War, but *because of it*.

Accordingly, the present analysis shares a normative concern typical of peace research (but not only that) – namely, the possibility that interpretations become potentially self-fulfilling prophecies that contribute to producing a threatening world while appearing as simple response to it; in other words, a concern about 'self-fulfilling geopolitics'.

The structure of the book is straightforward. The first part, consisting of three chapters, specifies the puzzle, along with the terms, central concepts and framework of the analysis. The second part provides six country studies. A concluding part first synthesises the empirical findings and then develops a constructivist understanding of process tracing and mechanisms so as to provide a way in which to conceive of the micro-dynamics of constructivist IR theories.

PART I

The analytical framework

1

Which puzzle? An expected return of geopolitical thought in Europe?

STEFANO GUZZINI

Was not a revival of geopolitical thinking only to be expected after the end of the Cold War? This would be the classical realist claim, suggesting that the aftermath of the Cold War showed clearly the eternal wisdom of the realist tradition, including its more geopolitical component. The analyses of Mearsheimer and Huntington are there, so the implication, because of the nature of world politics.[1] The revival comes as no surprise to political geography either, where 'geopolitics' has come to cover 'critical approaches to foreign policy practices and representations',[2] for in times of territorial change or even state redefinition it is only normal that geographical discourse should become more prominent.

However, the puzzle of this study is not just about a couple of more geopolitical references. To be sure, if 'geopolitical language can be recognized by the occurrence of words referring to boundaries and the conflict between territorially bounded interests',[3] then almost by definition the end of the Cold War had to increase geopolitical talk in Europe – as would the discussions by European Federalists after 1945 in their attempt to get the European countries to join each other in a federation. In itself, though, that is not a significant finding (at least, not any longer). The puzzle for this comparative study concerns the revival of a specifically classical and more determinist form of geopolitical thought; it is about a geopolitics that no longer shies away from using its arguments, or indeed its own name.

This chapter will therefore shortly discuss two possible rebuttals to the puzzle of this volume, informed by either realism or (critical) political geography. The realist rebuttal is unsatisfactory, since historical events underdetermine their interpretation. Realists are right, that the peaceful end of the Cold War does not naturally make everyone see the political expectations (and strategies) of peace research (*Ostpolitik*) confirmed. But for the same reason it is not in the nature of things that the end of the Cold War – a truly major historical event

---

[1] Mearsheimer, 1990; Huntington, 1993a.
[2] For this quote and for reference to the divide in the usage of 'geopolitics' between IR and political geographers, see Mamadouh and Dijkink, 2006, 350.
[3] Dijkink, 1996, 5.

achieved in an unexpected way for realists (despite later attempts to account for it) – would ultimately be considered of less importance than the Balkan wars, as realists would have it. And if political geographers are right to expect a flurry of geographic references in policy discourses after 1989, this does not necessarily require the more determinist version of geopolitics to (re-)surface. Finally, we need also to account for the fact that the revival did not happen everywhere. The puzzle remains.

1   '1989 and all that': realist politics after the Cold War freezer

Many citizens of former Yugoslavia may be forgiven for having a less glorious view of the end of the Cold War. Realists believed that their views had been swiftly vindicated by the many civil wars that took place in the Balkans, and stressed the need not to be lured by the peaceful solution of the Cold War. For them, the post-Cold War era was a dangerous peace, resurrecting a host of factors that almost required a revival in geopolitics.[4] Yet, as this section will argue, this does not invalidate the puzzle: it is not clear why geopolitics should so early and suddenly arise out of the ashes, both East and West. It is not self-evident why the peaceful end of the Cold War, an event of truly global proportions, would be overshadowed by the understandings and alleged lessons derived from the (regional) Bosnian wars.

For once, geopolitics as a distinct theory, and not just as a loose discourse, is akin to those very systemic and deterministic versions of realism that are usually considered unable to explain the behaviour of the Soviet Union at the end of the Cold War. We have no 'final' interpretation of the end of the Cold War, and given the far-reaching political implications of its historical lessons, the debate will probably stay 'essentially contested'. But it is quite safe to say that realist theories that concentrate mainly on systemic determinism (the balance of power) have been under severe attack within that debate.[5] In relative-power terms, the USSR was not weaker in the mid 1980s than it was at earlier stages of the Cold War. Moreover, a geopolitical outlook that would add more geographical emphasis, including a focus on territories, would have to explain the relative ease with which the Soviet government under Gorbachev let its sphere of influence go.

And, indeed, a Waltzian systemic response was swiftly discarded by realists themselves. An early rejoinder by William Wohlforth was more inspired by the realism of Robert Gilpin and Stephen Walt.[6] It mixed the idea of hegemonic decline and a moment of perception. Whether or not the relative-power

---

[4] For a laundry list of factors that self-evidently led to the revival after 1989, see Jean, 1995, 5.
[5] Kratochwil, 1993; Koslowski and Kratochwil, 1994; Lebow, 1994.
[6] See Wohlforth, 1994/1995 and the relationship to Gilpin, 1981 and Walt, 1987.

position was really as bad as it seemed, Gorbachev perceived a power decline and had to react by leaving some dead weight ('retrenchment'). Reagan's rearmament is seen as the catalyst.[7] This argument has recently been extended with another systemic factor, also taking into account the effects of globalisation and economic decline.[8]

It is debatable whether even that late realist fixing is persuasive – and historically it comes too late to justify an almost natural revival of geopolitics in the early 1990s. There is the question of timing, since the major shift appears in 1987, quite a while after the first Reagan administration, which had provoked only responses of Soviet rearmament, not retrenchment.[9] And it happened also with and after Reykjavik, that is, at a time when the much more accommodating second Reagan administration had started facing a crucial leadership change on the other side.[10] Moreover, why would a challenger in decline prefer simply to give up the battle rather than to opt for a preventive war before the situation deteriorated further? Even if such a realist reading rightly stresses the existence of constraints on Soviet policy, it cannot explain why they were interpreted in a particular way and which policy was to follow. There seems no compelling evidence to support the notion that the Soviet Union needed to give up Eastern Europe,[11] let alone to encourage the demise of communism there.[12] Against this mainly US power-politics story, it is perhaps not fortuitous that it is mostly US outsiders[13] who have been particularly keen to stress the influence of détente and 'common security' on the then new power elite in Moscow: social democratic ideas,[14] *Ostpolitik*,[15] 'non-offensive defence', the Helsinki process and confidence-building measures, which all helped to build up a remarkable reservoir of trust, in particular towards Germany.[16] European peace researchers certainly saw themselves vindicated by events.[17] Material explanations, if they are not just indeterminate,[18] simply do not suffice and might not even identify the most important components.[19]

Accordingly, realists derive the renewed appeal of geopolitical arguments not from the end of the Cold War, but from some regional events after the Cold War. However the end of the Cold War might have shattered realist

---

[7] Patman, 1999.

[8] Brooks and Wohlforth, 2000/2001. It is, however, somewhat curious that IR realists picked up this argument right then. In the meantime, the globalisation debate had moved towards conceiving of globalisation as a dependent variable, itself in dire need of being explained, rather than as a general systemic and independent variable to explain all possible national socialisation and convergence patterns. See Leander, 2001.

[9] McccGwire, 1991.   [10] Risse-Kappen, 1991.

[11] Evangelista, 2001.   [12] Kramer, 1999, 2001.

[13] But not just US outsiders; see Evangelista, 1999.

[14] Lévesque, 1995.   [15] Risse-Kappen, 1994.

[16] Forsberg, 1999.   [17] Wiberg, 1992.   [18] Lebow, 1994.

[19] For a general assessment of these debates, see Petrova, 2003.

explanations, the Balkan wars now stood paradoxically for realism's invigorated wisdom. For the Balkans marked a return to the 'normal' days of world politics, no longer muted by the transitory ideological contest of the Cold War. We were back to the future.[20]

Mearsheimer looks at the outbreak of hostilities and their ethnic content in terms of a 'freezer theory' of the Cold War. Here, first domestic and then international conflicts had become dormant as they were overlaid by superpower competition. Once the overlay was withdrawn, however, regional history picked up where it left off and territorial disputes, now in a new power context, inevitably came to the fore. This meant business as usual for the realist, although the Cold War had temporarily suppressed these eternal dynamics. 'You wanted the end of the Cold War – and look what you got.' With such an approach, a kind of cyclical determinism creeps in, one that would regard a revival of geopolitical thought as only to be expected.

There are many shortcomings in the assumptions that underlie this analysis, not least the fact that the sheer occurrence of conflict is not in itself an argument for realism. Like any other theory, realism needs to explain both conflict and cooperation. Conflict may arise for reasons other than realist ones.[21] Assuming that conflict is an a priori argument in favour of realism is thus deeply fallacious and usually not shared by realist theorists. It would reduce realism, as a famous quip has it, to the untenable '*shit happens* theory of international relations', always ostensibly confirmed when international relations sour.[22] It confuses, in Wendt's words, the description of *Realpolitik* with its explanation.[23]

But also the empirical part of Mearsheimer's analysis has been widely criticised, since it crucially hinged on his prediction about Germany as inevitably taking up a more aggressive and unilateral posture in Europe once the strictures of the Cold War had been removed and its recent unification seemed to justify a bigger role in Europe, in proportion to its accrued power position. This claim was unlikely from the start, as shown by other realists,[24] and the situation it suggested did not materialise.[25] And so, not much is left of the more determinate version of realism that would explain why the resurgence of geopolitical thought was simply following the necessities of world politics after 1989.

Most importantly, even if all had been accurate, this only begs the question in terms of the present research puzzle: how is it that in the predominantly

---

[20] Mearsheimer, 1990.

[21] Even the security dilemma can be explained by other than realist–idealist arguments (note that both of these traditions analyse that dilemma in the same way, but have different views on its possible solution). See Mitzen, 2006.

[22] This quip was made by Friedrich Kratochwil during a roundtable discussion with Mearsheimer at a meeting of the International Studies Association.

[23] Wendt, 1995, 76.

[24] See, for instance, the almost immediate reply by Van Evera, 1991.

[25] E.g. Banchoff, 1999.

Northwest-dominated IR discourse, the peaceful dismantling of the Berlin Wall and the end of the daily threat of a global war – that is, the major shift in world politics at the end of the century – was in some European countries ultimately considered less important than a partial reading of local ethnic conflicts in former Yugoslavia (as horrendous as the wars in the Balkans were)? In other words, even if not all states or their elites shared Germany's enthusiasm in the days of the then celebrated Paris Charter or the hopes of a genuinely common European security structure,[26] it is not self-evident that geopolitical thought, long scorned for its militarist and determinist vision of foreign policy, would rise up just after the Cold War finally came to a peaceful end.

2   Critical geopolitics: 1989 stirring up the geographical imagination

Shifts in world politics stir up geopolitical discourses. This is a quite common generalisation arising out of the study of the development of geopolitical thought over the last two centuries. Hence, like realists, more critical geopolitical writers also find little surprising in the reappearance not just of geopolitical thinking but also of the very term 'geopolitics' after 1989. Yet, it is important to look here at the exact reasons for such a revival, since they will give us a first clue for specifying the type of approach that will be most suited to our study.

Before coming to the analysis of the post-1989 environment done by critical geopolitics scholars, some background to this family of approaches seems warranted. Critical geopolitics can perhaps best be understood through comparison with classical or mainstream realist geopolitics. They all share a focus on the relationship between geography and politics, in that all geography is political and politics is always spatial. However, beyond this quite trivial common ground, they differ profoundly according to the ways in which their underlying meta-theories specify the relationship between the material and the ideational aspects of the social world and between the representation of social reality and that reality itself. Here, geopolitics is seen either as a first-order phenomenon (e.g. the 'factual' empirical relationship between geographic factors and state policies) or as a second-order phenomenon (e.g. the politics of its representation) that, in turn, can have an effect on the first-order phenomenon (reflexivity). In other words, the mainstream approach to geopolitics is about *the geography of politics*, where long lists of material factors usually provide the structural background within which agents make their hopefully optimal decisions. Critical geopolitics reverses this interest by problematising geography itself: it is about *the politics of geography*. A classical 'critical' version focuses

---

[26]   This enthusiasm (and early calls for political action to use the momentum for institutionalising it) could be found both in government (Genscher, 1995) and in academia (e.g. Senghaas, 1992).

on geography's role in supporting foreign policies, as well as its political and ideological function.[27] Applying a constructivist or post-structuralist turn, a second branch of critical geopolitics problematises the interplay between the politics of geography and the geography of politics – or, in their own terms, the 'geo-politics of geopolitics'; that is, how geographic representations in turn interact with social reality.[28] In this latter category, some approaches aim at a macro-historical understanding of how the modern geopolitical imagination influences the understanding and practice of world politics,[29] while others focus more on exposing the political implications of more (country-)specific geopolitical discourses.[30]

In so doing, critical geopolitics 'denaturalises' geography: the value of geographical factors is not naturally given. That means more than the argument that technological change influences the value of geographical factors, an argument already common in classical realist writings for which the value of resources was never fixed in their analysis of power.[31] Instead, a critical approach starts from seeing the role of geographic factors driven by the understandings actors have about them. Whatever the actual importance of certain territories in terms of natural or human resources, it is their place in the agents' representations that most strongly conditions their actual value for an agent. According to Yves Lacoste, within whose approach territorial conflict looms prominent for understanding geopolitics, the primary mover is not the 'natural data of geography' – to the extent that there is such a thing; rather, it is the claims made by nations on behalf of 'their "historical rights" or simply their desire to preserve their cultural identity or "environment"'.[32]

This interpretivist turn of geopolitical analysis focuses on representations. It opens up for a research agenda – such as John Agnew's – in which the historical development of a 'geographical imagination' as developed in Europe's modernity provides the general grammar within which particular periods of geopolitical thinking can be analysed. And it prompts the analysis of particular, usually national, geopolitical discourses or 'geopolitical visions', as well as how

---

[27] E.g. Lacoste, 1978.

[28] This does admittedly phrase critical geopolitics in the categories with which I characterise constructivism (in International Relations), but I think this is defendable. See Guzzini, 2000a and 2005.

[29] This would apply, although with different emphases, to the work of both John Agnew and Derek Gregory. See Agnew's self-definition as doing 'historical geo-politics': Agnew, 2003, 6 and Agnew in Murphy et al., 2004, 634–637, and Gregory's for being a 'historical geographer of sorts' in Gregory, 1998, 46. Again with different accents, both focus on the historical evolution of the relationship between knowledge and power (and a critique of the West), and favour a thick conceptual history understood either à la Koselleck or à la Foucault for studying 'the ways in which space is implicated in the operation and outcomes of social processes' (Gregory, 1998, 85).

[30] See e.g. Dalby, 1990b and Ó Tuathail, 1996.

[31] See e.g. Aron, 1962, 64.   [32] Lacoste, 1993, 9, 17.

they interact with each other and with international politics.[33] Although such an analysis rejects an objectivist understanding of geography and geopolitics, it does not amount to a subjectivist analysis, since these national interpretations are a socially shared discourse. And these discourses are themselves embedded within a historical and cultural context, whether that is general (i.e. modernity) or that of a particular state (or both), which enables the study of the conditions and processes with which such sets of representations evolve.

Armed with this very short *concis* on critical geopolitics, we can now return to our puzzle. Mainstream or critical geopolitics give two different answers to the question about the effects the end of the Cold War could have had on the development of geopolitical thought – that is, whether a revival was to be expected or not. For the more naturalised approaches, all there needs to be is 'shock experiences' produced by clear shifts in 'power position, its primary features like borders, and lost and gained populations', and geopolitical discourse tends to (re)appear.[34] But such a development has not always been forthcoming: in the Czech Republic, whose primary features have surely been changing through the split first from the Warsaw Pact and then from Slovakia, no revival happened.

A second answer would be more akin to the approach of the truly critical geographer, where the meaning of space (and of spatial change) is not given by an objective geography, but read into it by the actors' interpretations. The resurgence of geopolitics after 1989 was not a foregone conclusion: it was only to be expected if international events deeply affected the geopolitical imagination. Hypotheses for the resurgence of geopolitical thought after 1989 were supported not by the change in political factors as such, but by the latter's meeting with the modern geopolitical imagination (for a macro-historical analysis) or with particular national geopolitical visions.

Given the logic of Cold War discourses, the resurgence of geopolitical thought did not greatly puzzle scholars in critical geopolitics whose analysis focuses on the inertial effects of a pre-existing discourse in search of a new application. According to this, it was only to be expected that the established strategic discourse would find ways of reasserting itself: such discourses change slowly, and even major events do not necessarily undermine their basic logic. As I will argue, this rebuttal of the puzzle is partly justified. However, it does not really solve the puzzle, though it does provide an important element for its specification.

This can be exemplified with a short note on Huntington's famous thesis about a potential clash of civilisations. According to a critical reading, such a thesis is not just old hat with regard to classical geopolitics, it also simply rehashes Cold War dichotomies. Huntington divides the world into different

---

[33] E.g. Dijkink, 1996. [34] Van der Wusten and Dijkink, 2002, 21.

civilisations (poles) that occupy different cultural areas (blocs) at the borders of which (e.g. iron or bamboo curtains) friction is likely to occur. In particular, the Western world (democracy) will face the combined onslaught of civilisations that, by their own self-definitions, cannot compromise (totalitarianism). In this reading, Huntington seems to be looking for a new enemy to be slotted into an argument already given. In other words, it is not a new problem that spurs a Western response, but Western strategic solutions that are in search of a problem.[35]

In particular, Gearóid Ó Tuathail (Gerard Toal) has stressed the resurgence of such old-fashioned geopolitics in times of disarray in strategic thought (such as after 1989) – a disarray he refers to as 'geopolitical vertigo'.[36] Here, the resurgence of more spatial presentations of international dynamics is part and parcel of an attempt – not necessarily conscious and strategic – to regain ground in international politics. Faced with the partial dissolution of spatial references, the revival of 'geopolitics' is not simply an intellectual move: it is a reaction to the decline of the politics of geopolitics. Being intrinsically connected to militarism, so Ó Tuathail's hypothesis goes, geopolitics reappears at a time when, in response to the public's call for a Cold War 'peace dividend', military budgets are shrinking. It is the attempt to fix the disorientation, exacerbated by 1989, and to allow a return to 'business as usual'.

The general approach of critical geopolitics is clearly congenial with the analysis presented in this volume, though not with all of its hypotheses. Indeed, it helps to specify the puzzle. Even if it does not seem all too puzzling that geopolitics reappears – and indeed might even be the privileged expression of a pre-existing strategic discourse (and imaginary) in dire need of strong justification – this does not answer the question of why some foreign policy elites and discourses seem to have been much more receptive to a revival of geopolitical thinking than others. In some countries, geopolitical thought remained basically a dead letter – for example, in the Czech Republic, Germany and Sweden. Why was this? Was it because the foreign policy elites of those countries were not disoriented in the first place – in other words, 1989 did not affect them in the same way or simply did not mean the same for them? Or was it for other reasons that geopolitics could not play its usual role of 'fixing anxiety' in those countries?

3   Conclusion: the puzzling rise of 'neoclassical geopolitics'

Whereas the realist rebuttal is unconvincing both historically and theoretically, political geographers have better justification for being unimpressed by

---

[35] For this argument, see Guzzini, 1998, 234.
[36] For the following, see Ó Tuathail, 1996, chapter 7.

the post-1989 revival of geopolitical thinking. World political crises and their aftermath spur geopolitical imaginations, old and new. When borders shift, so does the territorial identity of the state or homeland/nation. After major political earthquakes, future landscapes are envisioned, or old ones restored. While perhaps puzzling to the non-realist scholar in International Relations, a revival of geopolitical thought after such a sea change as the end of the Cold War was quite predictable for political geographers.

Indeed, their findings are part of the very research design of the present study. They rightly point to the relationship between the revival of geopolitical discourse and the crisis of national security discourses when faced with new world political settings. Yet, it still needs to be explained why this geopolitical discourse is not just a rearticulation of space and (home) territory, a mere return of geography or spatial and/or territorial coordinates to the visible agenda of politics. For it is more: it is a revival of exactly that part of the geopolitical tradition with which many political geographers feel most uncomfortable. It is a revival of aspects of environmental determinism and of many of the late nineteenth- and early twentieth-century thinkers tainted by it. Geography surely matters in politics, but from there it is another step to start determining politics from a then naturalised geography. We are not just witnessing a return of *geopolitical discourse* in the sense of a visible return of geography to politics; we are dealing with *geopolitics* in its stronger more classical sense, or what Mark Bassin has dubbed 'neoclassical geopolitics'.[37] And such a development is in no way necessarily predestined to happen in times of crises. A more visible geopolitical imagination does not automatically translate into a geopolitics that no longer shies away from using its name.

[37] Bassin, 2004, 621.

2

Which geopolitics?

STEFANO GUZZINI

The puzzle, then, hinges on a thicker definition of geopolitics in terms of 'neo-classical geopolitics', as Bassin terms it, a definition the present chapter will elaborate. However, it will do so through a discussion of the classical vision of geopolitics, for two reasons. One reason is connected to the overall research design. If, as hypothesised, the revival of geopolitical thought in Europe affects the 'culture of anarchy' in such a way as to halt the movement to a more Kantian vision of European security, or indeed to reverse it towards a more Hobbesian one, then it is necessary to show the precise components in the neoclassical geopolitical discourse that are responsible for this.

The second reason has to do with the way in which neoclassical geopolitics is presented. For, as defenders of such a position will be swift to point out, my reference to classical geopolitics might stack the deck too much in one direc-tion, mobilising the guilt-by-association charges so typical of 'politically cor-rect' references to geopolitics. They see 'geopolitics' as far more innocent, no longer tainted by the theoretical and political pitfalls of its past. Such a defence usually comes in predictable guises. First, it tries to show that the almost neces-sary association of geopolitics with fascist foreign policy is mistaken. Either, as some argue, there was no strong link between Hitler and geopolitics, or, as others maintain, the German school was somewhat special and contemporary geopolitical approaches rarely rely on this particular branch. Also, in a second move, the defence of geopolitics concedes that environmental determinism does not work, and therefore claims that present versions do not rely on it. Hence, talking geopolitics today is relatively innocent and does not deserve all the fuss and criticism. So, which *geopolitics redux?*

For these reasons, the present chapter will need to engage the different attempts to define and redefine geopolitics in order to justify the working definition of neoclassical geopolitics found relevant to specify the puzzle of this comparative study. This will be done in three steps. First, I will discuss the relationship between the geopolitical tradition and its German *Geopolitik* branch. Here, I will suggest that although *Geopolitik* is not to be conflated with Nazism (though it was used by the latter), the core assumptions on which the German tradition relies are the same as those of the wider classical geopolitical tradition. Claiming that *Geopolitik* is special for its reference to organicistic explanations is not entirely wrong, but misses the point. What defines the classical geopolitical tradition is a reliance on what were then common versions of Social Darwinism. Pruning away the German tradition does not touch the common roots.

In a second step I will then discuss the exact relationship between the geopolitical tradition and realism. I share the usual assessment that geopolitics is a branch of the realist tradition because a key element these approaches have in common is a belief that power expansion is the default dynamic of world politics. Nevertheless, realism should not be reduced to, or conflated with, geopolitics, since it does not share the latter's reliance on Social Darwinism and some muscular version of nationalism (often linked to a special 'mission') as causes for that expansionism.

Finally, I discuss the claims made by present-day geopolitical scholars that their theories are not just devoid of any significant connection with *Geopolitik*, but also generally not 'environmentally determinist'. I try to show that this claim relies on a faulty definition of what such determinism would imply. To be sure, their theories are not using a determinism that is monocausal and makes clear predictions of behaviour. However, all that is needed for a critique of 'environmental determinacy' is to show that an analysis gives explanatory primacy to environmental factors. That geography or space generally matters is really not the point for which one would need 'geopolitics'; it is consistent with almost all IR theories. Hence, giving up this environmental primacy prompts a dilemma: either geopolitics is something specific, in which case such explanatory primacy is required and in need of justification – which, however, is now no longer provided by claiming that geopolitics is not determinist – or it is not something specific, a kind of looser materialist talk, and then it is redundant and insisting on the use of the label needs to be justified – which is also something that is not usually done. To conclude the discussion by geographers, I also take up the attempts by critical geopolitics to change the way we study this subject, suggesting we regard it not as a school of thought in statecraft but as the practices of spatialisation within that statecraft. Although this has opened up fascinating avenues of research, such a wide definition of geopolitics does not fit the purpose of the present study, as I will show.

The chapter will end by setting out a working definition of neoclassical geopolitics that takes into account these different components. And, although it is possible to make the case that there has been a revival of geopolitical thought that fits such a definition, it is important to stress that not every use of the concept 'geopolitics' does. As mentioned earlier, this thicker definition is necessary for the puzzle, since it specifies what makes the revival unexpected. And it is also fundamental for that revival having the potential wider historical effects on the European culture of anarchy.

1   Classical geopolitics, but no *Geopolitik*?

'It is not German *Geopolitik*', goes the mantra. It seeks to resist the reduction of geopolitics to its particular German branch, a reduction that would amount to an immediate disqualification. To be able to say geopolitics, this guilt by association with Nazism must be exposed and hence removed.

Yet although German *Geopolitik* cannot be blamed for Hitler, it is far less self-evident to claim that geopolitics and *Geopolitik* can be treated as having no close connection. To stay in the language of Darwinism, into which this section will delve here and there: whereas geopolitics might not derive from *Geopolitik*, it has the same ancestors. What exactly that implies is not resolved by removing the *Geopolitik* lineage. Also, if geopolitical explanations weaken their environmental determinism, either by including a vast variety of factors to which explanatory primacy is attached or by denying the very possibility of such more determinate explanations, they obviously undermine the very justification for using these explanations, rather than others, in the first place.

Accordingly, this study does see in the revival of geopolitics, where it happens, an attempt to invigorate a kind of environmental determinism, whether openly or in an implicit way. And it is that particular feature that makes geopolitics so appealing in times of foreign policy identity crisis. Laundry lists of factors with contingent effects will not do: such times need clear and determinate paradigms, like the 'clash of civilizations' thesis.

Geopolitics saved from the Nazi aberration

The German geopolitical school's bad name is closely connected to the work and actions of Karl Haushofer. Since Haushofer was close to, if not a supporter of, the Nazi movement from its earliest days, was a friend of Rudolf Hess, enjoyed a relatively privileged position once the Nazis came to power (although he then became increasingly marginalised), was widely published and even built a research institute, he is, for many, the closest one may get to a Nazi court intellectual in foreign affairs. As things turns out, however, the story is far more complicated than that, which provides a first step to opening up a legitimate space, as it were, for justifying a return to geopolitics.

It is not difficult to find ways in which to delink German *Geopolitik* from the Nazi government. Geopolitical defenders are quick to point out that the *Zeitschrift für Geopolitik* published a fairly wide range of authors, including Karl Wittfogel, a prominent communist scholar. Also, the 'legendary' research institute on geopolitics in Munich was a tiny enterprise, hardly deserving its reputation abroad. Nor was Nazi politics significantly influenced by Haushofer, not even the Molotov–Ribbentrop Pact of 1939, although that agreement looks as though it might have been inspired by his vision of a continental bloc to stem the perceived Anglo-American tide of power.[1] More profoundly, *Geopolitik*'s underlying environmental determinism, the role of nature in conditioning human existence and political organisation, was in many aspects at odds with the Nazi insistence on race as the main principle for understanding (and justifying) their *Geopolitik*.

Indeed, Friedrich Ratzel, often considered the father of German geopolitics, decided to end his first major work, *Anthropo-geography*, with a strong diatribe against the use of anthropological distinctions in which race was a qualitatively important category. For him, such racial claims were an indefensible relict of 'older days when little was known about extra-European peoples'. Instead, racial distinctions were only 'deceptive garments' (*täuschende Gewänder*), misleading the superficial observer.[2] Given the basic dynamic of human migration, there are no pure races; the differences between the various racial mixes are hard to establish; and their value for explaining the difference between peoples pales into insignificance when compared with ethnographic (i.e. cultural anthropological) and historical factors. According to Ratzel, humankind is fundamentally unitary in its anthropology – as well as in its destiny, which would see the increasing fusion of peoples into a common mankind.[3] Hardly the stuff of Nazi *Geopolitik*.

As Bassin shows, this tension between space and race led to an increasing marginalisation of academic geopolitics and of the (still opportunist) Haushofer under the Nazi government in Germany.[4] To be sure, Nazi ideologues thought about race in terms of 'nature', and since geopolitics included human and cultural geography, German 'academic' geopolitics and Nazi geopolitics were two of a kind. Nor did Haushofer always share Ratzel's strong opposition to racial theories. In fact, he later allowed racial argument to intrude into his analysis, if not as the motor, at least as a condition for state power – for example, when he questioned the longevity of the French Empire on account of its 'racial policies' (mixing) or tried to limit racial policies to the domestic arena, allowing cross-racial alliances abroad.[5] Yet, this does not change the fact that German *Geopolitik* was less driven by racist concerns than the Nazi government. However, as I will argue below, the mere fact that Haushofer did not influence Nazi politics, or did not share its racism to the full, does not hide important affinities in the argument, not least the justification for almost unlimited expansionism in the inevitable struggle for existence.[6]

[1] Diner, 1999, 173.
[2] Ratzel, 1882, 469. The general argument begins on p. 468. If not otherwise stated, all translations from French, German and Italian original texts are mine.
[3] Ratzel, 1882, 177.   [4] Bassin, 1987b, 125ff.
[5] Haushofer, 1934, 31 and 215 respectively.
[6] Diner, 1999.

Geopolitics avoiding the German path?

Contemporary defenders of geopolitics argue that there are particularities to the specific German branch[7] that explain the latter's affinity with Social Darwinism ('survival of the fittest'), and which are shunned by geopolitical writers today. This specificity can be found in the German tradition's constant references to states as organisms. In my view, however, this geopolitical defence is not particularly persuasive.[8]

Much has been made of the fact that the German tradition uses an organic metaphor in relation to the state, legitimating its growth and expansion as something 'natural' and hence inevitable. This analysis usually culminates in the reference to the concept of 'Lebensraum', taken up from Thomas Malthus by Ratzel (and also used by Nazi foreign policy), and what later came to be known as Ratzel's 'seven laws of the growth of states'. But, in what sense is such reference to the organic state, *both in itself and in its implications*, unique to the German branch of *Geopolitik*?

Without question, organic metaphors play a major role in German romanticism, but they are hardly unknown elsewhere. Indeed, the use of such metaphors is prominent in the work of Herbert Spencer who had a strong influence on American thinkers in the late nineteenth century.[9] Similarly, they abound in early French sociology, from Auguste Comte to Émile Durkheim, from whom Ratzel is said to have taken them. At most, then, the claim might mean that German defenders of geopolitics used the organic metaphor more prominently than their counterparts in the UK (Mackinder) or the United States (Mahan). But it remains to be seen whether that single characteristic would necessarily end up with qualitatively different geopolitical theories, that is to say, picking up on a unique feature is not showing that it is significant enough to set the German path apart, except, perhaps, if it were not used as a metaphor but as an essential explanatory concept. This was not the case here.

Indeed, there is a need for caution when interpreting what the German tradition's references to the state as an organism actually meant and implied. The metaphor was famously used in the opening pages of von Rochau's treatise on *Realpolitik*. However, the theme of the relevant passage in that work quickly shifts to an alleged law of the strong in political life, similar to the law of gravity in the physical world,[10] something at best akin to the idea of the reason of

---

[7] The German branch includes Rudolf Kjellén, the Swedish political geographer and intellectual disciple of Ratzel who coined the word 'geopolitics'.

[8] Not all recent geopolitical writers resort to this argumentative strategy. Carlo Jean, for instance, clearly states that Social Darwinism and organicism make the German branch no different from others. See Jean, 1995, 17–19. His own type of defence will be discussed later in this chapter.

[9] Hofstadter, 1944, *passim*. See also p. 34, where he cites the sales figures of Spencer's volumes between 1860 and 1903 in the United States, a staggering 368,755 copies!

[10] Rochau, 1972 [1853/1869], 25.

state.[11] Furthermore, Ratzel himself, the alleged father of geopolitical thought in that organicistic tradition, was very cautious regarding the use of this analogy. Although one of his short essays is repeatedly quoted for showing its central role in the German tradition[12] his early book *Anthropo-Geography* hardly mentions it, and his subsequent major work *Political Geography* contains a clear disclaimer regarding the use of a biological analogy.[13] When Haushofer published a selection of Ratzel's writings in late 1940, this did include a section on the state as organism. However, the passages selected by Haushofer show that, for Ratzel, it is the political *organisation* that turns soil and people into an *organism*.[14] Accordingly, it seems fair to say that Ratzel's position is ambivalent. On the one hand, his former training in zoology does not lead him to use an organicistic (biological) metaphor that was widely available in those times, but instead enables him to see the limits of such a metaphor more clearly.[15] At the same time, Ratzel allows the metaphorical force of the biological analogy to suggest explanations. It provides the necessary 'scientific' grounding for his approach to geography and the political justification for the expansionism and colonialism that he actively supported.[16]

In this apology of expansionism, this German tradition is however hardly unique. Ratzel's insistence on the importance of soil or territory ('homeland') for the definition of the state might sound dated in such times of presumed de-territorialisation as our own, but it is not a strange topos for his time, and was not limited to German minds. His understanding of the state as a whole more than the sum of its parts, is surely indebted to German (and other) idealism and to the national idea so powerful ever since the nineteenth century – and not just in Germany. And nor did those German idealists all turn into Social Darwinists, as the argument about the German organicistic path to geopolitics might have us believe. Quite the opposite. Talk about the 'growth' of nations easily picks up a body metaphor, but it was quite common in the historical discussions about the 'rise and decline' of nations in the early nineteenth century that, according to Ratzel, were the very reason geography returned to the limelight of science![17]

That Ratzel and Haushofer both accept the idea of a general *Kampf ums Dasein* (struggle for existence) as a vision of politics is not questioned here (even if Ratzel had a more qualified vision of that struggle). Nor is it disputed that such a vision almost inevitably slides into political prescriptions regarding the need to arm for that struggle and condones territorial expansion, including expansion by war, as 'natural'.[18] Yet, nowhere – or so I will argue – does this

---

[11] Haslam, 2002, 184.   [12] Ratzel, 1896.
[13] Ratzel, 1897, 12–13.   [14] Ratzel, 1940, 113ff.   [15] Hunter, 1986, 278.
[16] Bassin, 1987a, 488 and 485. See also Smith, 1980.
[17] Ratzel, 1882, 6.
[18] See Lindemann, 2000 for a study of how such *völkisch*-Darwinist ideas contributed to the perception of an inevitable (First World) war among German foreign policy elites.

Social Darwinism derive from any of the specific organicistic metaphors that are more prominent in Germany.

In fact, in Ratzel's first version of the rule (*Regel* understood as probability) that political units tend to increase – which also means to expand territorially and clash – all the arguments are de facto derived from a special reading of Malthus. The starting point is the general demographic increase, an empirical fact, and the alleged shortage of useable land that induces people to move and states to expand, a Malthusian assertion.[19] That is all that is required, no organicism is necessary. Indeed, the only thing that needs to be done is to change Malthus's classical strategy: rather than reducing the pressure through demographic restraint, as Malthus advocated, pressure is reduced through territorial expansion. Interestingly, for Ratzel, this tendency to greater increase in space goes hand in hand with a tendency to make borders coincide with nations and their territories through the political development of more federal systems where the two can be positively combined (Ratzel cites the United States as a positive model in this context).[20]

This is even more visible in Haushofer, who is far less subtle in his arguments. For Haushofer, the drive for expansion and Germany's need to obtain new (or recover old) *Lebensraum* in Europe originate once again in a mixture of Malthus and nationalism. Malthus shows up strongly in Haushofer's repeated argument that overpopulation lurks in the future, and, centrally, in his concept of the *Volksdruck* (Malthus: population pressure), measured as the number of inhabitants per square kilometre, a factor that, when high, 'explains' if not requires (and condones) territorially expansionist policies.[21] Nationalism is visible in Haushofer's assertion that Germany is 'crippled' (verkrüppelt) because its state borders do not coincide at the very least with the territory of the 'geschlossener deutscher Volksboden' (contiguous/unified German national territory) – if not with the sphere of linguistic and cultural influence – with the clear message that such an anomaly should be remedied.[22] Again, no reference to any organicism is needed, or indeed used. Nationalism can be culturalist, not just organicistic.

Alternative roads to Social Darwinism

That German metaphors of organic states are not that crucial for reaching Social Darwinism can also be shown by pointing to another path that leads to

---

[19] Ratzel, 1882, 116ff.   [20] Ratzel, 1882, 166.

[21] Haushofer, 1934, 27, 41. Haushofer conveniently included the colonies in the calculus for France and Britain, which allowed him to show that both Japan and Germany had the most population pressure to endure.

[22] See Haushofer, 1934, 57, including the inevitable map to bolster the claim. This corresponds almost literally to Ernest Gellner's 1983, 1, famous definition of nationalism.

the claim of the survival of the fittest, this time outside Germany. In addition to the approach of the classical geopolitical tradition, described above, which combines Malthusianism and nationalism to end up with the struggle for exist-ence, there is also a second, rather more economic (and Anglo-American) tradition, one that often passes unobserved. The approach here starts from the world of scarcity of liberal economics, where the inevitable competition ends up selecting the strongest to survive in the market. Again, this path to the 'survival of the fittest' can dispense with much of the biological overtones usually considered to be necessary for Social Darwinists (although Spencer's ideas came as a welcome support). The results, however, are strikingly similar. Whereas the pessimistic and cyclical visions of continental Europeans hardly enthralled US observers, market selection heralded a history of progress. It was not the (interventionist) liberal progress of perfectibility, where human inter-vention would assure progress, but the libertarian-conservative (or neoliberal) vision of progress, where the system itself, in its 'natural' selection that is most effective when left alone, would ensure that those unfit would eventually be left out or perish.[23]

Richard Hofstadter has shown how the certainly conservative Herbert Spencer, who coined the expression 'the survival of the fittest', made Social Darwinism palatable to much of US sociology and the educated public at large. Spencer recommended abstaining from any state intervention to help the weak, regarding such activity as counterproductive since it would enable unfit people or groups to survive. His evolutionary optimism and his 'scientific' – because now biological – defence of laissez-faire was almost instantly acceptable to suc-cessful businessmen, who intuitively recognised in the Darwinian terminology a portrait of their own conditions.[24] It caused Hofstadter to wonder 'whether, in the entire history of thought, there was ever a conservatism so utterly pro-gressive as this'. It was 'Social Darwinism as a conservative rationale' and a 'conservatism almost without religion'.[25] Hence, the same William Sumner that Jonathan Haslam quotes as showing how far the United States was from the European tradition of realism[26] was a conservative laissez-faire sociologist who strongly embraced Social Darwinism – that is, the least palatable part of the European *Realpolitik* tradition.

---

[23] Another indicator of this reading is the reception (and reduction) of Schumpeter to his famous phrase (borrowed from Werner Sombart's work on *War and Imperialism*) about the 'perennial gale of creative destruction' as being the essence of capitalism (Schumpeter, 1975 [1942], 84). This reduction is powerful enough to have entered the US public imaginary, when US President Bartlet of the TV series *The West Wing* can, in a defence of free trade, claim creative destruction as a fundamental tenet of his expertise as a graduate in eco-nomics. It has become 'progressive' common sense through its translation into neoliberal economics.

[24] Hofstadter, 1944, 44.   [25] Hofstadter, 1944, 8 and 7, respectively.

[26] Haslam, 2002, 183.

Such oddity did not go entirely unnoticed within International Relations. Indeed, E. H. Carr dedicates a whole section to Darwinism.[27] Strikingly, though, he does not locate it within realism. It forms part of his utopian category, because he derives it from the nineteenth-century attempt to save the liberal creed of laissez-faire economics in which the weaker are left to die.[28] Carr notes the fact that Darwinism hardly corresponds to the original 'harmony of interest', since progress that used to eventually benefit all is now said only to reward the chosen or combative few. And, yet, perhaps in a wry critique of British imperialism and hegemony, ready to paper over such blatant disharmony of interest by assuming some superior race or culture, he includes this thought that is most attractive to conservatives into the utopian category (while insisting also that this demonstrates how much IR thinking owed to the American tradition). However, this American utopianism is clearly not as the usual IR reception of the liberal/utopian/idealist school has it: it is a peculiar mix of liberal laissez-faire and a pragmatic justification of might, just as amenable to divorcing the realm of economics and politics from 'liberal morality' as was the conservative European tradition of 'reasons of state'. It is a conservative, not a Wilsonian, utopia (or nostalgia).[29]

Classical geopolitics: the inevitable clash of national expansionism in a finite world

As we have seen, German *Geopolitik* did not use the organicistic metaphor as strictly explanatory and its Social Darwinism could be derived from various sources. Indeed, classical geopolitics shares with *Geopolitik* a common root: Malthusianism, which explains (and justifies) a vision of perennial struggle, paired with nationalism – or indeed racism – which justifies a quest for, or defence of, superior status and rank. Although national ideational and political cultures shape this common stock in various ways, the (Western) geopolitical tradition is one, not many. Halford Mackinder's address to the Royal

---

[27] Carr, 1946, 46–50. See also the discussion in Sterling-Folker, 2006.

[28] Hans Morgenthau also remarks how Darwin's theory helped a 'scientific approach' to politics by suggesting that both nature and man are subject to the same natural (and hence perfectionist) laws. See Morgenthau, 1946, 28. What Morgenthau does not notice is the conservative twist that he himself at times applies to Darwin's theory, namely, how the 'lust for power' makes power politics – and indeed the 'survival of the fittest' – inevitable. This is equally scientific, but does not imply any progress.

[29] Still, this path to the survival of the fittest was coined with domestic politics in mind, and was not easily combined with militarism (whereas these two went hand in glove in the German tradition). Only when combined with a special nationalist mission can such ideas turn more militant, as in present-day neoconservatism. For a wider discussion of neoconservatism in IR, see Williams, 2005.

Geographic Society in 1904 on the 'geographical pivot of history' will serve as a further illustration of this unity.

Much of the first inspiration of geopolitics around the end of the nineteenth century was captured by Mackinder's celebrated address. Here, I am referring less to his famous discussion of the Heartland or his map, suggestive for generations to come, but rather to his grandiose opening, in which he refers to the historic change from a Columbian epoch, where the expansion of Europe (*sic*) met with almost negligible resistance, to a 'post-Columbian age' in which the world has become a 'closed political system' of worldwide scope: 'Every explosion of social forces, instead of being dissipated in a surrounding circuit of unknown space and barbaric chaos, will be sharply re-echoed from the far side of the globe, and weak elements in the political and economic organism of the world will be shattered in consequence.'[30]

This quote refers to two related ideas that are certainly fundamental for this particular speech, but arguably also for much geopolitics in general, and that have found an echo in later International Relations. The first is the idea that the world has become a whole, a 'total' where all politics has become interconnected.[31] It is no longer possible to simply disregard continents, even if they are 'far away' and presumably of no immediate significance for one's own country and its foreign policy. A wake-up call for Sleeping Beauties, many geopolitical scholars – though not only them – use this idea of connectivity to alert their compatriots of a world politics turned global. Mackinder employed it to connect all geopolitical threads to the defence of Britain's Empire. Haushofer was at pains to convince his German readers that the future centre of world politics might well lie in the Pacific, between the two major rising powers of his day (the United States and the Soviet Union) and/or, perhaps somewhat unexpectedly, in the new Pacific way of running politics, so different from the old Atlantic (gunboat) version.[32] Henry Kissinger, prominent in the revival of 'geopolitics' in the 1970s, and whose use of geopolitics has often been noted as being rather shallow,[33] similarly referred to geopolitics to tie all political developments around the world back to the central bipolar balance of power – whether the case in hand concerned, for instance, domestic politics, such as the rise of the Communist Party in a European country (Italy) or civil war, as with the decolonisation struggle in Africa (e.g. Angola), none of which were of major interest to the US public.[34] The world is a whole, no niche is left; for Kissinger, it has become *one* system, just as Mackinder said.[35] This totality informs the loose

[30] Mackinder, 1904, 422. Note the use of organism in a similarly loose way as in the German tradition.
[31] Geoffrey Parker sees in this 'Ganzheit' (totality or wholeness) 'the ultimate object and justification' of geopolitics today. See Parker, 1985, 2.
[32] Haushofer, 1924. [33] Hepple, 1986b.
[34] See, for example, Kissinger, 1979 and 1983.
[35] See also Jean, 1995, 58.

organism metaphor, which functions as a proxy for the holism of classical geo-politics, as well as of the later application of systems theory to International Relations.[36]

The second idea, related to this interconnectedness, concerns the finiteness of the world. If the expansion of great powers was previously almost uninhib-ited, which permitted an intricate system of compensations in terms of space and riches, further expansion would have to deal with a world in which all territories have been flagged. Symbolically starting with the Fashoda crisis in 1898, this finiteness implied that great powers could only 'win' territories at the expense of other great powers. And here the tone turns grim, as Mackinder predicts that this finiteness will have a shattering impact on the weaker parts of what he calls the 'organism of the world'. Yet, such an implication only fol-lows if expansionism in the international system is taken for granted: a limited world in which actors vie for a bigger slice of a cake whose size can no longer be increased.

It is this neo-Malthusian view that provides the determinism in the story: in a finite world with limited resources, seeking expansionism is the default position of any state, and its realisation is necessary whenever an opportun-ity arises to achieve it. Furthermore, the whole of Mackinder's text is imbued with nationalist references to the superior civilisational stage that justifies the British Empire's privileged place under the sun.

So, when all is said and done, not much of theoretical significance is left of the specific German path. To be clear again: this is not meant to belittle the atrocities and particularities of Nazi politics, nor some affinities between aca-demic *Geopolitik* and Nazi politics. But, precisely because the link between Nazi politics and *Geopolitik* is severed, the German *Geopolitik* tradition, not Nazism, appears as far more mainstream, inspired by the same roots of Malthus and nationalism as other branches in the classical geopolitical trad-ition. German *Geopolitik* was certainly characterised by a Social Darwinism most conducive to imperialism, but there have been other comparable roads to such Social Darwinism or the apology of Empire. Ultimately, lopping off the German branch does not resolve the problems of classical geopolitics, whose origins lie not in Germany but in the common roots of its tradition at large.

2   Geopolitics and realism

In a second step aimed at further elucidating the type of geopolitics with which this research project is concerned, I now set out to discuss and distinguish it from realism. For, given the previous section's reading of classical geopolitics in

---

[36] Merle, 1982, explicitly refers to this and the following idea of a 'finite' world as prerequisites for his system theory.

a fairly straightforward IR manner, I may have just needed to refer to the realist tradition. Yet, it makes a difference whether we speak about a revival of 'realism' or a revival of 'geopolitics'; the different expressions do not seem to allude to exactly the same types of explanations. Although all of the scholars that have been prominent in launching geopolitical ideas since 1989, such as Zbigniew Brzezinski, Samuel P. Huntington, Edward Luttwak and John Mearsheimer,[37] are realists, not all realists appeal to geopolitics, nor, as I will argue, do they need to. Hence the need for a comparison between geopolitics and the realist tradition if we are to properly understand the kind of geopolitics that revived after 1989 in Europe.

As this section will show, there is undoubtedly a common stock that justifies the inclusion of geopolitics within the large realist tradition. That stock consists in a materialist vision of the world, one in which human agency can at best adapt to the necessities of nature and power but not fundamentally alter them. In this world, the drive for relative status is given and power expansion the default option, just as in classical geopolitics. Yet, this expansionism does not need to derive from some version of neo-Malthusian analysis. Nor is the drive for status necessarily connected to ideas of nationalism, special missions or national primacy. In other words, whereas classical geopolitics is always part of the wide family of realist approaches, the reverse does not hold. Some versions of classical realism – and certainly the pluralist wing of the 'English School' – conceive of the power struggle less in terms of the inevitable expansionism of powers, and more in terms of the reproduction of a (European) diplomatic culture, where (limited) war is not the breakdown of international society, but has come to stand for one of its institutions.[38] Only when a contemporary realist watches the world with the gaze of the military strategist and only when that gaze is used for foreign policy advice in terms of national primacy or aggrandisement (whether territorial or not) does realism become akin to neoclassical geopolitics.

Realism: the necessity of power expansion (for rank maximisation)

As I see it, realism is best understood as a tradition of thought characterised by the repeated – and repeatedly unsuccessful – attempt to translate practical maxims of classical European diplomacy into general laws of a US social science.[39] In this tradition, it is possible to distinguish analytically between a more political branch and a more military branch, between the participant in the European diplomatic culture and the strategic thinker. The two are usually

---

[37] Brzezinski, 1997; Huntington, 1993a; Luttwak, 1990; and Mearsheimer, 2001.

[38] For the classical realists, see in particular Aron, 1962 and Kissinger, 1957. For the pluralist English School, the classical reference is Bull, 1977.

[39] Guzzini, 1998, 1.

combined, but the different combinations have quite different emphases. The more realism tends toward its political tradition, the more it is about the rules and conventions of (European) international society as that developed historically. The analysis is usually couched in terms of historical contingency, and often also includes normative discussions. Its understanding of theory is accordingly closer to a framework of analysis, providing the rationale for selecting significant factors, rather than to empirical generalisations and hypothesis-testing. Representative of this approach is the English School of International Relations, as well as classical realists like Raymond Aron and Arnold Wolfers, whose approaches allow for the ultimate indeterminacy of their frameworks.[40] In contrast, the more the realist tradition sees itself as being part of the strategic tradition, the more it tends to build rational explanations in terms of worst-case scenarios. The political branch tends to be open in its explanations, whereas the strategic branch tends to be more determinist. In the first tradition, the *reason of state* corresponds to a common language within which to understand (and justify) state behaviour; in the second, it becomes the expression for an individual *national security interest* for which more or less quantifiable costs and benefits are calculated.

In principle, some degree of environmental (or simply materialist) determinism could be reached by following either path. However, the default position of expansionism that undergirds classical geopolitics has been mainly reached by following the second, more strategic tradition. For classical geopolitics requires an element of materialist determinacy that the more contingent school does not provide. Not all realism is geopolitical.

Does this mean that power expansionism as a default option is not a core component of realism? It is quite a slippery slope for almost all realism to rely on it, since it provides the basic behavioural determinacy in the theory, as Wolfers showed long ago.[41] When a school of thought needs to justify its assumptions or empirical truth claims, mere references to 'historical experience' or tradition will not do: its assumptions or claims need to be shown to be better than other explanations or normative proposals. They have to persuade. And it is this necessity that has repeatedly led realists to opt for a more determinist, more 'scientist' version of realism, ever since realist approaches lost their self-evident grip on the discipline of International Relations. A more scientific turn is strictly speaking not necessary for all forms of realism, since

---

[40] This understanding of realism can be criticised as being too broad. Indeed, although the classical English School tradition is arguably realist, perhaps not all writers inspired by it today would best be described by such a label (particularly the School's solidarist wing). On the other hand, it would be unfair and reductionist to the realist tradition if one were to restrict it to the more 'scientific' writers or to the Hobbesian tradition. For an argument showing the similarities between the English School and classical realism, see Guzzini, 2001a; for an attempt to distinguish realism from the English School, see Copeland, 2003.

[41] Wolfers, 1962, 86.

realist thinkers could simply reject the very need to justify what they perceive as the superiority of realism's practical knowledge. However, in a scientific environment (less so in politics), this is hardly a tenable position. And so, whenever pressed to defend its own superiority, realism repeatedly ends up tending towards the ideas of a default position of expansionism or rank/status maximisation (relative gains) and a historically infinite struggle for power. This is certainly not the teleological determinacy of progress that is so much despised or deeply feared by realists. But determinacy it implies, if in a conservative and historically cyclical form. This determinacy, in turn, can stem from several origins. In many regards, closest to the classical geopolitical tradition, both chronologically and intellectually, is the *early* Hans Morgenthau.[42] At this stage, Morgenthau's realist theory includes the two central geopolitical facets: an understanding of politics as a struggle for survival and the belief in an inherently human lust for power or will for domination, both sufficient conditions for depicting a world in which power competition reigns. The struggle for existence is endemic since, in a world of scarcity, self-interests necessarily clash. Moreover, it is inherent, since the human drive for domination is a quest for rank; it is never assured and hence virtually insatiable. As a result, all agents necessarily try to increase their power, whatever their ultimate aims may be. The default position is therefore expansionist or a defence against such expansionism, resulting in a de facto strategy of rank maximisation.[43]

The notion of such an expansionist drive is quite commonplace in early realist writings, even those lacking anthropological undertones. Indeed, it has been more common to couch the idea of such a drive in physicalist language. Here, the expansion appears in what could be termed 'collateral pressure' or 'osmosis'. In the image of 'collateral pressure', the internal pressure (power) of a state pushes collaterally on others. If that collateral pressure is higher than the one of these other bodies, then the state will expand – until the precise point that its own internal pressure (which is declining as a result of its expansion) is balanced by the pressures around. A closely related image is one that might be said to describe the 'osmosis of power'. Here, the flexible outer skin of a body becomes in fact permeable. The mounting pressure is balanced not by expanding bodies, but by letting their content pass through the barrier. This means that whenever there appears to be a 'power vacuum', it will inevitably be filled by the strongest actor, often after a fight. Expansion is not necessarily a drive, but simply the natural result of a decreasing power level in the environment. The main metaphor is that of the natural tendency of liquids to even out their levels in contiguous containers. One of the most literary (and powerful) examples of such an argument can be found in the article by 'X' (George F. Kennan) on 'The

---

[42] Morgenthau, 1946, 192–200.
[43] This struggle for power is not reducible to territorial change only. See Morgenthau, 1948, Part II (11–69).

Sources of Soviet Conduct': 'Its political action is a fluid stream which moves constantly, whenever it is permitted to move, toward a given goal. Its main concern is to make sure that it has filled every nook and cranny available to it in the basin of world power.'[44] The idea of a logic of power filling a 'power vacuum' leaves basically no choice: either one expands power (internally or externally) to keep up the pressure or one is engulfed in the other's expansion. Such is the alleged logic of power politics.

And, yet, already in Morgenthau's early writings, one can see how such assumptions come from a political realism that no longer condones but rather opposes nationalism.[45] For nationalism is no longer a value, the necessary expression of a group's self-interest in a scarce world; it has become part of the problem. It is owing to all the different 'universalist nationalisms' that the moderation of European diplomacy has so much trouble asserting itself. The limitation of war – that is, the more or less common management of power expansions – has become difficult to achieve. It is not by accident that some realist writers look back to the Concert of Europe with nostalgia, as a time where the new nationalist forces were still being kept at bay, at least relatively speaking.[46]

Accordingly, within such a political realism, Hobbes (or Machiavelli) takes the place of Malthus, and nationalism drops out. Scarcity breeds competition in a world in which no World Leviathan has been given the right to enforce order by a social contract. Also, whether premised on the structure of human nature or of the international power environment, the behavioural effects can then be treated in broadly rationalist terms. Robert Gilpin argues that 'a state will attempt to change the international system if the expected benefits exceed the expected costs' (i.e. if there is an expected net gain) and 'will seek to change the international system through territorial, political, and economic expansion until the marginal costs of further change are equal to or greater than the marginal benefits'.[47]

Geopolitics, or: realism's military and nationalist gaze

Hence, whether intended or not, whether based on human nature or rational calculus, expansionism – and thus power competition – applies. However, the expansionism here is not necessarily the same as that in Social Darwinism,

[44] Kennan, 1951 [1947], 118.
[45] Morgenthau openly opposes geopolitics. Interestingly, however, he does not criticise its vision of power expansion or the struggle for power/survival as such, but the tendency of geopolitics to understand power purely in terms of geography – what he calls the fallacy of a single factor. He also rightly notes how such an approach can be easily used for nationalist purposes. See Morgenthau, 1948, 116–118.
[46] Most importantly with Kissinger, 1957.
[47] See hypotheses 2 and 3 of Robert Gilpin's version of Hegemonic Stability Theory in: Gilpin, 1981, 10 and as developed in his Chapters 2 and 3.

since the latter would require a direct connection between expansionism and some version of nationalism (superior culture, race, nation), something that realism can perfectly live without.[48] Indeed, some realist writings are clearly meant to detach the Social Darwinism of earlier writers from its post-1945 versions.[49] Determinacy based on a necessary power expansion as a default option is fundamental for the theory; its link to the 'survival of the fittest' is not (except in some tautological sense).

Yet, there is a special connection between some versions of realism and geopolitics. Again and again, a purely systemic theory of realism that would be able to deduce power competition (in a quest for security) from the simple fact that the international system has no common authority (its 'anarchy') has been shown to be indeterminate: a default position of expansionism, or any other behavioural rule for that matter, does not necessarily follow.[50] There are different realist ways of fixing this indeterminacy. One strategy, perhaps not always consistent with realist assumptions, consists in increasing the number of factors included in the framework of analysis. This can happen, for instance, through the inclusion of idealist factors (perception) or specific domestic variables for the relevant states.[51]

A second available strategy moves from the level of observation to the level of action and assumes that we simply cannot afford to ignore the possible worst case. This is an understandable – if often counterproductive – practical move, but it has quite pernicious implications, both theoretical and practical. It basically claims that whether or not there is some necessary tendency to power expansion can be considered secondary; we simply assume it, because, to quote former US secretary of defense Donald Rumsfeld, there are 'also unknown unknowns. There are things we don't know we don't know'.[52] On the theoretical level, this ultra-prudential statement does not resolve anything: we still do not

---

[48] See also Portinaro, 1999, 79–80, who defends the view that realism assumes that power 'by its nature' (in quotation marks in original) is expansive, and that hence such expansionism does not need to refer to any sense of a mission, which would be necessary for versions of Social Darwinism.

[49] See, for example, Aron's (overstated) critique of Max Weber, in Aron, 1967. For my own take on Weber, see Guzzini, 2007.

[50] The locus classicus of such a realist theory is, of course, Waltz, 1979. For a critique of such an attempt, predating Waltz's actual theory, see the realists Aron, 1962 and Wolfers, 1962. For a later critique of the indeterminacy of such a theory, see Axelrod and Keohane, 1986, Guzzini, 1998, Milner, 1991 and Wendt, 1992.

[51] It is impossible to name even the most important scholars here, hence some pointers will have to do. The work on perception was central to Jervis, 1976 and Wohlforth, 1993. Writers who try to reinsert domestic factors are usually part of the 'neoclassical' realist school. For an overview, see Rose, 1998.

[52] Donald Rumsfeld at a press conference at NATO Headquarters, Brussels, Belgium, 6 June 2002; available at: www.defenselink.mil/transcripts/transcript.aspx?transcriptid=3490. Although much fun has been made of this quote, it is meaningful in terms of worst-case thinking pushed to the extreme.

know whether or not the behaviour of states is characterised by a tendency to expand their power, and hence to collide. And, on the practical level, if every state behaves on the general assumption that such a tendency exists, the risk of a dangerous self-fulfilling prophecy looms large in the picture.

Still, this second move that seeks to rely on worst-case thinking is crucial for pointing to a special connection between geopolitics and the more military or strategic wing of realism. For worst-case scenarios think politics backwards from war. It immediately drags foreign policy into the realm of military planning, and quickly tends to reverse Clausewitz's dictum – in other words, it comes to think of politics as a prolongation of war by other means, rather than vice versa, with often deleterious effects for foreign policy in general.[53] With potential war planning as a backdrop, geographic factors, which would at best be generic factors of the analysis, acquire a particular salience. It is almost self-evident that military movement and defence are conditioned, often strongly so, by geography, and that the domination of space is a crucial strategic facet. Accordingly, through the back door of military worst-case scenarios, in an equivalent of the 'primacy of foreign policy', here reduced to the primacy of potential war (as compared to domestic politics and diplomacy), geographical or generally more materialist factors gain priority in the analysis.

It is in this symbiosis of expansionism and worst-case thinking that geopolitics becomes or represents realism's military gaze. Any usage of 'geopolitics' will almost immediately mobilise this particular bias of strategic thinking. The bias is particularly well mobilised in times of higher alert or international tension. In turn, its use, whether intended or not, feeds into an escalation that moves military factors – and everything that can feed into them – to the top of the agenda. Geopolitical discourse is hence 'securitising' in the terminology of the Copenhagen School of Security Studies.[54] And what a powerful tool it is. For it is not just abstract argument; it comes with the persuasiveness of the visual, the power of maps in which the world is laid out before one's eyes. Even Carlo Jean, defender of a geopolitical approach but wary of the alleged determinacy of geopolitical argument, notes that 'the temptation of determinism in geopolitics ... feeds off the enormous propagandistic value of the geographic map. It presents as an objective evaluation that which is only subjective'.[55]

And the military bias of geopolitics – which puts national security thinking first – also enables the mobilisation of the implicit nationalist biases of the

---

[53] This is Aron's central line of criticism of US foreign policy during the Cold War, many times repeated in Aron, 1976.

[54] See Buzan et al., 1998, Wæver, 1995. Of course, peace research has long been aware of the perverse effects of worst-case thinking and has sought to apply a reflexive turn to it: in several cases, worst-case thinking produces the very worst case to be avoided. For an overview, see Guzzini, 2004a.

[55] Jean, 1995, 19.

geopolitical tradition to 'rally round the flag'. This is visible in discussions about the need for primacy in international affairs. Such a need is obviously justifiable if power expansionism can be taken for granted, although nobody derives it theoretically any longer.[56]

3   Neoclassical and critical geopolitics

As the first chapter showed, in order for the post-1989 revival of 'geopolitics' to be unexpected, it needs to be understood as an approach that goes beyond the revival of sheer geographic imagination after the collapse of the Cold War system and include some sort of geographic determinism. In my attempt to reach what I regard as an adequate definition of 'geopolitics', which will be set out at the end of this second chapter, I have so far tried to show that this determinism harks back to the common neo-Malthusian roots of geopolitics, and not just some allegedly special German tradition. I have also shown that it should not be confused with realism at large, but with that part of realism that derives from its 'strategic' tradition, in which worst-case thinking mobilises realism's military gaze.

With this argument, have I not neglected the actual analysis by defenders of a neoclassical geopolitical revival? Have they not spent all their time debunking the relation to German *Geopolitik* and refuting the charge of environmental determinism by embedding their tradition in a moderate version of realism? Yet, as we have seen, although the geopolitical tradition is perfectly right to oppose any guilt by association with Nazism, I did not find the arguments against expansionism and determinism convincing. Indeed, as this section will show, they run into a basic dilemma. They are compelled to share the materialist conditioning of politics in general and the expansionist drive of states in particular if they wish to retain some distinctiveness and determinacy in geopolitical explanations. Without the primacy of the material, self-evident for a geopolitical approach, also realism would lose its self-definition when compared to idealist approaches; without some determinacy, often found in the inevitable struggle for power (and hence expansion), both forms of analysis would lose their persuasiveness when compared to alternative explanations. I will argue that neoclassical geopolitics does rely on a less demanding understanding of determinism – namely, the explanatory primacy of geographical factors in their widest sense – and that this is all that is needed to reapply the criticism against classical geopolitics as I developed it above. This gives rise to the dilemma of the (neoclassical) geopolitical approach: if geopolitics comes with a defence of (material) determinism, it is not credible; if it renounces such

---

[56] For the mobilisation of national primacy arguments, see Huntington, 1993b; for a critique, see Jervis, 1993.

a defence, this undermines the very basis of its approach and identity. Why would we then need geopolitics in the first place? By daring to say 'geopolitics' but allegedly renouncing some version of geographic determinism, the revival of neoclassical geopolitics tries to have its cake and eat it too.

But by the time they reach this page, not only neoclassical geopoliticians but also political geographers may find themselves sighing with disappointment. What started as a nice opening to political geography seems to have tethered itself down to the usual IR line, reducing the discussion of geopolitics to a branch of realism, an approach they had done so much to get beyond. But, that would be too hasty a conclusion. Indeed, critical geopolitics has been a major inspiration for the present study. But, that inspiration comes more in terms of the content of the analysis, the critique of the geopolitical tradition, and less in terms of the redefinition of 'geopolitics' in a new guise. Although I can sympathise with efforts, such as those of John Agnew, to contaminate the geopolitical discourse by appropriating it – a strategy that is certainly useful for redefining political geography – my understanding is that the geopolitical discourse goes on in IR academia and practice unscathed by such attempts. And, it is the power of that discourse – that is, neoclassical geopolitics – that is the one of the key interests of the present study.

Saving geopolitics by trivialising it? No way out of the determinism dilemma

Contemporary scholars who defend geopolitics criticise the 'environmental determinism' of the tradition's past. It is commonplace to find early passages in their analysis and conceptual clarification that clearly state that no such determinism exists and hence repeating the critique of the past is ill-applied.

One line of defence simply waters down the determinacy of geographic factors, but retains them for structuring the analysis. As a result, the definition of 'geopolitics' becomes rather vague (and for many quite trivial), and its theoretical import underexplored. For instance, after having rejected both classical geopolitics and the deterministic use of geographical space in formulating foreign policy, Saul Cohen – the doyen of geopolitics in political geography, and for a long time its lonely defender within the discipline[57] – defines geopolitics as 'the analysis of the interaction between geographical settings and perspectives, and international politics', where his own approach is specified as 'combining spatial theory with geographical content in its application to foreign policy-making'.[58] That is as vague as it can get. For the issue is not whether geography can play some role, but why it should be the primary explanatory approach, as a reference to geopolitics suggests.

---

[57] See Cohen, 1963.   [58] Cohen, 2003, 3.

When Cohen moves to the empirical analysis, he sees the world stratified in terms of geographical levels (from the 'geostrategic' level to subnational units) in terms of a hierarchy of states, ranked by orders of power. Illustrating the interrelationship between geography and politics, Cohen writes that

> [t]here is a strong relationship between a nation's foreign policy-making and geopolitical structure. Structures reflect such geographical dimensions as distance and access, patterns of resource use, trade, capital and migration flows, levels of technology, and cultural/religious differences. As these dimensions change, foreign policy must adapt to them. For example, the flow of capital and the out-sourcing of manufacturing from Taiwan, South Korea, Japan and the United States to coastal China, has forced these four countries to adapt their foreign policies to accommodate the new economic reality. Beijing, in turn, has adopted more flexible policies on economy and trade, and in foreign affairs.[59]

Here, determinism seems to have been avoided, since the relationship between structure and agency is only one of conditioning (which apparently only happens from structure to agency, not the other way round).

Yet, it is not quite clear how such an analysis evades the critique of determinism. Obviously, determinism does not imply a one-to-one relationship, where a certain cause (geographical change) invariably produces a certain effect (e.g. change of power structures or foreign policy change). Such a charge of determinism is indeed easy to counter, because it is absurd in itself. Rather, the crucial question regarding environmental determinism is whether in the geopolitical analysis, even allowing for a multitude of factors, it is geography that trumps all others, including in cases where such an argument comes with the proviso of 'in the last resort'. And here, Cohen seems rather to be reaffirming the primacy of geography for structuring our thought in international affairs. All other factors are residual or added to this core. The fact that he cites as theoretical inspirations Herbert Spencer's *The Social Organism* and von Bertalanffy's work, along with his insistence on equilibrium thought and the world system as a 'general organismic system',[60] again suggests not only the possible affinity of organicistic evolutionist and a system theory of dynamic equilibria, but also a functional determinism creeping in by the back door for the way systems evolve 'in predictably structured ways'.[61] Yet, this primacy of geography is now no longer justified, since – and here the circle closes – the approach does not assume determinism and can therefore dispense with defending it.

Logically speaking, there are two main strategies for opposing determinacy, both prominent within other materialist approaches in IR. The first is to leave the geopolitical effects strong, but weaken the necessity with which they come about: geopolitical factors are efficient, but only under certain conditions. This

---

[59] Cohen, 2003, 7.   [60] Cohen, 2003, 3, fn. 4.   [61] Cohen, 1991, 560.

is the classical move of many positivist writings, where determinacy is dealt with in terms of 'probability'. Alternatively, one adopts the opposite strategy: one keeps a general necessitous effect, but renders vague what that effect actually is, in a way that parallels Waltz's defence of structural realism. Geopolitical factors are said to be ubiquitous, but with diffuse effects. In the first strategy, one would need to add a series of scope conditions, permissive, intermediate or (other) process variables under which the probability either increases or not. In the second, one basically leaves it to others to make an analysis tailored to the empirical case at hand, remaining content with a kind of generic range within which the final outcome should fall.

When all is said and done, though, at this point it is no longer quite clear how geopolitics does the explanation.[62] For one thing, such an analysis hardly adds to the usual materialist studies in (realist) International Relations. In order not to be redundant, it would need to show the primacy of some particular geographical knowledge, which is something that it does not do. Moreover, the actual analysis leaves the ambivalence about the actual role of geographical factors untouched. Now, if such factors are just background conditions, then they are present in all theories – no geopolitics needed. If, on the other hand, they are more, if there is a primacy, then that would need to be shown and justified, and this is not the case.

This brings me to a second strategy for resuscitating a geopolitics that is not tainted by determinism. In this second defence, the analysis moves down to the level of cognition. According to this line of thinking, geography matters, but only through the representations that people and/or foreign policymakers have of it. This move is typical of the French School of geopolitics, which has done much to legitimate the term 'geopolitics' in a more critical environment. In his recent treatise on geopolitics, drawing on the approach of Yves Lacoste, Carlo Jean debunks a series of misconceptions held by geopolitical scholars themselves. In fact, he is aware of how much determinism lurks in the background of all geopolitics, and this by necessity. Since geopolitics, for Jean, is about the spatial representations and the lessons of history in the elaboration of a national interest that is never neutral, the geopolitical scholar is akin to the geographer of the Prince, proposing a 'voluntaristic geography with which to identify and define the policies that lead to a modification of the existing geographic order'. He adds:

> Because of this lack of neutrality, no geopolitician can evade the temptation – even if it is only unconscious – of scientism and determinism, whatever critical thoughts he or she may have regarding these. This temptation is a constant for all those who, in their quest to make their political or strategic choices acceptable, elaborate geopolitical theories, hypotheses or scenarios and who look for the acquiescence of the 'Prince' or of public opinion … Those who brandish a political programme and cannot enrol 'God' or the

---

[62] See also the response to Cohen by Lowenthal, 2003, 35.

'Idea' under their banner will try to enlist nature or history (along with just-ice, humanity, religion, etc.) in order to convince others of their proposals.

But, adds Jean, 'there are no objective geopolitical principles or laws'. Borders or regions are not natural; 'they only become so with regard to a certain agent, given his visions, values and interests'.[63] Presumably exasperated by a succession of self-anointed experts pontificating in the (Italian) public debate, Jean's reaction displays an 'anti-apparent' realism[64] at its best, arguing for the impossibility of evading determinism, often hidden or unconscious, and unmasking the ideological component of claims that pretend to 'naturalise' their particular perspectives. So far, so good.

However, there is a clear slippery slope here: once it has been ascertained that geopolitics is not science (but 'a metaphysics of the competition for the domination of space'),[65] and that, like the national interest, it is subjective, it seems one is basically free to propose whatever explanations one deems fit. On what basis are we to judge them? When should we mix which factors for the analysis? Once we have determined that the geographic factor, although always present as constraining or enabling, necessarily needs to be accompanied by almost everything from ideology, via technology to domestic legitimacy,[66] how much does this factor count? And does this strategy of unmasking the necessary determinism not end up condoning it whenever it creeps in – as, for instance, in the prediction (based on what?) that Japan and Germany, 'whether they want to or not', will transform into military powers (the exact meaning of the latter being unspecified)?[67] And does this type of objectivistic analysis not blatantly contradict Jean's Lacostian starting-point whereby all is filtered through representation and historical rights?[68]

The material world was said to always function through a subjective factor, but when push comes to shove conventional realism reappears – and can now pretend to need no further explanatory justification. It is difficult to see why Jean's particular ideological use of geopolitics should not prompt a new round of his unmasking attitude, now applied to his own version of geopolitics. A critical attitude that stops at itself slides easily into becoming the ultimate ideological move. Such self-contradiction seems to confirm Carr's early verdict that it is impossible to be a consistent realist.[69]

---

[63] Jean, 1995, 8, 20, 9 and 20, respectively. [The translations are all mine.]

[64] Norberto Bobbio distinguishes between anti-ideal (opposing the utopian) and anti-apparent (unmasking) realism in Bobbio, 1996 [1969], xiv–xvii, where the former stands for the more conservative, and the latter for the more critical tradition. For a discussion of that latter tradition, which includes E. H. Carr and Susan Strange, see Guzzini, 2000b, 2001b.

[65] Jean, 1995, 13. [66] Jean, 1995, 11. [67] Jean, 1995, 85.

[68] Admittedly, though, Lacoste cannot evade lapses into classical objectivism, either. See the critique in Ó Tuathail, 1996, 165.

[69] Carr, 1946, 89. For the unsuccessful realist attempt to evade a need to justify realist validity claims by questioning the validity of science, see the discussion in Guzzini, 2004b.

But, if this is the case, why even bother to apply the label 'geopolitics' to this loose realist approach that allows for the inclusion of all possible factors and would represent little new or unfamiliar to realist writers and readers in IR? One of the reasons has been mentioned by Jean: the mobilisation of an object-ivist or scientist appeal. 'Geopolitics' is a powerful rhetorical tool. But it is also a symbol. As such, it is related to the definition of the foreign policy – or, rather, security – expert. 'Geopolitics' is often part of the language to which one has to conform if one is to gain and retain the required legitimacy to perform as an expert. It is part of, and can be used to define, the terms of the common sense of the IR expert, just as 'power politics' used to be. Or, to use a fitting, if harsh, description in a critique of the balance of power from the early 1960s:

> [t]hese cases illustrate the widespread tendency to make the balance of power a symbol of Realism, and hence of respectability, for the scholar or statesman. In this usage, it has no substantive content as a concept. It is a test of intellectual virility, of he-manliness in the field of international relations. The man who 'accepts' the balance of power and who dots his writing with approving references to it, thereby asserts his claim to being a hard-headed Realist who can look at the grim reality of power without flinching. The man who rejects the balance of power convicts himself of softness, of cowardly incapacity to look power in the eye and acknowledge its role in the affairs of states.[70]

Hence, two lessons can be drawn from this discussion of neoclassical geopol-itics. For one, the approach is trapped in a dilemma somewhat similar to the identity dilemma of realism.[71] If it does accept environmental determinism, it needs to justify it, which it has avoided doing so far by pretending it does not need to. If it pretends not to be environmentally determinist but allows for a multiplicity of equal explanatory factors, or inflates the definition of geog-raphy sufficiently to include everything from historical lessons to state forms, then it is redundant, since it loses both a specific explanatory added value as compared to already existing approaches and, indeed, its geographical iden-tity: why call it geopolitics otherwise?[72] Therefore determinism, understood as explanatory primacy, is part and parcel of the tradition of neoclassical geopol-itics, even it comes by the back door. The use of the term 'geopolitics' alludes to that materialist and structuralist 'necessity' that agents can ignore only at their peril.

The second lesson is that the use of 'geopolitics' is indeed not innocent. In an environment where less laden words or concepts could be applied, where valuable time could be saved by not wading through a muddled past in search

---

[70] Claude, 1962, 39.   [71] See Guzzini, 2004b.

[72] For a related critique, as applied to Geoffrey Parker's wide definition of geopolitical thought, which ends up being unable to discriminate consistently what is part of it (including also world system analysis, for instance), see Østerud, 1988, 192.

of a tradition made acceptable (why bother?), where realism already provides a fairly developed language that overlaps almost entirely with a moderate version of geopolitics, a geopolitics that dares to speak its name comes with a purpose, whether or not it does so intentionally. It mobilises, much more strongly than just 'realism', the necessitous component of the analysis and hence empowers the proposed geopolitical analysis as having explanatory precedence. It has the potential of a discursive trump card.

From geopolitics to geo-politics?

Before we can finally reach the working definition of neoclassical geopolitics adopted for the present volume, we need to address another way of widening the definition of geopolitics. Critical geopolitics is well aware and critical of the past and present of classical geopolitics, yet it wishes to retain the word 'geopolitics' for its analysis. It can do so only because it consciously moves the analysis to the level of second-order observations. It studies not geopolitics as the relationship between geography and politics (first-order observation), but rather the 'geo-politics' of this geopolitical representation itself, as the latter interacts with the geography and foreign policy it analyses (here the hyphenation expresses the second-order observation of the first-order phenomena). Whereas neoclassical geopolitics, 'using geographical knowledge and representations to naturalise power, belongs to the realm of realist approaches', critical geopolitics, 'problematising the fusion of geographical knowledge and power, belongs to the realm of constructivist approaches'.[73] This has important implications for how geopolitics is defined. 'Geopolitics ... should be critically re-conceptualized as a discursive practice by which intellectuals of statecraft "spatialize" international politics in such a way as to represent it as a "world" characterized by particular types of places, peoples and dramas'. And, 'the study of geopolitics in discursive terms ... is the study of the socio-cultural resources and rules by which geographies of international politics get written'.[74] Consequently, the present comparative analysis, which focuses on 'neoclassical geopolitics', could be faulted for starting from a narrow or outdated understanding of geopolitics.

Differences in research aims provide the underlying reason for why we have chosen to work with a more 'classical' definition. The aim of this study is different from that of political geographers who wish to unmask the only apparent naturalness of geography. Their endeavour leads to quite wide definitions of geopolitics, like the one just mentioned, which would help to uncover the geo-political core of allegedly naturalist geography and gather together all discourses pertaining to it, whether or not these use the label 'geopolitics'. Such

---

[73] Mamadouh and Dijkink, 2006, 353.
[74] Ó Tuathail and Agnew, 1992, 192 and 193.

definitions are part of the attempt to redefine what it means to be a political geographer in the first place. The present study aims, however, at something different. It seeks to understand why, in several countries, it has been specifically the geopolitical tradition that has been mobilised for a spatialisation of politics, not any other approach. Just as there is no natural correspondence between particular representations and the geography they image, there is no natural correspondence between spatialising biases and the open use of arguments from the specifically geopolitical tradition. When Gearóid Ó Tuathail and Simon Dalby write that 'geopolitics is not a specific school of statecraft but rather can be better understood as the spatial practices, both material and representations, of statecraft itself',[75] they correctly wish to change focus. But they would probably not object to the proposition that geopolitics is *both* a first-order and a second-order phenomenon, both a specific school and the spatial practices of statecraft.[76]

Hence, it is the focus and aim of this study that guides the usage of 'geopolitics' in a more traditional way, for it is the revival of that more traditional form of geopolitical thought that triggers the puzzle we examine and, as we will see later, is also more pertinent for the second social mechanism developed in our study. For other research purposes, critical geography may be well advised to use another definition.

4   Conclusion: the meaning and functions of 'neoclassical geopolitics'

Chapter 1 specified the puzzling nature of the *revival*: why would the peaceful end of the Cold War revitalise a school of thought within International Relations that, by most accounts in the academic (and wider) community, was discredited by that event? For that puzzle, what is important is not just that the end of the East–West conflict would spur a new spatial imagination in Europe, something that could be expected, but rather: why would the more determinist tradition called 'geopolitics' reappear, no longer shying away from saying its name? And why would that happen only in some countries and not others?

The present chapter specified the object of the study: which *geopolitics* redux; or, more precisely, what forms of geopolitics in the aftermath of 1989 seem puzzling because they would lead to a more Hobbesian culture in European security. The discussion has identified basically three forms of geopolitics. One is 'critical geopolitics', with which the present book shares several assumptions. But this 'geopolitics' and its revival after 1989 is not the object of the study. It

---

[75] Ó Tuathail and Dalby, 1998, 3.
[76] Ó Tuathail, 1996, 16, also wishes to retain a narrower definition, although for different reasons.

would certainly not contribute to a more Hobbesian culture of anarchy; quite the contrary.

A second way of seeing the revival of geopolitics might simply refer to the use of the term 'geopolitics' in public debate. Although such usage will not be the primary object of the present study, it can affect foreign policy discourses, simply through the term's capacity, discussed above, to mobilise materialist or militarist visions of international security. But that mobilisation of bias is a weak force in and for itself. And, rather than to be regarded as contributing to this mobilisation of bias, the fact that it seems acceptable or even self-evident to refer to 'geopolitics' is rather an indicator of an already existing bias. Such a situation says something about the underlying discourse itself.

Finally, there is a third 'geopolitics', the one dubbed 'neoclassical geopolitics', which is the central object of study here. This can come in two forms. In one, there would be not simply open, if loose, references to past geopolitical thinkers, but also an open endorsement of some vision of neo-Malthusianism. This has been rare. In fact, such an approach would be just classical geopolitics reapplied. Yet, as the present chapter has shown, the fact that one does not repeat the classics does not of itself automatically move one out of this tradition, including some of its less warranted components. More centrally for this study, neoclassical geopolitics comes in another guise. In the definition that underpins our puzzle and research, neoclassical geopolitics is *a policy-oriented analysis, generally conservative and with nationalist overtones, that gives explanatory primacy, but not exclusivity, to certain physical and human geographic factors (whether the analyst is open about this or not), and gives precedence to a strategic view, realism with a military and nationalist gaze, for analysing the 'objective necessities' within which states compete for power and rank.*

Such a definition asks for some clarification. It implies that neoclassical geopolitics is characterised by a version of environmental determinism understood as explanatory primacy. For this is the discriminatory criterion that sets geopolitics apart from other versions of realism. By the explanatory primacy of certain geographic factors, I understand an analysis that reserves a special place for those geographical factors that are usually attached to the analysis of state resources, either because they set the stage for the whole analysis or because they are the argumentative 'trump card'.[77] As in classical geopolitics, this includes aspects of human and cultural geography (demography, relation of people to territory, or 'their' territory), as well as political and economic

---

[77] This is broadly compatible with other definitions, such as for example 'A geopolitics ... is a policy-oriented discourse about a state inspired by its position on the map' (van der Wusten and Dijkink, 2002, 20) if some determinacy is attached to that 'inspiration'; or: 'Geopolitics is understood broadly as a political worldview that privileges the metaphors of space for the self-understanding of the territorial nation-state, and sees the state's relative position within such space as conditions of possibility for power projection' (Bach and Peters, 2002, 1).

geography. In other words, geopolitical thought was never only just about seas and continental masses, but always included a cultural, if not civilisational, component. It is therefore nothing unusual that Mackinder, for instance, positively discussed issues of ethnic homogenisation as a means of conflict resolution, as indeed was practised in the aftermath of World War I in the Turkish–Greek population exchange.[78] In this regard, Huntington's thesis is hardly new within the geopolitical tradition, where it firmly belongs.

Finally, the definition includes a parenthesis about the claim and reality of such primacy in the analysis. We saw in the illustrative discussion of Carlo Jean's geopolitics that neoclassical geopolitics can come in a version that denies such a primacy in theory, even though the primacy reappears in the actual empirical analysis. The obvious puzzle here is that if geopolitics boils down to some kind of realism, why not take the easy route and use realism instead, without taking an approach that makes it necessary to weed out all of geopolitics' dubious Germanic or Social Darwinist connotations? The answer: because the label 'geopolitics' has a certain symbolic function and power stronger than realism. And this leads to the analysis of explanations with an open endorsement of 'geopolitics', whether or not their approach admits or indeed requires geographic primacy. If it comes as a version of realism but wishes to retain a different – albeit tainted – name, if, as often appears to be the case, writers pepper their papers with geopolitical jargon without necessarily being aware of its ancestry or use the geopolitical pedigree in a very loose way, this in itself is to be understood in symbolic terms of rhetorical power.

Hence, this book will compare different European countries after 1989 in relation to the revival of 'neoclassical' 'geopolitics' in its two components. To analyse the type of the revival, it will look for the 'neoclassical' components defined above, whether or not the label 'geopolitics' is explicitly used in the analysis. But, it will also look for 'geopolitics' when it dares to speak its name on account of that name's rhetoric and symbolic function. It is this neoclassical geopolitical revival that is the focus of the present book.

[78] Mackinder, 1944 [1919].

3

The framework of analysis: geopolitics meets foreign policy identity crises

STEFANO GUZZINI

How, then, can we best understand the puzzling revival of neoclassical geopolitics? Now that we have specified the puzzle and its central term, this chapter introduces the central concepts and theoretical framework of the analysis.

The nature of the puzzle places the present study in the wide research field that investigates the origins and development of theories, worldviews or, in a general sense, ideational structures. In the absence of a unified social theory that might have resolved the latent materialist–idealist divide that such a research focus mobilises, there are a series of research traditions from which hypotheses could be derived for our case studies.[1]

On the more idealist side, a first hypothesis derives from the history and institutionalisation of ideas, namely, the ideational path dependence of a given political culture. This hypothesis stipulates that a materialist tradition, of whatever kind, would be more conducive to a revival of geopolitical thought. Where geopolitical thought was not part of the common wisdom, it would have been more difficult for the events of 1989 to trigger a geopolitical revival.

On the more materialist side, two hypotheses come to mind. Stemming from a more materialist sociology of knowledge, one would stipulate that since classical geopolitics thrived in countries in need of a sense of legitimacy concerning their desire to maintain or acquire a great-power status, a similar process might be happening after 1989. Geopolitics would function as the ideology of a great power. Looking at sociological factors within countries, hypotheses could be derived from institutional and political economy factors – that is, how the foreign policy expertise field was structured in different countries. Geopolitics being usually connected to military thought, the place of the military within the foreign policy community could be important. Also, how is the expert system organised? For example, how independent are universities or leading

---

[1] For the first statement of research hypotheses, see Guzzini, 2003. Of course, one solution – one I am sympathetic towards – consists in denying the central status to this divide in the first place, showing how this very dichotomy has become part of the problem, not the solution to the antinomies of social theorising, and how both poles are always intertwined. Needless to say, such a solution is not yet generally accepted, certainly not within IR.

research institutes from targeted public or private funding; what is the role of peace research institutes?

Finally, on the basis of some case studies, a further factor proved important for understanding the revival of geopolitics, and particularly the vigour with which it could arrive. Though structural factors might suggest a revival, such factors can remain dormant if they are not mobilised by political actors. Hence, a further factor for understanding the revival or its absence was the domestic political game in which the different countries found themselves after 1989. Geopolitical arguments seemed to fit best for conservative forces who could use geopolitics in a 'rhetoric of reaction', as Albert Hirschman so nicely put it, where any attempt to stem the 'natural forces' would either be futile, produce perverse effects or jeopardise what had already been accomplished.[2]

However, the most important factor – indeed, the one that would define the entire framework of analysis – was to become foreign policy identity (to be defined below), as constructivist scholars in political geography and international relations would have expected. Many countries that had seen a revival of geopolitical thought, so the hypothesis initially ran, were in some sense 'new countries', either because they had never previously existed in their present borders or because they had experienced an interrupted statehood. The foreign policy elites and discourses of these countries were in search of a new or redefined identity. In that situation, any allegedly objective criteria, such as geopolitical factors, would be welcome to help foster a fitting identity. When we brought the case studies together, the major finding was that the revival of geopolitics seemed to be closely connected to the existence of what could be called an 'ontological anxiety' in the foreign policy field. Foreign policy elites, old or new, would feel insecure about the main coordinates not just of world politics, but of their own country: where is its place, what is its role? Although certainly no sufficient condition for the revival of geopolitical thought, an 'identity crisis' seemed centrally connected to all cases where such a revival happened. This moved the analysis of identity within foreign policy discourses to the centre of our study.

The initial thesis, derived after a first set of comparative studies, is then as follows: *the resurgence of geopolitical thought in Europe after 1989 occurs at the meeting point of possible foreign policy identity crises – that is, anxiety over a new, a newly questioned or a newly acquired self-understanding or role in world affairs – and the spatial logic of geopolitical thought (both physical and cultural), which is well disposed to provide some fixtures to this anxiety.* This thesis includes two steps. First, a foreign policy discourse or tradition experiences an 'identity crisis' when the smooth continuation of its interpretative dispositions encounters problems, as taken-for-granted self-understandings and role positions

---

[2] Hirschman, 1991.

are openly challenged, and eventually undermined. In our case, such a crisis occurs when interpretive dispositions within a given foreign policy tradition or discourse come to understand the end of the Cold War as challenging the self-understanding and role conception embedded therein. Second, such an identity crisis is more likely to revive geopolitical thought when at least some of the following factors apply: a materialist tradition of thinking foreign policy, the institutionalisation of such a tradition within the foreign policy expert culture, and a political game where such thought is rhetorically used for political gain (usually on the conservative side).

This explanatory framework, involving a trigger and further facilitating conditions, has a series of methodological implications. First, pre-existing interpretive dispositions become the central unit of analysis, because, when mobilised in efforts to understand the relevant event, they prompt the possible trigger of an identity crisis. To be a disposition means that even if a foreign policy discourse is, in principle, in crisis because pre-established roles have been jeopardised, and even if geopolitical discourse is well disposed to provide easy allegedly natural references for fixing the anxiety, it does not necessarily follow that a geopolitical revival will happen. For that to be the case, other factors – the more structural (ideational path dependence, great-power ideology), institutional (the political economy of expertise production) and political action-oriented (political game and rhetoric) – come into play. Second, this thesis asks for a certain kind of process tracing that opens up the black box of the domestic setting case by case. Moreover, a kind of classical outside-in process tracing, where the same international event might trigger different responses depending on the domestic process variables, is not possible. Rather, the very meaning of the event is part of the analysis and needs to be assessed on a case-by-case basis: it might literally not be the same in each case. The analysis is in an important sense bottom-up for the very understanding of the international factor. Finally, as this chapter will show, the set of process factors may not allow a more positivist version of process tracing: some factors are dispositional and not causal (ideational path dependence), interacting (between ideational traditions and institutional settings) and partly contingent (the political one). An interpretive and configurational analysis ensues.[3]

The thesis also has a major consequence for the theoretical context in which this book is placed. A cursory reading might locate the present work within a wider research agenda on 'ideas and foreign policy', because it studies ideational structures in IR at the level of the state. That would be partly misguided, however. When conducted within foreign policy analysis, the ideas and foreign policy research agenda, informed by psychology, cognitive or social, usually focuses on how certain ideational structures impact on action. It analyses

---

[3] The concluding chapter will further qualify the type of process-tracing.

the ideational factor in the decision-making of state actors and in their actual behaviour[4]– for example, how worldviews and perceptions systematically bias towards particular readings of reality and hence predispose to certain actions.[5] The focus of such analysis is the impact on foreign policy behaviour.

Although the present volume has obvious affinities with such studies, its aim is different. Given its puzzle, the present research needs to investigate why certain ideational developments took place in the first place – that is, how foreign policy discourses related to geopolitical thought in the aftermath of 1989. The final aim of the analysis is not to identify how (mainly) ideational structures help us understand certain behaviours, but to explain the ongoing development of structures themselves, that is, how events, actions and practices relate to the historical dynamics of certain (mainly) ideational structures, here foreign policy discourses. And although this is necessarily done on the level of the state, and of actors within the state, ultimately the analysis takes a good part of its significance from the way such foreign policy discourses in turn interact with the overarching 'culture of anarchy', to use Wendt's term.

In other words, by analysing the revival of geopolitics in Europe after 1989, the present study seeks to contribute to the theorisation and analysis of the micro-dynamics of social macro-structures, an issue so far under-theorised in (constructivist) IR. It suggests that the evolution of the culture of anarchy in Europe after 1989 is fruitfully analysed through an examination of the way in which interpretations of '1989' are driven by, and interact with, different national foreign policy discourses, and how those in turn interact with each other in the reproduction of the more general culture of anarchy. And from here derives the second main empirical claim. It is the very success of 1989, the 'desecuritisation' of European security relations, that, under certain conditions, triggers an identity crisis that mobilises geopolitical thought as an easy fix, which, in turn, mobilises realism's militarist and nationalist gaze. Hence, perhaps paradoxically, the very success of desecuritisation in the Cold War ('1989') ushers in conditions under which strong resecuritising dynamics can come to the fore.

This chapter will begin by introducing a conceptualisation of foreign policy discourses in terms of a foreign policy imaginary.[6] Such an imaginary constitutes

---

[4] This can take different forms, investigating either general ideas or belief systems, or more individual beliefs or perceptions. For a general survey, see Smith, 1988. See also George, 1979 and Goldstein and Keohane, 1993. For a first step beyond a classical causal analysis, see Yee, 1996. For an overview of psychological approaches to IR, see Stein, 2002.

[5] For the wealth of literature, see, for example, Frei, 1985; Jervis, 1976; Larson, 1985; Lebow and Stein, 1994; Steinbruner, 1974.

[6] The concept is derived from 'security imaginary' as it is employed in security studies. For stylistic reasons, and where the difference is not significant, I will therefore use foreign policy imaginary interchangeably with security imaginary and foreign policy tradition in the remainder of the volume.

the main intersubjective dispositional unit of analysis for this comparative study. Then, the chapter introduces the study's methodological assumptions, tentatively termed *interpretative process tracing*. Next, the chapter derives a series of hypotheses about the ideational, institutional and political-rhetorical conditions in the foreign policy expert field that enable or facilitate the revival of neoclassical geopolitics, before finally discussing the specific selection of cases used for the study.

It is important to note already here that the framework set out above will be further qualified after the empirical analysis. Such a methodology is typical for a constitutive or ontological approach to theorising, where central concepts are continuously qualified by the empirical context in which they are used. As much as we need definitional work to get the empirical analysis started, that empirical analysis also feeds back into the ongoing definition of the initial concepts and their theoretical relation to each other.[7]

1   The trigger: 'foreign policy imaginaries' meet 1989 in a foreign policy identity crisis

> It is not surprising that the fading of Cold War antagonisms since the middle of the 1980s has put pressure on these countries to adopt a new, meaningful vision of external relations. The process evokes problems of identity and hesitations in establishing new foreign policy lines.[8]

The resurgence of geopolitical thought in Europe after 1989, according to the thesis, occurs at the meeting point of foreign policy identity crisis – that is, possible anxiety over a newly questioned or newly acquired self-understanding or role in world affairs – and the spatial logic of geopolitical thought, which is well disposed to provide some fixtures to this. This section will provide the general framework needed for its analysis.

Foreign policy roles and self-conceptions

To understand both the diverse reception and the variety of political lessons of 1989, we need to start from the relevant and diverse communities of interpreters. How were they disposed to understand the events of 1989 in one way rather than another? For this, we need to look for the prevailing debate and discourse on national foreign policy, the reservoir of past lessons and scripts that inform the understanding of what international politics is fundamentally about and the country's specific role therein: the national discourse on the national interest. With this, the analysis moves onto the terrain of foreign policy roles

---

[7]   See Leander, 2008, for an elaboration of this in Bourdieusian terms.
[8]   Dijkink, 1996, 140.

and identity, understood mainly as self-understandings/self-conceptions (*Selbstverständnis*).

The concept of identity, however, is riddled with problems (for the methodological ones, see below).[9] One problem is connected to the risk of anthropomorphising states. Although it is possible to argue that representatives of states do refer to other states *as though* they had an almost human identity – attributing intention, agency and hence responsibility – this kind of a collective identity is surely different from an individual one.[10] Also, there is the well-known tendency to see identity as something relatively given and homogeneous, even among constructivists.[11] After all, that would constitute its explanatory attraction. Once it has been shown that any argument in terms of the national interest basically begs the question – why was the interest elaborated and perceived in this particular way and not differently? – and once it has been argued that identity comes before interest, since one needs to know who one is before one knows what one wants,[12] identity explanations seem persuasive. But, if identity is heterogeneous – and it usually is – then almost anything goes, if the analysis is carried out in causal terms: any outcome could be explained by cherry-picking that part of the identity that fits the story, just as with 'national interest'. Identity would have simply opened up a further conceptual regress.[13]

Luckily, foreign policy analysis has started to address the study of foreign policy identity and to at least mitigate some of these problems, that are anyway not all necessarily pertinent for the present research. A first step consists in seeing foreign policy identity as part of the ideational predispositions of the foreign policy expert field. It is that field that gives meaning to '1989', possibly in such a way as to prompt neoclassical geopolitical thought. Hence, 'identity' does not refer to the general level, let alone a property, of the state or nation, but to those particular discourses among political actors, their observers (media and academia) or the public at large within which the subject-position of the country in world politics is negotiated.

Second, the very term 'identity' is to be used in a circumscribed way. It corresponds to what Rogers Brubaker and Frederick Cooper have termed 'self-understanding' and 'situated subjectivity', and is understood as a dispositional concept.[14] This is the way in which most constructivists have used the term within IR. Such an understanding has two inter-related facets. On the one hand, the idea of self-understanding refers to the ongoing process that aims to answer the question(s) 'for what/whom do we stand?', looked at from the inside.

---

[9] Brubaker and Cooper, 2000.
[10] See the Forum on 'Is the state a person? Why should we care?' with Jackson, 2004; Neumann, 2004; Wendt, 2004; and Wight, 2004a.
[11] For a critique, see, for example, Brubaker and Cooper, 2000; and Zehfuss, 2001.
[12] See, for example, Jepperson *et al.*, 1996 and Wendt, 1992 and 1999.
[13] Guzzini, 1997 [1995].   [14] Brubaker and Cooper, 2000, 17.

In IR, this has usually been the concern of scholars and practitioners who want to define the national specificity of foreign policy – in the extreme case: its mission. On the other hand, it refers to the slots available in international society, a socially ascribed function, as it were: 'what is our role in world affairs?' Foreign policy analysts have established a number of such role conceptions in international affairs. This more circumscribed understanding of identity can therefore be approached from two angles. The first is international. Most countries with some diplomatic history have built up a certain diplomatic personality that provides the references for answering the above-mentioned questions. In International Relations, a research line addresses diplomatic identity in terms of foreign policy 'roles' (e.g. a balancer, a mediator, a civilian power) – a suitable term, since international society, at least historically, has had a far more limited number of recognisable subject-positions than other, more differentiated societies.[15] The other understanding is more societal, seeing foreign policy identity with an emphasis on domestic history, the dual struggle for coherence of the tradition and for primacy in its definition.[16]

A third qualification consists in specifying the role this more limited concept of identity has in the actual explanation of our research puzzle. This is necessary to avoid explanatory overstretch or infinite regress. To introduce this, it may be illustrative to take a small detour to the literature on 'strategic culture'.[17] This latter concept has been used mainly to capture national differences in the understanding of security. Such an understanding is seen as shared by its political and military elite, nurtured by different histories and memories, and accounts for the way military doctrines and/or behaviour differ when strategic constraints should lead them to converge.[18]

Yet, by implication, much of the strategic culture analysis follows the classical setup of the realist–idealist debates, which opposes more materialist or idealist theories of action (making moreover the ideational moment the mere residual category to explain the otherwise unexpected). The underlying thrust is to understand how culture embeds ideas that, in turn, influence preferences and hence choice or behaviour. The behavioural setup of much of the strategic culture literature, however, is not the research focus of the present analysis, which seeks rather to understand why a particular idea – neoclassical geopolitics – arises (or not) under particular conditions; in a sense, it seeks to understand the link from one set of ideas to another, not from ideas to behaviour.

---

[15] For the *locus classicus*, see Holsti, 1970. For the development of the approach, see Walker, 1987. For further development and an application close to the present research, see Le Prestre, 1997.

[16] For such a discursive approach to foreign policy identity, see also Wæver, 2002. For an approach stressing 'societal identity' (which goes justifiably further than the more institutionalist setting proposed later in this chapter), see Hopf, 2002.

[17] For an overview, see Johnston, 1995.

[18] See, for example, Gray, 1986.

Therefore, the present study needs to look at theories that elaborate on the cultural and ideational level itself. In other words, rather than setting out to explain the causal link from identity to behaviour, it seeks to understand how shared meanings are affected in the reproduction of a foreign policy discourse with its embedded subject positions. More precisely: how may one ideational structure (the security/foreign policy imaginary), under certain circumstances, give rise to another (neoclassical geopolitics)? The study does not take identity for granted, but looks at how it is reconstituted through the understanding of salient international events. This is a dialectic or constitutive relation, not a causal one, if we understand causality in the classical Humean way.[19] Not being causal in this sense, its path dependency is no infinite causal regress. Rather, the research looks at how it was possible for such a crisis and the possible geo-political revival to arise.[20] Only when analysing how such a geopolitical revival may affect the international culture of anarchy will there be a link that includes foreign policy behaviour. This will be taken up in the concluding chapter.

Foreign policy imaginaries and foreign policy discourses

Central to this approach is an intersubjective unit of analysis that catches the interpretive predispositions of the foreign policy expert system. Jutta Weldes has introduced such a unit in her study of the Cuban Missile Crisis. She calls it a 'security imaginary', which is defined as a 'structure of well-established meanings and social relations out of which representations about the world of international relations are created'.[21] In the process of representation and interpretation of world affairs, actors mobilise this reservoir of raw meanings embedded in the collective memory of the expert field, including historical scripts and analogies (what Weldes calls 'articulation'), together with the embedded subject-position of a country in the international system ('interpellation'), which is the concept most directly related to the present study.

The use of such a concept, however, does not imply that such an imaginary must be homogeneous, that it entails only one way of heeding the lessons of the past or one particular national self-understanding or understanding of a given country's role in the world. Rather, there are shared features in the ways that debates about the past are conducted, or in the potential roles of a country in the world that can be conceived of. In the United States, there is the often-used divide between interventionists and isolationists, who both refer to the same historical event with different implications or who place different values on

---

[19] On constitutive analysis in IR, see Wendt, 1999, 77–90. On the critique of Humean causality in IR, see, for example, Dessler, 1991; Kurki, 2008; Patomäki, 1996; Wight, 2006.

[20] For this usage of *how* causality rather than *what* causality, or of research designs in terms of 'how possible' rather than 'why' questions in IR, see, for example, Doty, 1993.

[21] Weldes, 1999a, 10.

the same events. But they share a definition of the boundaries, and hence the legitimate contenders, of the debate. Similarly, among the interventionists, there is a debate over foreign policy containment versus engagement – which again pits two camps against each other. These rely on different lessons from the past: the argument for containment (against an inevitable expansion) being derived from the lessons of World War II, and for engagement (avoiding an escalation nobody wanted) from the lessons of World War I.[22] Pitting these two against each other justifies, whether openly or not, that it is those lessons that are authorised to structure the debate.

Hence, a foreign policy imaginary is not 'shared' in the sense that it produces just one opinion: there are always many scripts and different subject positions. Nor is it that actors are all predisposed to weigh the different scripts in the same way. What characterises a foreign policy tradition is not a ready-made ideational toolkit, making debates unnecessary; on the contrary, the existence of such a tradition is what allows political debates to happen in the first place, since it defines the stakes, draws the boundaries of relevant/competent debate, and ensures that people speak the same language when they dispute each others' points. A foreign policy tradition is not about a single shared opinion, albeit a system of references that frames and authorises certain opinions as parts of the debate. Foreign policy experts will disagree on issues, but within the terms that are already agreed upon by their sharing a foreign policy field and its imaginary. This is part of 'the concession to a social universe that one makes by accepting to become acceptable'.[23]

Central for the understanding of such foreign policy traditions are metaphors.[24] Such analogies work as quasi-logical scripts and are mobilised in and through foreign policy debates. For instance, in the discussions surrounding the US intervention in the Kuwait war (just as in the context of the recent war in Iraq), realist critiques saw a resurgence of Wilsonianism, because the military action was interventionism using an idealist cloak[25] – whether or not it had actually anything to do with the multilateral setup envisaged by Wilson in the first place. But the debate was framed in such a way that there were only two categories at hand from which the interpreter had to choose: liberal interventionist and conservative realist. Also the extremely rich symbolic capital of World War II gave rise to many analogies, mobilised in the debate ('articulated'), that made certain actions seem almost necessary, and surely more legitimate. As Timothy Luke describes:

[22] For still one of the most elaborate exposition of these two positions, see the spiral model and the deterrence model elaborated in Jervis, 1976.
[23] Bourdieu, 2001, 114, my translation. For an analysis in IR along these lines, see Ashley, 1987, 1988, 1989, and more recently Leander, 2005 and 2010.
[24] In IR, see, for instance, Drulák, 2006d; Hülsse, 2003; and Milliken, 1996.
[25] Tucker and Hendrickson, 1992. For a similar argument about the recent Iraq War (from a less realist position), see Rhodes, 2003.

> Like Hitler, the seemingly mad butcher of Baghdad cowered in his German-built *Führerbunker* as he directed his almost *Waffen-SS*-like Republican Guards to fight to the last man. Whereas Hitler gassed millions of Jews in sealed death chambers and rocketed Allied cities with V-1s and V-2s, Saddam shot SCUDs against Israel, where Jews sat in sealed rooms wearing gas masks against chemical warheads made possible by West German-built factories in Iraq.[26]

When a story distributed by Interfax reported that Saddam Hussein had had his top air-force commander executed on 24 January 1991, the Iraqi government denied the allegations, and even the coalition admitted that it could not verify the news. But the story had already been sent out, and the Gulf War got its 'nearest equivalent to a Stauffenberg plot'.[27] Harking back to the same collective memory, the official announcement of 'Desert Storm' paraphrased Eisenhower's famous radio address on 6 June 1944, as White House spokesman Marlin Fitzwater announced that 'the liberation of Kuwait has begun'.[28]

Inserting an event into the World War II script also mobilises a certain subject-position for the United States. In this case, the country appears as a liberator, the defender of morals and values, making, as in the past, the world – 'and nothing less', as George Kennan quipped[29] – safe for democracy. Such a subject-position guides the official reading, rationale and legitimation for the 1991 US intervention in Iraq. It is hence closely connected to the interpretations of particular historical events. Indeed, this touches on the very puzzle from which Weldes starts: how is it that one particular interpretation of the Cuban Missile Crisis – namely, as being about the defence of Cuba – was never even seriously considered among US decision-makers in the ExCom, although a perfectly valid case could be made for such an interpretation? Explaining this taken-for-grantedness, indeed the counterfactual, is Weldes' pointer for establishing the content of the security imaginary. Her thesis is that such a defensive Cuban interpretation would have seriously challenged the subject-position and self-understanding of the United States; accordingly, given the pressure for consonance between identity, interests and acts, the debate was predisposed against such a view.

In other words, prevalent subject-positions will provide the basis for interpretations of foreign policy events and actions, and will only be overruled in special cases, when a given event is truly unexpected or produces a large anomaly, as can be hypothesised for the end of the Cold War. Another possible source of change, one that is not followed up in the present study but will be discussed

---

[26] Luke, 1991, 331.   [27] Taylor, 1992, 77.
[28] Smith, 1992, 250. This can obviously have an effect on preferences. A Hitler–Saddam Hussein analogy implies that negotiation will not work and that only war and defeat can be a solution.
[29] Kennan, 1967, 323.

in the concluding chapter, stems from the fact that such self-understandings can become a source of diplomatic weakness when other actors try to exploit what could be interpreted as tensions between different self-understandings, or between them and foreign policy acts. Representational blackmail pushes actors either to give up their own self-understandings in order to remain consonant with the prevalent interpretation of their acts – a particularly painful exercise – or to maintain their subjectivity by conceding to the pressure to change their behaviour. Janice Bially Mattern defines this as 'representational force', a power politics with and through identity.[30]

This subject-position – the self-understanding and international role of a country, embedded in the discursive practice of a foreign policy tradition is hence the central focus of the present study. A foreign policy imaginary provides the intersubjective background, the life-world, as it were, within which identity is discursively renegotiated.[31]

That leaves a final point for qualification. A security imaginary is a discursive practice. This implies that we cannot understand it independently of its 'enactment'. The 'enactment' of the language of foreign and security affairs can be found in three connected but different settings: within the government or political system; within the media, schools and cultural institutions; and within the expert system of private or public think-tanks, research institutes and universities of a given country.[32] Critical geopolitics similarly distinguishes between three levels: a formal geopolitics, which is mainly the one produced by researchers; a practical geopolitics, which is the one used by practitioners; and popular geopolitics, which is the one to be found in the wider public space, usually the media and public culture.[33] The interplay of these three settings is not the same in all countries, depending on the particular way the foreign policy field is organised.

1989 and a foreign policy identity crisis

How can we then understand a 'foreign policy identity crisis' or a state of 'ontological anxiety' within such a framework? In order for such a crisis or such anxiety to occur, there must be a misfit between the significance of a certain event and the subject-positions or roles that are embedded in a foreign policy imaginary. This means something more than that the event 'obviously'

---

[30] Bially Mattern, 2005, in particular 95–102. The strategy of 'shaming', even though it works primarily through the threat of exclusion from international society (see, for example, Risse et al., 1999), can arguably also work through such blackmail on the prevalent self-identification of the target country, as for instance in Mahatma Gandhi's strategy against the British Empire.

[31] For a related point, see also Wæver, 2002, 26–33.

[32] Weldes, 1999a, 108–109.   [33] Ó Tuathail and Dalby, 1998.

contradicts the relevant identity. For it is perfectly possible for security imaginaries to provide material for interpreting particular events in ways that would fit their predispositions. Whereas conservative scholars on US foreign policy would see in Reagan's arms race one of the main conditions for the shift in Soviet foreign policy under Gorbachev, German peace research and détente politicians would see the long-term effects of *Ostpolitik*. Since facts are often underdetermined by theory, many interpretations are feasible and no dissonance prompted merely by the event itself need appear.

Hence, for a crisis to occur, interpretations given to the event must be such as to make role conceptions no longer self-evident – in other words, those conceptions need to justify themselves. An identity should come naturally; the moment it needs consciously to justify its assumptions, we can say that a crisis has occurred. Such a definition is weaker than one that would add that such justification should turn out to be impossible. The research puzzle starts with a demand for an identity fixing, not with the impossibility of a solution to the identity crisis.

As applied to our case, a crisis could hence be prompted in several ways:

(1) *The embedded self-conception or international role of a country's security imaginary is closely connected to the Cold War scenario.* Although such a circumstance does not entail that the self-conception will be profoundly affected by the end of the Cold War, in most cases the foreign policy identity narrative cannot simply go on as though nothing has happened. Only if it appears self-evident that no substantial change has occurred (a new Cold War scenario), will no crisis ensue. However, the degree to which the events of 1989–1991 were received as a major change was sufficient that, at least in the 1990s, one could expect many countries to see debates about their place in the world, regardless of how that debate ended. On the level of self-conceptions, this is a scenario that is applicable to neutral states, such as Austria, Finland, Ireland and Sweden: what does neutrality mean when the previously opposing camps are no longer there?[34] But, it could also be applicable to other states, such as Italy or Turkey, who defined their 'importance' much in terms of the strategic role they could play for the Western Alliance, as well as to France or Germany, who defined their diplomatic role much in relation to the existence of two security blocs in Europe. And it does apply to Russia, to the extent that that country sees itself as a continuation of the Soviet superpower that no longer is.

(2) *Debate over a country's foreign policy identity was suppressed during the Cold War, but this is no longer the case.* This would apply to all countries of the former Warsaw Pact, possibly also including Russia (if Russia is seen as

---

[34] See, for example, Joenniemi, 1988 and 1993; and Kruzel and Haltzel, 1989. For an analysis that shows historically how questions of neutrality can become a central part of the self-representation of a country, see Malmborg, 2001.

having been suppressed by the Soviet Union, a line that had some prominence in the 1990s) and potentially also Italy.

(3) *A country did not exist in its present shape during the Cold War.* This is a relatively heterogeneous category, since it covers countries that basically did not exist for the Cold War decades, such as countries from the former USSR or former Yugoslavia, as well as countries that changed their shape after 1989, such as the Federal Republic of Germany, the Czech Republic and Slovakia. Whereas, in the first case, existing foreign policy imaginaries and identity discourses run into anomalies, in the last two cases (with the exception of Germany), new elites had more actively to look for establishing such a tradition in the first place. But, in all these cases, it could be expected that discussions about who 'we' are now in world (or European) affairs would surface, often strongly influenced by concerns of societal identity.

Let me summarise at this stage. The claim of this book is that the revival of neoclassical geopolitical ideas in Europe after 1989 takes place at the meeting point of foreign policy identity crises – that is, possible anxiety over a new, a newly questioned or a newly acquired self-understanding or role in world affairs – and the spatial logic of geopolitical thought, which is well disposed to provide some fixtures to this anxiety. I have specified three categories of countries for which an identity crisis could be expected. However, the occurrence of such an identity crisis is not a sufficient condition for the revival of neoclassical geopolitics. On the basis of existing research, one can hypothesise a series of process factors that would condition the revival, or indeed make it possible in the first place.

2   How identity crises meet neoclassical geopolitics: ideational, institutional and rhetorical process factors

With its spatial metaphors and determinist outlook, neoclassical geopolitics has many resources that can provide a possible fix for a foreign policy expert field debating a country's self-understanding and international role – that is, its identity. That, however, does not make their use unavoidable. Some foreign policy discourses that could have experienced an identity crisis have not seen a significant development of neoclassical geopolitics, such as those of the Czech Republic, Finland, Germany and Sweden. Hence, the next step is to specify factors that play a role in the very way relevant expert fields deal with crises in the reproduction of their security imaginaries.

Three main types of factors seem to be important. First, it could be expected that the revival of a strongly materialist theory (or ideology) would be path-dependent on the existence of a pre-existing political culture that is materialist or indeed has known a prominent geopolitical past. In addition to such ideational path dependence, there is also the factor of how the foreign policy expert field, including its recruitment, is organised. Finally, geopolitics is a tool in politics itself, mobilised by actors in their political struggles. Some of the characteristics of geopolitical thought make it a welcome rhetorical resource mainly, but not only, for conservative ideologies. In addition to these three main factors comes the one that is connected to geopolitics almost as its original sin and with which the discussion will begin. Geopolitics has been used as an imperial ideology, and accordingly countries that find themselves in the position of having or keeping expansionist aims might find that the ability to rationalise such aims in geopolitical terms comes in handy. In a sense, this is not really a domestic factor connected to debates of self-conceptions, but an international process factor when countries use geopolitics to claim that they should be accorded greater recognition for their role in world affairs.

This section will introduce these various factors, indicating for which European countries one could have expected particular factors to play a key role. Before doing so, however, I will clarify the type of process tracing within which these factors will be used.

Interpretivist process tracing

The puzzle of the present study is of a kind that requires the analyst to open up the 'black box' of domestic politics, as well as, more generally, that of the process by which a given initial input (in this case, the events of 1989) is transformed into a particular output (here, the revival of geopolitical thought). In the social world, there are situations where knowledge of what happened within the political processes of a government – or within the brain of an actor, for that matter – can be assumed to be secondary. Arnold Wolfers illustrates this with the example of a 'hotel fire'.[35] Imagine a room packed with people, where there is only one exit and a fire has broken out. For most research interests, it is not really necessary to look into the personal interpretations given to such an event in order to understand the outcome: a general rush to the door. Such black-boxing produces hence an analysis along the lines of the behaviouralist stimulus–response scheme: input/fire alarm–output/rush to the exit. To be a permissible approach, that is, for such situations to exist in the social world, at least one of two conditions needs to be met. Either: we must be able to assume almost perfect unit homogeneity (that is, the actors all share the same characteristic, one that is truly fundamental for the explanation). Or: we are explicitly interested in research questions which deal only with the aggregates of individual actions and can legitimately assume that individual differences 'wash out' (or can be expressed in probability statements).

---

[35] See Wolfers, 1962. For a more recent application, see Krasner, 2000.

Yet, in the social world, we must be prepared for the eventuality that the very same outcome can be the result of different factors or different paths.[36] This can be illustrated even with the hotel fire. There might be cases where individuals do not react and rush to the door: for instance, small children might not understand the meaning of the fire alarm and need to be dragged by their parents. Or there might be cases where people do the expected rushing to the door, but for other reasons: deaf people might not have heard the fire alarm, but might imitate what everyone else does, even before they can read on the lips of the people around what is going on. In both cases, it is not the fire alarm (input) that is prompting the behaviour of the individual (output). Depending on the actual research question, the simple input–output analysis, typical for behaviouralism, would now be misleading. The analysis would now need to control for equifinality – that is, the possibility that 'several explanatory paths, combinations and sequences lead to the same outcome'.[37] In other words, in the social world, an analysis that assumes a black box is a special case whose conditions need to be carefully established, on a case-by-case basis.

For the present research design, the implication is straightforward. Since we are interested in the reasons why the end of the Cold War triggered a revival of geopolitical thought, and, relatedly, why this occurred in some countries but not in others, we have to control the unfolding of the process both for finding out why the same event did not effect the same outcome, and, when it did, whether we have cases of equifinality. As a result, the underlying methodology is at least akin to 'process tracing', 'a procedure for identifying steps in a causal process leading to the outcome of a given dependent variable of a particular case in a particular historical context'.[38]

But, it is a process tracing of a particular kind. For one thing, the start of the process is not some neutral or easily objectifiable phenomenon. Usually, a process-tracing exercise assesses the different causal mechanisms through which one phenomenon affects another. It is in such a manner, for example, that Jeffrey Checkel provides a very thoughtful setup whose aim is 'to theorize and document a set of socialization mechanisms as intervening variables linking input (international institutions) and output (socialization outcome or internalization)'.[39] And, indeed, at first sight, the present research puzzle seemed straightforward enough in terms of the usual methodological toolbox of comparative analysis. All cases start from the same event (1989 or the end of the Cold War) and ask whether that event would produce the same outcome (geopolitical revival). This would give us the typical research design of process

---

[36] For an analysis of the methodological implications resulting from a different ontology of the social world, see, for example, Hall, 2003.
[37] George and Bennett, 2005, 20. See also pp. 161–162.
[38] George and Bennett, 2005, 176.   [39] Checkel, 2005, 805.

tracing, since the same input does not produce the same output in all countries, producing a variance to be controlled for.

However, the starting point for the process in our cases was not always the same. For Russia, 1991 was more important than 1989. Germany's little geopolitical flurry occurred not after 1989, but mainly in the mid 1980s, when, encouraged by a governmental shift to the right and alarmed by the pacifist mobilisation against the NATO dual-track decision, the *Historikerstreit* saw a formerly quiescent conservative intelligentsia intervening in the debate about German national security. Although international events are obviously not disconnected from the creation of ontological anxiety, such events alone are not enough to create it; indeed, which international event would prove significant would be determined more by the nature of the state identity embedded in domestic national security discourses and the battles around that identity. In other words, instead of having a typical design, where the varying effects of a given international phenomenon would be traced through a series of domestic mechanisms, we needed to start the analysis in terms of an internal process of identity recreation that interacted with the outside to create the triggering event in the first place. International events can *mean* different things within different foreign policy discourses, and hence at some point might indeed *constitute* different events for them. In a sense, what constitutes the input into this process is endogenous to the process itself.

By the same token, the process cannot comply with the approach of naturalist process-tracing research, which would disaggregate the process into mechanisms that can be subsumed under covering laws, qualified by scope conditions.[40] There are several reasons for this. Identity explanations are dispositional, as noted earlier by Brubaker and Cooper, leading to 'how possible?' rather than 'why?' questions. Also, the ongoing evolution of the foreign policy imaginary and its embedded subject-positions is not independent of those process factors; indeed, through the analysis of the latter, we also access the former. We are in a version of a hermeneutic circle.[41] When Jutta Weldes focused on the discussions in the ExCom and inferred the content of the US security imaginary from things not said and arguments taken for granted by the political elite of the time, she needed to have some preconceptions of what such a security imaginary could be in the first place in order to make sense of those omissions.

---

[40] Although perhaps not the intention, that would be the implication of George and Bennett, 2005, 226ff.
[41] This is a model of the process of interpretation, which begins from the problem of relating a work's parts to the work as a whole: since the parts cannot be understood without some preliminary understanding of the whole, and the whole cannot be understood without comprehending its parts, our understanding of a work must involve an anticipation of the whole that informs our view of the parts while simultaneously being modified by them. I am indebted to Catherine Schwerin for this formulation.

She needed to have a reservoir of meanings to make sense of the meaning of the deliberations. Such meanings are hence paradoxically both the base and the result of the analysis. But, then, how can we check the validity of these meanings on which the inferences are based? Here, the analyst must rely on some type of path dependence of ideational structures. For instance, Weldes' inferences are based on common themes in US foreign policy identity discourse, as these developed through and after the early post-1945 period. It is against the background of a belief system that came into place at the onset of containment – as studied by, for example, Deborah Welch Larson – that her inferences, in turn, must make sense.[42] As with path-dependence explanations more generally, this produces a virtually infinite *historical*, but not *logical*, regress. And since the basic question of Weldes' study is not of a classical causal type, but of the 'how possible' type, more akin to a more contingent understanding of mechanisms (see Chapter 11), such regress in not pernicious. With this background, we can now turn to the individual process factors and the hypotheses that can be derived from them.

Geopolitics and the sociology of knowledge: the ideology of a great or dissatisfied power

The classical sociology of knowledge tradition was an attempt to 'take account of the rootedness of knowledge in the social texture'.[43] It is this more materialist understanding of the sociology of knowledge that has been often used in IR for analysing the rise of certain ideas or ideologies. Applied in a relatively straightforward (and slightly crude) manner, it states that foreign policy ideas are nothing but the rationalisation of national interests (left usually insufficiently defined). In this manner did E. H. Carr argue that the conception of a 'harmony of interests' in which states share a common interest (e.g. in peace or in the expansion of international free trade) could only appear in satisfied powers that had much to win from the continuation of the status quo, such as Carr's own Britain.[44] Writing from within critical geopolitics, Simon Dalby has used such an argument in his discussion of the Second Cold War, where the geopolitical perspective could be understood 'as an ideological representation of imperial drives in a period of declining hegemony'.[45] Inversely, rising powers, such as Nazi Germany, would use just any ideology that could command

---

[42] Larson, 1985.
[43] Mannheim, 1936, 33. For a critique of this earlier tradition, see Berger and Luckmann, 1966.
[44] Carr, 1946. For an analysis of the link from Mannheim to Carr, see Charles Jones, 1998. It is this heritage that lets also Gramscians show affinities to Carr. See Cox, 1986 [1981] or Germain, 2000.
[45] Dalby, 1990a, 181.

some wider resonance in order to justify their attempts to expand further or to improve their ranking within the society of states.[46]

Applied to the revival of neoclassical geopolitics, a first hypothesis would hence double-check whether neoclassical geopolitics, or a geopolitics that dares to speak its name, can be found mainly with countries whose foreign policy discourse treats them as great or superpowers. This hypothesis derives from a historical analogy. John Agnew and Geraoid Ó Tuathail stress the historical moment of the rise of 'geopolitics' during the heyday of imperialism. Geopolitical theories accompany the attempt to reconcile expansionist nationalism with what was then becoming an increasingly 'finite' world.[47] The underlying Social Darwinism of such theories justifies the position of the few chosen under the sun, and their ruling over the world.

There are no obvious cases for this hypothesis in post-1989 Europe, although self-understandings might be different and therefore need to be empirically checked (for the Russian case, see below). A possible exception could be the EU as a whole. So far, however, and certainly in the 1990s, the EU has staked its reputation on being an anti-geopolitical unit. In the memorable phrase of Ole Wæver, 'Europe's other is Europe's past',[48] the EU being a peace organisation, a 'civilian' or 'normative' power,[49] aimed precisely at overcoming the militarism and nationalism, historically associated with classical geopolitical thought, that had plagued Europe's early twentieth century.[50] That said, the very same 1990s did see growing concern about a possible more global role for the EU and a concomitant start in the use of the term 'geopolitics'.[51]

---

[46] For a critique of Carr's argument that just any ideology would do, see Guzzini 1998, 21–22. It was certainly difficult for a racist ideology like Nazism to credibly use 'internationalist' justifications, as in the attempted 'new Europe'. Social Darwinism was more congenial to Nazism, but foreclosed a higher degree of international legitimacy. At a minimum, domestic and international justifications must meet to stay credible, but that does not always serve the legitimating purpose.

[47] Agnew, 2003; Ó Tuathail, 1996.   [48] Wæver, 1996.

[49] The term 'civilian' power was initially used for Europe (Duchêne, 1973), as well as for post-1945 Germany and Japan (Maull, 1990/1991). For a theoretical elaboration on the concept, see Kirste and Maull, 1996. Needless to say, the concept and its use has drawn wide criticism, not the least from Bull, 1982. For a short review of the debates, see Orbie, 2006. On normative power, see Manners, 2002 and the more recent discussion in Diez and Manners, 2007.

[50] The United States would belong here too, but is outside the comparative scope of this study. After 1989, the United States had shrugged off earlier concerns about its decline. Being often perceived as the only remaining superpower, this apparent selection of the fittest is understood to vindicate a sense of general national superiority and to establish a right to go it alone. Such a view is shared by US neoconservatives; see for example Kagan 1998 and Krauthammer, 1991 and 2002–2003. For a discussion of neoconservative foreign policy ideology, see Williams, 2005. For a discussion of the ideological and/or performative use of power in arguments about US primacy, see Guzzini, 2006.

[51] Diez, 2004.

For the scope of the present study, a perhaps more relevant and connected second hypothesis would involve looking at countries whose elites are dissatisfied with the power status of their countries, and who feel that the international community is not giving them their due. Since recognition is a social phenomenon between peers, dissatisfied partners tend to insist on some objectifiable indicators to support their claims for higher recognition. Should countries base their claim on perceived advantages in natural and material resources, one can expect them to highlight the necessitous facets of geopolitics. Such a move is often accompanied by a conscious attempt to remilitarise international affairs, if the perceived distribution of military power would merit a reassessment of international rank. Hence, a further hypothesis would look at the possible relationship between state dissatisfaction and geopolitical arguments, since the latter can provide an allegedly scientific shield for claims to rank maximisation. Such a hypothesis could suit the Russian case both after 1989 and, as some have argued,[52] for some centuries.

This quite materialist sociology of knowledge could also apply to a 'geopolitics of irredentism'. The latter seems to inspire a few Hungarian scholars with no problems referring back to a geopolitical tradition à la Mackinder.[53] For many Hungarian nationalists, and not just them, the Treaty of Trianon remains a traumatic event. It drastically reduced Hungary's territories, made Hungarians a sizeable minority in nearly all of the neighbouring countries – Slovakia, Vojvodina (Serbia), Transylvania (Romania) – and nurtures until today a kind of Hungarian irredentism. Although not calling for any form of secession, Gusztáv Molnár used Huntington to good purpose (at least in terms of his own position) in his writing on the Transylvanian issue – an intervention that quickly spurred major rebuttals, all taking issue with the allegedly scientific use of Huntington's geopolitical scheme.[54] And, in an even more materialist reading, such an irredentism would also apply to countries whose improved international position would almost automatically prompt a claim for higher recognition, such as is arguably the case with the Federal Republic of Germany after its unification.

Having said this, a concern with rank does not need to express itself in this manner. For instance, rather than attempt to justify a particularly defensive identity in terms of their small size, some small states choose to embrace the European peace project, in which their sovereignty is arguably further diluted.

[52] Neumann, 2008.

[53] Molnár, 1997. The Transylvanian Gusztáv Molnár headed the Geopolitical Research Group of the Teleki László Foundation-Institute for Central European Studies in Budapest.

[54] Andreescu, 1998; Mitu, 1998; Molnár, 1998. In contrast to the lavish treatment of Huntington in many Central and Eastern European states, the Romanian translation of his *Clash of Civilizations* was prefaced not by a politician but by an academic, Iulia Motoc, an international lawyer and IR theorist, who went on to heavily criticise the very book she introduced.

Luxemburg might refer to geographical size and position in its foreign policy identity, but not necessarily to neoclassical geopolitics. Hence the latter effect is tied to self-understandings or role conceptions that have evolved in a form that is closely intertwined with natural indicators (or borders), and/or that perceive international society as legitimating so materialist a vision. In turn, such geopolitical argumentation is empowered by the predispositions of the security imaginary and hence found attractive. Geopolitical thought becomes an expression of the underlying foreign policy imaginary, and the use of geopolitical statements thereby a justified solution to the identity crisis.

Hence, the basic hypothesis is that neoclassical geopolitics could appear useful in situations where a country's self-understanding seems not to be matched by a corresponding role within international society (the external identity misfit) and where materialist indicators of size and power are the prevalent means for establishing rank in a country's foreign policy discourse.

Geopolitics and intellectual traditions: the continuity of materialism

There is the rather obvious hypothesis that a geopolitical renaissance is more likely in countries in which a geopolitical tradition has existed at an earlier point in time. In other words, when faced with an identity crisis, the expert field will tend to rely on already 'well established' intellectual resources in its attempts to address the crisis. Yet, this varies from country to country.

In some countries, most notably France, a rather vigorous geopolitical debate has been taking place for quite some time. The participation of elite military schools and many military figures in public debate has ensured the continued presence of more classical geopolitical themes. Yet, concomitantly, France has seen one of the most original attempts to redefine geopolitics, namely Yves Lacoste, editor of the journal *Hérodote*. This version of a more left-wing geopolitics has included a series of conceptual changes, including an analysis of the strategic use of geography for political purposes, that make geopolitical research more acceptable outside of its usual audience (the first issue of *Hérodote* featured an interview with Michel Foucault). Within the French debate, references to 'geopolitics' are both more ubiquitous, and do not necessarily refer to a version of 'neoclassical geopolitics'.

In other Western European countries with strong geopolitical traditions, geopolitics has been marginalised since 1945 on account of its connection to fascism and Nazism. So, in a sense, here the geopolitical past could, in principle, also play against a revival. Yet, there is quite a compelling difference between, on the one side, Germany (and Sweden), where geopolitics as a coherent theory is still barely acceptable and references to it almost inaudible, and, on the other, Italy, where, as already mentioned, 'geopolitics' has become a buzzword within academic and political discourse and geopolitical publications a major commercial success (more on this difference later).

Still different is the case of some countries in Central and Eastern Europe – either new, founded anew or with a new foreign policy outlook – that are searching for new inspiration. In this quest, they can look abroad or else reach back to thinkers of their own who may have been writing at times when their countries were pursuing more independent foreign policies. Thus, the attempt to find a more independent voice can lead to a revival of earlier ways of thinking. Since many countries in Central and Eastern Europe had their last days of truly independent foreign policy in the inter-war period, this reaching for a national tradition can easily find itself mobilising the fashion of that period: geopolitics.

Indeed, the inclusion of Central and Eastern European countries adds a further twist to this hypothesis of an ideational path dependence of materialist policy discourses. In many regards, geopolitics (or geo-economics) is not too different in outlook from a vulgarised historical materialism.[55] Accordingly, a related hypothesis would be that the predominance of an unbroken materialist political tradition within a country would make a geopolitical renaissance more likely. What remains to be explained then, of course, is why such a renaissance did occur in some countries (e.g. Russia, and to a more limited extent Hungary), but not in others (e.g. the Czech Republic).

Geopolitics and sociological institutionalist analysis: the 'field' of foreign policy expertise

So far, the research hypotheses about the diverging geopolitical revival in national foreign policy and security discourses have been derived from more long-term historical and sociological theories. A next step is to look at the sociological environment in terms of the institutional setting within which foreign policy expertise is generated. 'Ideas do not float freely', as Thomas Risse-Kappen so nicely put it.[56] The analysis of the institutional context is important, since it specifies the conduits for the creation and dynamics of ideas.

In order to investigate why certain ideas find an easier way into the foreign policy expert field, an institutionalist analysis would start by looking at the context within which foreign policy experts are socialised and work. This leads again to a series of hypotheses. These are related insofar as they focus on the reproduction of classical international thought as it used to be prevalent in earlier foreign policy and security expert systems. Yet a full-blown analysis would imply a field analysis of the entire foreign policy expert system, whether as a kind of network analysis or, perhaps more suitably, a Bourdieu-inspired field analysis (more suitable, since Bourdieu's approach encompasses questions

---

[55] Even during the Cold War, analysts of Soviet foreign policy thought were astonished by the many parallels with realism. See Light, 1988 and Lynch, 1989 [1987].

[56] Risse-Kappen, 1994.

of doxa and symbolic power). This is beyond the scope of the present study. Still, a series of indicators can be used that provide at least first pointers.

A first research avenue focuses on the existence of strong peace research traditions and their institutionalisation in research centres that have challenged the traditional foreign policy establishment in the later decades of the Cold War. The existence of such alternative expert systems, so the hypothesis goes, could go hand in hand with a much weaker geopolitical revival. For this reason, the revival of geopolitical thought was meagre even in some countries with strong geopolitical traditions, such as post-Kjellén's Sweden and post-Haushofer's Germany. On the other hand, in countries like Italy, so the hypothesis would go, where an alternative expert culture was never allowed to join the official discourse, the diplomatic and military corps was able to isolate itself more efficiently and geopolitics could stay unchallenged and/or more easily rise.

Obviously, the existence of peace research institutes or non-mainstream security think-tanks is both cause and effect in this scheme. Such institutions appear in countries whose political debate and culture have made it possible for them to be created in the first place. In turn, their research and intervention can help to cement such a culture and pre-empt the revival of neoclassical geopolitics, either by undermining its 'scientific' credentials or by proposing alternatives, such as wider and/or non-military understandings of security (as in German or Scandinavian peace research).

A second related hypothesis focuses on the way in which the discipline of International Relations is generally taught, since this will affect future generations of leaders to a greater or lesser degree. Here, there are different contexts that would make a geopolitical revival more or less likely. In some countries, the relevant teaching is carried out mainly 'in house', within the military or diplomatic corps, an approach that often reproduces previous traditions. Similarly, if International Relations is mainly taught as a practice (and by practitioners) – and particularly as historical practice rather than legal practice – then, so the hypothesis would go, this could enhance the appeal of geopolitical thought. Finally, where International Relations theory is taught mainly in terms of a realist or materialist tradition (particularly in those institutions from which future leaders are usually selected), geopolitical arguments would have less of a problem catching on.

Central to these hypotheses is that the peace research tradition and approaches such as constructivism (which existed in IR before it was labelled as such)[57] are not just reflective, in that they impose a distance between observer and actor; they are also reflexive, that is, they take into account how the way we conceive the world affects that very world. This imposes an analytical distance to tradition and practice, and problematises the interaction effects between

---

[57] Guzzini, 2004a.

knowledge and social reality. In such an environment, neoclassical geopolitics would find it more difficult to be accepted as anything else but an ideology.

A final type of hypothesis in this context relates to the possible international influence for establishing the status and authorising expertise within national foreign policy elites. This goes two ways: demand and supply. Countries in which an expert is considered such only if he or she is connected to certain international institutions, say military ones like NATO or research institutions like RAND, will see their expert culture obviously influenced by this. Looking from the outside in, international actors – particularly international organisations whose role and scope has grown in post-1989 Europe – will more easily become conduits for the passage of policy processes and norms, as well as playing an increasingly important role in defining what knowledge and outlook defines the expert.

This hypothesis is in principle applicable to all European countries. So far, though, it has been mainly applied to the socialisation of Central and Eastern European foreign policy elites into international organisations such as NATO, the EU, the OSCE and the Council of Europe.[58] In this context, so the hypothesis goes, if the socialisation of foreign policy elites (which include security elites) happens mainly within institutions, such as NATO, that look at the world with a more military gaze, neoclassical geopolitical arguments will find it easier to surface.

All of these hypotheses – the existence of non-mainstream security research institutions and thoughts, the role of theoretical reflexivity in the teaching of IR within academia and elsewhere, and the socialisation of elites into international institutions – eventually focus on how institutions are related to the ideational dispositions in the field and practice of foreign policy expertise and the ways in which these enable, legitimate or empower the possible rise of neoclassical geopolitics.

Geopolitics and rhetorics: mobilising geopolitics in political debate

Finally, the rise of neoclassical geopolitics, or the lack of it, relates back to political actors and their particular field. For, as already mentioned in the above hypotheses, there are some characteristics of geopolitical argument that can come in useful in political debate. Again, one can establish a series of hypotheses about these intrinsic qualities of neoclassical geopolitics, that is, when peppering a discourse with 'geopolitics' could be useful, and for which actors.

A first hypothesis is related to geopolitics' link to territorial politics or, more precisely, to territorial conflict – a link emphasised both by Yves Lacoste and

---

[58] See, for example, Flockhart, 2004; Gheciu, 2005; and Schimmelfennig and Sedelmeier, 2005.

later by Carlo Jean. In countries where territorial borders are either not secure or contested, where open territorial conflict is in proximity, there is a probability that political actors will have to deal with geopolitical arguments, either by endorsing them or by refuting them.

A further hypothesis has to do with the possibility of connecting geopolitical discourse with a language of threat. Here, geopolitics can be used for 'stifling domestic dissent: the presence of external threats provides the justification for limiting political activity within the bounds of the state'.[59] On a somewhat related note: since, as mentioned earlier, 'geopolitics' can be used for all three aspects of a rhetoric of reaction, where any attempt to stem 'natural forces' would either be futile, produce perverse effects or jeopardise what has already been accomplished, it is functional for conservatism – and Bassin shows the parallel rise of neoclassical geopolitics and conservative forces in Europe.[60] In other words, when conservative politics is on the rise, geopolitical argument finds a more receptive audience (and, inversely, in countries where the political culture or intellectual tradition is receptive to geopolitical thought, conservatism is rhetorically empowered).

Perhaps the most important feature of geopolitical discourse is its apparent determinism. As seen in Chapter 2, the usage of 'geopolitics' and the revival of classical thought in this tradition has much to do with its appeal to structural conditions and long-term dynamics, that is, to the physical components of power and the rise and fall of states (or nations). This can have clear conservative overtones, in that it downgrades the place of active political agency ('change') in favour of a passive adaptation to the mighty course of history in structural conditions that are always already given. But, the rhetoric use is not always conservative. Indeed, neoclassical geopolitics' reference to an essentialised human and cultural geography is most helpful in debates about nationality, which may well stretch beyond the conservative political wing.

In a similar vein, when political actors – experts or politicians – invoke 'geopolitics', they often wish to alert the public and decision-makers to the primacy of foreign policy. This is obviously a classical realist argument, famously advanced in the German historicist tradition.[61] And it can play a similar role today. Here, the intention is not to make an argument in favour of a more conservative worldview, but to assert the importance of international politics *tout court*, whether or not this politics is seen as profoundly unchangeable.[62] This mobilises the normative agenda of the primacy of foreign policy in times of democratic control, where formerly sovereign decisions have come under wider public scrutiny.

[59] Dalby, 1990a, 172.   [60] Bassin, 2004.
[61] Meinecke, 1916; Ranke, 1916 [1833].
[62] Ó Tuathail and Dalby, 1998, 6, note geopolitics' capacity for political mobilisation in favour of 'world politics', since the world is interconnected and total.

Related to this quality of geopolitical rhetoric is another, a quality that could be one of the reasons why strategists, whether militarily educated or not, tend to favour it. 'Geopolitics' lifts the debate above the day-to-day bickering, to more long-term 'interests' or policy concerns. Here, the use of geopolitical rhetoric emphasises the need for strategic thinking in the definition of foreign policy, rather than tactical finesse. The military has no choice but to engage in long-term planning: weapons systems and strategy cannot be changed quickly. Hence, the rhetoric of geopolitics helps to rescue international politics from the short-term vagrancies of crisis management – driving the political agenda, rather than being driven by it. To use a metaphor often encountered in relation to statesmanship: whereas the diplomat is often reduced to steering a ship through the latest storm, the foreign policy strategist must steadily rebuild the ship to keep it able to face future storms.

Of course, this series of hypotheses about the rhetoric usefulness of geopolitics – dealing with territorial issues; being part of a threat rhetoric; controlling domestic dissent and strengthening conservatism; establishing the primacy of foreign policy and the need for long-term strategy; providing a foreign policy language for nationalist claims – do not come all together. Not all political or civil society actors will resort to 'geopolitics' for the same reason, nor with the same intentions, or mobilising the same purpose. Often, indeed, geopolitical language will appear natural, not consciously chosen. Yet, although various actors might be using geopolitical language for a range of different reasons, the revival of geopolitical language generally has similar effects. It empowers a look at the world in terms of maps, or – to use the title of a French TV programme on international affairs – 'beneath/behind the maps' ('le dessous des cartes').[63] It empowers views of international affairs led by the naturally 'given', whose effects are extrapolated over time, not by the diplomatically changeable. It does what geopolitics did to realism: it encourages a view on the world with the military strategists' gaze.

Summary of this section

This section has specified a series of factors that *can* make geopolitics a welcome fix for addressing a crisis of self-understanding and role recognition in a country's foreign policy practices: (1) ideational path dependence of materialism in the wider public discourse and/or academic lineages (popular and formal geopolitics); (2) a certain organisation of the foreign policy expert field,

---

[63] This series of short ten-minute features, which has been running for several years now, can be watched on ARTE, but is also shown on other channels. In association with the TV producers, a French publisher has produced schoolbooks for the four last years of high school based on the TV programme. See www.arte.tv/fr/Comprendre-le-monde/le-dessous-des-cartes/1632212.html.

and how it defines its most appropriate knowledge; and (3) the mobilisation in a political debate in which the rhetorical characteristics of geopolitics can play into the hand of some contenders. All of the country studies that follow will have to examine these factors in order to ascertain not only what type of geopolitics was revived in countries that experienced a post-1989 geopolitical revival, but also how such a revival could take place, how it became possible. In combination with the existence of a foreign policy identity crisis within the respective security imaginaries, these process factors provide the framework for analysing which neoclassical geopolitics revived in some countries, but not others.

3   Summary of research design and case selection

Puzzle

How is it that exactly as the Cold War came to an end, in a series of developments that illustrated the historical possibility of peaceful change against all (determinist) odds and seemed to herald the superiority of non-realist approaches within the discipline of International Relations, many European countries, both East and West, experienced a revival of a distinctively realist tradition, namely geopolitics – a tradition that suddenly dared to speak its name? That puzzle derives from more than the idea that the end of the East–West conflict would spur a new spatial imagination in Europe. Rather, why would the more determinist tradition called 'geopolitics' reappear, and why would this happen only in some countries and not others?

For this study, neoclassical geopolitics is defined as a policy-oriented analysis, generally conservative and with nationalist overtones, that gives explanatory primacy, but not exclusivity, to certain physical and human geographic factors (whether the analyst is open about this or not), and gives precedence to a strategic view, realism with a military and nationalist gaze, for analysing the 'objective necessities' within which states compete for power and rank (see pp. 43).

Thesis

The resurgence of geopolitical thought in Europe after 1989 takes place at the meeting point of potential foreign policy identity crises – that is, anxiety over a new, a newly questioned or a newly acquired self-understanding or role in world affairs – and the spatial logic of geopolitical thought, which is well disposed to provide some support to this anxiety. The hypothesis proceeds in two steps. First, a foreign policy discourse or tradition experiences an 'identity crisis' when its interpretative dispositions face problems in their smooth continuation, because taken-for-granted self-understandings and role positions are openly challenged, and eventually undermined. In the present research, an identity crisis ensues when interpretive dispositions come to understand the end of the Cold War as challenging the self-understanding and role conception embedded in a national foreign policy tradition. Second, such an identity crisis is more likely to revive geopolitical thought when at least some of the following factors apply: the existence of a materialist tradition of thinking foreign policy, its institutionalisation within a country's foreign policy expert culture, and the existence of a political game where such thought is rhetorically used for political gain (usually on the conservative side).

Framework of analysis and methodology

This study understands the revival of geopolitical thought after 1989 in the context of how national security imaginaries or foreign policy discourses and their embedded subject-positions interact with international events. It therefore shares an interpretivist approach, since the event itself is insufficient to impress a single meaning and effect on agents; rather, agents give meaning within the interpretative context. Moreover, focusing on the dispositional factor of identity prompts a dispositional type of explanation that seeks to understand how a certain phenomenon has become possible. In this explanation, an identity crisis would be a trigger whose realisation is however dependent on a series of process factors. Accordingly, the study relies on an interpretivist version of process tracing, and its comparative framework is case-oriented.[64]

Particular research questions for the case studies

First, country studies need to establish whether a revival took place, and if so of what kind: has there been a revival of neoclassical geopolitics? If so, what is the exact content of the neoclassical geopolitical thinking involved? Also, on what level has the revival been taking place (formal geopolitics, practical geopolitics or popular geopolitics)? How important is it? Carefully establishing the content of the revived geopolitics is also important for further study of the possible micro-dynamics of the European 'culture of anarchy'.

Second, the case studies need to establish the kind of foreign policy identity crisis that occurred in the country studied. Was the end of the Cold War understood as constituting a challenge either to the country's self-identification or to its foreign policy role recognition, or both?

Third, each study needs to establish how such a crisis, if it happened, was related to the rise of geopolitics by checking out a series of factors. Derived from the sociology of knowledge, one research avenue would examine cases in

---

[64] For the distinction between case-oriented and variable-oriented comparisons, see Ragin, 1987.

which a country's self-understanding seems not to be matched by a correspond-ing role within international society (the external identity misfit) and where materialist indicators of size and power are the prevalent means used for rank-ing legitimacy within the relevant country's foreign policy discourse; in such cases, neoclassical geopolitics can be expected to be revived. For establishing ideational path dependency, the study would ask: was there a geopolitical trad-ition in the country beforehand? How 'compromised' by the German tradition does it seem to be? Does the country have a political culture that is strongly materialist, whether realist or Marxist? In order to investigate how institutions are related to the ideational dispositions in the field and practice of foreign pol-icy expertise, as well as the ways in which these enable, legitimate or empower the possible rise of neoclassical geopolitics, the country studies would look at the existence of non-mainstream security research institutions and thoughts, the role of theoretical reflexivity in the teaching of IR within academia and else-where, and, if possible, the socialisation of elites into international institutions. Finally, the revival of neoclassical geopolitics can be linked to its usefulness in political games, where its rhetorical power can show when dealing with terri-torial issues, being mobilised in a threat rhetoric, controlling domestic dissent and strengthening conservatism, as well as establishing the primacy of foreign policy and the need for long-term strategy.

Case selection

A comprehensive study of the interaction effects between the end of the Cold War and national foreign policy discourses in Europe would have potentially included all European countries. That being beyond the financial possibil-ities of the present project, a case selection was necessary.[65] This selection, in turn, had to respond to two expectations. First, it needed to allow for a plausi-bility probe of the main thesis. Hence, the selection needed to include both cases where neoclassical geopolitics experienced a revival and cases where it did not. Second, since the analysis would be dispositional and the compari-son case-oriented, the case studies would need to cover a set of identity cri-ses and processes that were sufficiently diverse as to make it possible to check the potentially different paths towards the occurrence (or absence) of such a revival.

The cases selected were those of the Czech Republic, Estonia, Germany, Italy, Russia and Turkey. These correspond to the above-mentioned criteria in the following way. First, the selection includes countries that have not experienced a significant revival of geopolitical thinking (Czech Republic, Germany). Second, it includes different potential types of identity crisis. Given the cen-trality of territory and borders, this meant including both countries that have

---

[65] Comparable research of other cases does exist. For a congenial study see Mälksoo, 2010.

seen their borders changed (Czech Republic, Estonia, Germany, Russia) and countries that stayed the same (Italy, Turkey). Also, the selection needed to include countries where potential identity crises could be linked to the different ways in which a country's national foreign policy identity discourse could have been challenged, distinguishing between countries that understood their status as being challenged – 'no longer an identity' (Italy, Russia, Turkey) – and those where such an identity needed to be re-established in the first place – 'not yet an identity' (Czech Republic, Estonia). Finally, the selection needed to have some variance on the process factors, to tease out the configuration of these factors on the different paths. Hence, the selection included countries with a strong geopolitical tradition (Germany, Italy, Russia, Turkey) and those without (Czech Republic, Estonia), as well as countries with a Marxist past after 1945 (all formerly communist countries, to some extent Italy) and those without. It also included countries with different structures in their intellectual production (academic and other) and different civil–military relations (Russia and Turkey being different from the others). For the final process factor, political games, the selection needed to include countries that have seen dynamic national-conservative (not just generally right-wing!) forces who could use the rhetorical power of geopolitical thinking and those that have not. Having said this, such forces are present in virtually in all countries, yet with different strengths, ranging from rather weak (Germany) to strong (Turkey). Obviously, since this research has left space for inductive and case-specific contributions, the process tracing had not to exclude further factors that could play an important role in each individual case, and to allow the specificity of such factors to be teased out in the final comparison.

Theory development

As with all more interpretivist analysis, and as with all comparisons that are case-oriented and rely on process tracing, the relationship to theory development does not come in a hypothesis-testing manner, where a pre-given middle-range theory is operationalised, applied to a set of cases and then empirically tested. In interpretative studies, the empirics and the theory are far more intertwined, because interpretivists approach theories mostly through their constitutive character: it is through theory that the empirical analysis becomes possible in the way that it does. Therefore, much of the defence of the selection of theories has to happen on the level of its meta-theoretical and theoretical assumptions. If theories are shown to be inconsistent, then they will be discarded in favour of others; and only those should be applied in empirical analysis. In other words, the test comes largely before the empirical application. On account of the internal relation between observation and the object of study and the theory dependence of facts, the empirical analysis alone cannot consistently invalidate the underlying theory (although the empirical analysis can be wrong, of course). The high level of meta-theoretical critique in constructivist writings is not merely the brainchild of abstraction-obsessed scholars, but a scientific check at the level where it is necessary. And, more often than not, this is one that the scholar has reached with some despair, because lower-level adjustments would simply not work.[66]

Still, also for such an interpretivist design, the terms of the analysis, its central concepts and framework need to be clearly delineated. Hence, the empirical study does not come unprepared. The analyses are also fallible, both in their theoretical logic and in their empirical reach. The proposed thesis would be contradicted by cases where neoclassical geopolitics would have revived without any type of foreign policy identity crisis.

Being not hypothesis-testing but puzzle-solving, using not a variable-oriented comparison but a case-oriented one, and endogenising the input of the analysis into the process tracing itself, the theoretical contribution of the present study can only be twofold. On the one hand, the empirical analysis can contribute to fine-tuning the underlying framework of analysis, including its meta-theoretical assumptions. On the other hand, the theoretically informed analysis can establish new or different social mechanisms, or qualify the significance and roles of known ones. Although these mechanisms are about empirical phenomena, they are inherently theoretical in that they are about the specific relationship between selected empirical phenomena, and in that regard not too different from ideal-types. After the input of the empirical analyses, two such mechanisms will be presented in the concluding chapter of this work: a mechanism of foreign policy identity crisis reduction and a self-fulfilling mechanism that is called the 'vicious circle of essentialisation'.

---

[66] Moreover, at times, the reflexive interaction between the observation and the observed is relevant for the research question itself, just as here with the potential relation between geopolitical analysis and the rise of a generally more Hobbesian security culture in Europe.

PART II

Case studies

4

Czech geopolitics: struggling for survival

PETR DRULÁK

Introduction

This chapter is about a dog that did not bark. Whereas in many other European countries, geopolitics again became popular after 1989, the Czech Republic is one of those countries which did not experience any strong revival. Although there have been some isolated attempts, neither the academic, nor the political, discourse have been much shaped by it.

Yet, most of the factors, which were identified in Chapter 3 for understanding a possible revival, seem to apply to the Czech case. For one, and with regard to the core factor of this book's analytical framework, the Velvet Revolution in 1989 and the end of the Cold War brought about a fundamental redefinition of the country's international role. Therefore, it can be seen as an example of a 'foreign policy identity crisis' in which the loss of well-established and reified identities produces a state of 'ontological anxiety' which could then be fixed with reference to seemingly objective givens of geography. Apart from such external factors, also prevailing foreign policy discourses were prone to prompt an identity crisis. To some extent the Czech 'security imaginary' tends to picture the Czech nation as a perennial victim of territorial ambitions of the two neighbouring great powers: Germany in the West and Russia in the East. In this respect, the expulsion of the Sudeten Germans from Czech territory after 1945 and the withdrawal of Soviet troops after 1989 can be seen as recent Czech triumphs in the battle for space. However, given the power asymmetry between Czechs and Germans as well as between Czechs and Russians, these territorial triumphs are at the same time seen as fragile and reversible which can again provoke ontological anxiety and may make the geopolitical arguments relevant in the political discourse.

Some of the ideas addressed by this chapter have already been analysed in Drulák (2006b). However, despite some overlaps, this chapter differs from the previous text both in its scope and in its focus. I am grateful to Stefano Guzzini and other participants in the seminar on self-fullfilling geopolitics at the Danish Institute of International Relations (5–6 June 2006) for their helpful comments.

Also several of the hypothesised process factors did apply to the Czech case. Forty years of communism left behind the intellectual tradition of 'vulgarised historical materialism' in Czech minds. This materialism was the only social theory which was published and taught at schools and at universities for such a long period. This materialist ideational path-dependence could provide grounds for an emergence of equally materialist geopolitics. Finally, the 'field of foreign policy expertise' has been newly founded after 1989 with a weak academic background and under a heavy influence of practitioners. Moreover, the essential academic input came from historians. As Guzzini argues in Chapter 3, the practical orientation and the historical background could 'enhance the appeal of geopolitical thought'.

How come then, that the Czech geopolitical revival was less strong than one could expect? A closer look reveals that none of the above factors is as unambiguous as it may seem. In particular, I will argue that a strong anti-geopolitical tradition both pre-empted the development of a widely shared identity crisis, and lessened, if not neutralised, the impact of process factors, such as a materialist ideational path-dependence or the closeness of the new foreign policy expert system to practitioners.

First, the Velvet Revolution produced the feelings of crisis and ontological anxiety only in the old communist elite. In contrast, the new elite embraced the change as a moment of liberation and new opportunities. The interpretation of the Czech communist experience by the new elite was very much in tune with Milan Kundera's metaphor of a 'kidnap'.[1] In this perspective, Czechs, together with other Central Europeans, were kidnapped and then taken hostage by the Soviet imperialists for forty years. Therefore, the fall of old certainties was seen as a break out from prison. Moreover, Kundera's definition of Central Europe was cultural rather than geographical: 'its borders are imaginary and must be drawn and redrawn with each new historical situation'.[2] This intellectual insight was then reinforced by the events of the Velvet Revolution which was started by students and representatives of culture – actors, musicians and writers among others.

In the Czech case the renewal of political and administrative elites was more radical than in most other countries in the region (with the exception of Eastern Germany) as completely new networks took over: dissidents around Václav Havel, many of whom came from the field of culture, and neoliberal economists around Václav Klaus.[3] The members of the old elite who could not or did not want to change allegiances disappeared from public life. Thus, the new political and intellectual elite did not feel any ontological anxiety which would push them towards geopolitical certainties. In contrast, their 'can-do' experience of the Velvet Revolution was at odds with geopolitical determinism.

[1] Kundera, 1984, 33.   [2] Kundera, 1984, 35.   [3] Drulák and Königová, 2005.

In their thinking they relied either on their artistic and cultural experience or on their neoclassical economic expertise.

Still, there were later two brief geopolitical revivals which can be linked to foreign policy identity crises. The new elite went through its first such crisis at the time when Czechoslovakia disintegrated. At this moment, geopolitics briefly emerged as a respected template for international thinking. Later on, an influential part of the Czech political and intellectual elite succumbed to anxiety which is brought about by the new international assertiveness of Putin's Russia. At that time doubts were raised about the usefulness and effectiveness of the EU and the NATO as possible shelters. For a brief period, geopolitical arguments reappeared again.

But, and this is central to my argument, the state of the security imaginary greatly contributes to the explanation of why the two geopolitical revivals were so brief. Even though the Czech security imaginary has a clear geopolitical dimension which has been sketched above, it also has a strong anti-geopolitical dimension. Below I argue that it is the anti-geopolitics that has traditionally prevailed in the Czech political thinking. I also show that after 1989 the Czech security imaginary has been shaped by two streams of political thinking which correspond to the composition of the new political elite: the humanism of Václav Havel and the neoliberalism of Václav Klaus. While the former is an offspring of the Czech anti-geopolitical tradition, the latter takes distance from both geopolitics and anti-geopolitics.

Besides pre-empting the development of a major identity crisis, this anti-geopolitical tradition of Czech political thinking also undermines the impact of process factors in this study. Referring to the ideational path-dependence, one should not overestimate the impact of vulgarised materialism after 1989. The official ideology has not been taken seriously by almost anyone in the last years of communism. Havel fittingly describes the condition in which people pay lip service to the official slogans without actually believing them.[4] Hence, even though the Marxist-Leninist ideology was the obligatory reference point in political and scholarly discourse, its intellectual influence was limited. A variety of rules of thumb which originated from the experience of the decay of the communist society were probably more important in this respect. However, their theoretical conceptualisation would be quite difficult. Moreover, I will argue that the ideology was applied to the official version of the Czech history in an outspokenly anti-geopolitical manner. This does not mean that the communist ideology would not leave any trace in the Czech intellectual tradition but it did not prescribe a specific path of intellectual evolution which would favour geopolitics.

Finally, practitioners and historians who contributed to the establishment of the 'field of foreign policy expertise' were mostly related to the new elite having

---

[4] Havel, 1978/1985.

being persecuted under the communist system.[5] Therefore, even practitioners had a limited experience with the practical foreign policy and its geopolitically oriented common sense. Moreover, most of them drew on the anti-geopolitical tradition of the Czech political thinking.[6]

The main argument of this chapter is about the weakness of the Czech geopolitical revival. At the same time, just as the other chapters, it analyses the content of the (here: few) geopolitical interventions. Since the chapter's main argument relies on the distinction between geopolitics and anti-geopolitics, I start with the conceptual elaboration of these concepts. Following this, I present the Czech anti-geopolitical tradition arguing that anti-geopolitics has been the mainstream of Czech political thinking since the nineteenth century when modern politics comes into being. I then analyse the most important contributions to Czech geopolitics and argue that its intellectual peaks are linked with periods of ontological anxiety when the territorial integrity of the state is called into question, just as initially hypothesised. And yet, when my last section finally addresses the two modest revivals of Czech geopolitics after 1989, it provides further evidence of the lingering impact of anti-geopolitics.

Geopolitics, anti-geopolitics and common sense

Given that geopolitics 'is notoriously difficult to define,'[7] a brief introduction of the basic concepts is in order. I introduce the concept of geopolitics together with its opposite, anti-geopolitics. Both concepts are then contextualised within the IR debates. Finally, I point to the significant contribution of geopolitics to 'common sense' international relations. This close connection between geopolitics and common sense allows us to distinguish between practical geopolitics and formal geopolitics. Moreover, it turns geopolitics into one of many default theories in IR, which are difficult to avoid when thinking and speaking about international politics.

The chapter argues that no significant revival of (neoclassical) geopolitical thought occurred in Czechoslovakia or the Czech Republic after 1989. To do this fairly, I try to cast a wide net for finding possible evidence of such a revival, by operationalising the concept of geopolitics in a less stringent manner than 'neoclassical geopolitics'. Yet, having thus more incidences of geopolitical talk, much of the chapter then deals directly with them, assessing their meaning and significance with the aim of distinguishing between more rhetoric usages and a true geopolitical discourse (which would be akin to neoclassical geopolitics).

For the sake of my analysis, I will hence define geopolitics as 'a policy-oriented discourse about a state inspired by its position on the map'.[8] Although less

---

[5] Drulák and Drulaková, 2000.   [6] Drulák and Drulaková, 2000.
[7] Ó Tuathail and Agnew, 1992/1998, 79.   [8] van der Wusten and Dijkink, 2002.

demanding (and 'conveniently' vague) than the reference definition in Chapter 2, such a definition is sufficient for raising several claims that are fundamental for setting up the central dichotomy of this chapter. The central claim of geopolitics is objectivity. Supposedly, this factor is guaranteed by its focus on 'the enduring conditions of the physical environment'.[9] On this basis, geopolitics claims to provide an impartial perspective on international politics cleansed from ideology and any other discursive factors in general. In this sense, geopolitics is 'a foil to idealism, ideology and human will'[10] representing a determinist discourse which analyses politics on the basis of geography and evokes the unchanging, natural features of geography.[11]

In contrast, anti-geopolitics stresses the role of ideas, human agency and the possibility of change despite the constraints of objective conditions.[12] Moreover, it shows how deeply ideological the geopolitical claims can be; it reveals 'the hidden politics of geopolitical knowledge'.[13] The distinction between geopolitics and anti-geopolitics can be contextualised within the IR debates. First, geopolitics is on the side of realism and anti-geopolitics is on the side of idealism in the first great debate. Being an offshoot of realist thinking, geopolitics conceptualises the realist struggle for power in more specific terms, such as those of the struggle for territory. Second, the anti-geopolitical critique of determinism and materialism shares a common denominator with a reflectivist critique of neoliberalism and neorealism.

Geopolitics, along with realism, also has an important function in the public discourse regarding international relations. Like realism, it contributes to what is usually seen as the common sense aspect of international politics, thus providing IR claims that are often taken for granted and informing much of IR thought.[14] Guzzini[15] shows that realism, as a discipline of social research, represents Hans Morgenthau's[16] attempt to translate the older common sense aspects of European diplomacy into the language of American social science. Thus, the neorealism of Kenneth Waltz is just another step towards the formalisation of 'common sense' international politics.[17] This observation helps us to understand to what extent the language of practitioners of International Politics and other significant parts of IR research are, indeed, realist.[18]

A similar case can be made with respect to geopolitics, in the sense that it formalises beliefs about a decisive function of physical space in international

---

[9] Bassin, 1987b, 120, quoted in: Ó Tuathail and Agnew, 1992/1998, 79.

[10] Ó Tuathail and Agnew, 1992/1998, 79.

[11] These features may refer to physical geography (rivers, mountains, resources). But as Huntington shows, they can also refer to cultural geography.

[12] Routledge, 1998, 245–254.   [13] Ó Tuathail, 1998, 3.

[14] Ó Tuathail (1996, 168–169) makes a brief observation on the links between geopolitics, realism and common sense in regard to international relations.

[15] Guzzini, 1998.   [16] Morgenthau, 1948.

[17] Waltz, 1979.   [18] Beer and Harriman, 1996, 6–7.

politics. Geopolitics can often point to powerful political figures, such as Napoleon or Bismarck, who voice these beliefs. In this connection, a distinction can be made between a *practical* geopolitical reasoning 'of a common sense type'[19] and a theory-based, *formal* geopolitical reasoning. The very existence of practical geopolitics can serve as evidence for the importance of geopolitical thought in common sense international relations.

The presence of geopolitical discourse in common sense international relations has several consequences. Most importantly, common sense functions as a discursive structure that makes one kind of statement possible or understandable while precluding other statements.[20] In this respect, it facilitates geopolitical arguments while discriminating against anti-geopolitical reasoning. Hence, like realism, geopolitics serves as one of the default theories of international thinking. The grasp of realism and geopolitics over international thinking makes them (realism and geopolitics) somewhat inevitable in the public discourse, especially when it comes to discursive contributions which advocate a specific opinion and are aimed at general audiences or at practitioners of international politics.

In this respect, even thinkers whose theoretical background is anti-realist and anti-geopolitical sometimes use the language of realism and geopolitics when trying to reach a wider audience. An occasional embrace of geopolitical language cannot be equated to the speaker's adherence to geopolitical thinking. On the contrary, the language of geopolitics can be used to support reasoning that is basically anti-geopolitical. Thus, Jacques Derrida and Jürgen Habermas refer to the realist 'balance of power' vocabulary when they argue that Europe should 'balance out the hegemonic unilateralism of the United States',[21] despite the fact that their own theoretical work is clearly at odds with what realism stands for. Similarly, Václav Havel, a textbook example of an anti-geopolitician,[22] claims that 'our geopolitical position cultivated in us the sense for a moral dimension of politics'.[23] In other words, the mere reference to space does not pass for geopolitics.

This tension between practical geopolitics and formal anti-geopolitics must be taken into account when assessing the role of geopolitics in political thought, especially on the basis of what key actors may write or say. Thus, geopolitical statements which arise from the discourse of these figures must be contextualised with respect to their basic tenets, as they are revealed on other occasions and with respect to their target audience at the time such statements were made. Such a contextualisation makes it possible to distinguish between geopolitical discourse, which is embedded in true geopolitical thought, and

[19] Ó Tuathail and Agnew, 1992/1998, 79.
[20] Milliken, 1999; Weldes, 1999a.
[21] Derrida and Habermas, 2003.
[22] Routledge, 1998.   [23] Havel, 1999b, 43–64.

geopolitical rhetoric which relies on commonsensical templates created to drive anti-geopolitical arguments home.

The anti-geopolitical mainstream

The dominant tradition of Czech thought on international relations is anti-geopolitical. This argument is substantiated by a review of four highly influential figures, all of whom are both public intellectuals and politicians who have shaped political thought and practice in the Czech countries since the second half of the nineteenth century: František Palacký, Tomáš Garrigue Masaryk, Zdeněk Nejedlý and Václav Havel. I will start with a brief introduction for each of them and then explain their individual contributions to Czech political thought. Following this, I outline the most important anti-geopolitical arguments that have been shaping Czech mainstream political thought.[24]

Figures

František Palacký (1798–1876) was the great national historian whose *History of the Czech Nation*, published in 1836, still influences the prevailing understanding of Czech history, based on the view that Czech history is defined by never-ending contacts and struggles between the Czechs and the Germans. Moreover, he was the political leader of the Czech liberal conservative party, who was seen as *pater patriae* by his contemporaries at a time when the Czech countries belonged to the Austrian Empire. He is also a member of the 'pantheon of national heroes' and is respected by all important forces in the Czech society, including communists, as a continuous source of inspiration for Czech political thinking.

Palacký greatly inspired Tomáš Garrigue Masaryk (1850–1937), who transformed his legacy into a political programme for an independent Czechoslovak state.[25] Masaryk started out as professor of sociology; however, he turned into the political and intellectual leader of the Czech emancipation movement prior to World War I. During the war, his exile negotiations with the Entente contributed to the fall of the Austro-Hungarian Empire and the rise of Czechoslovakia. He became its first president. The impact of his influence is nicely captured by Gellner, who observes that Czechoslovakia 'dominated by the spirit of Masaryk ... had a foreign policy based on [his] philosophy'.[26]

Zdeněk Nejedlý (1878–1962), one of Masaryk's students, was a historian and musicologist.[27] Before World War II he was an influential public intellectual

---

[24] For a more detailed account, see Drulák, 2006b.
[25] Šolle, 1999, 473.   [26] Gellner, 1995, 49.
[27] Basic information about Zdeněk Nejedlý can be found at www.libri.cz/databaze/kdo20/search.php?zp=2&name=NEJEDL%DD+ZDEN%CCK.

who defended the Marxist-Leninist perspective on a variety of political, social and cultural issues within the public discourse. After having spent his war years exiled in Moscow, he became the first communist minister of education and social affairs in the Czechoslovak government. In the 1950s, he headed the Czechoslovak Academy of Science and supervised research activities. In this way, he was responsible for the Stalinisation of Czechoslovak education and research. When the communists took over, Nejedlý was their most prominent intellectual and the only person among the communist top officials with a scholarly background. He laid the groundwork for the official Czechoslovak communist ideology, which was based on the Marxist-Leninist interpretation of Palacký and his former mentor, Masaryk.

Václav Havel (1936–2011), playwright, anti-communist dissident and democratic president of Czechoslovakia and the Czech Republic, was also inspired by Masaryk, with whom he also shared the fate of fighting against undemocratic regimes in the name of the truth, democracy and morality.[28] Even though Havel's influence over political thinking has never been as strong and uncontested as Masaryk's, he exercised clear leadership in foreign policy discourse and practice throughout the period of post-communist Czechoslovakia (1990–1992).

In many respects, these figures are strange bedfellows. Still, they have several features in common. First, each was recognised, at least for some time, as the ultimate authority in the public discourse. Hence, their work gives us valuable insights into the beliefs and practices of the given period. Second, they all belong to the tradition of thought that began with Palacký. Both Masaryk and Nejedlý considered themselves to be students of Palacký, each of them reinterpreting Palacký's reading of Czech history in a particular way. In addition, Havel liked to draw on what he saw as Masaryk's legacy, especially after he became the Czechoslovak president. Third, the core of their thinking is anti-geopolitical and based on either religious, moral or social perspectives. Still, geopolitics is not totally absent from their discourse, especially when they address the general public or decision-makers in times of crisis.

From Jan Hus to human rights

The main argument of the Czech anti-geopolitics thinkers is traditionally based on a particular interpretation of Czech history which identifies the Hussite period in the early fifteenth century as the nation's greatest historical achievement and, ultimately, a benchmark for the most important political projects. This reading of history makes little sense from a geopolitical perspective. The

---

[28] Masaryk is the person Havel referred to most frequently in his speeches in the 1990s (Havel, 1999b).

Hussite period is not connected with the territorial expansion of the state, like the Great Moravian period or the period of the rule of Přemysl Otakar II, nor is it connected with the peak of the nation's political influence, which most likely took place during the rule of Charles IV. On the contrary, the Hussite period was a time of civil war, huge material destruction and foreign intervention.

The Hussite movement is connected with the teachings of the Czech scholar and preacher Jan Hus. Inspired by the English Church reformer John Wycliff, Hus gave a voice to a growing dissatisfaction with the institutional governance of the Catholic Church, especially with its corruption and accumulation of property. Hus argued for a Church which would be pure and poor, emphasised a personal interpretation of the Holy Scripture and defied the Church hierarchy. In 1415, he was invited to Konstanz, where the Church Council took place, to defend himself against charges of heresy. However, he lost his case and was immediately burned there.

The death of Jan Hus together with the ensuing repression of his followers and political confusion in the country provoked a public anger which turned into a revolt against the Church and against the king. The years 1419–1434 mark the period of civil war in which significant parts of the Bohemian kingdom, including the capital, Prague, were freed from the control of these traditional authorities and were governed by Hussite communities led by radical preachers and lower nobility. Some of these communities organised themselves on radically egalitarian principles (e.g. individual property was banned, all members were equal). Others introduced new hierarchies. Importantly, most of them were surprisingly efficient in military affairs, resisting four crusades which were called by the pope against the Hussite heretics. They were defeated when a moderate wing of the movement made a deal with the Catholics which ended these exhaustive wars of huge destruction.

Why then is the Hussite movement so highly valued? Palacký considers Jan Hus' attempt to reform the Catholic Church as avant-garde and as a precursor to the European reformation a century later. This makes it possible to interpret the Hussite movement universally as an early advocate of humanistic and democratic values.[29] In this respect, Palacký also makes a careful distinction between the Hussite movement as a battle of ideas that he looks upon favourably and the Hussite wars, which he harshly criticises for being destructive,[30] although he notes that the wars were at least driven by ideas and not material interests.[31]

Masaryk elaborates on this conception, arguing that the Czech reformation introduced democratic ideas into theocratic Medieval Europe. The difference between democracy and theocracy is central to his political thinking.

---

[29] Válka, 1999, 95.   [30] Čornej, 1999, 131–133.
[31] Bednář, 1999, 64 and Palacký, 1868, 65.

While the former is defined in moral terms as individual responsibility and self-limitation which does not need any external enforcement, the latter is associated with the worship of hierarchy and power politics as embodied by the Catholic Church, or by what Masaryk calls the Prussian *caesaropapism*, which, according to him, overwhelmed German culture, thinking and politics in the nineteenth century.[32]

He interpreted the ongoing World War I as a fight between democracy (France, UK and United States) and theocracy (Austria, Germany). The Czechs sided with democracy due to their Hussite tradition. Moreover, Masaryk understands history in a teleological way, as a march from theocracy to democracy – to which Czechs were early contributors. This contribution allows Masaryk to argue for Czech independence from the Austrian Empire from an ethical perspective and not from a geopolitical or economic perspective.

Nejedlý shifts this view by interpreting the Hussite movement as a revolutionary force in a reactionary Europe.[33] In this respect, he replaces Masaryk's liberal dichotomy and teleology of democracy/theocracy with a Marxist dichotomy and teleology of revolution/reaction. Thus, Hussites turn from early democrats into early revolutionaries striving for a classless society. Moreover, Marxism-Leninism defined itself as anti-geopolitical, rejecting any kind of geographical or cultural determinism while replacing it with the teleological determinism of world revolution leading to a classless society.

After the Hussite movement underwent decades of heavy abuse from official communist propaganda, Havel did not attempt to resurrect its Masarykian interpretation. More generally, he is sceptical of great theories, thus 'put[ting] his trust, not in overall historical theory, but in the eventual victory of simple decency'.[34] Instead, his anti-geopolitics is developed on Masaryk's concept of democracy, which is based on morality.[35] In this sense, Havel offers his personal credo 'Living in Truth' – a credo he used to fight the communist regime, which is also similar to Masaryk's favourite slogan 'Truth Prevails'.

Thus, Havel argues that politics has to be anchored in the moral awareness of individuals and in the responsibility for the world as a whole. Therefore, a country cannot pursue its own narrow interests at the expense of others. What he calls the 'spirit of our foreign policy' is defined as a campaign for human rights and their universality and indivisibility.[36] Havel seems to conceive of the Czechoslovak foreign policy as a continuation of the Velvet Revolution on a global scale. The peaceful struggle for human rights and democracy against all kinds of totalitarian or authoritarian regimes constitutes the fundamental precepts of the new foreign policy.

---

[32] Masaryk, 1925, 410–420.   [33] Nejedlý, 1951.
[34] Gellner, 1995, 55.   [35] Gellner, 1995, 56.
[36] Havel, 1999a, 487.

Even his comments on contemporary events are full of explicit rejections of geopolitical templates. The indivisibility of freedom provides Havel with grounds on which to defend Czechoslovak participation in the first Gulf War or his meeting with the Dalai Lama. He warns against 'collective hatred in the shape of nationalism', claiming that Central and Eastern Europe needs time to get used to the 'otherness'.[37] Havel also stresses friendship with Germany. He considers Germany a pillar of European spirituality, he appreciates that Germany started to tear down the wall which divided Europe and he even equated traditional anti-German feelings with anti-Semitism.[38] All in all, Havel tries to avoid any externalisation and territorialisation of the negative other. Instead, he constructs the other (of hatred and intolerance) as being inside individuals, and therefore it needs to be suppressed by their self-reflection.

Anti-geopoliticians' geopolitical trips

All of the four figures occasionally use geopolitics. They are aware of its rhetorical power (see Chapter 3, this volume) and strengthen their arguments by referring to the realities of the map and physical power. However, this is done without any consistency and only when reacting to the territorial challenges of the day in newspaper articles, speeches and pamphlets.

Thus, when Palacký proposes federalisation of the Austrian Empire, he argues that the Empire has been functioning as a geopolitical shelter of Central European nations, including Czechs, first against the Turkish threat, and later against Prussia and Russia. However, when his proposals fail, Palacký suggests that the Czechs act as a bridge between the West and the East, calling for closer contacts between the Czechs and Russia. Similarly, when pushing for the break up of the Austrian Empire during the war, Masaryk presents a variety of isolated geopolitical arguments (about a Slavic alliance, against pan-Germanism, or defending the particular shape of the Czechoslovak borders) targeting leaders and diplomats of the Entente, as well as Western public opinion.[39] However, these arguments do not add up to any consistent geopolitical perspective of international politics which could be compared to his anti-geopolitical thought.

On the other hand, Masaryk's very conception of history and democracy is open to a geopolitical reading. His concepts suffer from a contradiction between a positivist, Comtian law of history (transition from theocracy to democracy) and a moral and metaphysical understanding of democracy (responsibility and human agency).[40] This contradiction has made it possible to read Masaryk in a purely positivist and geopolitical manner,[41] namely against the concept that 'the

[37] Havel, 1999a, 249–263.   [38] Havel, 1999a, 94–103.
[39] Krejčí, 1993.   [40] Patočka, 1991.   [41] Gellner, 1995.

Spirit of World History' (in the shape of a march towards democracy) was located in the West and that the Czechs pragmatically chose an alliance with Western powers to be on the winning side of history. The geopolitical reading of Masaryk also facilitated an intellectual acceptance of the communist regime by slightly redefining 'the Spirit of World History', as was done by Nejedlý. In this reading, the Spirit of History (taking the form of a march towards a classless society) was located in the East, and on this basis the Czechs pragmatically chose an alliance with the Eastern power to be on the winning side of history again.

Even though Havel gives up on any kind of simplified teleology, he occasionally uses geopolitical arguments as well. This may be connected with the audience. In Poland, Havel argues for Central European cooperation 'to fill the power vacuum which came after the fall of the Habsburg empire'.[42] Similarly, he reminds the American audience that Czechoslovakia is in the centre of the continent, and its political stability is important for Europe.[43] Moreover, geography becomes unavoidable when the end of Czechoslovakia is discussed. Thus, when warning his fellow citizens against splitting up, he points to such threats as floods of immigrants from the East, doubts about borders, or the revival of divisions in Europe.[44] However, none of these statements refer to any underlying principles comparable with his concept of human freedom.

Czech geopoliticians: lingering on the margins

Even though anti-geopolitics tends to prevail in Czech mainstream political thought, this generally anti-geopolitical mainstream has had its own geopolitical margins in the past. And these were occasionally quite broad. It was especially in times of ontological anxiety provoked by territorial changes that geopolitics gained some influence. In this respect, three periods are especially important: the foundation of Czechoslovakia (1918), the destruction of Czechoslovakia by the Munich conference (1938) and the split of Czechoslovakia (1992).

In the early 1920s, Viktor Dvorský (1882–1960), a leading geographer, a member of the Czechoslovak delegation at the Versailles conference, and the founder of formal geopolitics in the Czech environment, provided the arguments for the existence of a sovereign Czechoslovakia against the claims made by Austria or Germany. In the late 1930s, Jaromír Korčák (1895–1989), an economic geographer and the founding father of Czech demographics, was motivated by the belief that the official Czechoslovak anti-geopolitical thought was unable to engage the German geopolitical claims, which doubted Czechoslovak sovereignty and territorial integrity.[45]

---

[42] Havel, 1999a, 44–53.   [43] Havel, 1999a, 59–72.
[44] Havel, 1999a, 311–319, 714–718.
[45] Korčák, 1938, 7.

Unlike Dvorský and Korčák, Emmanuel Moravec (1893–1945) was not an academic. He was a soldier, serving as a colonel in the Czechoslovak general staff, and a prolific commentator on international politics in the 1930s. Even though he started out as a leading advocate of Masaryk and Beneš in public debates,[46] he is now remembered as the Czech Quisling, personifying the worst kind of collaboration with the Nazi occupiers, due to his infamous activities as minister of education under the German occupation. This reversal was connected with his deep disappointment following the Munich conference in September 1938. The fact that France betrayed Czechoslovakia and that the Czechoslovak government accepted it without a fight shattered his deepest beliefs. Moravec reacted with a series of essays in which he criticised the 'naive idealism' of previous Czechoslovak foreign policy thought, outlining alternatives based on geopolitics.[47]

In the aftermath of the division of Czechoslovakia in the 1990s, Oskar Krejčí presented a dissident geopolitical perspective which draws on pre-war Czechoslovak geopoliticians and heavily criticises the decision to split the state. Despite his rich publishing activity, Krejčí was barred from any academic job in the Czech Republic from 1990 until recently because of his close connections with the communist establishment and intelligence services in the 1970s and 1980s. In this respect, Krejčí represents that part of Czech society that perceives 1989 as the foreign policy identity crisis to which geopolitical recipes may provide appealing remedies.

Despite the diversity of their thought, Czech geopoliticians share at least three tenets. First, they criticise the idealism of the anti-geopolitical mainstream, which they contrast with their own scientific analyses of objective facts. Second, they define the state identity in geographical terms, and they do not see the Hussite movement as particularly important. And third, they focus on their country's conflictual relationship with Germany.

Reality of power

Czech geopoliticians insist on a clear distinction between the normative approach of the mainstream and what they see as a scientific approach of their own. Their supposed science is based on the reality of geography and material power. This corresponds to the realist critique of idealism in the first great debate in IR. While the contributions of Dvorský predate the debate, Moravec's book was published only less than a year before E. H. Carr's *Twenty Years' Crisis*.

Thus, Dvorský presents geopolitical reasoning as part of a new 'science of states' or 'biology of nations'[48] and is dismissive about international law in

---

[46] Veber, 1939/2004, 5.   [47] Moravec, 1939/2004.
[48] Dvorský, 1918, 63.

general and about the League of Nations in particular. Similarly, Moravec criticises the Czechoslovak government for consistently pursuing idealist policies, cooperating with democratic countries while avoiding contacts with non-democratic ones, and sticking with the League of Nations while failing to recognise that the Western democratic powers pursued such policies only as long as it fit their geopolitical interests.[49] He rejects any foreign policy based on 'Masaryk's ideas of humanity, liberty, democracy and international tolerance' that lacks 'realism' and gets carried away by ideology.[50] Also, Krejčí criticises the 'ideological' approach to foreign policy of both Havel and Klaus, who disregard Czechoslovak national interests in his view.

Identity of a geopolitical centre

Czech geopoliticians seek the justification of the existence of the state as well as its identity in geography. They connect this identity with the Great Moravian state rather than with the Hussite movement. This idea is introduced by Dvorský. He uses the concept of river-defined basins to argue that Czechoslovak territory consists of three such areas: the Moldau-Elbe basin, the Morava-Thaia basin and the Danubian basin. The Morava-Thaia basin gave rise to the Great Moravian state, where the Czechoslovak nation was born, in the eighth century. After the Hungarian invasion in the tenth century, the Great Moravian territory was split, and the centre of the Czechoslovak nation moved to the Moldau-Elbe basin in the northwest, which was better protected by surrounding mountains. The Czechoslovak state with its centre in Prague on the Moldau is thus 'a restitution of the Great Moravian state in the same sense as current Italy is a restitution of the Roman Empire'.[51]

Korčák uses the concepts of 'tribal area' (kmenová oblast) and 'action centre' to elaborate on Dvorský's argumentation. While the former refers to a geographical area with a very long continuity of human settlement where a distinctive ethnic group had been formed, the latter is an established tribal area with an especially high concentration of people emanating 'geopolitical energy'.[52] Great empires in European history correspond to such action centres.

However, Central Europe, defined as the Central Danubian floodplain, has never been an action centre itself. This is because a large chunk of its territory actually does not fit in with the rest of it.[53] Korčák contends that Alföld (the great plain east of the Danube containing most of Hungary's current territory) is completely different from the European plains that host European action centres. Geologically, it is comparable with the Asian steppes, which are not

---

[49] Moravec, 1939/2004, 36 and 53.
[50] Moravec, 1939/2004, 61 and 268.
[51] Dvorský, 1918, 22.   [52] Korčák, 1938, 16–17 and 39–40.
[53] Korčák, 1938, 45–47.

suitable for a sedentary life based on the cultivation of land. As a result, Alföld was inhabited by nomads that disturbed European progress for millennia.

The most powerful tribal area in central Europe gave rise to the Great Moravian state. The state fell after the Avarian invasion from Alföld which divided the tribal area and which Korčák considers as 'the greatest geopolitical loss' of Czechoslovak history.[54] After 1918, Czechoslovakia integrated a significant part of the Great Moravian tribal area with the two neighbouring tribal areas (along the rivers Elbe and Danube), creating a natural geopolitical entity and restoring what was destroyed by Alföld a millennium before.

Similarly, Krejčí considers the Great Moravian state to be the greatest achievement in Czech history: the state controlled vital, pan-European merchant routes and was able to balance the German influence by intensive contacts with the Byzantine Empire.[55] Its fall brought about several adverse effects, which shaped Czech statehood for centuries to come. First, the core of the state shifted northwest from the Moravian tribal area, where conditions had been optimal, to the Elbe plain, which was harder to control and consolidate. Second, the Czech and Slovak territories were split. Third, the Hungarian–German alliance cut off the Czech state from the Byzantine Empire, making the German Empire the exclusive focus of Czech politics.

Moravec derives the centrality of the Czech territory from its location on an important geopolitical crossroads. Three avenues of geopolitical pressure intersect in Central Europe: the one from the south to the north (Roman), the one from the north to the south (German) and the one from the east to the southwest (Mongolian, Russian).[56] He considers Prague a political and military centre for Central Europe, saying that he who rules over Bohemia also rules over Europe.[57] In 1918, Czechoslovakia was constructed to serve as a dam built by Western powers against German expansion to the southeast, acting as a forward guardian, at the Danube and Elbe, of the Black Sea straits and of British air-bases in the Middle East.[58] It was supposed to be a bar on a 'Eurasian axis' through which non-Europeans used to penetrate into Europe (Tatarský průsmyk). He ascribes to Czechoslovakia three geopolitical tasks – to face German pressure in the West, to be an offensive Slavic advanced guard to Alföld, and to defend the Danubian area against communism from the East.[59]

German threat

Czech geopoliticians see the conflict with Germany as the key issue of Czech politics. Dvorský argues that the Czech–German tension is geographically inevitable, representing a clash between a basin state, whose centres are

---

[54] Korčák, 1938, 101.   [55] Krejčí, 1993, 22–26.
[56] Moravec, 1939/2004, 95.   [57] Moravec, 1939/2004, 48.
[58] Moravec, 1939/2004, 44.   [59] Moravec, 1939/2004, 77.

around rivers with their borders in mountains, and a dorsal state, which occupies mountains and has its borders in valleys. In this respect, he claims that the Czechoslovak western border is the site of an inevitable tension between the German dorsal strategy (to draw the border inside the Elbe-Moldau basin) and the Czechoslovak basin strategy (to draw the border in the surrounding mountains).

Korčák is ambiguous in regard to this issue. On the one hand, writing in the late 1930s, he sees Nazi Germany as a mortal threat to Czechoslovakia. On the other hand, he admiringly identifies Germany with the Baltic action centre, which is the youngest and the most dynamic of all the European action centres, being a source of inspiration for a more dynamic Europe.[60] In this respect, he appreciates the otherwise negative historical role of Alföld, as its repeated interference prevented Central Europe from falling into the Western trap of 'effeminacy of urban life' and materialism.[61] This makes Central Europe 'young' and similar to the new Germany.

A similar ambiguity can be found in Moravec. On the one hand, he speaks about the tragedy. Due to its idealism, Czechoslovakia was neither willing nor able to fulfil its geopolitical tasks which put it at odds with German demands for living space. As such, it was unable to resist the 'success of the German will'.[62] On the other hand, he argues that Czech historical experience taught that enmity with Germany is detrimental to Czech interests. Therefore, Czech interests should always be aligned with those of the Great Germany.

Krejčí is unambiguous. He identifies three geopolitical orientations for Czech foreign policy, German, Western and Eastern, to reject the German one, which embraces the pan-German ideology and subordinates Czech interests to it.[63] In contrast, the Eastern tradition fares best because it draws on the Great Moravian connection with the Byzantine Empire. The orientation eventually boils down to a quest for an Eastern ally (Russia) against Germany. The Eastern bloc, cemented by Slavic ideology or proletarian internationalism, is deemed unbeatable. The Western tradition is second best, to be applied only when the great Eastern power is too weak or when it allies itself with Germany.[64] The tradition also argues for balancing against Germany but does so by looking for Western allies behind Germany. On this basis, he rejects the split of Czechoslovakia, which inevitably pushes the Czech Republic into the German orbit. This push is exacerbated by careless political elites who deny the Slavic orientation of the country, suffer from Russophobia and rely on Western powers, whereby these are either too weak (France and Great Britain) or ignorant about the threat of German dominance (United States).

---

[60] Korčák, 1938, 158.   [61] Korčák, 1938, 160.
[62] Moravec, 1939/2004, 176.   [63] Krejčí, 1993, 120.
[64] Krejčí, 1993, 121.

Fragile revivals of geopolitics after 1989

The Czech political discourse has recently experienced two revivals of geopolitics: a short-lived revival connected with the fall of Czechoslovakia (1992–1993) and a recent revival brought about by the Czech participation in the US missile defence (2006–2008). Neither of these are connected with the above tradition of Czech geopolitical thought, whose most important current representative, Krejčí, has remained marginalised in the Czech academic and political discourses. In contrast, the revivals are connected with the entry of right-wing neoliberals into the Czech government (1992 and 2006) and with the ontological insecurity provoked, first, by the birth of a new state and, second, by US–Russian spats.

The neoclassical economics which shapes the neoliberal worldview is not easily reconciled with the geographical determinism of geopolitics. Therefore, these revivals do not rely on any formal geopolitical reasoning and only take place at the practical level. This may explain the fragility and limited influence of the Czech geopolitical reasoning.

Moreover, this practical geopolitics differs from the Czech geopolitical tradition in two important respects. First, the Czech territory is not assigned any special role. On the contrary, its marginality is emphasised. Second, neither a German threat nor a relationship with Germany is the issue. Instead, a Russian threat and instability in Eastern and Southern Europe are emphasised.

Fall of Czechoslovakia

The first revival took place as the crisis of the Czechoslovak state deepened in the early 1990s and the anti-geopolitical mainstream, shaped by Havel, was challenged by geopolitical arguments. After the 1992 elections, the former dissidents surrounding Václav Havel were succeeded by neoclassical economists led by Václav Klaus, who were more open to geopolitical reasoning than the previous dissident elite. However, their brief embrace of geopolitics can be explained according to their need to differentiate themselves from the previous elite, which they criticised for neglecting Czech interests and for stubbornly insisting on keeping Czechoslovakia together. Hence their geopolitics came into being as a negation of Havel's anti-geopolitics while also providing justification for the splitting up of Czechoslovakia.

In 1992–1993 the public discourses of Prime Minister Klaus and Foreign Minister Josef Zieleniec frequently relied on a variety of geopolitical arguments. This new discourse delimited itself against the Czech anti-geopolitical tradition. Thus, not only has Klaus often criticised Havel for his idealism, but he also took on Masaryk, reproaching him for focusing too much on normative theory without standing up for the national interest.[65] However, he did not provide any geopolitical definition of the national interest. As before, the supreme policy goal remained the 'return to Europe', meaning transition to democracy and a market economy and integration into the EU and NATO.

Even though the foreign minister saw geopolitics as 'the most important factor of foreign policymaking',[66] the geopolitical statements were usually only a matter of political expediency. For example, they helped to justify the split of Czechoslovakia and to demonstrate that Czechs belong in the West. It was thus claimed that after the split, the Czech Republic re-orientated itself towards the West, losing contact with the post-Soviet and Danubian spaces and making the state more stable and more transparent to the West.[67] Similarly, it was often emphasised that the Czechs 'have been part of Western Europe for 1000 years, with the exception of 40 years',[68] which is occasionally supported by the contestable claim that Christianity came from Rome, and not from Byzantium.[69] Thus, the discourse did not dwell on any geopolitical specificity of Central Europe. On the contrary, Czech territory was not pictured as having any particular significance apart from belonging to the West. The Western orientation of the official geopolitics also included good relations with Germany, which Klaus saw as the basis of the Czech national existence.[70]

The official geopolitics also had some support in academia. Bořek Hnízdo, a lecturer in political geography at Charles University who introduced Anglo-American geopolitical theories to Czech students and researchers,[71] provided several geopolitical arguments supporting official policy without, however, integrating them into a formal geopolitical theory. Hence he argued that the Czech Republic is in Central Europe no matter how the region is defined and that due to its location, Central Europe has to be included in any scheme of pan-European integration.[72] Similarly, he argued that the communist Eastern orientation was unusual in Czech history and that it was Slovakia which drew the Czech lands to the East. Therefore, the split of Czechoslovakia was beneficial in bringing the country to the West. In this respect, he argued that the building of a new oil pipeline from Germany and the connections to West European highway networks are likely to facilitate a 'geopolitical transition' of the Czech Republic from an 'East European' to a 'West European' country.[73]

Despite this, geopolitics provided only occasional templates for the official discourse without leaving any persistent impact there. This can be explained by the fact that the geopolitics of the new elite was not embedded in any systematic geopolitical way of thinking. On the contrary, their favoured social

[65] Klaus, 2000.   [66] Zieleniec, 1993.
[67] Zieleniec, 1992a and 1993.   [68] Zieleniec, 1992b.
[69] Klaus, 1992.   [70] Klaus, 1992.
[71] Hnízdo, 1995.   [72] Hnízdo, 1995, 85.   [73] Hnízdo, 1995, 96.

theory came from neoclassical economics.[74] For several reasons, neoliberalism, based on neoclassical economics, is much closer to anti-geopolitics than to geopolitics.

First, the neoliberal world is the world of economic agents (individuals and companies) who meet in the markets, where, thanks to the invisible hand, they make one another richer. Political agents may provide useful regulations, but they usually disturb the efficiency of markets. In contrast, the geopolitical world consists of political agents (states) whose conduct is determined by geography and who are engaged in a zero-sum game struggle over territory. Second, neoliberals do not particularly care about geography. It is only one of many possible sources of comparative advantages without any decisive role. For geopoliticians, geography is the only advantage or disadvantage that really matters. Third, the neoliberal hero is a free and inventive individual. Geopolitics deals with territories and the big collectivities which are determined by them.

Still, a shared emphasis on competition provides a possible meeting ground between geopolitics and neoliberalism and may explain why neoliberals were more open to geopolitics than the previous elite. However, it is obvious that each side speaks about a very different kind of competition, a zero-sum game of political collectivities against a positive-sum game of economic individuals, which makes any alliance between geopolitics and neoliberalism fragile.

Klaus and his peers believed in the Czech uniqueness. However, they did not derive the claim for uniqueness from any geopolitical category (such as geographical position or cultural tradition). They derived it from what they saw as the unquestionable success of their liberal market reforms, believing that these reforms should inspire the rest of the world. Not only were they to guide post-communist countries in their transformation, but European social market economies were also called upon to follow the Czech role model and to consequently deregulate their economies. Therefore, the official geopolitics was quite thin while the neoliberal economics defined the official common sense of the period.

US missile defence

After the elections in 2006, a new right-wing government informed the public that the previous government led by social democrats had favourably responded to an American offer and started secret consultations with the United States about the Czech participation in the US system of ballistic missile defence. Both governments explored the possibility of locating one or two elements of the system on the Czech territory. Once made public, the project

---

[74] Drulák, 2006a; Drulák and Königová, 2005.

met with negative public opinion, and the social democrats, now in opposition, rejected it.

The project turned out to be divisive inside the governing coalition as well, having the support of the dominant party of right-wing neoliberals while being criticised by their junior partners. Eventually, the government endorsed it on the condition that the missile defence would turn into a multilateral NATO project rather than being only an American project with the additional participation of a few willing countries. Despite that, a bilateral treaty between the United States and Czech Republic was signed in 2008 which would establish an American anti-missile radar station in the Czech Republic. However, at the time of the signature the treaty did not have a sufficient support in the Czech parliament and its ratification was repeatedly postponed. In 2009, the new Obama administration decided that it was no longer interested in the project and the non-ratified treaty became history.

Even though the missile defence project eventually failed, its discourse is revealing. The argumentation of Czech neoliberal Atlantists for the Czech participation in the missile defense project provides an interesting insight into the most recent geopolitical revival.[75] However, unlike the previous revival, which took place in public and could be documented with rich references to speeches of political leaders, this revival was mostly observable in private conversations and off-record discussions with policy makers.

At first glance, the arguments for the presence of the US radar in the Czech Republic were not really geopolitical. The Czech participation in the missile defence project was argued to be a Czech contribution to improved transatlantic relations whose good quality was essential for freedom and democracy in the world. Moreover, the missile defence was presented as purely defensive and not of any threat to anybody. Also, it would provide security to a host of other countries, and Europeans should take the opportunity offered by the American readiness to pay for it. Finally, it would be part of the NATO defence systems and could contribute to the reinvigoration of this essential but ailing institution.[76] Thus, to some extent, the Czech participation could have been justified on anti-geopolitical grounds, and that is what was going on in the Czech public discourse.

Now the technology of the system had clear geographical implications. It was supposed to protect a clearly delimited territory of the Northern part of Europe against possible attack from the area of the Middle East. This division was based on geopolitical considerations about which territory needed to be protected and which territory needed to be contained.

However, this geopolitical division and the threats from the Middle East were irrelevant in the thinking of Czech Atlantists. They embraced a very different

---

[75] Drulák, 2006c.   [76] Drulák, 2007.

kind of geopolitics. For them, the main rationale of the Czech inclusion in the system was protection against Russian expansion. An American military facility on the Czech territory was a tangible proof of an American commitment to defend the territory, although the United States would otherwise not care much about it. Their vision of the world was gloomy. They pointed to a revival of Russian imperialist ambitions since Putin, which could not be contained by a toothless EU or by appeasing great European powers. NATO itself was becoming less and less efficient and could not provide a sufficient guarantee of Czech security. The only hope would be a direct tangible American involvement on the territory. In this respect, the purpose of the installation was secondary. The only thing that really mattered was that it was an American strategic asset whose location in Czech Republic increased the strategic value of the territory in American eyes.

This vision was rarely presented in public. Still, several hints pointed to it. Thus, Jan Zahradil, a member of the European Parliament and a leading neo-liberal foreign policy expert, argued that the Czech participation in the system was the most important foreign policy decision since 1989, more important than NATO or EU membership.[77] Alexandr Vondra, deputy prime minister and the strong man in the then Czech foreign policy making, justified his support for the project by pointing to 'the Czech historical experience in the space between Germany and Russia', referring to 'geographical reality', which 'cannot be changed'.[78] In this connection, he warned against 'the power vacuum' in Central Europe which had brought about troubles in the past. Off-record discussions allowed politicians to elaborate on these insights. High officials argued that Czech Republic was in a 'no-man's-land' (despite its EU and NATO memberships) and that Russia was waiting to seize the opportunity to assert its interests there. Therefore, Russia needed to be 'balanced' and 'kept within its borders', and the installation of the American radar was seen as just such a balancing act. It seemed to be a common wisdom among the Czech foreign-policy makers that 'geopolitics returned'.

Why was the geopolitical revival hidden from public discourse, and what was it caused by? A reluctance to use geopolitical arguments in a more open manner was connected with the anti-geopolitical mainstream. For example, Deputy Prime Minister Vondra's remarks were provoked in a parliamentary debate about his presentation at the Heritage Foundation, and he was immediately chided by the chairman of the Foreign Relations Committee for embracing 'the 19th century vision of Europe'.[79] Hence, geopolitical arguments were not easily accepted in the Czech political discourse, which helps explain the half-hidden nature of the revival. Also, as argued above, even though a rhetorical common

[77] Haslingerová, 2007.
[78] Alexandr Vondra, Czech Parliament, 29 November 2007.
[79] Jan Hamáček, Czech Parliament, 29 November 2007.

ground between geopolitics and neoliberalism exists, it is rather thin on a conceptual level. Therefore, it is difficult to make a coherent geopolitical case without abandoning neoliberal principles.

Among the possible causes for the geopolitical revival, three are especially important. To start with, Russia became more assertive under Putin, especially when using its oil and gas exports as a political weapon, and its reaction to the US–Czech negotiations about the missile system was aggressive, as it promised to target its missiles against the radar. The new assertiveness gave rise to feelings of ontological anxiety in Czech Republic. Moreover, the Atlantist foreign policy elite which came to power in 2006 had in general been more sensitive to the Russian threat than its predecessors and more open to geopolitical argumentation.

Finally, geopolitical rhetoric was imported, literally, from friend and foe. As for friends, the geographical implications of the missile defence obviously invite a geopolitical reflection. Concerning foes, Russia used geopolitical rhetoric for some time. Czech Atlantists believed in fighting against the Russian geopolitical perception that former Warsaw Pact countries represented an area which was still sensitive to Russia. They challenged this perception by accepting the Russian framework of geopolitical reasoning, within which they argued that the border of Russian influence needed to be pushed as much to the East as possible. They considered as naive the anti-geopolitical challenge to this argumentation that emphasised partnerships which will make borders less and less relevant.

Contested institutionalism and irrelevant geopolitics

Geopolitics has played a limited role in the Czech political and academic discourse since the 1990s. After its modest revivals in 1992–1993 and in 2006–2008 it faded away. The main message of the first revival was that the Czech Republic is more Western than other post-communist countries because it climbed out of the Danubian mess. This might have been good PR at the time, but it became redundant when most of the Danubian countries were also invited into NATO and the EU. The main message of the second revival was that an American radar was, for Czechs, a more important anchor to Western security and prosperity than either NATO or the EU, which was a statement which was too controversial to be publicly argued for.

The general political debate has been marked by the clash between two kinds of liberalism: the right-wing liberalism of Václav Klaus and the left-wing liberalism of Václav Havel, which was to some extent taken over by the social democrats since the late 1990s. Their perspectives on international politics differ in a few important respects. While the former emphasises the role of self-regulating market forces in all human activity and is sceptical about any international or supranational attempts at their regulation or institutionalisation, the latter argues that international norms, whether universal or regional, need to be enhanced and developed by international and supranational institutions. This debate has had important implications for Czech thinking about the EU and about other international institutions. The right-wing liberals tend to see them as clumsy bureaucracies that often create more problems than they solve. The left-wing liberals consider them as the only legitimate agents of international action.

However, no matter how contested international institutionalism is between right-wingers and left-wingers, neither embraces geopolitical arguments. The debate is between profit, on the one hand, and human and social rights, on the other. Geography is not attributed any special role in this. The same goes for research and academic discourse, which focus on institutional reforms, procedures and policies rather than on the spatial dimension of international politics.

This is hardly surprising. A brief review of the Czech geopolitical thinking of Dvorský, Korčák, Moravec and Krejčí showed that this kind of geopolitics is especially difficult to reconcile with the respect for democracy and international law that constitutes Czech political thinking after 1989. None of the revivals drew on this undemocratic tradition and, therefore, there was no clash with democracy or international law. Instead, they relied on a somewhat oxymoronic neoliberal geopolitics which did not develop any alternative concepts and stayed at the superficial level of political statements or even semi-private statements.

Conclusions

The foreign policy identity crisis seems to provide a plausible explanation of geopolitical revivals. Czech geopolitics usually asserts itself in such crisis conditions. The Czech position on the map is supposed so serve as a guide through these difficult periods. Academic geopoliticians stress the unique location of the Czech and Slovak lands as a gateway to the Danubian area, where important expansionist pressures from the West and from the East tend to meet and clash throughout history. On this basis, they draw attention to the Great Moravian state, which was the first state-like political entity originating in the area and which is traditionally considered the origin of Czech statehood. Geopolitics has thus been an important undercurrent in Czech security imaginary, succumbing to brief moments of dominance in times of turmoil and perceived insecurity (1918, 1938, 1992, 2007).

However, in stable times the anti-geopolitical dimension of the Czech security imaginary prevails, emphasising freedom, responsibility and agency at the expense of determinist constraints of the geopolitical kind. Thus, Palacký and Masaryk focus on the medieval Hussite movement, interpreting it as a proto-democratic force serving as an inspiration for the future. Nejedlý uses the same logic when interpreting the Hussites as proto-communists. Havel, who at the end of the twentieth century was wary of similar grand historical generalisations, looks for something more immediate and finds the Velvet Revolution to be a triumph of freedom and democracy over tyranny, an event which also constitutes his political legacy. Even Klaus, whose neoliberalism puts him at some distance from both geopolitics and anti-geopolitics, emphasises the Czech economic reform, considering this transition from a command economy to a free market economy as unprecedented and unique in the history of mankind. The strength of anti-geopolitics in the Czech intellectual tradition may help us understand why the geopolitical revivals were so short-lived there.

Interestingly, 1989 itself did not bring about almost any geopolitical revival. The public discourse has been dominated by the winners of the Velvet Revolution who saw the events not as their own crisis but as their enemy's crisis. In this respect, 1989 served for the construction and vindication of their anti-geopolitical stress on freedom and agency. On the other hand, some of the losers of the Velvet Revolution, who more or less disappeared from the public discourse in 1990, fell for geopolitics and their arguments drew some attention during the disintegration of Czechoslovakia two years later.

5

The theme that dare not speak its name: *Geopolitik*, geopolitics and German foreign policy since unification

ANDREAS BEHNKE

The purpose of this chapter is to trace the emergence of a new security imaginary in the foreign policy discourse in Germany during the 1990s and to determine whether it constituted a return of *Geopolitik* in German foreign-policy making. Does the reappearance of geopolitical terms and expressions in the official and the academic discourses in post-unification Germany indicate such a shift? To wit, critics of the Schröder/Fischer foreign policy accused the administration of abandoning the traditional German foreign policy orientation of 'civilising politics' (*Zivilisierungspolitik*) in favour of a newly assertive 'power politics' (*Machtpolitik*)[1] and of reverting back to (US dominated) geopolitical calculations by participating in the Kosovo Campaign in 1999.[2]

The guiding questions for this chapter are therefore: to what extent did the foreign policy of the post-unification governments in Germany display a departure from the foreign policy orientations of the Federal Republic of Germany before unification; and to what extent can we discern a new *geopolitisch* defined security imaginary in this new paradigm? The chapter will argue that the claims about a return of *Geopolitik* cannot be sustained. To the extent that the rhetoric of German government officials changes during the 1990s, this does not produce a coherent *geopolitisch* security imaginary that stands diametrically opposed to the definition of political and institutional spaces of the *Bonner Republik*. The *Berliner Republik* did not experience a revival of the traditional German discourse on *Geopolitik* of the first half of the twentieth century, or an articulation of a neoclassical version of geopolitics, as defined by Guzzini in Chapter 2. Instead, it was a powerful narrative of historical continuity and vindication for Germany that rendered *Geopolitik* irrelevant. Over time, it was the German insistence on continuity in the face of radical changes in the global political environment that would lead to tensions between Germany and

---

[1] Hellmann, 2007.
[2] Bittermann and Deichmann, 1999; Elsässer, 1999.

its allies, and to a rearticulation of the German security imaginary in response to these changes.

A note on methodology

Given the peculiar absence of any significant (re-)articulation of *Geopolitik* or neoclassical geopolitics, this chapter relies on a slightly modified methodology compared to the other chapters of this volume. The 'process tracing' outlined in the Introduction gives way to a systematic investigation of the dominant security imaginary that 'inoculated' the political elites in post-Cold War Germany against the intellectual temptations of *Geopolitik*. Moreover, the analysis is extended beyond the 1990s into the 2000s, in order to include the new foreign policy discourse of the Schröder/Fischer administration that came to power in 1998. As noted above, a number of critics accused the new administration of a shift towards power politics, and a return to *Geopolitik*. Finally, the analysis is disaggregated into three levels, in order to capture any articulation of geopolitics within different contexts. Even in the absence of a coherent geopolitical 'culture' of foreign policy, individual speech acts, articles or publications by academics or politicians might point to a *geopolitisch* counter-narrative that should be investigated in terms of its critical or dissident potential. These three methodological modifications serve the purpose to cast the analytical net as wide as possible and to support the chapter's claim about the absence of a revival of geopolitics in post-Cold War Germany.

The concept of *Geopolitik* itself plays a peculiar role in the German foreign policy discourse of the 1990s. While the logic of geopolitics is acknowledged as relevant for policy making, to speak of *Geopolitik* remains problematic, if not prohibited. As late as 2002, Karsten Voigt, then coordinator for German–American cooperation in the German Foreign Office, reiterates this linguistic embargo imposed upon an inherent feature of foreign-policy making when introducing a theme, 'namely geopolitics [*Geopolitik*], that since the end of the Second World War wouldn't be called by this name in Germany'.[3] The problem of translating his statement correctly already illustrates the very problem at the heart of the German geographical imagination. Clearly, geopolitics is relevant, yet *Geopolitik*, its proper name in German, must not be mentioned.

This tension between an official discourse that rejects *Geopolitik* on one hand, and political knowledge that draws on geopolitics on the other, suggests the existence of different levels of geopolitical imagination. As the German case demonstrates, the embargo imposed upon the concept of *Geopolitik* on one level might on occasion be challenged on another in response to the perceived need to redefine the spatial structure of international politics and to articulate

---

[3] Voigt, 2002.

a new framework for European geopolitics in response to the demise of the old bipolar order.

We may think of the spatialisations of power, national interests and identities in terms of 'security imaginaries'. A security imaginary is defined as 'a structure of well-established meanings and social relations out of which representations or the world of international relations are created'. Through such imaginaries, 'the total world given to a particular society is grasped in a way that is determined practically, affectively, and mentally, that an articulated meaning is imposed upon it'.[4] A security imaginary provides the 'cultural raw material' out of which interests, identities and relations of states are fashioned.

The concept of 'security imaginary' is helpful for establishing the 'constructed' nature of national identities and interests and in studying their discursive transformations in crisis moments such as the end of the Cold War. For the purpose of this chapter, however, it needs to be amended in order to account for the peculiarity of the German discourse on *Geopolitik*/geopolitics. In particular, the tension between the official rejection of any reference to *Geopolitik*, the recognition of the general relevance of spatial or geopolitical categories, as well as the renewed emergence of explicit references to it in parts of the academic discourse in the 1980s and 1990s suggests the need for an analytical scheme that allows us to address the relevance of geopolitical imaginations without reducing them to particular historical and ideological instantiations, such as the German context of the 1920s and 1930s, and to be analytically open to broader articulations of geopolitics. It is therefore helpful to turn to a model developed by Gearóid Ó Tuathail,[5] which outlines three analytical levels.

The ontological assumptions about international politics, about the spatial sovereignty of states and its consequences, are located on the *basic level*. The intermediate, or *meso* level, pertains to embedded national discourses that underpin both political and academic discourse. Here we find the *Geopolitical Culture*, containing interpretations of the state as a foreign policy actor in world affairs, and the communicational culture of foreign-policy making. This level also encompasses *Geopolitical Traditions*, historical schools of foreign policy theory and practice. And finally, on the phenomenal or *micro* level we find storylines, narratives and particular speech acts by foreign-policy makers about national identity and security.

The added analytical value of this model for the German case is that it offers a theoretical structure within which the general relevance of geopolitics can be reconciled with the particular taboo imposed upon particular concepts. As the basic level indicates, any foreign and international politics is geopolitics, as the international system is constituted as a spatial structure.

---

[4] Weldes, 1999a, 10; quoting Castoriadis, 1987, 145.
[5] Ó Tuathail, 2004.

On the *meso* level, we can locate the academic or intellectual debates on foreign policy and their respective references to particular spatialisations of foreign
policies, among them those that refer to the particular tradition of *Geopolitik*,
or those that could be characterised more broadly as neoclassical geopolitics.
A conceptual clarification is in order at this point: with *Geopolitik* I refer to the
particular version or tradition of geopolitics as it emerged in Germany after
World War I and which is usually associated with the name of Karl Haushofer.
Geopolitik is therefore a particular version of geopolitics, located on the *meso*
level. It should be emphasised that this tradition is but one among a number of
'geographies' relevant for the analysis of German foreign policies. *Geopolitik* is
but one way to inscribe a spatial order upon the contingency of international politics, characterised by distinctive ontological and epistemological assumptions.

The Finally, on the *micro* level we find 'Geopolitical Discourses', i.e. storylines and
narratives, and particular speech acts by foreign-policy makers about national
identity and security. On this level, the official representation of identity and
space takes place. Its relationship with the meso level needs to be conceptualised in terms of its contingency. Theoretically, we might find the discourse on
the latter level largely in agreement with the micro-level's discourse, or contradicting it. Thus, for most of the Cold War, German geopolitical discourse was
defined by an isomorphic relationship between meso and micro level that produced an agreement about the invalidity of the concepts and strategies associated with traditional *Geopolitik*.[6]

The following analysis will focus on the relationship between micro and
meso level in the German foreign policy discourse from the time of unification
to the end of the Schröder/Fischer administration in 2005. The time period
under investigation here comprises the transition from the '*Bonner Republik*' to
the '*Berliner Republik*' and the reformulation of a German foreign policy with a
stronger emphasis on German national identity and interests than before. This
transition has been identified and mapped by a number of scholars.[7] Of interest
here is the role of geopolitical imaginations in general and *Geopolitik* in particular, in this transition.

The meso level I: re-reading *Geopolitik*
after the end of the Cold War

With the end of the Cold War and German unification, the 'wretched existence' of *Geopolitik* that had condemned it to speechlessness and insignificance[8] ended. 'Since then, the geopolitical role of Germany in Europe has

---

[6] This consensus was briefly undermined by the *Historikerstreit* of the 1980s.
[7] The best analytical overview is Hellmann, 2000.
[8] Reuber and Wolkersdorfer, 2002, 59 [fn. 24].

been increasingly and openly a topic for debate in the political and the public arena.[9]

Reuber and Wolkendorfer's observation is overall correct, yet it oversimplifies matters a bit by condensing a decade into a brief summary. The 1990s witnessed a discursive evolution regarding the historical version of *Geopolitik*, which deserves to be analysed in some more detail. I will therefore begin by briefly sketching out the debate at the time of the German unification.[10] *Geopolitik's proponents* had to overcome the taboo that was imposed upon it due to its alleged intellectual association with Nazi ideology. Overall, we can discern two such strategies.

First, there is the rendition of *Geopolitik* as a universal and de-historicised source of knowledge. Claim about a *Geopolitik* competence in Plato, Aristotle, Machiavelli and other great theoreticians of the state is supplemented with the claim that it also produces crucial insights into virtually any issue of contemporary international politics, such as environmental politics, economic transition processes and political regionalism.[11] The historical association of *Geopolitik* with Nazism is usually dealt with in a short and limited fashion, pointing to the 'ways it went astray' or defining some of its elements such as theories about *Lebensraum* as 'pseudo-scientific' and thus not representative of the tradition as such. Only in this perverted form did it serve the leadership of the Third Reich to legitimise their aggressive foreign policy.[12]

This strategy, then, attempts to de-contextualise *Geopolitik* and cleanse it of any 'contamination' by Nazi ideology. This universalisation of *Geopolitik* however significantly reduces its analytical purchase power. These arguments 'are leading us astray, because they displace the relationship between *Geopolitik* and our century in favour of some vague common-places such as: *one has always thought about the relationship between power and geography*'.[13] The argument that all (international) politics takes place within a spatial structure and that geographical conditions have long been considered relevant in politics is hardly constitutive of a distinctive paradigm of *Geopolitik*.

Arguably, the substantial contributions of *Geopolitik* are more closely linked to the historical context of the early twentieth century. To salvage and reconstruct this tradition for contemporary politics therefore requires a different, more demanding rhetorical strategy that locates the substance of *Geopolitik* within its historical context while at the same time extracting it from this context and making it relevant for contemporary politics. For instance, in Frank Ebeling's reading of Haushofer's work, *Geopolitik* is placed within the particular historical context of the massive changes and transformations of the early

---

[9] Reuber and Wolkersdorfer, 2002, 46.
[10] I have dealt with this in greater detail in Behnke, 2006.
[11] Boesler, 1994/1995, 75–87.
[12] Brill, 1993, 5.   [13] Sprengel, 2000, 148.

twentieth century.[14] At the same time, however, *Geopolitik* exceeds the logic of its historical situation, as it also claims contemporary significance. Once again, the argument goes, we find ourselves in a situation of 'tremendous changes and re-organisation of spaces'.[15] In this context, a 'recollection' of geopolitical basics will help to better understand, control and steer political developments. 'To put it succinctly, if the re-organisation of spaces is to succeed this time without plunging the world into a disastrous conflictual order (*Gegeneinanderordnung*), one cannot do without *Geopolitik*.'[16] In order to salvage the latter from its contamination by Nazism, Ebeling tries to uncover an original, authoritative text that can provide the historical lessons relevant for current international politics. *Geopolitik* is here defined as inherently conservative and sceptical towards excessive idealistic policies that pretend to be able to overcome the limitations of space; it therefore constitutes a powerful critique and rejection of Nazi foreign policy.

Yet the attempt to construct an original, authoritative edition of *Geopolitik* must ultimately fail. Concepts and ideas within this approach exceed the control of one particular author, as they can be mobilised within different contexts and horizons. Thus, in the 1990s, we find a reiteration of assumptions about the organic nature of political communities and their need for *Lebensraum*. We can also observe the rehabilitation of the concept of *Zwischeneuropa*, used to designate the political space between Germany and Russia as tentative and provisional, and thus once more the object of German strategic imaginations. These 'offensive' elements re-emerge in the 1990s, contradicting Ebeling's assertions about the inherently conservative nature of the approach.[17] Moreover, even Ebeling's own sympathetic treatment of Haushofer's argument for a German *Sonderweg* is based on a number of problematic assertions. In Haushofer's narrative, Germany assumes a civilisational and cultural superiority that sets it apart from its neighbours, and warrants its role as the embodiment of the European identity. Germans were after all 'the true European people'.[18] As such, they had the historical task to unite the continent. Threatened and harassed by the Western powers and the League of Nations, Haushofer's argument included a 'right' to realise this mission by military means. While the integration of Europe should ideally be accomplished through the pure force of (German) ideas, given the reality of politics, this process might very well include the use of military power.[19] Germany has a *Sonderweg* to pursue, a special destiny to fulfil, because culture and geography set it apart from the West as well as the East.[20] And against the universalist arrogations of authority and legitimacy by

---

[14] Ebeling, 1994, 22.   [15] Ebeling, 1994, 24.
[16] Ebeling, 1994.   [17] Bassin, 2003, 358–361.
[18] Quoted in Ebeling, 1994, 115.   [19] Ebeling, 1994, 117.
[20] Ultimately, *Geopolitik* does not seem to be able to maintain its own claim that geography determines political destiny, as a lot of explaining the latter rests on cultural rather than strictly geographical assumptions.

the liminal powers, Germany must lead *Mitteleuropa* into a more powerful and therefore integrated future.

Any current invocation of *Geopolitik* will therefore conjure up the central assumptions of a German *Sonderweg*, and thus the possibility of an anti-Western orientation and aggressive intentions towards the East. Even if we accept the argument about the non-identity of *Geopolitik* and Nazi ideology, the particular structure of this discourse with its constitutive distinction between the West, the East, and Germany itself, becomes anathema to a German political leadership that in the context of German unification faces a particular challenge. While for other countries, the end of the Cold War constituted a time of ontological crisis in which a new national identity and political orientation had to be articulated, for Germany this historical rupture presents a challenge to demonstrate the continuity of its (Cold War) identity and political orientation.

Micro level I: *Geopolitik* as the Other

For Germany, the end of the East–West conflict did not produce the same existential crisis as it did for countries, the identity and foreign policy orientation of which were defined by the Cold War. The end of the Cold War meant the successful conclusion to Germany's national purpose as stipulated in the West German constitution's preamble, 'to achieve … the unity and freedom of Germany'. Or in the famous dictum of ex-chancellor Willy Brandt on the day after the Berlin Wall was opened: 'Now what belongs together will grow together.'[21] Rather than an existential crisis, Germany faced an existential *challenge* in the form of demands by its allies and by neighbouring countries to explicitly confirm its continued commitment to its Western identity. What was required from the German government and the foreign policy elite was not so much the redefinition of German identity, but rather its reassertion under dramatically new circumstances. The challenge therefore was to demonstrate that the end of the Cold War and the regaining of full sovereignty would not lead Germany once again down a *Sonderweg*.

Second, this challenge emanated not from a sense of existential crisis *within* Germany, but was triggered by the revival of old historical concerns in neighbouring countries about the role of a unified Germany in Europe. In many of these countries, public and political debates looked to past experiences with Germany to better assess the future of Europe. Against the sense of historical vindication within Germany stood the scepticism and concern of its neighbours.

---

[21] Merseburger, 2002, 837.

The continued *Westbindung* of Germany, its lasting embeddedness within the Western civilisation, had to be asserted constantly. As the former German foreign minister Hans-Dietrich Genscher wrote in his memoirs, 'I was under the impression that Mrs. Thatcher had reservations against German unification. Her repeated warnings against any changes in the status quo suggested that she came to terms with these developments only reluctantly'.[22] France and Great Britain were concerned that Germany had now regained a 'freedom of choice – towards the West as well as towards the East'.[23] In response to these concerns, the German government produced a narrative about the meaning of German unification that centred on three *topoi*: '*Verantwortungspolitik*', '*Westbindung*' and 'A European Germany'.[24]

The last of these commonplaces constructs an essential correspondence between German and European identity. First, the Cold War division of Germany becomes embedded in the division of Europe, and both could only be overcome together. Second, the correspondence between the division of Europe and of Germany leads to an affirmation of the European(ised) identity of the latter. 'We don't want a German Europe, we want a European Germany.'[25] Germany's national and its European interests are identical.[26] 'Our policy is more national, the more European it is. History tells us: only as good Europeans can we be good Germans.'[27]

There is a remarkable resonance here with a central theme of traditional *Geopolitik*, i.e. the identity of German and European interests. Germany still speaks 'in Europe's name', continuing 'the habitual conflation of German and European interests' that characterised its foreign policy during the Cold War.[28] This de-nationalisation of Germany's identity itself, however, does not establish a particular spatial order. While *Geopolitik* located European identity proper only within Germany and in opposition to the other powers in Europe, the Cold War narrative and the narrative on German identity at the time of unification emphasise the infusion of Western and European identity in Germany. In a sense, the 'flow' of identity is here reversed. While *Geopolitik* sought to create a European space from within Germany's 'essence', the *Bonner Republik*'s narrative constructed a Europeanised Germany that has absorbed the civilisational values and norms of its environment. And while the former projection of identity justifies, indeed necessitates, the German *Sonderweg*, the latter constructs Germany as an integral part of the European space. Here, the concepts of *Geopolitik* serve as the negative backdrop against which Germany

---

[22] Genscher, 1995, 676.   [23] Thies, 1993, 524.   [24] Behnke, 2006, 412–415.
[25] AA 1995, doc. 238, 710. References here list source, document number, and page number. The source is a collection of documents pertaining to German foreign policy 1949–1994, published by the German Foreign Office (Auswärtiges Amt) in 1995.
[26] AA 1995, doc. 206, 614.
[27] AA 1995, 616.   [28] Garton Ash, 1994, 71.

now defines its identity, as any notion of a *Sonderweg* destroys this homologous relationship.

The *topos* of a European Germany is supported by the invocation of the second *topos, Verantwortungspolitik* (politics of responsibility), as opposed to *Machtpolitik* (power politics). German foreign policy, the argument goes, is responsible for the whole of Europe, and not just for Germany's national interests. Placed at the heart of Europe, the geographical position of Germany determines the course and purpose of its diplomacy. Above all, Germany bears a particular responsibility for the future of Europe and the overcoming of its division. *Verantwortungspolitik* for Europe is routinely contrasted with national *Machtpolitik.*[29] Germany cannot pursue its own national interest or exercise its power without regard for the repercussions of such a policy for the whole of Europe. Even before the end of the Cold War, both German states were joined in a community of responsibility (*Verantwortungsgemeinschaft*) 'for the peace in Europe'.[30] However, Germany now faces a widely held fear that its reunification would entail a return to the old traditions of the first unified German nation-state.[31] Responsibility now has to be exercised as a part of Europe, not as a separate agent.

The final *topos, Westbindung*, combines and reinforces the Europeanised identity and responsible policies of a unified Germany within the network of European and transatlantic institutions, such as the EC and NATO. This network serves as a further safeguard against any German *Sonderweg* and claims to sole leadership or superior status. Germany is now a part of the West, linked 'in friendship, and cooperating in a close and trusting partnership, with the Western Allies, the USA, France, and Great Britain'. This belonging 'was, is, and will remain of existential significance for Germany'.[32] Germany 'has become a thoroughly Western country. Our political culture is and remains formed by Western values'.[33] As it is no longer based on mutual dependencies, mutual trust will henceforth be the cornerstone of this community.[34] 'The bitter lessons of history' are the incentives to make the 'firm and enduring "anchoring" (*Verankerung*) of Germany in the Atlantic Alliance and within the community of values of the free peoples of the West irrevocable'.[35] As for the European Community, Germany declares its willingness to transfer national sovereignty to the EC level with the goal to create a United States of Europe.[36] As for NATO, it will serve as the cornerstone of the security order to be created in Europe. In both cases, German 'embeddedness' in Western institutions guarantees that

---

[29] AA 1995, doc. 202, 595; doc. 204, 601; doc. 206, 615; doc. 216, 654; doc. 233, 686.

[30] AA 1995, doc. 194, 574; cf. doc. 197, 579.

[31] AA 1995, doc. 202, 593–594.   [32] AA 1995, doc. 199, 585.

[33] AA 1995, doc. 202, 595.   [34] AA 1995, doc. 202, 598.

[35] AA 1995, doc. 206, 611; cf. doc. 206, 614; doc. 219, 662; doc. 227, 678; doc. 243, 719; doc. 244, 722; doc. 245, 729; doc. 258, 786.

[36] AA 1995, doc. 253, 768.

the trajectory of its foreign policy is pointing to the future of a united and stable Europe. Germany is no longer 'a wanderer between East and West'.[37]

The early 1990s, then, witnessed a dominant official foreign policy discourse defined by these three commonplaces. Paradoxically enough, the dramatic transformations in the political environment in Europe were framed in a way that emphasised the continuity of one of its central powers, i.e. Germany. Neither unification, the regaining of complete sovereignty, the end of the Cold War, nor the emergence of new security political issues within Europe and beyond were affecting the national identity and purpose of Germany. This was still the *Bonner Republik*, a state adamantly indistinguishable from the West as such. But there is an inherent tension built into this discourse that on one hand acknowledges the historical changes in Europe, yet at the same time reiterates and insists upon a German identity that remains defined by the Cold War. The tension between a stable Germany and the West eventually becomes too problematic because after the end of the Cold War, the West itself loses its ontological stability. In fact, as early as 1990/1991 a first fissure appeared between the West and Germany when its allies and neighbours decided to use military force to expel Saddam Hussein's troops from Kuwait. In this case, the German government found itself unable to contribute *Bundeswehr* forces to a UN authorised military campaign. A brief and ultimately rejected consideration to contribute naval forces to a WEU task force in the Persian Gulf, and the decision not to withdraw German soldiers from NATO during a support operation for the NATO ally Turkey quickly led to criticism from the political opposition in the *Bundestag*, which reflected the dogmatic commitment to the anti-*Geopolitik* discourse: 'This is, I am afraid, only the beginning of a new development. For the first time, we don't deal with the defence of our own country; instead our government engages in *Geopolitik* by military means. The Green Party rejects this with a clear "no".'[38]

This tension between a radically transforming environment and the dogmatic commitment to an essentially unchanged German national identity and foreign policy is picked up and problematised in a series of interventions on the meso level of geopolitics, which demand a different geopolitical culture for Germany. Predominantly produced within the conservative part of the political spectrum of German politics, these interventions offer a political critique of contemporary German foreign policy, rather than a call for a renaissance of *Geopolitik*. This critique ends up demanding an 'affective' rather than spatial re-orientation of German foreign policy, and therefore tends to address the rhetoric, rather than the substance, of German policy making.

---

[37]   AA 1995, doc. 206, 611; cf. doc. 202, 595.
[38]   Fischer, 1991, 6.

The meso level II: a new *Geopolitik* as political critique

This conservative critique of the Kohl administration's continued commitment to the tenets of the *Bonner Republik* focused on the political purposes and normative constraints that defined the goals and means of the latter. Arguments were targeting the alleged *Machtvergessenheit* (an oblivious attitude towards power) of a German foreign policy that continued to insists on 'a politics of responsibility' and that allegedly continued to demonstrate an unwillingness to confidently assert the German national interest in international politics. In particular, *Westbindung* was interpreted as a wilful and ultimately counterproductive denial of certain geopolitical facts that determine the role Germany has to play in Europe. While the Cold War allowed Germany to hide behind the rigid logic of a bipolar international order, the breakdown of this order now enables, even necessitates, a reassessment of the costs and benefits of this central tenet of her foreign policy. Against the idealisation of the *Westbindung* its critics assert the reality of Germany's geopolitical location in a *Mittellage* in Europe. The West as a community of values can no longer provide any purpose for Germany's foreign policy; it is erroneous to believe that 'decisions about foreign, security, and alliance policies can be grounded in specific societal (*gesellschaftspolitische*) preferences and options'.[39] The orthodox commitment to the West as the cultural and ideational point of reference for Germany and the taboo imposed upon *Geopolitik* after World War II have to be understood as part of the peculiar structure of world politics during the Cold War and the trauma of Nazism. Yet with the collapse of this order, Germany is caught in a historical position 'between a no-longer and a not-yet', between a West, no longer identical with itself, and an East in transition. Germany rediscovers its *Mittellage*.[40]

The rhetorical force behind the rejection of the 'utopian and totalitarian'[41] dogma of the *Westbindung* and the assertion of a newly *selbstbewusste* German nation, able to define her national interest without the tutelage of Western powers and institutions, would easily suggest the radical opening of new options for German foreign policy.[42] Significantly, the positive revalorisation of the notion of *Sonderweg* now even suggests a political course away from the strong bonds with Western institutions and values, and a rejection of Germany's *Sonderrolle* as the bridge between East and West.[43]

---

[39] Großheim *et al.*, 1993, 14.   [40] Schlögel, 1993.
[41] Großheim *et al.*, 1993, 10.
[42] Schwilk and Schacht, 1994. The translation of the term 'selbstbewusst' reveals an interesting ambiguity. Its conventional translation is 'self-confident' or 'self-assured'. A more philosophically inclined translation, however, would render it 'self-conscious', or even 'conscious about one's self', thus linking the demand for a more assertive politics with the notion of a distinctive German identity.
[43] Bassin, 2004, 623.

Yet despite the vigorous critique of *Westbindung* and the renewed fascination with Germany's *Mittellage* and its historical *Sonderweg*, many of the alternatives outlined by the proponents of this apparently renewed *Geopolitik* are in
effect remarkably modest and conventional. The greatest danger conceivable
in Ludwig Watzal's analysis, for instance, is the pursuit of a 'utopia of a total
Western integration of Germany into a European federal state',[44] yet at the same
time, it is repeatedly recognised that the '*orientation* towards the West' offers
many chances and opportunities for German foreign policy.[45] Specific discussions of political issues often demand a modified strategy, but hardly ever question the institutional framework itself within which Germany operates. While
EU integration as outlined in the Maastricht Treaty is considered a mistake
(*Irrweg*), German membership in the EU and the overall logic of European
cooperation is never cast in doubt.[46] With regard to NATO, Karl Feldmeyer
argues that Germany needs to leave the tutelage of the Four Powers and the
dependency on the United States behind. The traumatic attitude towards
power that led Germany to accept an inferior position within the Alliance has
to be overcome in favour of a clear formulation of German national interest.
At the same time, the European security structure is inconceivable without the
Alliance, and the option of Germany leaving NATO is not even contemplated.[47]
And for Thies the 'new perspectives of German foreign policy' include the
cornerstones of a 'Europe-friendly orientation towards the West' and 'a close
partnership (*Schulterschluß*) with the United States of America'.[48] Germany is
encouraged to articulate its own interests more assertively, while at the same
time retaining a positive attitude towards European integration. Should the
process of European integration fail, Germany should be prepared to become
an actor on the world stage once again.[49] Generally, Germany will have to give
up its reservations about power politics, while remaining sensitive towards its
own history.

Some references to *Geopolitik*'s commonplaces appear in this debate. 'The
reality of the new *Mittellage* in Europe, the correlation between geography
and politics, one could also say: *Geopolitik* cannot be disputed. Directly at
Germany's Eastern border begins a great crisis zone (*Erdbebenzone*, literally
"earthquake zone") that reaches all the way to Vladivostok.'[50] Out of this zone
emanates the most significant challenge facing Germany and Europe: migrants
and asylum seekers.

Overall, however, the invocation of *Geopolitik* remains subordinated to
the apparent concern by most of the authors to remain 'policy-relevant' and
to outline political alternatives that do not exceed or dismantle the extant

---

[44] Watzal, 1993.   [45] Großheim *et al.*, 1993, 15.
[46] Watzal, 1993, 477–500.
[47] Feldmeyer, 1993, 459–76; cf. Inacker, 1994, 364–380.
[48] Thies, 1993, 527.   [49] Thies, 1993, 534–535.   [50] Thies, 1993, 528.

institutional structures. Given this policy-orientation, and the absence of the distinctive 'organicistic' rhetoric of classical *Geopolitik*, one might label this critique a weak neoclassical geopolitics.[51] It certainly displays conservative and nationalist overtones, and gives explanatory primacy to geographical factors, above all Germany's *Mittellage*,[52] yet it lacks the 'symbiosis of expansionism and worst-case thinking' that Guzzini[53] identifies as underlying the military gaze of neoclassical geopolitics, not to speak of *Geopolitik*. In fact, the critique's implications for Germany's security imaginary are limited. For all its acerbic criticism of the *Westbindung* orthodoxy and its allusions to the German *Sonderweg*, this discourse offers a shift of emphasis at best. *Westorientierung* replaces *Westbindung*, and an assertive expression of German national interest (a faint echo of the *Sonderweg*) is to supplant the alleged wilful submission to the tutelage of Western powers and institutions. It is only on the most radical margin beyond this critique that *Geopolitik* completely rejects the normative basis of Cold War Germany's foreign policy and returns to the expansionist and revisionist policies it advocated in the 1920s and 1930s. Here, a project of territorial readjustments in the East reflects an unmitigated commitment to a notion of power politics that finds its origins in revived and highly problematic notions of *Lebensraum*, organic state and historical calling.[54]

Underlying the 1990s 'neo-*Geopolitik*' are ontological assumptions about the nation-state as the constitutive and privileged entity of the spatial order in Europe. For the supporters of neo-*Geopolitik*, there exists a dichotomy in international politics that places statehood, power and rationality against transnational integration, obliviousness towards power and utopianism. If there is one concern they share and express clearly, it is the alleged need of Germany's foreign-policy makers to forego the idealistic and value-based orthodoxy of *Westbindung* for a realist(ic) assertion of German national interest. Germany, the argument goes, should first and foremost pursue its own national purpose within Europe. Its growing self-confidence and 'self-awareness' will lead to a new appreciation that the geopolitical space best suited for democracy political stability remains the nation-state.[55] Neo-*Geopolitik*'s primary concern is arguably the proclamation of a 'normal' and 'self-confident' German nation-state. To the extent that it actually offers any empirical analysis, it is based on and reflects this ultimately metaphysical commitment.

In summary, this weak neo-*Geopolitik* combines a realist/statist ontology with a nationalist mode of thinking, setting it apart from the traditional *Geopolitik* and its conflation of European and German interests and identity. Contrary to this, the new version emphasises the egotism of states, the predominance of national interests, and the continued sovereignty of states over their

---

[51] Guzzini, chapter 2.   [52] Großheim *et al.*, 1993, 13.
[53] Guzzini, chapter 2.   [54] Cf. Bassin, 2003, 358–361.
[55] Hahn, 1994, 340.

integration in supranational structures. Against the three commonplaces of the official discourse identified above it sets its own triad. *Westorientierung* replaces *Westbindung*, power politics challenges the notion of *Verantwortungspolitik*, and a German nation-state conscious of its own national interests dissolves the idea of a European Germany.

Once Germany's interest and purpose are distinguished from those of Europe, once, in other words, a rift in terms of identity has taken place, Germany can be identified as a *Mittelmacht* or *Zentralmacht* (central power) within Europe. As such, the European space is no longer an ontological structure within which Germany is embedded; rather, it becomes the geopolitical object of its political, economic and strategic interests. Germany's commitment to European integration is no longer the expression of the European identity of Germany; instead it is now based on the economic and political benefits that this process offers its participant states.

Overall then, this weak version of neoclassical geopolitics only echoes its old predecessor in terms of putting Germany at the centre of the spatial structure again. Yet this renewed focus does not translate into a *Sonderweg* for Germany as defined by traditional *Geopolitik*. The realist ontology introduced with the new *Geopolitik* focuses above all on the 'normalisation' of German politics in terms of a reassertion of national interests and power, rather than on any responsibility for Europe. There is, in other words, nothing *besonders*, nothing 'un-normal' about Germany foreign policy anymore. Neo-*Geopolitik*, to put it succinctly, amounts to a realist geopolitical critique of the perceived misguided idealism of German foreign policy.

The themes developed here found some strong resonance in the writings of prominent academic German historians and political scientists. While the academic discipline of Geopolitics remains irrelevant in terms of institutional support, it is within History departments that an institutionalised dissemination of these commonplaces begins to emerge. Christian Hacke (Hamburg), Gregor Schöllgen (Erlangen), Hans-Peter Schwarz (Bonn) and Michael Stürmer (Erlangen) are arguably the most prominent among these scholars that offer a historically rather than explicitly geopolitically informed critique of German foreign policy.[56] Geopolitical considerations enter these works via the constant reference to Germany's *Mittellage* in Europe as a historically constant fact, and the insistence on the ontological as well as political priority of German national interest and identity. Yet again, the institutional structure of Europe, above the relevance of NATO and the EU, is never denied or rejected. There is a consensus that the problems associated with Germany's central position can only be solved within an established institutional framework that has to be adapted to the new historical circumstances. As such, then, Germany inhabits two spaces: its geopolitical situation in the centre of Europe, and an institutional space as

[56] Cf. Hacke, 1993; Schöllgen, 1992, 1993; Schwarz, 1994; and Stürmer, 1992.

the easternmost country of the Western institutions. As a result it has a particular role to play in the integration and stabilisation of the countries to its East.[57]

Overall, notions of *Geopolitik* play only a subdued role within this debate. Despite the provocation of an open problematisation of Germany's *Westbindung*, and thus of its existential European identity, ultimately it only delivers an argument with no immediate radical consequences. And the overall rhetorical focus on 'responsibility', 'normalcy' in contra-distinction to an allegedly oblivious attitude towards power produces ultimately only a call for an 'affectively' rather than substantially redefined German foreign policy. It should therefore come as no surprise that some of the conservative critics of Kohl's foreign policy initially applauded the more assertive style of the Schröder/Fischer administration.

Micro level II: towards the geopolitics of the *Berliner Republik?*

While the rhetoric of the conservative critics went more or less unheard in the German capital, a voice in the German province heeded its call. On 2 November 1993, at the beginning of the provincial elections campaign for the Bavarian Parliament, then Bavarian prime minister Edmund Stoiber explained in an interview to the Munich daily *Süddeutsche Zeitung* that a European Federation was no longer on the agenda, that there was a need to re-discover a proper German national identity, and that the conservative parties CDU and CSU would have to break with their traditional foreign policy towards Europe. The purpose of the EU would no longer be defined by a continued integration process and the creation of a European identity. Instead, a Europe of nations would be based on the expediency and efficacy of its institutions.[58]

Similar to the debate on the meso level, Stoiber's argument dismantles Europe as an ontological space. Germany's belonging to Europe and its participation in the EU integration process is now a matter of expediency, interest and calculation. The 'search for a European identity' is considered 'obsolete'.[59] German attempts to dissolve their national identity within the European one reflected but the nation's hopes to escape its historical liabilities. 'After German unification, we now face a different situation – and we have to become aware again what German identity truly is.'[60]

Stoiber's argument does not produce a coherent ontology to replace the Cold War geography of Europe. The statement about the obsolete nature of a European identity and the preference for national, indeed regional (Bavarian), identity is contradicted by the proposition that the problem with the EU integration process is that it is simply going to fast. And while the EU as a

---

[57] Schwarz, 1994, 88.   [58] Stoiber, 1993.
[59] FAZ, 1993a.   [60] Stoiber, 1993.

confederation is not supposed to be more than the sum of its member states, which can choose to leave the EU, Stoiber nonetheless foresees a European government with authority for a joint foreign and security policy. Arguably, Stoiber's intervention is remarkable not because of its intellectual or political coherence, but because of the first explicit renunciation of the Germany's Cold War security imaginary by a prominent politician.

Stoiber's remarks caused a stir in the public debate in Germany, precisely because they called into question the basic official commitments concerning Germany's identity and location within the institutional structure of the West.[61] Ultimately, his arguments did not lead to the re-orientation of German foreign policy as he had demanded.[62] While it did open up a discursive space that allowed some notions from the meso-level's critique to enter public and political speech acts and narratives, overall the responses to his intervention demonstrated a firmly established discourse that continued to construct a 'European Germany'. Predictably, for Stoiber's critics, this questioning of traditional assumptions about German foreign policy constituted a breach of the very commitments made by the Kohl administration in 1990 about Germany's identity and place in Europe.[63] Once more, the ruling discourse asserted itself against a challenge. Yet within a year, and in response to this eruption of discursive struggle over the relationship between Europe and Germany, the then head of the CDU faction in the German Parliament Wolfgang Schäuble, together with the foreign policy expert the faction, Karl Lamers, published a paper entitled 'Reflections on European Politics'.[64] Published in September 1994, the paper develops a new geopolitical map of Europe. It places Germany within the 'core' of EU member states, which share a positive attitude towards further integration and cooperation. The 'semi-periphery' is composed of those EU member states like Italy, Spain and Great Britain, which are for a number of reasons unwilling to fully engage in this process.[65] Finally, beyond the EU lies the space of Eastern Europe and Russia, the Mediterranean, and the transatlantic relations with the United States. The problems and issues in this space define the necessity to further integrate and strengthen the Common Foreign and Security Policy of the EU. In other words, the core of the EU needs to be further strengthened in order to find an effective strategy through which Europe can confront these issues.[66]

Embedded within this call for further integration itself is the articulation of an alternative political future of Europe, should the integration process fail. Due to its 'geographical location', Germany, the authors assert, has a strong interest in preventing Europe from 'drifting apart'. Historically, its *Mittellage* has made it difficult for the country to define its internal political order in unambiguous

---

[61] Cf. Joffe, 1993.   [62] FAZ, 1993b, 1994.   [63] FAZ, 1993c.
[64] Schäuble and Lamers, 1994.   [65] Schäuble and Lamers, 1994, 6.
[66] Schäuble and Lamers, 1994, 8ff.

terms and to establish a stable and balanced foreign policy. Attempts to overcome this conundrum by establishing a German hegemony over Europe have failed, with the 'military, political, and moral catastrophe of 1945' demonstrating that Germany did not have the power to accomplish this, and that a different, cooperative security structure was necessary for Europe. Hence the integration of Germany in the EC/EU and in NATO provided a political stability in Europe that allowed the country to become a part of the West, both in terms of its internal order as well as its foreign policy orientation.[67]

Moreover, 'there was no alternative to this extra-ordinary stable and successful post-war system for Germany, because the East-West conflict and the total defeat of 1945 deprived Germany of the option of an independent policy towards the East (*Ostpolitik*) or even a political orientation towards the East (*Ostorientierung*)'.[68]

There is an interesting ambiguity in this statement as to what constitutes Germany's *Westbindung* during the Cold War: its identity as a Western(ised) state and society, or the absence of any political alternatives, given the constraints of the bipolar order of the Cold War. Whether Germany belonged to the West because it now *was* a Western country, or because it faced no other options, remains unresolved. This ambiguity is further exacerbated when the authors turn to the end of the Cold War. Now the stability of Eastern Europe, and consequently of Europe as a whole, is once again on the agenda, and with it the identity and foreign policy orientation of Germany. Regarding the possibility of a stalling European integration process that would exclude the countries east of Germany, a dire alternative is conjured up: 'Without the further development of the (West-) European integration process Germany might be called upon, or be tempted by its own security needs, to bring off the stabilisation of Eastern Europe by itself and in the traditional way.'[69]

Germany, in other words, does have choices again. Above all, the German *Sonderweg* rears its head again, as Germany considers the possibility to take on the responsibility for European stability and integration by itself. Here, geopolitics re-appears in a neoclassical guise – including worst-case thinking and expansionism – in a complex fashion that intertwines ontological stipulations with political strategy. European integration or *Sonderweg* are theoretically equivalent options for Germany; albeit a clear *political* preference is expressed for the former path. Its own identity seems to be contextual rather than essential. Germany acquired a Western identity through its embeddedness in the institutional framework of the Cold War; yet with the end of this historical period, new possibilities emerge, among them a return to the German *Sonderweg*.

---

[67] Schäuble and Lamers, 1994, 2.
[68] Schäuble and Lamers, 1994, 2.
[69] Schäuble and Lamers, 1994, 3.

Thus, a classic *topos* of *Geopolitik* reappears in the Schäuble and Lamers paper. While the official discourse had defined it as its historical ontological Other, the *Sonderweg* now appears as a if not necessarily favoured, yet nonetheless theoretically conceivable, strategy. In other words, no extant membership within the West and its institutions provides automatic safeguards against such a course of action.

Again, it should be emphasised that during the chancellorship of Helmut Kohl, these potentially radical theses were not adopted as the official stance of German foreign policy. Moreover, the Schäuble/Lamers paper also needs to be understood as a performative speech act *within* the context of EU integration, as a 'wake-up call' to prevent a stalling of the institutional reform process within the EU. *Geopolitik* is deployed in a negative fashion in order to provide support for its alternative.

Until 1998, therefore, no coherent alternative discourse on German identity and international purpose emerged, no new *Geopolitik* security imaginary articulated a new Germany with a different position and subjectivity vis-à-vis its allies and partners. Such a new imaginary appeared to emerge only within the subsequent Schröder/Fischer coalition government. Yet exactly how different this *Weltbild* was, and what role *Geopolitik* played in it, quickly became a matter of contestation.

The security imaginary of the *Berliner Republik*

As Günter Hellmann has argued, a significant rhetorical shift regarding Germany's role in European and world politics emerged with the Schröder/ Fischer administration. Assertions of Germany's national identity and political purpose are now articulated in a different key.[70] Chancellor Schröder set the tone in his first government address to Parliament when he describes a Germany that possesses 'the confidence of a grown-up nation, which does not have to feel superior, nor, however, inferior to others. [It is a country] that faces up to its history and its responsibility, but for all its willingness to engage with it critically, still looks ahead'.[71]

In terms of its relationship with Europe, this new confidence translates into a definition of Germany's European identity as a matter of choice and volition: 'We are today democrats and Europeans not because we would have to, but because we really want to.'[72] Clearly, Schröder here echoes the structure first introduced by Stoiber and the Schäuble/Lamers paper. Germany's relationship with Europe is now defined by a willed orientation, a political choice, rather than an ontological identity. This apparently new geopolitical imagery of the

---

[70] Hellmann, 2000, 48–79.   [71] Schröder, 1998, 28.
[72] Schröder, 1998, 29.

Berlin Republic can be further demonstrated through an analysis of then foreign minister Joschka Fischer's famous speech of May 2000 at the Humboldt
University in Berlin. Here too we find the notion of a core Europe that drives an
integration process not supported by other, marginal, EU member states. Once
again, the stability of East and Southeast Europe is at stake, with a strengthened
and expanded EU as the central lynchpin of a future order. And crucially, 'the
enlargement [of the EU] is in Germany's highest national interest. Germany's
size and central location (*Mittellage*) define *objective* risks and temptations,
which can be overcome by the enlargement and simultaneous deepening of the
EU'.[73] Here too a different, yet familiar Germany looms as a potentiality that
has to be contained by an integration process, the logic and direction of which
is defined by Germany itself. Arguably, the logic of *Geopolitik* takes on even
more ontological depth here than it does in the Schäuble/Lamers paper. In the
latter it defines an alternative strategy for the German government, should
the European integration process not go according to its design. In Fischer's
rendition, *Geopolitik* can be interpreted not only as another political option,
but also as an underlying *objective structure* with its own logic and imperatives. European integration as a *political* project is therefore always in peril of
succumbing to the objective imperatives of Germany's *Mittellage*. If we accept
this interpretation, then Fischer's argument amounts in effect to a 'blackmail' of Germany's European partners, as it offers them a deal they cannot,
indeed must not, refuse.[74] For the alternative to the European integration process (on German terms) is not only defined as a different political strategy, but
also determined by the objective necessities of *Geopolitik*. Again the Germany
of old, the one that adhered to the 'objective' imperatives or temptations of
Geopolitik, still serves as the ontological Other against which the new Germany
is set off. In other words, Fischer here continues the by now familiar negative
deployment of *Geopolitik* with the aim to defuse its purported logic.

In this sense, we can still observe continuity with the discourse on German
identity and purpose as it emerged in 1989/1990. Both the arguments by
Schäuble/Lamers and by Fischer fold this alternative into the present and
future of politics as a potentiality. The Germany of old, that the Cold War discourse had represented as a historicised and therefore distant Other, is now
turned into a spectral entity that haunts current politics in Europe. This spectre
requires constant containment through a permanent strengthening of those
ties that bind Germany to its Western/European space. As such, its supplica-
tion does not so much deny or reject the relevance of the EU for the German
security imaginary as in fact confirm and reassert it.[75]

---

[73] Fischer, 2000, 4 (emphasis added).
[74] On the blackmail implied in this logic see Schmierer's (1996, 135) discussion of the
Schäuble/Lamers paper.
[75] Cf. Fischer, 1999b.

Afghanistan and the end of *Geopolitik*

Critics of the Red-Green coalition's foreign policy have often focused on the definition of Germany's role and interest in the speeches and texts produced by chancellor Schröder. And on this level, a clear pattern emerges that the critics identify as a 'power political re-socialisation process' (*machtpolitische Resozialisierung*) and a shift from a civilising foreign policy towards a power political orientation.[76] If this were to be a valid analysis, the consequences would be quite significant in terms of a different security imaginary and the return of *Geopolitik*. Hellmann associates the ideal type of *Machtpolitik* with Heinrich von Treitschke's philosophy of the state, thus opening the door for a reassertion of a distinctive nationalist *Geopolitik*.[77] His argument about this re-socialisation process is based on a systematic analysis of the foreign policy vocabulary of Schröder (and in a second study, of the foreign policy elite in Germany), and on a critical evaluation of particular German foreign policy decisions and practices, which he interprets in light of this rhetoric and as examples of this shift.

Regarding the analysis of Schröder's political rhetoric, there is little to disagree with. Compared to his predecessors, Schröder's willingness to refer to words and phrases previously only used in the conservative critique of the *Bonner Republik*'s foreign policy is certainly evident. The description of Germany as a 'great power in Europe' and its geographical position or *Mittellage*, the constant references to 'national interests', to 'responsibility' (in terms of the use of German armed forces), 'pride' and 'self-confidence' create a certain pattern that re-produces the ontological distinction between Germany and Europe and the West.[78] There is also the fascinating reference to the *deutschen Weg*, the 'German way', a barely hidden allusion to the German *Sonderweg*, that Schröder introduced in his opening speech of the Federal election campaign in 2002.[79] Hellmann's analysis is also very good in demonstrating the 'erratic and haphazard' quality of Schröder's statements, revealing a personality that dealt with the complexities of foreign policy and international relations through instinct and gut-level responses.[80] Yet this very insight unravels his larger argument, as he conflates the micro and meso levels of geopolitics. For rhetoric does not make discourse; the personal (erratic) statements about foreign policy by a single actor, even if this is the chancellor himself, do not constitute a new security imaginary that can articulate a whole set of subject positions and purposes. A broader and more systematic analysis of German foreign policy discourse would be needed to sustain such an argument. Such an analysis remains to be conducted, yet Hellmann at least alludes to it and the 'split' assessments of

---

[76] Hellmann, 2005 and 2007.   [77] Hellmann, 2007, 463.
[78] Hellmann, 2005; cf. Schröder, 1999, 2002a and 2002b.
[79] Schröder, 2002b, 2 and 8.   [80] Hellmann, 2005, 16–17 [fn. 18].

Schröder's foreign-policy making.[81] Even more interestingly, Hellmann initiated a debate on German foreign policy in general in the pages of *WeltTrends*, a German language journal located between academia and public discourse, to which a wide variety of scholars responded. If the resulting debate demonstrates anything, it is a general disagreement over the basic principles of current German foreign policy.[82]

The absence of any clear security imaginary becomes evident already in the first major foreign policy decision of the new administration. Germany's participation in NATO's 1999 Kosovo campaign produced contradictory and ambiguous justifications, not least by the new foreign minister, Joschka Fischer. A ferocious critic of the *Bundeswehr*'s deployment to the Balkans in the early 1990s, he now justified the German participation in the campaign on moral, as well as on 'realist', grounds. Against critics from his own Green Party, Fischer mobilised Germany's historical experience and his personal commitment to two principles: 'never again war' and 'never again Auschwitz, never again genocide'.[83] While these principles had been mutually reinforcing during the Cold War, the Balkan War necessitated a discursive renegotiation.[84] For Fischer, the moral imperative to prevent another genocide now takes precedent over the rejection of war. Only through this commitment can continuity with the principles of German foreign policy be maintained. Yet to the members of the German Council on Foreign Relations, a distinctly different audience, Fischer downplays the relevance of morals in the decision to support NATO operation *Allied Force*. In his words: 'Moral principles played … a large role, but regarding Kosovo the primary concern was regional security in Southeast Europe, which has consequences for the whole of Europe.'[85] And finally, as Fischer reveals in his memoirs, regarding the decision to support NATO's operation against Yugoslavia, 'Germany could not stand aside and risk a fissure in the Alliance'.[86]

Westbindung, European stability and moral *Verantwortungspolitik* combine here in a somewhat contradictory explanation of German foreign and security policy. Yet together they reinforce the impression that the new government emphasised continuity and reliability over change or transformation. While it was a crucial moment in German foreign policy to commit military forces for combat operations for the first time since the end of World War II, the underlying security imaginary invoked remains within the traditional parameters. These, however, had incrementally changed with earlier 'out-of-area' deployments of the *Bundeswehr* and the decision of the *Bundesverfassungsgericht* from July 1994, which permitted these deployments.

---

[81] Hellmann, 2005, 19–20 [fn. 35] and 2007, 455–460.
[82] Hellmann, 2005.   [83] Fischer, 1999a.
[84] See Zehfuss, 2002 for an analysis of the processes involved.
[85] Fischer, 1999b.   [86] Fischer, 2007, 107.

A more radical change in the German security imaginary takes place after 11 September 2001. 'Afghanistan' becomes the event that occasions a significant redrawing of Germany's geopolitical space and purpose. As Murphy and Johnson argue, 'German policymakers saw September 11 as an opening through which to shed the post-war yoke of geopolitical quiescence'.[87] While the notions of 'yoke' and 'quiescence' might be exaggerated, the statement nonetheless points to an interesting shift in the geopolitical imagination of the German government. In a speech at the World Economic Forum 2002 in New York, Chancellor Schröder explicitly links the German participation in Operation *Enduring Freedom* and the military campaign against terrorism to a radical 'breach' in Germany foreign and security policies:

> I feel it is important to express in an international forum the extent to which we have broken with the traditions of the old Federal Republic in foreign and security matters. A very good tradition, in light of the events of the Second World War and fascism in Germany, was the pursuit of a foreign and security policy that ruled out involvement in military interventions ... The changes that have taken place in the world have forced us to think anew about this question ... As a consequence we had to change our foreign and security policy; our partners in Europe and everywhere in the world expected solidarity in an unrestricted sense and expected, as a last resort to be sure, but also without restrictions, our participation in joint military interventions.
>
> I hope this makes clear the extent to which change in operative policy has become possible [...] in Kosovo, later in Macedonia, and now in Afghanistan within the United Nations framework, but also through our willingness to participate in Operation Enduring Freedom and, as such, in the military action being undertaken against terrorism. That was, as it were, the foreign and security policy aspect of our response and adjustment to changed conditions in the world.[88]

The emergent post-9/11 security imaginary defines a changing geopolitical map and a transformed role for Germany. Regarding the latter, we can observe what critics have called a *Enttabuisierung des Militärischen*, a 'removal of taboos' concerning the use of military force.[89] In Schröder's words, '"secondary assistance" such as providing infrastructure support or granting of financial means in support of international efforts to secure freedom, justice, and stability' would no longer suffice.[90] More active forms of security policies gain in significance.[91] Military action is now no longer the exception; it becomes an integral part of German foreign and security policy.

Concerning the geopolitical map, the spatial 'preference' for Europe, which made the military deployment in support of the UN Mission in East Timor in

---

[87] Murphy and Johnson, 2004, 2.
[88] Schröder, 2002a.   [89] Geis, 2005.
[90] Schröder, 2001.   [91] Voigt, 2002.

1999 an exceptional measure,[92] has been dissolved in favour of a global geo-political imaginary defined by the threat of 'international terrorism'[93] and the 'international totalitarian challenge'[94] it poses. German security is now defended through multilateral actions, and in a global space. Realising that 'risks no longer emanate from our immediate neighbours, but that there are dangers beyond Europe, which affect directly or indirectly European secur-ity',[95] German geopolitics now far exceed the limits of *Geopolitik*.

With regard to the topic of this chapter, the consequences are significant. Defence Minister Struck's 2002 claim that Germany's security is defended at the Hindu Kush[96] in fact constitutes the end, rather than the return, of *Geopolitik*. To the extent that the deployment of *Bundeswehr* forces to Afghanistan reflects a new, if still evolving security imaginary, it no longer invokes the three defin-ing features of *Geopolitik*: Germany's *Mittellage*, a German *Sonderweg*, and the focus on national *Machtpolitik*. 'Hindu Kush' can be seen to stand for the 'return of geopolitics' in German foreign and security politics, if we take this to mean the return of political space as a problem, and the emergence of a new spa-tialisation within which Germany's role becomes 'globalised' and in which its geographical position within Europe becomes irrelevant. As part of this devel-opment, the civilisational discourse that articulates a German identity in terms of a *Mittellage*, distinct from East and West, fades into oblivion. In a similar fashion, 'Hindu Kush' represents the end of a German *Sonderweg*. The deploy-ment of German forces reflects a mission defined by a common transatlantic purpose to fight a common enemy. In practical terms, the deployment repro-duces their dependency on US forces for airlift and protection, demonstrat-ing the deep security interdependence that defines German security politics in the twenty-first century.[97] If there were any hint of a *Sonderweg* observable at all, it would be the German forces' focus on 'peacekeeping' missions and the refusal by the German government to deploy the bulk of the forces in the more dangerous South of Afghanistan. But as such, these represent more of a continuity with *Verantwortungspolitik*, one of the traditional *topoi* of German foreign policy discourse, than an emerging shift towards power politics. While Schröder's rhetoric cited above suggests abandoning, of traditional notions of *Verantwortungspolitik* and *Westbindung*, a closer investigation of German for-eign policy under the Schröder/Fischer administration reveals a more complex picture. The exercise of (military) power, as the deployment to Afghanistan demonstrates, is still significantly circumscribed by such commitments to civilising power and the necessary embeddedness of both German forces and policies within international institutions. Moreover, Schröder's critique of, and resistance to, the US invasion of Iraq in 2003 reflected a continued (and

---

[92] Fischer, 1999b.   [93] Schröder, 2001.   [94] Fischer, 2001.
[95] Voigt, 2002.   [96] Wagener, 2004, 14 [fn. 37].
[97] Wagener, 2004, 31.

popular) rejection of mere power politics and a policy characterised by a commitment to the peaceful settlement of conflicts, as well as a strengthening of the international legal order.[98] *Verantwortungspolitik* reappears, adjusted to the now global context of German foreign policy.

The deployment of the *Bundeswehr* to Afghanistan as part of the NATO-led International Security Assistance Force (ISAF) also reaffirms the continued relevance of Germany's *Westbindung*. Far from returning to a classical power politics based on a nationally defined geopolitical security imaginary, the deployment of German armed forces remains tied to the political purpose and institutional context of Western institutions. Moreover, if Fischer's autobiographical recollections regarding the concern about NATO's stability in light of the Kosovo crisis are to be trusted, we find further evidence for the continuity of this *topos* of German foreign policy, if under changed circumstances.

It is perhaps only the commonplace of a 'European Germany' that vanishes in German foreign policy formulation with the change of power in 1998. 'European-ness', Schröder explains, is a matter of choice and volition, not an existential given anymore. And as some researchers have pointed out, under Schröder, Germany experienced a significant level of 'de-Europeanisation' of its foreign policy, in effect turning from a 'vanguard' to a 'laggard' with regard to EU integration.[99] Yet as the authors are careful to emphasise, this 'new' policy is not the result of a unilateral decision or volition on the part of the German government, or even the German chancellor. Rather, it is the outcome of an intricate interplay of changing EU structures of governance and particular German structures, such as the increased involvement of the *Länder* (the German federal units) in EU politics which led to a re-assessment of the German position on EU asylum policies, and the continued commitment to a conscription-based *Bundeswehr*, which made a full-fledged support for the European Security and Defence Policy (ESDP) more difficult. Moreover, as Thomas Risse[100] has pointed out, Germany's continued commitment to the EU was expressed in the German support for the Eastern expansion of the Union, and for the EU's 'constitutional' reform process. Thus, while Germany's European identity might have become a matter of choice, political realities 'on the ground' seem to suggest it is the only credible alternative.

Conclusion: the spectre of *Geopolitik*

To put it succinctly, *Geopolitik* did not experience a renaissance in post-unification Germany's security imaginary, neither in its traditional, nor in a neoclassical, version. The country in which *Geopolitik* was first articulated

---

[98] Risse, 2004.   [99] Hellmann *et al.*, 2005.
[100] Risse, 2004, 26–28.

and institutionalised as a scientific endeavour in the 1920s and 1930s, did without this tradition when attempting to find a new national identity and purpose, a new security imaginary after the Cold War.

To be sure, German foreign and security policy underwent significant changes since 1990, and a new spatialisation emerged, most dramatically after the events of 9/11 and the deployment of German forces to Afghanistan. Geopolitics, in the sense of a geo-spatial imaginary, mattered, as it always does in international politics. But then the Cold War too was a particular geopolitical structure with Germany firmly, politically as well as existentially, embedded in the West.

Most of the outspoken proponents of *Geopolitik* remained on the margins of academic and political discourse, and those writers, academic or not, that pushed for a different, more self-conscious, more 'powerful' German foreign policy, only referred to *Geopolitik* hesitantly, using some of its central terms, yet almost invariably recognising the continued reality of the institutional structures within which Germany would continue to conduct its foreign policy. Against this quest for a 'different' German foreign policy, a strong alliance of scholars and academics in Frankfurt, Trier and Berlin insisted on the continued desirability and necessity of a foreign policy that orients itself towards a civilising purpose rather than power politics. Here, *Geopolitik* again appears as a spectre of the dangers that a misguided 'normalisation' of German foreign policy would produce. Finally, speeches and narratives by officials occasionally, but in a thoroughly unsystematic fashion, refer to tropes and *topoi* that are part of the *Geopolitik* vocabulary. In Fischer's 2000 speech, the logic of *Geopolitik* emerges as a potentiality and an unwanted alternative to European integration. In Schröder's 2002 election campaign speech, the *deutsche Weg*, the German way, serves to provide an emotive focus for a list of domestic and international challenges that Germany allegedly faces. The allusion to the *Sonderweg* is as blatant as it is irrelevant – Schröder is never able or willing to argue the case for a German identity and role in Europe similar to the one of *Geopolitik*.

The failure of *Geopolitik* on both the meso and the micro level of German foreign policy can be explained in a fairly straightforward way. First, there is the continued collective memory of the Nazi regime and the excesses of nationalist power politics.

Second, unlike many other states in Europe, Germany did not experience an 'existential crisis' with the end of the Cold War. Hence the temptation to find easy answers in response to an ontological crisis did not present itself in Germany. Instead, *Geopolitik* defined at this moment precisely what was to be avoided, the dark spectre of history against which the new, yet same, Germany would define its identity and purpose.

Over time it became clear that the continued recognition of Germany as a full member of the Western institutions depended on a change in the German security imaginary. And it is within a changed institutional context that

Germany has to develop its new security imaginary. Yet as discussed above, this happened in a reactive, often 'gut-level', and not necessarily coherent, fashion. Given this particular dialectic between continuity and change, *Geopolitik* was simply irrelevant.

The analysis also suggests that 'Hindu Kush' is a harbinger of the 'end of (traditional) geopolitics', an example of the discursive 're-territorialisation' that attempts to translate the threat of a globalised and non-territorial enemy into traditional 'patterns of thought' of realist geopolitics. As a consequence, a complex and 'viral' enemy is rendered amenable to the use of traditional military strategies, tactics and means. Geopolitics itself, with its insistence on a territorial ontology, now becomes a problem rather than a heuristic or analytical solution – a turn recognised also by German representatives of Critical Geopolitics.[101] While geopolitics might have provided a (temporary) solution to the existential crises of identity in some European states after 1989, it does nothing to elucidate the changing identity of global politics.

[101] Reuber and Wolkersdorfer, 2003, 8–10.

6

Geopolitics 'in the land of the prince': a *passe-partout* to (global) power politics?

ELISABETTA BRIGHI AND FABIO PETITO

La geopolitica può servire da bussola per orientarsi nel futuro imprevedibile del mondo [Geopolitics can serve as a compass to navigate the unpredictable future of the world].[1]

The revival of geopolitical thinking and practice in Italy since the landmark events of 1989 is at once a relatively uncomplicated and yet ultimately perplexing affair. While there is no doubt that a revival of some kind has taken place, its meaning and implications for the wider academic debates around IR in Italy – let alone for the country's foreign policy – are much less clear. To start with, over the last two decades geopolitics has been invoked by its own supporters and scholars in a startling variety of ways – as a discourse, a doctrine, a set of theories, or even a science – to the effect that the term itself has inevitably become both ubiquitous and exceedingly vague. Secondly and more interestingly, despite its undefined meaning, the 'geopolitical approach' to international politics has managed to gain and retain a powerful status in Italian IR academia and public debates – it has, in fact, become a legitimate discourse in itself and, to some extent, a legitimising discourse for those who practice it. In the public debate, often without much questioning, geopolitics has been elevated to a vital asset, a veritable master-key, or *passe-partout*, for the understanding of the intricacies of international politics, old and new.

Thus, one has witnessed not just the proliferation of a number of reviews and journals dedicated to the study and/or application of geopolitical reasoning

We would like to thank Franco Mazzei, Alessandro Colombo, Rosario Sommella, Sonia Lucarelli, Christopher Hill, Michele Chiaruzzi, Pascal Vennesson, Elsa Tulmets and Marco Antonsich for their useful comments and pertinent suggestions on an earlier draft of this chapter. Elisabetta Brighi would like to acknowledge the support provided by a research grant awarded by the Istituto Italiano di Scienze Umane during the writing of this chapter. The title alludes to the contribution of Lucarelli and Menotti, 2002a, although using the expression for a different purpose, as will become clear in what follows. All translations are by the authors.

[1] Jean, 2004, back cover.

to matters of international politics, but also the affirmation of a few scholars and the rise of 'experts' often from the military/diplomatic background, whose reputation was generally boosted (or a few times established *ex nihilo*) thanks to their alleged geopolitical expertise. Several geopolitical 'classics' were also translated for the first time or re-edited in Italian and, more generally, over the last fifteen years countless works have been published on the 'geopolitics of …' – focusing on either a region, the foreign policy of particular states, or particular issue-areas. All in all the body of literature on geopolitics, or at least broadly inspired by it, has grown at an exponential rate.[2]

This chapter sets out to investigate the issue of how and why geopolitics has come to attract such wide attention in the Italian public and academic debate since 1989. As it will be argued, a series of long-term and short-term developments combined to ensure that this development could take place. On the one hand, confronted with the much more uncertain environment of post-bipolarism, a series of long-forgotten anxieties concerning Italy's status in the world resurfaced, triggered by the seismic changes of 1989 and by the way these were interpreted in the political and intellectual debate. Once problematic questions such as those of nation, identity and nationalism were reintroduced in the public discourse, after decades of utter oblivion during the Cold War, the field was ready to witness the confluence of two strong strands of materialistic thinking, realism and Marxism, around the only approach believed to be able to provide clues able to orient Italy's foreign policy and secure its place in the post-bipolar world. The scene, in other words, was ready for the come-back of geopolitics as a welcome fix to address the Italian foreign policy identity crisis. A series of enabling conditions or process factors, such as the particular state of IR academia and the evolution of Italy's domestic political system, further ensured that in the span of only a few years, and in spite of its dubious pedigree and vague agenda, geopolitics re-emerged to affirm itself as a suitable, legitimate and legitimising framework through which to analyse the contemporary world politics and Italy's place in it.

To develop this argument, the chapter will proceed in two main stages. Its first two sections examine the history of Italy's geopolitical tradition and the substantial content of its present revival. The first section shows the roots of Italian geopolitical thought in the first segment of the twentieth century, its distinctive features and original agenda and draws our attention to the way in which elements of this story have resurfaced in the contemporary debate. The second section will illustrate the main features of the renaissance of geopolitics

---

[2] Suffice it to say that about 200 volumes have been published with the word 'geopolitics' in the title over the relatively brief span of the last twenty years. Considering the relatively small size of the IR academic publishing market, an average of ten books a year is rather remarkable. Data from the national catalogue of libraries accessible from the Ministry of Education's website (www.internetculturale.it).

in Italy since 1989, looking at its different strands and manifestations both in the intellectual debate and in the arena of foreign-policy making. In particular, it will discuss three in-depth examples of the revival of geopolitics, analysing the success of *Limes: rivista italiana di geopolitica* and the writings of the two figures who have most contributed to this revival, namely Carlo Jean and Carlo Maria Santoro. As we shall illustrate, in the Italian debate geopolitics has been taken to mean many different things;[3] yet, this ambiguity has not substantially detracted from the popularity of the term/approach – quite the contrary has been the case. The second part of the chapter, also in two sections, deals with the reasons for this revival and what it tells us concerning the case of Italy. The third section investigates the basic contention of this volume, namely that such a revival happens in the content of a foreign policy identity crisis by discussing the nexus between history, identity and foreign policy in post-1989 Italy. Here, geopolitical thought has come to serve, to some extent at least, a revisionist or even irredentist function within a security imaginary where Italy's world political role has been continuously seen as precarious and undervalued. The final section analyses a series of process factors which have enabled this crisis to develop a geopolitical response, namely a materialist ideational path dependency of political culture, the state of the Italian public and academic debate around foreign policy and the particular political field and struggles of Italy in the post-1989 period. Finally, the conclusions will serve the purpose of summing up the argument of the chapter as well as delineate the possible future trajectory of geopolitics in Italian foreign policy and in the debates around it.

Italy's geopolitical precedents, amnesia and awakening

As with German and French geopolitics, Italian geopolitics has a distinctive pedigree, though perhaps less celebrated or well-known.[4] Intimately tied to the nationalist project climaxing in the fascist *ventennio*, geopolitical arguments started to emerge at the turn of the twentieth century just as Italy was joining the scramble for colonies in the very last phase of European imperialism. As in many other European countries at this time, public interest in geography significantly increased and political geography strengthened itself as an academic discipline. Geopolitical scholarship capitalised on this general interest to grow into a prominent strand of thought in the years following World War I, eventually to become a major influence on the country's foreign policy during Mussolini's regime, especially from the 1930s.

Interestingly, just as fascism did not invent nationalism but rather built on themes and tendencies which had run through the late liberal era,[5] fascism

---

[3] Stanzione, 1995.
[4] For good overviews, see Antonsich, 1997b and Atkinson, 2000.
[5] Bosworth, 1979; Chabod, 1951, 546–548 and Salvatorelli, 1923.

did not really create geopolitics *ex-novo* but rather magnified and celebrated a mode of thinking whose main tenets had already been set out in practice, if not fully systematised in theory during the late liberal period.[6] Despite the rather natural association between geopolitics and fascism, there is in other words much to substantiate yet another 'continuity thesis' – the geopolitical thread clearly running through the two periods, rather than sharply delineating one from the other.

Both in its late liberal and fascist variant, geopolitical thinking essentially vehicled a vision of international politics which greatly borrowed from a realist, indeed an 'arch-realist', understanding of international relations. Thus, for instance, the justification of Italy's expansion into Libya eventually achieved in 1911 – not an insignificant adventure, effectively setting off the chain of events leading to World War I[7] – was given in typically spatial and antagonistic terms. It was a matter of once again 'dominating the Mediterranean, which meant dominating the world', as the nationalist Francesco Giunta proclaimed[8] or, as Foreign Minister Antonino Di San Giuliano urged, 'to join the great contest of peoples' and achieve a much-longed-for 'relative place in the world'.[9]

Fascism only came to reinforce and systematise such an approach – and most importantly use it to justify its revisionist projects. The definitive institutionalisation of geopolitical thinking came in the early 1930s with the establishment of a network of political geographers with radical geopolitical leanings at the University of Trieste, and with the publication of the first-ever Italian review of geopolitics, *Geopolitica: rassegna mensile di geografia politica, economica, sociale, coloniale*, between 1939 and 1942. Publicly greeted by Karl Haushofer as the sister-journal of the German *Geopolitik*, in the mind of its founders the Trieste-based and state-funded review provided a means to promote the country's geopolitical awareness, *coscienza geopolitica*, about the rapidly changing features of the international politics of the inter-war period. According to the two leading figures of the 1930s revival of geopolitics and editors of *Geopolitica*, Giorgio Roletto and Ernesto Massi, beyond political geography was the complex and urgent task of considering how the global distribution of power and natural resources combined with a set of important factors to generate change – and especially 'cultural factors, spiritual factors, and the will to power and empire'.[10] This was the remit of geopolitics: to take into account the dynamic and competitive elements of international politics, and assist an increasingly revisionist actor such as fascist Italy in the articulation of its foreign policy.[11]

---

[6] See Knox, 2002; on Di San Giuliano and geopolitics, see Bosworth, 1979 and Cerreti, 1997.
[7] Childs, 1990.   [8] Quoted in Rumi, 1968, 128.
[9] Quoted in Bosworth, 1979, 282.
[10] Roletto and Massi, 1938, 10.   [11] Pagnini, 1987.

In fact, one could well argue that the fatal encounter between fascism and geopolitics revolved precisely around the issue of agency and change. The peculiarity of Italian geopolitics was that instead of focusing on the 'geo-', using static concepts or a fixed spatiality, it foregrounded the shifting character of 'politics', and its contingent developments – typically solving the traditional debate between 'static' and 'dynamic' geography in favour of the latter. The emphasis on change and agency tied in extremely well with the fascist ideology of action, and in particular with the dogma of freedom of action in foreign policy. According to Mussolini, action was not only a 'vehicle of implementation of ideas, but a good in itself',[12] hence in foreign policy Italy ought to 'reclaim its freedom of action, taking care of its interest'. Radical revisionism thus offered an excellent common ground on which fascism and geopolitics would meet.

It was of course not long before the imagery conjured up by the Italian geopolitical scholarship of the 1930s translated itself into foreign policy practice. As Mussolini's speeches make abundantly clear, the *Duce* himself was a keen reader and eager practitioner of the geopolitical theories of the day.[13] Two regions in particular became the objects of constant geopolitical and rhetorical attention: the Mediterranean and the Balkans. As for the former, the geographical tropes used by Mussolini changed with the degree of expansionism of the regime: while the Mediterranean was characterised as *mare nostrum*, or even simply 'our lake' in the 1920s, it became 'a path' to Empire in the mid 1930s and finally a 'prison' from which Italy had to escape in order to march towards the Oceans in the late 1930s, as the war approached.[14] As for the latter, expansion into Albania was justified with a formula reminiscent of Mackinder's more famous expression: 'He who holds Bohemia, holds the Danubian basin. He who holds Albania, holds the Balkans.'[15] In both cases, geopolitical arguments were used in the process of planning and carrying out expansion and military aggression – the invasion of Ethiopia in 1935, that of Albania in 1939, and finally that of Greece in 1940, with World War II already underway.

Just as the war came to mark the dramatic end of the fascist experiment in Italy, so did it also signal the sudden loss of popularity of geopolitics among the elites and public at large. Inevitably marred by its fascist contaminations, geopolitics was summarily sentenced to an oblivion which was to last for almost half a century. Indeed, the *morte della patria* which followed the armistice of 8 September 1943[16] meant not only the death of the nation – and the origin of a long-lasting taboo around the very term of 'nation' and 'national interest'[17] – but also, by extension, the death of geopolitics. In the public and academic debate alike a veritable amnesia rapidly set in. Even the very few exceptions to

---

[12] Quoted in Moscati, 1963, 102; cf. also Kallis, 2000, 57.
[13] E.g. Mussolini, 1934, 61.   [14] Cagnetta, 1994, 257.
[15] Quoted in Lowe and Marzari, 1975, 326.
[16] Galli della Loggia 1996 and 1998.   [17] Galli della Loggia 1996.

the rule (e.g. the publication of *Hérodote-Italia* between 1978 and 1984) were short-lived and passed by relatively unnoticed.

Given the long parenthesis of almost total oblivion during the Cold War it is certainly surprising that only a few years were enough to bring geopolitics vigorously back in fashion after 1989. However, the magnitude of the changes which followed the fall of the Berlin Wall was short of dramatic for Italy and justified many transformations.[18] The end of bipolarism brought to an abrupt collapse of Italy's self-conception and 'clear' international role: by losing its key domestic and international frames of reference, as we will analyse below, the well-established Italian security imaginary of the Cold War was put into deep question and the country found itself in a state of ontological insecurity and anxiety.

In this scenario, interest in geopolitics suddenly re-emerged. Crucially, this paralleled the rapid emergence of another big theme in the public debate, namely the question of Italy as a *nation*, with its interests and identity. Not coincidentally, the two questions were often referred to in tandem by the main protagonists of this debate to make the case for a discussion, indeed for a major reconsideration of Italy's national interests. A wealth of publications was dedicated to launching a debate on Italy's role in contemporary international relations, as well as Italy's capacity to project its interests abroad in a unitary and coherent fashion. A number of these were funded through a major research programme launched by Carlo Jean, then president of the most important Italian military think-tank (*Centro Alti Studi Difesa*, CASD),[19] while some others were the individual works of well-known figures from the world of diplomacy or military historians.[20] The rationale for this sudden revival of interest in these themes was aptly captured by Ernesto Galli della Loggia, one of the most prominent and vocal historians on these very issues: 'The end of bipolarism allows everyone to be oneself. It brings back Italy to its autonomous responsibility, since the international system which kept the country on its feet has fallen. Now we have to decide who we want to be.'[21]

The encounter of geopolitics and the theme of nation ('national interests', 'national identity') became not only natural but also mutually reinforcing. On the one hand, it was precisely the more fluid and dynamic international politics of the post-Cold War that allowed for, indeed seemed to command, a re-evaluation of Italy's national interests. This in turn produced the resurfacing of recurrent anxieties about the 'status' of the country in the world, as well as its identity as a nation. On the other hand, the re-evaluation of Italy's place in

---

[18] Cf. Andreatta and Hill, 2000 and Guzzini, 1995 for the debate on the sources of these changes.
[19] E.g. CeMiSS, 1997 and Corsico, 1998.
[20] E.g. Ilari, 1996 and Incisa di Camerana, 1996.
[21] Caracciolo and Orfei, 1993.

the world rather naturally came to involve the use of geopolitics as a discursive/ practical means to imagine and cope with this new politics. Just as in the inter-war period, in a post-bipolar world in which cultural and 'spiritual' factors had risen to prominence after decades of 'exile', geopolitics had come back to cast its spell on intellectuals and policy makers alike, and to present itself as the most immediately available toolkit at their disposal.

Let a thousand flowers bloom: the renaissance of geopolitics in post-1989 Italy

In the public debate of the early to mid 1990s the need to come to terms with Italy's 'national interest' developed soon into a fixation and geopolitics became perhaps the most important buzzword in the debate. The sudden resurgence of interest in geopolitics progressively invaded newspapers, reviews, the book market and academia itself. Only towards the mid 1990s did the revival start to lose some of its momentum, partly as a response to changes in the political context, both domestic and international, partly because of the rather unnat-ural way in which much of it was carried forward at the beginning of the dec-ade – involving only a small section of the intellectual elite, and by and large failing to command the attention of the larger, more average public. It is diffi-cult not to agree with the warning of former Minister of Defence Beniamino Andreatta:

> Italy has interests because it is an important actor in the international arena, *and not the other way around.* Otherwise we would run the risk of creating artificial and ephemeral interests, as if made in a laboratory, which would not be in tune with the country and thus would not be perceived as such.[22]

But before attempting to discuss more in detail the issue of where this leaves us today, and what it tells us concerning the case of Italy, its foreign policy and the field of production of foreign policy expertise, it might well be useful to give more detailed indications of the renaissance of geopolitics in post-wall Italy and, in particular, analyse three of its various manifestations.

Limes *and co.: the birth of a geopolitical 'fad'*

An account of the resurgence of geopolitical writing in Italy cannot but start acknowledging the central place of *Limes: review of geopolitics* in this pro-cess. Its first issue published in March 1993, the journal quickly managed to attract a number of high-profile intellectuals from a variety of backgrounds, all concerned with re-launching the debate around the changing character

---

[22] Andreatta in Corsico, 1998, 137 (emphasis added).

of post-bipolar international politics and Italy's place in it. Under the editorship of left-wing journalist Lucio Caracciolo and *Hérodote* exponent Michel Korinmann, and under the aegis of the father of French post-war geopolitics Yves Lacoste himself, the journal provided a forum for well-known historians, political scientists, diplomats and journalists – with the ambitious mission, so read one of its advertisements, to make readers 'understand the world as it is'.[23]

In pursuing this mission, the journal received support not only from the world of academia and public intellectuals, but also from the Ministry of Foreign Affairs and the world of business. Regarding the former, in particular, the former Secretary General Bruno Bottai played a key role – just as his father, the fascist Minister of National Education Giuseppe Bottai, had played in the success of the review *Geopolitica* in the late 1930s, many commentators noted. More generally, the world of Italian diplomacy was rather close to the review from its origin. Former ambassadors Sergio Romano and Luigi Vittorio Ferraris were regular contributors especially in its first years, while today many diplomats in service are periodically used to publishing their views, under pseudonyms, in the pages of the journal. As for the world of business, *Limes* was too successful an editorial product to be ignored by big public firms such as Finmeccanica, Alitalia, Enel and Telecom, who all financed the journal by buying advertising space.[24]

If this is the anatomy of *Limes*, one should certainly delve further into its contents and editorial style, for it is here that it becomes clear what kind of geopolitical scholarship the journal promotes. Variously defined as 'pragmatic', 'concrete', 'realistic' and 'a-theoretical' by its own editor,[25] the geopolitics of *Limes* intends to be first and foremost a 'mode of reasoning' able to account for the genuinely global and increasingly fluid nature of post-bipolar international relations by combining a thorough consideration of the evolving spatiality and territoriality of post-wall international politics with an appreciation of elements as diverse as nationalism, culture, identity and ethnicity, power and the global economy. The real vocation of geopolitics *à la Limes*, however, is not merely descriptive. It is not enough to understand the world, surely, and since theorising is considered beyond its remit, what remains is the important task of aiding political practice. Geopolitics for *Limes* is first and foremost a *Realgeopolitik* at the service of decision-makers.[26] The aim of the debate around Italy's national interests and foreign policy has the explicit aim of helping decision-makers to identify what and where these interests are, and act accordingly. *Limes* performed this task often with zeal and at times with surprisingly bullish statements as well.[27]

---

[23] Atkinson, 2000, 108–109.   [24] Antonsich, 1997a.
[25] See especially Caracciolo and Korinmann, 1993.
[26] For the term see Antonsich, 1997a.
[27] See for instance Caracciolo and Korinmann, 1998.

Naturally, the journal's approach spurred some criticism, mainly from two different standpoints. On the one hand were those who held theory in far greater consideration. Thus, for instance Carlo Maria Santoro lamented the lack of a conceptual *fil rouge* and of a firm anchorage in the analytical categories of more traditional strands of geopolitics,[28] while Marco Cesa reiterated the criticism of many early realists who condemned geopolitics as a 'pseudo-science' in eternal oscillation between description and prescription.[29] On the other hand were those who lamented the political bearing of the project in which *Limes* embarked: the rediscovery of Italy's 'national interests' could not but lead to a growing nationalism, which the discourse and practice of geopolitics would justify as normal.[30]

Be that as it may, the proof of the enormous success of *Limes* are not only its average sales[31] and the enviable place it has acquired in the market – the journal is certainly one of the key, if not *the* reference publication for issues of foreign policy and international relations – but rather the contagious 'geopolitical fad' it has launched. Thus, a number of reviews and journals (such as *Eurasia* and *Imperi*) tried to capitalise on this mood and adopt a geopolitical approach similar to that of *Limes*, but none matching its success so far. Beyond journals, however, geopolitics has spread further afield to the world of communication, mass media and even to more institutional fora such as universities. Thus, it is now a common practice for TV broadcasts in cases of international crises to interview 'experts' on geopolitics or geostrategy – sometimes well-known and respected, other times self-proclaimed. Even more interestingly, geopolitics has entered the world of undergraduate and postgraduate curricula. The prestigious University of Rome 'La Sapienza', for instance, now offers a Masters of Science in 'Geopolitics and Global Security',[32] while courses in geopolitics and geostrategy are offered as options in more than a few universities at the undergraduate level.

The popularity of the geopolitics that *Limes* has launched is however no more evident than in the proliferation of published books dedicated to the subject or, more broadly, claiming to adopt a 'geopolitical approach' to specific aspects of international affairs. First, since the early 1990s a variety of books have been devoted to examining the changing geopolitics of regions such as the Balkans,[33] the Middle East[34] and Far East Asia.[35] Second, geopolitics has been used to make sense of the foreign policy of specific actors, such as the United States,[36] or of the domestic politics of others, i.e. the crisis of the First Republic

---

[28] Santoro, 1996b.   [29] Cesa, 1995.   [30] Bonanate, 1997.

[31] These days, the sales are around 30,000 per issue (oral communication with *Limes* editorial team, 18 June 2010).

[32] See http://w3.uniroma1.it/scpol/stpagina.asp?id=249.

[33] Antonsich *et al.*, 2001 and Jean and Favaretto, 2004.

[34] Anzera and Marniga, 2003.   [35] Mazzei, 2000.   [36] Polanski, 2005.

in Italy.[37] Third, the recent writings of the 'French school' of geopolitics, and especially of Yves Lacoste, Philippe Moreau-Defarges and Pascal Lorot have been promptly translated into Italian by publishers no doubt eager to exploit the general state of infatuation with geopolitics in the Italian market,[38] just as there has been an all-too-evident increase in the rate of translation of contributions from American IR realists-cum-geopolitical leanings such as Mearsheimer, Brzezinsky, Kissinger, Luttwak.[39] Fourth and last, not only have classics been translated for the first time in book form, but there are now a good number of journal contributions or monographs discussing in detail the legacy of specific authors such as Nicholas Spykman and, most recently, Halford Mackinder.[40]

Needless to say, the degree of self-consciousness about what geopolitics is or about the specific nature of the chosen geopolitical approach varies greatly across publications. If a few contributions are very clear about the distinctiveness of their approach, others simply treat geopolitics as a form of 'realism-cum-geography'; others still consider it merely as a synonym for international affairs. But the two figures who have more lucidly – though not entirely unambiguously – contributed to the academic revival of geopolitical analysis in Italy after 1989 are no doubt Carlo Jean and Carlo Maria Santoro. Because the two alone have published about ten books on the subject and because their scholarship has been (respectively) widely read and particularly unique, it is worth examining their main claims in detail. Together with more popular discussion well exemplified by the *Limes* phenomenon, this provides a good insight into what geopolitics has come to mean for post-1989 Italy.

The Machiavellian, half-critical (and all-realist) geopolitics of Carlo Jean

Carlo Jean is a general who has held very prominent positions within the Italian Army as well as within the Italian political establishment as military advisor. He is, however, most well-known by the larger public in Italy for his books on contemporary geopolitics that are probably the most widely read books in international relations written by an Italian. Together with the review *Limes*, Jean represents the other immediate association that is likely to come up in the mind of the average Italian questioned about the revival of geopolitics in his own country. In fact, no one in Italy has written (and published reprints) as much as Jean on geopolitics in the last fifteen years.[41] But what is geopolitics about for Jean?

---

[37] E.g. Caracciolo, 2001 and De Michelis, 2003.
[38] E.g. Claval, 1996; Lorot, 1997 and Moreau Defarges, 1996.
[39] E.g. Brzezinski, 1998; Kissinger, 1996, 2004; Luttwak, 2001 and Mearsheimer, 2003.
[40] E.g. Dossena, 2002.
[41] Jean, 1993, 1995, 2003 and 2004.

In his main theoretical contribution to geopolitics[42] Jean recognises that geopolitics does not enjoy a common accepted definition or a clear academic status.[43] While in a previous work he had subscribed to the traditional distinction between a 'restricted' and an 'enlarged' conception of geopolitics[44] – the former referring to the German school of Munich associated with the Nazi foreign policy and the latter to a form of applied political geography studying the constraints and influences of geography on politics and, in particular, foreign policy – in his most recent and complete book on the topic, he has more assertively argued that the only meaningful classification applicable to geopolitics is among different national schools whose particularities can be traced to the specific situation of their respective states. This is why, he adds, 'while it doesn't make sense to talk of a Marxist or social-Catholic or liberal geopolitics, it is indeed correct to talk of a German, Russian, American, French or Italian geopolitics'.[45]

To Jean, in fact, geopolitics, is not science – whereby for example political geography is – but rather 'a system of reasoning' (*sistema di ragionamento*) that draws on different academic disciplines, such as geography, history, economics and other social sciences, in order to identify the national interests of a particular state and suggest appropriate foreign policy strategies.[46] According to Jean, three different moments can be distinguished in the elaboration of a geopolitical hypothesis: the analysis, as objective as possible, of the international situation; the definition of the interests; and finally 'the action of communication and propaganda to obtain the international and internal consensus necessary for the action'.[47]

It is worth noting that the properly geopolitical approach to the analysis of international relations (to be used in the first stage of elaboration of a geopolitical hypothesis) is admittedly inspired to a form of political realism[48] which however takes into consideration also geographical, historical, economic, cultural, social and political elements. The traditional prevalence given to the geographic dimension should be reduced, according to Jean, in favour of a more balanced and eclectic multidisciplinary approach that pays attention to factors such as the return of culture and identity politics in international relations as well as the role of military force (geostrategy), the competition for world markets (geoeconomy) and the growing role of information linked to technology (geoinformation). The geopolitical nature of Jean's analytical approach, hence, does not really follow from a clear theoretical proposition: rather, it seems to be essentially a form of realism updated in an eclectic and sometimes syncretic way to the international reality of the contemporary globalised and post-bipolar world.

---

[42] Jean, 1995 [2003].   [43] Jean, 2003, 7.
[44] Jean, 1993, 275.   [45] Jean, 2003, 9.
[46] Jean, 2003, 25.   [47] Jean, 2003, 12.   [48] Jean, 2003, 24.

And yet there is another, possibly more important, meaning in which Jean's approach is indeed 'geopolitical'. This has to do with the primarily 'political function' of geopolitical discourse, which Jean promptly acknowledges. For Jean geopolitics is never neutral, rather it is essentially a '*geography of the prince*', a 'voluntaristic' geography meant to identify a state's national interest and its foreign policy strategies. This function is central to any geopolitical discourse and theorising. Even more interestingly, Jean argues that the very central role of the geopolitical theorist is that of 'advisor to the prince'. This explains inter alia why geopolitical analyses have been often declined in deterministic and quasi-scientific tones, traditionally in the form of great geographical (meta-geography) or historical generalisations (meta-history). To put it simply, if the aim is that of persuading the 'prince' (or public opinion) to accept a proposed foreign policy strategy then, echoing Morgenthau's classic strategy, the deterministic/scientist argument is undoubtedly the most useful, given its forcefulness and cogency.

Now the point is that, according to Jean, geopolitics as a *mobilising device/discourse* has become to some extent even more relevant in today's mass media societies. Geopolitical/geographical representations have indeed the capacity to crystallise a political position into something similar to a slogan, and therefore manipulate public perceptions and possibly build a consensus. Or in other words, as Jean continues in an unmistakably military jargon, today geopolitical representations 'have a considerable propagandistic content, of informative and dis-informative nature'.[49]

It is not completely striking, therefore, that in the revised edition of his *Geopolitica* (2003) Jean entertains a very unnatural and unexpected flirt with the deconstructionist argument put forward by recent 'critical' geopolitical approaches focusing on revealing the hidden politics of geopolitical knowledge created by practising statesmen and intellectuals of statecraft.[50] While agreeing on the inescapability of the power/knowledge nexus and even praising the 'new humanism' of this approach, Jean, of course, cannot subscribe to its normative ('critical') dimension.[51] Yet, Jean fully endorses Gearóid Ó Tuathail's view that the main challenge for critical geopolitics in contemporary international relations is to problematise how global space is incessantly re-imagined and re-inscripted by centres of power and authority – first of all the United States.[52]

Given all these theoretical premises, what becomes interesting is to briefly scrutinise the politics and practice of Jean's geopolitics. This can be done easily by looking at his later book *Geopolitica del XXI secolo* (2004) where it is clear

---

[49] Jean, 2003, 9–10.   [50] Ó Tuathail, 1998.
[51] In Jean's reading, its critical ethos is nothing but the fruit of a form of ingenuous post-modern idealism searching for a politics beyond the state (Jean, 2003, 117–119).
[52] Ó Tuathail, 1996.

that Jean is addressing the larger public opinion rather than academia. Without hesitations and with a certain aura of acquired authority, as announced in the back cover blurb Jean aims to introduce the reader to 'geopolitics (now without any further qualification as a kind of "scientific" approach) as a compass (*bussola*) to navigate the unpredictable future of the world'.[53] Rather than any theoretical sophistication, or rich analytical frameworks, Jean here clearly prefers putting into action the propagandistic power of geopolitical representations with the aim of influencing the political debate in Italy on the post-9/11 geopolitical scenarios and the country's necessary foreign policy response.

Never entirely articulating his analysis explicitly (and thus ultimately in contradiction with his own self-declared critical/reflexive sympathies), in *Geopolitica del XXI secolo* Jean weaves the threads of a geopolitical argument aimed at supporting a particular course of Italian foreign policy whose lines can be summarised as follows:

(1) reinforce a pro-Atlantic and Eurosceptic Italian foreign policy;
(2) emphasise the need for a renewed bilateralism against the traditional multilateralism of Italian foreign policy;
(3) identify the entrance of Italy in the European *directoire* wanted by France, Germany and the UK as priority; by the same token, avoid the marginalisation of Mediterranean Europe into a buffer zone to protect central and northern Europe from the arc of instability of the Greater Middle East by strengthening the bilateral relationship with the United States and opening the EU to Turkey and Russia.[54]

Jean's intention is clearly that of implicitly suggesting an Italian 'grand strategy' (*sic*) for coping with the post-9/11 international conjuncture, which is to some extent natural given that Jean has been one of the most vocal protagonists of the debate around Italy's 'national interests', as seen, and certainly the most resolute in lamenting the lack of strategy – grand or otherwise – for the country's foreign policy. His engagement, however, is now closer to the one of the 'propagandist in action' whom rather than *arguing* for a particular course of Italian foreign policy – which he has done in different contexts – is primarily trying to gain the 'hearts and minds' of his readers. To do so, Jean turns to geopolitics, and uses it as a mobilising discourse/device – advancing attractive slogans and making unsubstantiated points often presented as self-evident truths. Therefore, for example, Jean's well-known view that the United States is absolutely central to the protection of a stable international order, and that Europe is unfit to perform it, is put in the astonishingly vague but compelling statement that 'Europe needs a global sheriff to defend globalisation'.[55] Further, we also learn that the success of Bush foreign policy strategy in Iraq is necessary

[53] Jean, 2004, back cover.
[54] Jean, 2004, 95.   [55] Jean, 2004, 106.

to avoid 'a clash of civilisation',[56] which is, Jean continues, a real objective threat to the Western political community. Although not explicitly articulated, this last point cannot but be interpreted as a powerful rhetorical strategy to actually defend the presence of the Italian contingents in Iraq.

Even ignoring the problematic nature of Jean's more empirical assessments, the picture that emerges is rather complex and ambiguous. Jean's geopolitics heavily borrows from realism and yet it is fluid enough to put him in the all-too-cherished position of 'advisor to the prince'. Yet, it is precisely when performing this role that Jean ends up in propaganda and *intentionally* ignores the lesson of those whom he dubs 'post-modernists', i.e. that behind every geopolitical sketch, and especially behind those claiming an objective status, there is always a political design and one which should be brought under the scrutiny of the 'prince' and, one needs to add, of the public.

Carlo Maria Santoro: the last classical geopolitical theorist

For more than ten years Carlo Maria Santoro taught in the faculty of Political Science at the University of Milan. By holding one of the only five IR Chairs in the Italian university system he has been one of the main actors in the process which Luigi Bonanate referred to, at the beginning of the 1990s, as the still unfinished pioneering phase of the discipline in Italy.[57] Santoro began his career as a diplomat, and then combined his academic engagement with a prolific activity as journalist and consultant for the Ministry of Defence for more than twenty years. In the 1990s, he taught at the two main Italian military research institutes and towards the end of his career he was undersecretary in the Ministry of Defence under the Dini government.

As a response to a dissatisfaction with the IR theorising of the second half of the twentieth century as well as with the prevalence, in the post-1989 'globalised' era, of liberal and universalistic approaches, Santoro developed a peculiar theoretical approach to international relations. According to Santoro, these theories have fundamentally overlooked the role of 'space' in international politics, and this means primarily the role of territorial, time and cultural *differences*.[58] Heavily influenced by the thought of conservative figures such as Carl Schmitt, Julius Evola, René Guénon as well as by the geopolitical classics, Santoro urged for a new IR paradigm able to recover the *forces profondes*, that is 'the rights of geography, history and culture'.[59]

---

[56] Jean, 2004, 62.
[57] Bonanate, 1990 and Lucarelli and Menotti, 2002a.
[58] Santoro, 1996a.
[59] Santoro, 1998, 23. Santoro might have derived the emphasis on the *forces profondes* directly from the work of first French (historical) IR school of Pierre Renouvin and Jean-Baptiste Duroselle and the school of the *Annales* or, most likely, indirectly through Raymond Aron's works such as his *Paix et guerre entre les nations*.

Given that the end of the Cold War has reinforced the liberal paradigm with its emphasis on globalisation, universalism and a linear conception of history, Santoro's argument is that IR requires a fortiori a new realist and cyclical approach able to, above all, foreground the spatial dimension of international politics. Only such an approach can uncover the liberal-universalistic theorising for what it really is, that is, the winning ideology of an American 'imperial' design aimed at reconstructing the international system according to a model inspired by institutions and democracy; a model which is economically, technologically and militarily superior; a model, most essentially, which is based on indirect forms of control rather then conquest, and is primarily centred on the Oceans.[60] This is what Santoro calls the 'Oceanic model' of the twenty-first century or, in one word, *Oceania*: 'a system of communication and control among the three oceans [as] the optimal solution of delocalisation and deterritorialization for a global sea power'.[61]

Rather than geopolitics, Santoro predicates the need for a 'geo-theory'. Admittedly drawing from that tradition of classical geopolitical thought stretching from Mackinder and Haushofer to Mahan and Spykman,[62] Santoro's 'geo-theory' is based on an interpretative framework revolving around three couples of 'metaphors': Sea and Land, Eurasia and Oceania, Occident and Orient. To be fair, we are never told with a reasonable degree of analytical preciseness what 'metaphor' actually means in this geo-theory. However, two basic assumptions emerge rather clearly. On the one hand, the assumption is that the history of international relations can be boiled down to the most essential opposition between Sea and Land, that is, insular sea powers and continental land powers. On the other, that the opposition between Occident and Orient is an historically and culturally valid one. In the economy of Santoro's geo-theory these two statements seem to function as the two main *arcana* of international politics – two macro-interpretative keys, or hidden laws of international relations revealed in the empirical patterns of world history.

This original geopolitical/geotheoretical framework has also been applied by Santoro to more empirical questions, such as the issue of Italian foreign policy and of its history since the unification of the country in 1861. *La politica estera di una media potenza* (1991) is not only one of Santoro's most widely-read texts but also one of the most comprehensive and compelling works ever written on the subject. In this book Santoro analyses Italian foreign policy with the help of, once again, his favourite conceptual pairing, that is Sea and Land, to 'discover' the basic 'structures' of Italian foreign policy. His main finding, needless to say, is that geographical factors such as Italy's very positioning between Europe and the Mediterranean offers the key to the country's various diplomatic oscillations, what Rinaldo Petrignani calls Italy's 'pendulum' policy[63] – between

---

[60] Santoro, 1999 and 2000.   [61] Santoro, 1998, 149.
[62] Santoro, 1998, 50.   [63] Petrignani, 1987, 37.

Germany and France in the nineteenth century, between the Triple Alliance and the Entente later, between Europe and the United States more recently. According to Santoro, the country's ambiguous and 'amphibious' peninsular positioning naturally reflects itself in the dual and at times contradictory orientation of its foreign policy. Further, the proverbial weakness and volatility of the country's foreign policy is not really imputable to individual figures – to the point that fascism, Santoro argues, only changed the style, not the substance, of Italian foreign policy[64] – or to the country's political culture. Rather, it needs to be understood as a product of its 'structural', geographical marginality and vulnerability.

Whether in the form of his 'geo-theory' or in his more empirical statements about Italian foreign policy, Santoro seems to rely boldly on geopolitics to uncover the essential, almost Archimedian points from which a theorisation of the subject becomes not only possible but natural and objective. This fascination with theoretical 'purity', this almost esoteric search for the secret *arcana* of international relations, finally revealed in metaphors, clearly sets Santoro apart from other contemporary geopolitical scholars – Jean *in primis* – and offers yet another face of the revival of geopolitics in post-1989 Italy, the one, perhaps, of the last 'classical geopolitical theorist'.

Geopolitics as the new orthodoxy? Some hypotheses

As the chapter has shown, the popularity of geopolitical arguments in the Italian public debate on IR has been such that, to paraphrase Martin Wight, 'we are all geopoliticians now, and the term in this sense needs no argument'. Yet, after questioning what geopolitics is taken to be in the debate, it is time to investigate more in detail why geopolitical analysis has (once again) emerged as an orthodox, legitimate and legitimising discourse around issues of foreign policy, and what this says concerning the case of Italy.

A number of hypotheses are of course possible. First, there is certainly an argument to be made regarding the concomitant revival of geopolitical arguments and the re-emergence of a series of questions pertaining to the idea of 'nation' in post-1989 Italy, and especially issues of 'national identity' and 'national interests'. As mentioned throughout the chapter, in no way can this parallel development be considered coincidental. The fact that the taboos which had originated in the aftermath of World War II have all been broken at once in the span of just a few years is simply too significant to be ignored.

Arguably, and not differently from other countries, Italy's gradual awakening in the post-Cold War environment has prompted a complex foreign policy identity crisis and ongoing reassessment of the country's strategic and

---

[64] Santoro, 1991, 159.

diplomatic 'relative place in the world', as well as of its identity and interests *as a nation*. The greater fluidity of the post-1989 international system has meant a greater freedom in orienting and re-orienting foreign policy as well as a greater propensity to ask 'big questions' concerning the nature and direction of its foreign policy. Now, because of its particular history, these are especially complex questions for Italy. In particular, the incomplete nature of the nineteenth-century nation-building process has not only determined a clear vulnerability to authoritarian experiments in the past, but still plunges the country into cyclical phases of self-doubt and inquiry into its identity and, even more significantly, its 'status'.

Be that as it may, however, there is nothing in this argument able to explain why such a reassessment has been specifically carried out via rather shifty geopolitical notions. In fact, somewhat against the tide, Italian post-1989 geopolitics has not been used, except in a few cases, as a tool to secure national identity, as has been the case in so many other countries. Very few and rather unpopular have been the attempts to frame the issue of national identity as a 'self'/'other' business, and for its most part national identity has been investigated in inclusive and rather open terms.[65]

Why geopolitics then? An enabling function has been certainly played by the rather strong materialistic tradition in Italy's intellectual history, which is still very much present in the public debate. As mentioned previously in the chapter, geopolitics has often been understood as a form of realism up-to-date, or *Real-geo-politik* – an approach which is, not surprisingly, still popular in the land of Machiavelli. Even more interestingly, the post-1989 Italian geopolitics has been the result of a confluence of not one but two strands of materialistic traditions – realism and Marxism. *Limes* embodies such a 'transversal' combination of intellectual traditions most clearly, with left-wing post-communist contributors standing side by side with figures from right-wing, conservative and military backgrounds.

To find the single most important reason why geopolitics has been elevated to the master-key, the *passe-partout*, of international relations in post-1989 Italy, however, one needs to look elsewhere, and in particular at the two functions which geopolitics has more frequently played in the history of Italian foreign policy. First, the function of *socialising* the country in the international system and providing a synthetic, powerful mode of thinking through which to analyse the country's place in the world. In this sense (and in this sense only), the intention of 1930s *Geopolitica* to enhance the country's *coscienza geografica*

---

[65] The one big exception is, of course, the position of one political actor, the Lega Nord, which has explicitly used the dubious geopolitical notion of '*Padania*' to affirm a specific identity common to the north of the country (and connecting this to the rest of continental Europe), while at the same time separating it off from the south of the country, and increasingly of Europe.

is strikingly similar to the 'mission' of *Limes*, to 'understand the world as it really is'. Today just as yesterday geopolitics retains its charm as a supposedly powerful analytic tool able to lay bare the *arcana*, the 'secret' and 'hidden laws' of international relations – a field sufficiently remote and mysterious, and at the same time terribly critical to the country's self-definition.

Second and perhaps more importantly, not by chance the kind of geopolitics which has re-emerged in the post-1989 environment is mainly 'voluntaristic' in nature or, in Jean's iconic words, the *'geography of the prince'*. This version of geopolitics is especially concerned with agency and change, allowing and indeed contemplating a degree of revisionism in foreign policy. Although revisionism has certainly not been one of the main features of Italy's foreign policy through the Cold War – although even then there were revisionist phases, suffice it to mention the case of Giovanni Gronchi – it is striking that just as before 1945 nationalism, geopolitics and revisionism came to form three aspects of the same phenomenon, after 1989 all three of these terms have made a sudden comeback, although naturally in much lighter fashion. But in what way could Italy be considered a 'dissatisfied power'? What is Italy's revisionism aimed at? Central to these questions are the issues of 'status' and 'prestige'. The fear of marginalisation, the anxiety regarding the country's status in world politics, the apprehension to make it in the 'first division' of powers are all rather traditional concerns of Italian foreign policy, manifesting themselves once again today and calling for a discursive apparatus and security imaginary able to devise strategies to enhance and secure the country's role in world politics – which is where geopolitics plays a role.

Indeed, many scholars have identified these concerns and desires and the related form of nationalism as the single most important dimension of Italy's foreign policy since its unification in 1861.[66] Naturally, in the history of Italian foreign policy such concerns have come in waves. They animated the liberal period right up to World War I, convulsed the fascist *ventennio* through and through, only to subside partially after 1945, during the Cold War decades thanks to the identity stabilisation and unique 'situation rent' provided by joining the West and its institutions, the EU and NATO. Italy's gradual awakening in the post-Cold War era has arguably been marked by the return of some of these apprehensions which have been, however, constitutive of the Italian security imaginary since its entrance in the European power game in the second part of the nineteenth century.

This identity crisis and the anxieties about 'our relative place in the world'– as in 1913 the then Italian Foreign Minister Antonino di San Giuliano would put it speaking in front of the Chamber of Deputies in Rome[67] – combined with the overall desire to 'count more' have made the Italian security imaginary

---

[66] Bosworth, 1996; Santoro, 1991 and Vigezzi, 1997.
[67] Bosworth, 1979, 282.

particularly vulnerable to 1989 and have made geopolitics such a useful tool to mobilise at first hand. Confronted with a less certain environment, Italy is at pains to renegotiate its role and identity in world politics, just as it was in the first half of the twentieth century, before the 'iron certainties' of the Cold War put Italy's neurosis to sleep.

However, if this analysis can be considered a more fitting explanation as to why geopolitical arguments have made a comeback in Italy one must not exaggerate the elements of continuity in such a line of argument and assert its 'inevitability'. After all, the reaffirmation of geopolitics in the Italian debate around foreign policy was crucially facilitated by a number of factors regarding the particular political context of the early 1990s, as well as the peculiar state of the field of foreign policy expertise in Italy.

From theory to practice? Contextual factors in the revival of Italian geopolitics

The ascendance of geopolitical thinking in the early 1990s was greatly helped by a number of important contextual and institutional factors. Three of these stand out, and will be analysed in detail in what follows: two concern the political context and games of the 1990s and how this evolved, both domestically and internationally, while the third regards the state of the field in which expertise around foreign policy and international relations is produced in Italy. These factors have not only mediated the process of affirmation of geopolitics in the Italian political debate, but have influenced the degree to which these ideas have played out in the practice of Italy's foreign policy.

It goes without saying that the international relations of the 1990s provided the first great catalyst for the return of geopolitics in Italy. Italy's concerns with the crises which erupted in the Balkans at the beginning of the decade, for instance, clearly combined a political and a geographical component. The instability which then started to characterise the arc of countries stretching from the North of Africa to Central Asia and the Gulf had clear repercussions for a neighbouring country such as Italy in terms of rising number of migrants, greater exposure to illicit international trafficking, and a more general sense of insecurity at its borders. All these elements objectively combined new political and geographical elements, making geopolitics perhaps an easy candidate for a revival.

However, an even bigger role as permissive condition was played by the transformation of Italy's domestic context over the last twenty years. In particular, the affirmation of new political actors on the political scene was instrumental in affirming a bland yet unmistakable form of neo-nationalist discourse in the political arena, and re-legitimising geopolitics as part of that discourse. In order for geopolitical ideas to establish an hegemony over the field, in other words, it was essential that political actors interested in capitalising upon its arguments, such as the centre-right, emerged and quickly became dominant. Arguments which were previously available, but politically marginal in the public debate, were then used at the level of political discourse – but also as justifications for a 'new' foreign policy practice.

To start with, the period which goes from the end of the Cold War to roughly 1995 corresponded to a time of great fluidity in Italy's domestic political situation, with all major parties undergoing at best structural transformations or, at worse, a complete collapse. It was precisely at this time, under the leadership of Gianni De Michelis (1989–1992), that Italy launched a number of rather short-lived yet significant initiatives, such as the *Pentagonale*/Central European Initiative (May 1990), the Conference on Security and Cooperation in the Mediterranean (CSCM, September 1990), as well as the rather surprising proposal for a European seat at the UN Security Council (September 1990). Of these, the first two were clearly cast and justified in bland yet unmistakable geopolitical terms by De Michelis himself.[68] One needs to add that the figure of De Michelis was key in prompting a certain discourse around Italy's 'national interests' and geopolitics. Indeed, he anticipated and in part at least inspired what was to follow – as his numerous contributions in *Limes* and *Affari Esteri* in the early 1990s demonstrate.

A less inventive and more muscular foreign policy was carried forward by Antonio Martino (1994–1995), for the new Berlusconi-led centre-right coalition. This was perhaps the time when the public debate around 'national interests' and the revival of geopolitics reached its climax. And it was in this context, for instance, that the issue of national borders became once again contentious, with the right-wing party *Alleanza Nazionale* (AN) campaigning for a redrafting of the Treaty of Osimo which had decided upon Italy's Eastern border. Together with the ill-fated demand to be part of the then forming 'Contact Group' for Bosnia, this was perhaps the most visible manifestation of how the more clamorous, indeed extreme views expressed in fora such as *Limes* could rather unproblematically translate into foreign policy practice.[69]

After the electoral victory of 1995 the centre-left coalition in government pursued a foreign policy certainly less inspired by the *rhetoric* of 'national interests' although, at times, not necessarily less assertive.[70] Especially under the Prodi government, the emphasis was clearly not so much on the opportunities to expand the country's influence in the regions, but rather on proving that it was a 'good citizen' of the international community, actively participating

---

[68] See especially De Michelis, 2003; for a critique, see Ferraris, 1993.

[69] See Romano, 1996.

[70] It was under the government of Dini that Santoro was called to the post of undersecretary of defence, where he served until the government's fall, in May 1996.

in multilateral fora such as the EU and the UN, and contributing to peace, stability and order.[71]

Lastly, since the victory of the centre-right in 2001 Italian foreign policy has once again experienced a reversal, this time back to the muscular tendencies of the early 1990s, although adapted to a different international context – with geopolitical ideas once again providing a source of inspiration. Most evidently, the three main tenets of the second Berlusconi's government in foreign policy, namely Atlanticism, neo-nationalism and Euroscepticism correspond to the strategy put forward, as seen, by one of the most active Italian analysts of geopolitics, Carlo Jean, in his latest works.[72]

But an analysis of the enabling conditions for a revival of geopolitics would not be complete without mentioning the third set of contextual factors which have crucially facilitated the success of geopolitics. These have to do on the one hand with the particular features of the foreign policy process and, on the other, with the state of Italy's 'epistemic community' that provides foreign policy expertise.

By and large dominated by a rather heavy bureaucratic apparatus and increasingly centralised in the hands of the 'executive dyad' – President of the Council and Foreign Minister – the foreign policy process in Italy has been traditionally at the margins of parliamentary scrutiny, with very few debates high on the political agenda except in times of international crisis.[73] The rather conservative diplomatic culture of the Foreign Ministry, the *Farnesina*, has traditionally meant an extraordinary impermeability to progressive, let alone reformist, instances while allowing an exceptional (if not embarrassing, at times) closeness to the world of business and finance,[74] and a high degree of interpenetration with the Defence Ministry and military institutions. The job of discussing foreign policy issues and elaborating foreign policy strategies is for its most part kept in-house (a job which pertains especially to the *Unità di Analisi e Programmazione*, part of the General Secretariat), and relies on a very few external think-tanks, the most prominent of which is of course the partially Ministry-funded Istituto Affari Internazionali (IAI), in Rome.[75]

---

[71] D'Alema's more 'realist' foreign policy leanings, especially manifest in the case of the Kosovo intervention, would fit uneasily in this account. Suffice it to reiterate here, however, that 'realist' foreign policy assumptions often cut across political groupings and really present the default foreign policy paradigm.

[72] For a more comprehensive assessment of Berlusconi's 'new course' see Brighi, 2006.

[73] Studies on the Italian foreign policy *process* are in notoriously short supply and most of them are written in Italian by former personnel (see for instance Serra, 1984 and 1999). The notable exceptions in English language are, unfortunately, not up-to-date but still worth reading (Kogan, 1963; Sassoon, 1978).

[74] See Fossati, 1999 and, for an example in practice, Dini, 2001.

[75] For a general study of IR think-tanks in Italy, see Lucarelli and Menotti, 2002b; for interesting though brief remarks on Italy's foreign policy epistemic community, see Andreatta and Hill, 2000, 258–262.

The resurgence of public interest in international affairs which has accompanied the end of the Cold War has put an increasingly participatory pressure on the foreign policy process and its machinery, which has however failed to determine any substantial changes so far. In sum, Italy remains a country where foreign policy is still perceived not only as a distant and complicated subject, but as a domain where by and large only 'experts' are allowed to have a say – and that category usually includes only diplomats, military figures, and a very few IR (preferably American) analysts.

If these are the broad features of the foreign policy process itself, a process far from being pluralistic in terms of ideas or actors, the current state of the field of production of foreign policy expertise is also to be investigated, in that it provides the last enabling condition for the revival of geopolitics. Briefly put, the particular magnitude of this revival depended on the peculiar characteristics of the field of foreign policy expertise in Italy – had this been bigger, more pluralistic and open; had there been alternative policy paradigms on offer; had the epistemic community around foreign policy issues been more articulated; and lastly, had the discipline of IR enjoyed a stronger academic status both in quantitative and qualitative terms, then geopolitics would have encountered greater challenges on the path to its revival. In a different intellectual and cultural environment, it would not have risen to provide the automatic default prism through which Italian intellectuals and policy makers look at international relations.

After all, in the English-speaking world geopolitics represents the stage of infancy, almost the pre-history of IR as a social science, hence its revival is not surprising in a case such as Italy where IR remains heavily underdeveloped. Even more importantly, the success of enterprises such as Limes had in fact the perverse effect of further isolating the world of IR academia from both the arena of policy making and that of public debates, making the already deplored gap between theory and practice even wider. With its maps and sweeping arguments, Limes gave many diplomats and policy makers the false impression of completely mastering international politics at very low intellectual cost (i.e. no need to engage with complex theoretical arguments). Arguably, geopolitics has made it even more difficult to bridge this gap in the future.[76]

Another interpretation is also possible, however, which concerns the broader cultural traditions dominating the political debates among intellectuals. Given the special attention that some Italian intellectual circles (especially on the left) have always paid to the cultural and political debates happening in France, it is not so far-fetched to hypothesise a direct influence of the French understanding and revival of *géopolitique* – intended as an approach with an

---

[76] We are indebted to Sonia Lucarelli for this insight.

autonomous disciplinary status, parallel to that of IR, and mainly linked to the study of geography, military doctrines and area expertise – on *Limes* and the other main protagonists of the geopolitics debate in Italy. It was precisely the unpredictable convergence of the two most powerful and traditionally opposed constituencies – the world of 'progressive' intellectuals and the 'arch-conservative' world of foreign policy experts (diplomats and militaries) – which made geopolitical discourses in post-Cold War Italy so remarkably successful and legitimate, and hence provided a further enabling condition for its outstanding revival.

Conclusions

Perhaps it is not completely surprising that the end of the Cold War has brought about a revival of geopolitical thought in Italy. Both Jean and Santoro would agree that the end of the Cold War, by destroying the clear-cut divisions and geopolitical representations of the bipolar confrontation, was first of all a true 'spatial catastrophe'[77] and, as a consequence, paved the way to the reopening of 'the struggle for space'. Their neoclassical versions of geopolitics, however, together with the more popular discussion well exemplified by the *Limes* phenomenon points to a more limited national story: the re-emergence of the national discourse on the national interest (and its geopolitical corollaries) in the context of a double crisis; a crisis of foreign policy identity and security imaginary in the wake of the end of the West–East bipolar confrontation, on the one hand, and a crisis of domestic politics, and in particular of the two universalist rival political cultures that dominated Italian politics since World War II, on the other.

Be that as it may, the aim of this chapter was to advance some reflections on the nature and causes of the renaissance of geopolitical thinking and practice in post-1989 Italy. As it has been argued, geopolitical themes have re-emerged in a variety of publications as well as, more generally, in the public debate around foreign policy and international relations. The surprising convergence of progressive and conservative intellectual sectors around the 'unholy geopolitical alliance' most clearly embodied by *Limes* has, finally, sanctioned the affirmation of geopolitics as a kind of new orthodoxy in the Italian debate – an ubiquitous and trendy term of reference, although often one with equivocal meanings. This has in turn partially fed into foreign policy practice, following a trajectory which the chapter has tried to outline. Most importantly, the appeal of geopolitical arguments in the Italian debate needs to be understood in the context of a deep post-1989 foreign policy identity crisis and with reference

---

[77] Colombo, 1996.

to both the background history of Italian foreign policy as well as the current state of the field of production of foreign policy expertise, as well as of IR academia broadly speaking. The rudimentary yet compelling assertions typical of geopolitical writings, as well as its essentialist claims to pure knowledge of 'profound forces' in international relations, are all arguments to which Italy has proved, somewhat inevitably, still particularly vulnerable.

7

Turkey's 'geopolitics dogma'

PINAR BILGIN

A first look at Turkey's case reveals it to be an 'ideal' one, which affirms the hypothesis 'tested' in this volume: that a 'revival' of geopolitical thought occurs in those settings where a crisis of foreign policy identity coincides with a pre-existing disposition to materialist foreign policy thinking, active involvement of key actors fluent in geopolitics-speak and their employment of this discourse in pursuing a conservative agenda. A second look, however, calls for qualifying this hypothesis in that geopolitical discourse has been employed in Turkey by a variety of actors in pursuit of political agendas that are conservative/radical in different ways – so much so that the same set of notions and images driven from classical geopolitical thought have been invoked in justifying policy agendas diametrically opposed to each other. For example, in the post-Cold War era, whereas a coalition of 'Eurosceptic' actors have tapped geopolitics to make a case for Turkey remaining outside European integration, those wishing to make a case for Turkey joining European accession have employed the same discourse. This, I offer, could be understood as a function of the historical centrality of geopolitical assumptions and language to Turkey's security imaginary – heretofore referred to as the 'geopolitics dogma'.

The chapter begins by laying out the main features of Turkey's 'geopolitics dogma' in an attempt to highlight the mutually constitutive relationship between security imaginary, (foreign policy) identity and (re)production of geopolitical thought. While it may seem counterintuitive to begin with 'the geopolitics dogma', I have chosen to do so to underscore my finding that the post-1989 'revival' of geopolitical thought in Turkey is more one of quantity and less of quality. That is to say, references to geopolitical assumptions and language have never been far from central to Turkey's security imaginary. The end of the Cold War has only reinforced an already existing propensity to invoke geopolitics in support of policy choices of various kinds – conservative and radical.

Put differently, the chapter begins with 'the geopolitics dogma' not because this is how I began my research, but because this is where the process of tracing the changes in the practical, formal and popular discourses of myriad actors in

Turkey has led me – i.e. historical ubiquity of geopolitical assumptions and language to Turkey's foreign policy discourse. In what follows, I outline the main features of the dogma and highlight its historical centrality to Turkey's security imaginary. Next, the chapter shows that the post-1989 period in Turkey witnessed a proliferation of publications and think-tanks seeking to provide a 'geopolitical perspective'. While there was not much that was new in terms of ideas (after all General Suat İlhan, Turkey's foremost geopolitician since the 1960s and Professor Ahmet Davutoğlu, current Minister of Foreign Affairs and author of the best-seller *Geopolitical Sensitivity*, while coming from different professional and ideological backgrounds, tap into the same set of ideas), what was new was the widespread dissemination of these ideas. In the third part of the chapter, I locate this quantitative revival in Turkey's geopolitical thought in international politics – namely, the post-1989 crisis in Turkey's already fragile 'Western' identity.[1] The argument comes full circle in the fourth section where I highlight the domestic politics dimension as bringing about the centrality and persistence of geopolitical assumptions and language to Turkey's foreign policy discourse – namely the role of the military, the state of International Relations as an academic field, and the project of locating Turkey in the 'West'. The fifth and final section further illustrates this inter- and intra-national complex with reference to post-1989 debates on Turkey's accession to European integration, where the versatile yet ultimately indeterminate nature of geopolitics as discourse is highlighted with reference to myriad actors' resort to geopolitics in the struggle over locating Turkey in the 'West' (read: EU) or elsewhere, with radically different implications for the country's domestic politics. As such, the chapter has implications beyond Turkey's case in that, while underscoring the versatility of geopolitics as discourse in fixing (foreign policy) identity it also highlights the fragility of such a 'fix' – contrary to assumptions of determinacy flaunted by geopoliticans.

Turkey's 'geopolitics dogma' (identifying a 'pre-existing materialist disposition in foreign policy thinking')

In accounting for Turkey's actors' (pre-)disposition towards geopolitics, I offer the concept of 'geopolitics dogma', defined as a structure of well-established assumptions as to what geography tells one to do and why this makes sense. Different from any geopolitical truth-claim that is likely to enjoy some authority warranted by the ostensibly 'scientific' and/or 'god-given'/'natural' quality of geopolitics (as in Classical Geopolitics), the 'geopolitics dogma' is a structure of geopolitical truth-claims, the constituent parts of which support one another

---

[1] This is not to suggest that foreign policy identity is not precarious elsewhere.

in a tautological fashion thereby rendering it impossible to verify the truth/falsity of statements emerging out of this structure.[2]

In identifying the main features of Turkey's geopolitics dogma, I draw from formal geopolitics as shaped by Turkey's two foremost geopoliticians, namely, General (Ret.) Suat İlhan and Professor Ahmet Davutoğlu while pointing to inter-textuality between formal, practical and popular forms of discourse.

General İlhan is a well-known public commentator and prolific author who has published some twenty-one books[3] including several studies on various aspects of Turkey's geopolitics.[4] Professor Davutoğlu is the author of the 2001 non-fiction best-seller, *Stratejik Derinlik* (Strategic Depth).[5] Professor Davutoğlu's ideas deserve particular treatment not only because of their apparent popularity, but also because he has had access to the 'Prince's ear' during the AKP's (*Adalet ve Kalkınma Partisi* – Justice and Development Party) term in office (since November 2002). Davutoğlu was appointed as Ambassador-without-portfolio by the AKP government and served as advisor to both the Prime Minister and the Minister of Foreign Affairs 2002 through 2009. In 2009, he was appointed as Minister of Foreign Affairs.

The first feature of Turkey's geopolitics dogma is the understanding drawn from Classical Geopolitics that geographical elements are 'natural' and 'constant' 'facts' that are 'out there' waiting to be 'discovered' by the geopolitician and that politics driven by the 'facts' of geography is a foil to idealism, ideology and human will. Adopting such an unreflexive approach to geography helps to establish geopolitics as the 'view from nowhere' that offers a 'scientific' and 'objective' outlook on world affairs. Once geopolitics is established as a 'privileged perspective', alternative views are marginalised by default, as they come to be considered 'unscientific', 'idealistic', 'political' or outright 'ideological'. Indeed, General İlhan considers geography to be the only 'constant' component of geopolitics (other components being the human and temporal dimensions).[6]

---

[2] Given Turkey's current divide between the so-called 'secularists' and 'Islamists', it is difficult to underplay the dogma's appeal to and authority over both those favouring 'scientific' and/or 'divine' justification for their truth-claims.

[3] See İlhan, 1971, 1989, 1999, 2000, 2002 and 2004.

[4] There is also a distinct Ottoman/Turkish tradition. For instance, the chronicles of the seventeenth-century Ottoman historian Naima are replete with the metaphor of 'state as an organism'. See Thomas and Itzkowitz, 1972.

[5] Davutoğlu's book went through several printings in a manner unusual for a book of academic nature and was lauded by the Turkish media (see, for example, Akyol, 2003; Kömürcü, 2003 and Yılmaz, 2001). As of this writing, the book was in its twenty-ninth printing. Most of those who purchase the book are likely to be university students who are assigned the book on Turkish Foreign Policy courses – which also begs explanation. That a book of such polemical nature is assigned to university students as required reading in courses on Turkey's Foreign Policy says less about the reception of the book than the state of International Relations (IR) in Turkey (see below).

[6] İlhan, 1989.

Geopolitical analysis is a 'search for truth', he writes; it is a way of looking at the world that is untainted by personal or political ambitions or cultural procliv-ities.[7] Accordingly, İlhan portrays geopolitics as 'the only branch of knowledge that could uncover and help to establish' such 'realities', which he views as 'the means and ends of threats to security'.[8]

The second feature of Turkey's geopolitics dogma is the axiomatic nature of widely held views about the primacy of geography as a factor shaping world politics. Since geographical knowledge is portrayed as the 'view from nowhere', policy recommendations that are justified with reference to geo-politics are portrayed as 'fait accompli of geography'.[9] 'Geopolitics is polit-ics shaped by geography', writes General İlhan, 'sensitivities of countries are determined by geographical factors'.[10] Professor Davutoğlu concurs: strategies should be rooted in 'geopolitical, geocultural and geoeconomic realities'.[11] As such, the essentially political character of policy making is denied; geopolitical truth-claims are offered in place of political outcomes – geopolitically correct policies, as it were.

The third feature of the geopolitics dogma is the assumption that Turkey's geographical location is somehow more unique than others and that it some-how has more deterministic power over Turkey's policies than other countries. The extra-determinism of Turkey's geography is considered to stem from its 'uniqueness'. For, it is a 'central' state that 'constitutes the hinge of the world island that is made up of three continents. It is both the lock and the key to this hinge. It connects the Mediterranean and the Black Sea ... It brings together and keeps apart the Balkans, Caucasus and the Middle East'.[12]

İlhan assumes Turkey's geography to hold extra-determinism over its foreign as well as domestic policies when he maintains that only 'strong unitary nation states' can survive in Turkey's geographical location.[13] Needless to say, İlhan understands state strength in solely military terms, and not in terms of the strengthening of democratic norms and practices and state–society relations in addition to the military. The argument that Turkey should become a 'strong state' rests upon a transformed version of the 'state as an organism' metaphor drawn from Classical Geopolitics.[14] Whereas Classical geopoliticians under-scored geography's determinism over a country's 'needs' and 'interests' in the inter-national arena (as with Lebensraum), the transformed version as found in İlhan's work stresses the determinacy of geography over state structure and domestic policy making (i.e. intra-national relations).[15]

---

[7] See also Davutoğlu, 2001; Olcaytu, 1996 and Sezgin and Yılmaz, 1965.
[8] İlhan, 1989, 5 and 30.   [9] İlhan, 1989, 55.
[10] İlhan, 1989, 3 and x.   [11] Davutoğlu, 2001, 58.
[12] İlhan, 2000, 34.   [13] İlhan, 2000, 36. See also Işık, 1987.
[14] See Bilgin, 2007.
[15] For a discussion on the South American context, see Hepple, 1992.

The transformed version of the 'states as an organism' metaphor is invoked in both the high school 'National Security' textbook (see below) and the 2005 fiction best-seller *Metal Fırtına* (Metal Storm).[16] The novel tells the story of an imaginary US invasion of Turkey in the year 2007. The plot begins with the collapse of Turkey's defences against the invading US forces. The military failure is represented as a consequence of a political failure; the latter is seen as having been caused by politicians who have overlooked the exigencies of Turkey's geography that 'demand' a 'strong state' understood in the above-mentioned narrow terms.[17]

The fourth feature of the geopolitics dogma is the prevalence of representations of Turkey as surrounded by 'enemies' and occupying a geographical location that is the 'envy' of friend and foe alike. İlhan writes:

> Turkey occupies a very significant position according to both the heartland theory [of Mackinder] and the rimland theory [of Spykman] … No matter which theory you adopt in your analysis Turkey is one of those countries that demand priority at both the regional and global levels.[18]

In a similar fashion, at the end of *Metal Fırtına*, the great powers' decision to put together a coalition led by Russia and to press on the already embattled United States to withdraw from Turkey is explained again through appealing to geopolitical truth-claims: 'These lands have a strategic significance', Turkey's fictional prime minister wryly notes: '[n]o powerful country would want another to get hold of these territories all by itself'.[19] As such, other states are portrayed (in Turkey's formal and popular geopolitical discourse alike) as having malicious 'goals' and 'intentions' whereas Turkey innocuously responds to their actions.[20]

Having identified the main features of Turkey's 'geopolitics dogma', the remainder of this section highlights its centrality to Turkey's security imaginary.[21] One way of doing this is to look at the classics of Turkey's foreign policy,

---

[16] The novel's title, 'Metal Storm', invokes a parallel with 'Desert Storm', the US-led coalition war against Iraq (1991). *Metal Fırtına* took Turkey's close observers by surprise not only because of the outrageousness of its plot but also due to its record sales. At the time of this writing, the *Metal Fırtına* was in its sixth printing with 50,000 copies published each time. Although this figure may not seem so high for a population of over seventy million, given Turkey's not-so-strong readership, the significance of this sales record by two (until then) virtually unknown authors cannot be underestimated.

[17] For analyses of popular geopolitics in Turkey, see Yanık, 2008 and 2009.

[18] İlhan, 1989, 61. See also Doğanay, 1989; Gürkan, 1987a, 1987b; Harp Akademileri Komutanlığı, 1963; Işık, 1987, and Ü. Özdağ, 2003.

[19] Uçar and Turna, 2005, 160.

[20] Such a portrayal of Turkey's international relations does not only render invisible the agency of Turkey's policy-makers, but also that of their global counterparts. After all, if Turkey is a 'central' state, then others' policies too should be considered as exigencies of politics as determined by geography.

[21] See also Bilgin, 2003b.

Man: 'Germany has harsh winters. They have to plan ahead. This has resulted in German
   advance in development and planning'; 'The English have a small country, they have
   travelled to other lands. As a result, they have advanced in seafaring and science'; 'In
   Israel water and land are scarce; they have developed new irrigation techniques'; 'the
   United States is far from Europe. To be able to monitor from far, they have advanced
   in information technology.'

Boy: 'But then what did we develop?'

Man: 'Nothing. For we are a country of immense geopolitical significance.'

Figure 7.1. Political cartoon by Behiç Ak demonstrating 'geopolitics as common sense'
in Turkey. Reproduced by kind permission of the artist

which invariably begin with discussions on the primacy (if not determinacy)
of geography.[22] A more recent and widely used textbook on Turkey's foreign
policy is by Baskın Oran (2005). The two-volume textbook's singular moment
of reflection on the primacy of geopolitical truth-claims in Turkey's foreign
policy discourse is a political cartoon (reproduced in Figure 7.1).

   Another way of highlighting the centrality of geopolitics dogma to Turkey's
security imaginary is to point to those instances when geopolitical truth-claims
are marshalled to respond to the challenges directed against various arguments
emerging out of the imaginary. In what follows, I will resort to the latter course
and focus on post-Cold War foreign policy debates.

   A significant component of Turkey's security imaginary has been the
Republican leaders' answer to the identity question: 'Who are we?'.[23] 'Western'
was the answer the founders of the Republic offered.[24] During the inter-
war period, they sought to write Turkey's 'Westernness' into 'race' and

---

[22] See Gönlübol *et al.*, 1989 [1967] and Sander, 1982.
[23] Weldes, 1999a.   [24] Bilgin, 2009.

'language' – tapping then prevalent theories of identity.[25] Later, during the Cold War, the ideological stance of anti-communism and NATO membership served as the marker of Turkey's 'Western' identity.[26] Turkey's geographical location meant its ideological stance mattered even more. For years, Turkey assumed a key role in the choreography of NATO defence against Soviet expansionism. In the post-Cold War period, challenges to Turkey's 'Westernness' have increasingly been met by writing it into 'space'. For instance, in response to Valéry Giscard d'Estaing who declared that 'Turkey's capital [is] not in Europe, 95 % of its population [lives] outside Europe, and it [is] not a European country',[27] various actors have pointed to Turkey's Cold War contributions to security in Europe and what it has to offer towards advancing European Security and Defence Policy (ESDP). Needless to say, both qualities are considered to be a function of Turkey's geographical location and its implications for politics.[28] The assumption being that, if not culture, religion, ideology or civilisation, geopolitics secures for Turkey a place in the 'West' and/or 'Europe'.[29]

What renders geopolitics discourse particularly powerful in Turkey has also to do with its 'Westernness'. Turkey's geopoliticians treat as a 'timeless truth' the prominence British geopolitician Halford Mackinder ascribes to Turkey's geography. Although Turkey is not located in the 'heartland' as plotted by Mackinder, it somehow emerges, in the writings of Turkey's geopoliticians, as a 'central state'.[30] Turkey is a 'central state', various authors assure their readers, not because we, as Turks, would like to think so, but because world-renowned Western geopoliticians, such as Mackinder, say so. While Turkey's geopoliticians begin their studies with an overview of the ideas and ideals of 'Western' geopoliticians, the substance of what the canons of classical geopolitics say is somehow considered less important when compared to what cursory references to them allow Turkey's authors to 'say'.

The relationship between the geopolitics dogma and the Sèvres metaphor, another component of Turkey's security imaginary, further illustrates its centrality.[31] The Sèvres Treaty[32] marked an attempt by the Allies to divide up the

---

[25] See Aytürk, 2004 and Göksu-Özdoğan, 2001.

[26] Yılmaz and Bilgin, 2005.

[27] 'Turkey Entry "Would Destroy EU"', 2002.

[28] See, for example, Bir, 1998 and Ministry of Defence of the Republic of Turkey, 2000.

[29] Bilgin, 2004.

[30] See, for example, Doğanay, 1989; Hacısalihoğlu, 2003; Harp Akademileri Komutanlığı, 1963; Ü. Özdağ, 2003; Türsan, 1971b and Uzun, 1981.

[31] The Sèvres metaphor has a rather paradoxical relationship with Turkey's actors' claim to a Western identity. Whereas being 'Western' requires identification with other Western actors, the effect the Sèvres metaphor seems to have on the psyche of many is symptomatic of a failure to trust those very same actors. Yet, this paradox is explained away through resort to geopolitics: since it is geography that drives world politics, neither Turkey nor other state actors can resist faits accomplis of geography. Past 'Western' advances on Turkey are therefore understood as exigencies of politics determined by geography.

[32] The Sèvres Treaty, 1920.

Ottoman Empire following World War I. The Treaty comprised clauses that allowed for the division of most of the Empire's territories between Britain, France, Italy and Greece. It also recognised the right of self-determination for the Armenian and Kurdish populations thus rendering the Empire a shadow of its former self. In present-day Turkey, the Sèvres metaphor is frequently invoked to remind the audiences of the destructive effects of the Treaty, thereby reinforcing the trauma. In the novel *Metal Fırtına,* for instance, one phase of the US military operation (whereby Turkey's territories are carved up between a US mining corporation, the Greek Orthodox Church and Armenia) is dubbed 'Operation Sèvres', in an all-too-obvious reference to the Treaty.

Lest the continuing relevance of the Sèvres metaphor as a guide to Turkey's foreign policy are questioned, the timelessness of 'Western conspiracies' as such is written into space. Consider the textbook of the high school course, 'National Security' (Milli Güvenlik Bilgisi). This course, which is compulsory for all high school students, has been a part of the curriculum since 1926. Previously it was called 'Military Service', reflecting its post-Independence War purpose of generating awareness of the 'virtues of military service'. In time, the title as well as the content of the course has changed. The most recent version[33] devotes a significant number of pages to Turkey's international relations.[34] What is interesting for the purposes of this chapter is that Turkey's international relations are represented as a function of its geography. The first few sentences of the textbook read as follows: 'The Turkish Republic, because of its geopolitical position, has experienced [political] ploys by external powers. The Turkish youth need to be prepared to confront such ploys.'[35]

In the rest of the book, the schemes laid out by 'external powers' are discussed in detail with recourse to geopolitical truth-claims while Turkey's foreign policies are represented as mere responses to the aggressive behaviour of others; thus erasing the agency of Turkey's policy makers and representing them as mere slaves to the exigencies of geography.

The significance of the 'National Security' textbook cannot be underestimated not only because it is required reading for all high school students, but also because, as Ayşe Gül Altınay[36] has highlighted, it is the only course in the high school curriculum that takes up current affairs issues. It is not only substance but also style that the 'National Security' textbook disseminates. For, the only language high school students learn to use when making sense of international relations is that of geopolitics as taught by military officers following a textbook written by the military. Young men who do not have access to high school are exposed to this language during compulsory military service, as a part of which they attend seminars on Turkey's international relations couched

---

[33] Lise Milli Güvenlik Bilgisi, 2004 [1998].
[34] Altınay, 2005.   [35] Lise Milli Güvenlik Bilgisi, 2004, 7.
[36] Altınay, 2003.

in geopolitical terms. Although it is difficult to know the extent to which course material is carried over to their life after school and/or military service, it could be surmised that the course's bearing for current affairs issues makes it somewhat more interesting to students/conscripts compared to other course material that has less palpable relevance to the 'reality' 'out there'.

The chapter so far has identified the main features of Turkey's geopolitics dogma and highlighted its centrality to Turkey's security imaginary. The next section is designed as an exposé of the ubiquity of appeals to geopolitical truth-claims in post-Cold War Turkey through which the dogma and the security imaginary of which it is a central part has been re-produced.

Post-Cold War ubiquity of geopolitical truth-claims (a 'revival or not?')

In recent years, close observers of Turkey have witnessed a proliferation of publications, publishing outlets and think-tanks that claim to provide a 'privileged' perspective on world politics by virtue of their 'geopolitical outlook'. There is, for instance, the journal *Jeopolitik* (Geopolitics, 2003ff.) and the two in-house journals of ASAM, *Avrasya Dosyası* (The Eurasian Dossier, 1994–) and *Stratejik Analiz* (Strategic Analysis, 2000ff.). All three are policy journals that publish articles on world politics in general and Turkey's international relations in particular. They come out regularly and are distributed widely to bookshops and newsagents around the country. There is also *Strateji* (Strategy, 2004ff.), the weekly supplement of the centre-left daily, *Cumhuriyet*, published in cooperation with a privately funded think-tank, TUSAM (Center for the Study of National Security Strategies, established in 2004) that specialises in research into 'national security strategies'.[37] Although it is difficult to know what kind of readership these new publications have, the very fact that they have been coming out with minimum interruption may be considered indicative of interest in the kind of 'geopolitical outlook' they purport to provide.[38]

---

[37] *Cumhuriyet*'s readership is not strong but loyal; for years, it has been the newspaper of Turkey's state elite and other bearers of a statist conception of politics. For TUSAM, see www.tusam.net.

[38] Past examples tended to be short-lived. The only exceptions are those published by publicly funded universities (such as the more academically-oriented *The Turkish Yearbook of International Relations*, published since 1960 by Ankara University's Faculty of Political Science) and publicly funded think-tanks (as with the policy-oriented quarterly journal *Foreign Policy*, published since 1974 by the Ankara-based Foreign Policy Institute). Both are specialised journals unlikely to be (physically and/or intellectually) accessible to those who are outside the field. There is also the new privately funded academic journal *Uluslararası İlişkiler* (International Relations). The latter's success warns against reading too much into the longevity of geopolitics journals and magazines.

Among Turkey's new think-tanks, the now defunct ASAM is the one that first comes to mind – not always for the right reasons: the bold manner in which ASAM pushed for a military-focused foreign policy led some to quip that 'the centre has a lot of tanks and not-so-considerable novel thinking'. ASAM stands for 'Avrasya Stratejik Araştırmalar Merkezi' (Eurasian Centre for Strategic Studies). It was set up in 1999 as Turkey's first privately funded think-tank specialising in strategy and security issues. During the decade it was functional, ASAM did not merely claim to provide a privileged 'geopolitical perspective' on and insight into international relations, but also actively sought to carve out an intellectual space wherein citizens' 'geopolitical consciousness' would flourish – to quote the centre's website.[39]

Over the years, ASAM published several monographs and edited volumes on 'geopolitics', including the Turkish translation of an edited volume by Colin Gray,[40] perhaps the most prominent contemporary representative of the Classical Geopolitics tradition, and the collected works of Colonel Muzaffer Özdağ.[41] Late Colonel Özdağ, besides being the father of ASAM president, Professor Ümit Özdağ, is better known as a prolific author and a prominent figure in Turkey's ultra-nationalist right.[42] When Colonel Özdağ initially began to air his views on Turkish nationalism and the need to reach out to Turkey's Central Asian brethren, it was still during the Cold War and flaunting such ideas was not without its dangers; those who dared risked being branded as a threat to national security.[43] Geopolitics proved a safe outlet for Colonel Özdağ's ideas; after all, it was not he, but the 'science' of geopolitics that made these recommendations. Arguably, it was in and through geopolitics that Özdağ found a broader audience for his otherwise potentially destabilising views and reach beyond his traditional (ultra-nationalist) constituency. His ideas were aired once again in the aftermath of the dissolution of the Soviet Union when ASAM reprinted his collected works.

Another prominent geopolitician whose works have reached broader audiences in recent years is General (Ret.) Suat İlhan, who, as noted above, is no ordinary retired general; he is also a prolific author and a public commentator. During 1967–1969, he set up and taught the first geopolitics course at

[39] See ASAM's mission statement at www.avsam.org.tr/misyon.asp (accessed 26 May 2006).

[40] Gray, 2003.

[41] Following Özdağ's death in 2002, ASAM published his collected works in four volumes. See M. Özdağ, 2003. See also Özdağ, 2000 and 2001.

[42] Colonel Özdağ first came to prominence as a low-ranking military officer partaking in the 1960 military coup. When dissent surfaced among the coup-makers, he was one of the first to be forced to early retirement. Özdağ became a central figure in Turkish nationalist right until he retired from active politics in 1971.

[43] The nature of the threat was understood as ethnic irredentism at home and Soviet wrath in response to perceived expansionism on the part of Turkey. These threat perceptions, in turn, are rooted in the trauma of World War I whereby 'pan-Turkist' adventurism on the part of some Ottoman statesmen led to disastrous losses on the Russian front.

the Military Academy. His lecture notes were later published in book form[44] and have, since then, been used as teaching material at the Military Academy and the National Security Academy.[45] His classical work, *Jeopolitik Duyarlılık* (Geopolitical Sensitivity) was published in 1989 by the state-funded Turkish Historical Society but soon after sank into oblivion save the aforementioned institutions. It was as part of post-Cold War debates on Turkey's accession to European integration that İlhan and his 'geopolitical outlook' gained a new lease of life. His 2000 book, *Why 'No' to the European Union: The Geopolitical Perspective* was widely distributed and read. Volume II of the same book followed in 2002. In 2003, *Geopolitical Sensitivity* was reprinted; this time by a commercial publishing house.[46]

In his early works, which are replete with approving references to Classical Geopolitics, General İlhan had called for adopting geopolitics as the guide for shaping Turkey's domestic and foreign policies. To emphasise how 'accurately' geopolitics describes the world, İlhan referred to the case of Germany and its search for colonies in the late nineteenth and early twentieth centuries. Yet in a typically unreflexive fashion, he failed to note that if geopolitics is able to describe 'accurately' such developments, this is because geopolitics – like realism during the Cold War – 'has helped to *construct* some of that reality'.[47] In his later publications, İlhan focused more on specific foreign policy issues, as with the prospect of Turkey's EU membership, which he is staunchly against. Notwithstanding his conviction that the 'EU won't let Turkey in' ('because of its Muslim identity', İlhan's point of convergence with Samuel P. Huntington), İlhan nevertheless leaves open the possibility that Turkey may become a full member, but only as part of a 'Western conspiracy' designed to carve out some of its territories and/or render it defenceless.[48] In this scenario, EU conditionality is portrayed as part of a conspiracy designed to weaken Turkey's military and therefore render defenceless the secular unitary make-up of the Republic – yet another instance of Turkey's geopoliticians invoking the Sèvres metaphor to justify their scepticism toward Turkey's accession to European integration.[49]

Another geopolitician who has called for modifying Turkey's almost exclusively Western orientation is Professor Ahmet Davutoğlu, currently Minister of Foreign Affairs. In his 2001 best-seller, *Stratejik Derinlik* (Strategic Depth) Davutoğlu maintained that Turkey's Cold War foreign policies 'denied' the country its 'natural sphere of influence' and its 'strategic depth'. This is because, he argues, the aforementioned policies were designed to make the most of

---

[44] İlhan, 1971 and 1989.
[45] The National Security Academy was set up in the aftermath of the 1960 military coup to provide in-service training to high-level civil servants and media representatives.
[46] Ötüken, which is well known for its ultra-nationalist leanings, reprinted İlhan's other early works as well.
[47] Booth, 2005, 5 (original emphasis).
[48] See İlhan, 2000, 40–42.   [49] See Bilgin, 2005.

Turkey's geographical location for the purposes aiding Euro-Atlantic policy making – that is, deterring 'Soviet expansionism' – whereas Turkey's own interests demand tapping into its 'strategic depth' – that is, opening up to former Ottoman lands as well as other areas where Muslim and Turkic peoples live. The solution to Turkey's foreign policy problems, according to Davutoğlu, is to be found in a 'new strategic theory' that would help Turkey's policy makers make use of the opportunities provided by the post-Cold War 'geopolitical and geoeconomic vacuum' in Turkey's zone of 'strategic depth'.[50]

To recapitulate, although there has been, in the post-Cold War era, a proliferation in publications and publishing outlets that provide a professedly geopolitical perspective, there is very little new thinking that warrants calling it a revival of geopolitical thought. Of the some 101 international relations books (in Turkish) during 1989–2005, thirty-four of them have 'geopolitics' either in the title or among their keywords.[51] Just under 34 per cent is not an insignificant figure. Yet, going beyond the title and the keywords of these books reveals that the discourse of geopolitics is used to regurgitate ideas and formulae developed in earlier periods. What is new, then, is the ubiquity of geopolitical thought thanks to the widespread availability of writings on foreign policy thinking already embedded in a materialist tradition.

What is also new in the post-Cold War era is myriad actors' recourse to geopolitical truth-claims in support of a Eurosceptic agenda, better known as 'Eurasianism'. In Turkey's context, 'Eurasianism' serves as an umbrella term whose very ambiguity seems to have allowed for coalitions to be formed among otherwise unlikely fellows (see below). General İlhan, Colonel Özdağ and Professor Davutoğlu, despite differences in emphasis (İlhan and Özdağ on geography and national identity, and Davutoğlu on Muslim identity and geography) share the conviction that Turkey should relocate 'eastwards' if it is to fulfil its 'destiny' of becoming a great power. What has allowed such coalitions to be formed and justified, in turn, is Turkey's geopolitics dogma and the security imaginary of which it is a part; both of which have been re-produced in and through Turkey's post-Cold War 'ontological insecurity'. This is what the chapter turns to next.

Turkey's post-Cold War crisis in foreign policy identity

Until 1989, the prevalence of 'ideological geopolitics'[52] as the 'organizing script and defining drama' of world politics[53] had meant that by virtue of the anti-communist posture it adopted, Turkey was ascribed the role of a 'Western'

---

[50] Davutoğlu, 2001, 71 and 115.
[51] This number is derived from database research at the National Library in Ankara, which is a deposit library.
[52] Agnew, 1998.   [53] Ó Tuathail, 1996, 225.

state. Whereas the United States, in the absence of the Soviet 'enemy', experienced a 'widespread sense of uncertainty about how to organise world politics',[54] for Turkey the crisis was one of a shadow being cast upon its highly-prized 'Western' identity. Many in Turkey had, until then, thought that their country had succeeded in locating itself firmly in the 'West' by virtue of the role it assumed within Western institutions in general and NATO in particular. Indeed, NATO membership was viewed by many in Turkey as not only ending the anxieties caused by post-war Soviet demands[55] but also bringing Turkey into the Western security system as a fully recognised 'Western' state.[56] In time, acceding to European integration came to be seen as the next logical step on the Westernisation path – pretty much like joining 'economic NATO', as one external observer wryly noted.

Earlier signs of the fragility of Turkey's 'Western' identity had been witnessed during the 1980s when Turkey–EC relations took a downward turn following the 1980 coup d'état and the promulgation of the 1982 constitution, which the EC had found wanting in terms of political rights and freedoms. The EC's 1989 'no' to Turkey's application for full membership, and the calls for a 'special arrangement' (i.e. less than full membership) had already signalled the widening gap between Turkey's preferred location (in the 'West'/'Europe') and the location it was being assigned by others (in the 'Middle East' or the 'Mediterranean'). The decision to welcome some former 'Eastern' bloc countries into the EU while 'Western' Turkey was waiting at the doorstep, when coupled with EU actors' mid-1990s approach to Turkey within the Euro-Mediterranean partnership framework, was particularly worrying for some; it was invariably viewed as signalling that Turkey was being located in the 'non-West' and/or 'non-Europe'.[57] The website of Turkey's Ministry of Foreign Affairs put into words this post-1989 feeling of rejection and betrayal: 'Having played an active role in the demise of the Soviet bloc, it was only natural for Turkey to aspire for inclusion in the new European architecture which it helped to build' (Relations between Turkey and the European Union n.d.).

In all their haste, many in Turkey failed to reflect upon their own shortcomings (as with Turkey's domestic problems being exported to 'Europe' thereby further troubling the already troubled relationship) or to appreciate the transformation the EU had begun to go through since 1989.[58]

During this period, Turkey experienced troubles in its relationship with the United States as well. In the immediate aftermath of the Cold War, successive US administrations had become less accepting of the limits of Turkey's

---

[54] Agnew, 1998, 119.
[55] In the aftermath of World War II, the Soviet Union made demands on Turkey's Eastern provinces and joint control of the strategic waterways of the Straits.
[56] Yılmaz and Bilgin, 2005.
[57] Bilgin, 2004.   [58] For a discussion see Bilgin, 2001.

democratisation efforts and the not-so-bright human rights record. Coupled with the end of US grants after 1993 and the decline in US economic aid after 1994 (which increasingly began to come with strings attached), little room for manoeuvre was left for Turkey's policy makers who were desperately in search for a 'Western' ally that would reaffirm Turkey's 'Westernness' without any reservations.[59]

It was within such a climate that there emerged heated debates in Turkey on the country's identity and role in post-1989 world politics. What is significant for the purposes of this chapter is that the participants to these debates articulated their views through tapping geopolitics. During the 1990s, it was invariably argued that Turkey had made great contributions to securing Europe throughout the Cold War and was likely to contribute further in the post-Cold War era by virtue of its 'significant' geographical location. Consider the words of Hikmet Sami Türk (then Turkey's defence minister) who maintained that:

> Geographic destiny placed Turkey in the virtual epicentre of a 'Bermuda Triangle' of post-Cold War volatility and uncertainty, with the Balkans, the Caucasus, and the Middle East encircling us. Rather than isolating ourselves from the pressing conflicts at our doorstep, Turkey decided to assume a pivotal role in promoting regional peace, stability and cooperation in contributing to vital efforts to end human suffering and conflict.[60]

The point being that in recent years various actors have invoked geopolitical truth-claims within a context characterised by the EU's ambivalence towards Turkey's membership and less-accommodating policies by the United States, which rallied myriad actors to the cause of reminding the 'Western' allies of Turkey's 'geopolitical significance' lest they had forgotten in their post-Cold War euphoria.

There is one caveat: perhaps one should not make too much of such emphasis being put by Turkey's actors on their country's geography. The widely shared assumption in Turkey is that throughout the Cold War, it was Turkey's contribution to security in Europe (which is understood to be a function of its geography and military prowess) that helped to locate the country in the 'West'. Is it not only 'natural' for Turkey's actors to emphasise what they consider to be their greatest source of strength? After all, EU actors make similar points through deploying analogous notions in the attempt to convince the sceptics within the EU of the virtues of Turkey's membership.[61] That is to say, there may

---

[59] These dynamics in Turkey–US relations have changed since the 2001 economic crisis in Turkey and the 9/11 attacks.

[60] Türk, 1999.

[61] See, for example, 'The Impact Assessment Report of October 2004' and 'Recommendation of the European Commission on Turkey's Progress towards Accession'. Available at www.europa.eu.int.

be little that begs an explanation here: if you have a significant geographical location (Mackinder says so, it must be true!) you try to make the best of it.

One problem with this line of reasoning is that it explains away the contradictions (geography as Turkey's greatest source of strength and weakness; geopolitics as pushing towards and pulling away from Europe/Eurasia) in Turkey's geopolitical discourse.[62] Whereas analyses sensitive to political agency and socio-economic context would expose such contradictions as (unintended) consequences of ('nested'[63]) games being played by multiple actors in the international and the intra-national realm.[64] Another problem, more significant for the purposes of this chapter, is that such reasoning leaves unanswered the question: 'Why geopolitics but not another set of notions and theories as to how the world works?' In the following section, the chapter maintains that if geopolitics has come to occupy a central place in Turkey's security imaginary, this should be considered as an unintended outcome of two main factors: namely, the military's entrenchment of its own central role in Turkey's politics, and the way in which the field of International Relations has evolved in Turkey.

Why geopolitics (but not another materialist explanation as to how the world works)?

Geopolitics as a field of study and discourse was introduced to Turkey for the first time during World War II in a series of articles published in mainstream newspapers that called for developing its study in Turkey.[65] By the time World War II came to an end, the study and discourse of geopolitics had become stigmatised in the 'West' because of its links with Nazi expansionism. However, in Turkey, there was little if any sign of such stigma being attached to geopolitics. Far from it, Turkey's aspiring geopoliticians presented geopolitics as a 'science' that was studied at 'Western' institutions of higher education and used for shaping post-war policies in the West and elsewhere.[66] The implication of these writings being that both Turkey's 'Western' orientation and its foreign policy interests required achieving mastery over this new 'science'.[67]

---

[62] Such contradictions are not unique to Turkey. See Ò Tuathail, 2002.

[63] Putnam, 1988.   [64] Bilgin, 2007.

[65] Eren, 1964; Sezgin and Yılmaz, 1965; see also Fahri [Fındıkoğlu], 1946. It is likely that officers of the Ottoman Army were exposed to classical geopolitical thought during their training. Many of Turkey's founding leaders had served in the Ottoman Army had military background. Yet their public discourse did not invoke classical geopolitics when justifying foreign (or domestic) policy. See Bilgin, 2007.

[66] See, for example, Eren, 1964; İlhan, 1986; Öngör, 1963; Osmanağaoğlu, 1968; Sezgin and Yılmaz, 1965 and Turfan, 1962.

[67] Western authors' reservations regarding the 'contamination' caused by the close links between Classical Geopolitics and Nazi expansionism were not totally lost on Turkey's geopoliticians. Yet, this did not prevent them from making explicit and approving references

Although geopolitics was not shunned in Turkey as in the West, interest in geopolitical notions and theories nevertheless remained confined to the military well until the late 1960s. Following World War II, the Military Academy (and the National Security Academy after 1960) introduced a series of lectures on geopolitics to the curriculum.[68] The majority of the texts that were published during this period are written up versions of the lectures delivered at these two military institutions by professors from leading universities in Turkey.[69]

The military's attraction to geopolitics is not 'unique' to Turkey. In other parts of the world such as South America where militaries have a track record of intervention in politics, geopolitics has emerged as the preserve of military actors and provided 'a more conceptual and comprehensive foundation for an ambitious political-military vision and theory of the state'.[70] Had the afore-mentioned texts remained confined to military institutions and outlets, the military's interest in geopolitics could perhaps be likened to a typical military bureaucracy that seeks to enhance its understanding of and control over space to fulfil its duty of defending the state. However, the military in Turkey has not stopped there but played an active role in introducing geopolitics to civilian audiences, disseminating the idea of geopolitics as a 'privileged perspective' and representing itself as enjoying unrivalled command over this perspective. Indeed, in formal writings by military officers that came out in the aftermath of the 1960 (the first) coup d'état, geopolitics is presented as a 'view from nowhere' that 'shows the way' when civilians fail because of their 'ideals and ideologies'.[71] Instrumental in the popularisation of these ideas and assumptions has been the aforementioned high school course on 'National Security', which is designed and taught by military officers, compulsory military service for the male population over eighteen years of age, and the National Security Academy.

This is not to suggest that the military is solely responsible for the emergence of the geopolitics dogma or its centrality to Turkey's security imaginary. Geopolitics has its own attractions; the field of International Relations in Turkey has its own weaknesses (see below). Rather, the point is that the military's role in this process cannot be denied. For, in the post-World War II era, the military tapped geopolitical discourse to justify its interventions (1960, 1971, 1980, 1997) and its forays into the political sphere during times of 'civilian rule'.[72] Yet, pointing to the agency of the military goes only so far in responding to the question 'why geopolitics but not any other alternative?'.

---

to the ideas of German geopoliticians such as Haushofer and Ratzel. See, for example, Eren, 1964; İlhan, 1989; Öngör, 1963; Sezgin and Yılmaz, 1965 and Turfan, 1962.

[68] İlhan, 1989, 12.
[69] See, for example, Bilge, 1959; Eren, 1964 and Turfan, 1962.
[70] Hepple, 1992, 139. See also Dodds, 2000.
[71] See Harp Akademileri Komutanlığı, 1963. İlhan, 1971, iii–iv, makes a similar point in the immediate aftermath of yet another military intervention in 1971.
[72] Bilgin, 2007.

There may be a very straightforward explanation for this. The appeal of geo-politics may be the appeal of geopolitics. Classical Geopolitics offers a neat and seemingly parsimonious explanation of world politics ostensibly devoid of 'politics'. It is an account of the world as driven by geography, which, in turn, is taken as 'god-given'/'natural' and therefore 'untainted' by ideals and ideologies. How can one not be attracted to that? Especially if alternative explanations as to how the world works (i.e. International Relations theory) are found too complicated, lacking or even irrelevant.

This brings me to the second explanation for the weakness of alternative accounts of world politics, which has to do with the way in which the field of International Relations has developed in Turkey. For years International Relations was considered in Turkey as a vocational programme for training high-level bureaucrats for the state. As the entrance examination of govern-ment institutions (the Ministry of Foreign Affairs in particular) have empha-sised knowledge of law and history, the curriculum of International Relations departments were structured around these subjects.[73] Consequently, concep-tual training and reflection has never been on equal footing with law and his-tory in the study of International Relations in Turkey.[74]

The third and related explanation has to do with the 'standard' textbooks (and the concepts and theories introduced by those books) used for teaching International Relations at universities. As with other non-Western contexts, the instructive value of such textbooks remains rather limited for Turkey's con-text. Turkey, after all, is a part of the developing world about which 'stand-ard' theories of International Relations have very little to say.[75] When they read the canons of the discipline, students often do not recognise their own world. Yet, in the absence of reflection on the suitability of these imported textbooks, concepts and theories for Turkey's context, International Relations/Theory has remained a course that has to be studied but not necessarily internalised. In the absence of suitable conceptual tools to make sense of the vast realm of world politics, the appeal of geographically determinist accounts on world politics for minds trained in history should not be underestimated. Indeed, practical, popular and formal discourses of various actors suggest that there currently exists very little space outside geopolitics in Turkey's foreign policy discourse.[76] As such, the chapter proposes a qualifier to the hypothesis of this volume regarding the use of geopolitical discourse by conservative actors. For, in Turkey it was not merely in support of a 'conservative' agenda that geopol-itical discourse has been utilised. Rather, actors with myriad political agendas have tapped geopolitics in making their case.

[73] Ataöv, 1961; Eralp, 1996, 8–9.
[74] See Bilgin, 2008b and Bilgin and Tanrısever, 2009.
[75] See Bilgin, 2008a; Holsti, 1992 and Tickner, 2003.
[76] For an analysis popular discourse, see Yanık, 2008 and 2009.

The point here is not the same as that of Sidaway *et al.*,[77] who has highlighted that conservative actors' agendas often call for radical changes in foreign or domestic policies of their governments in the attempt to 'preserve' certain things. Rather the point here is that in Turkey's case actors who seek to preserve/change different aspects of Turkey's foreign and domestic policy have tapped the same discourse. In other words, in Turkey it is not the case that conservative actors alone have tapped geopolitical discourse; all actors did. While this has to do with the pre-existence of 'the geopolitics dogma', the reason why it became a 'dogma' to begin with begs for an explanation. The reason, I have argued elsewhere, has to do with the fragility of Turkey's Western 'identity' and geopolitics having allowed for locating Turkey firmly in the 'West'. While the fixing of Turkey's 'Westernness' has been a cornerstone of Turkey's security in both the international and domestic arenas[78] throughout the Republican era (since 1923), it was during the Cold War that Turkey was able to firmly locate itself in the 'West': by virtue of standing against the Soviet bloc (the 'East') together with the United States. The end of the Cold War proved the fragility of Turkey's 'Western' identity and geopolitical discourse as a fix. For, following the dissolution of the Soviet Union (i.e. the 'East' against which Turkey had located itself in the 'West') Turkey's claim to 'Western' identity received a decisive blow. Also significant in bringing about this crisis was the transformation of European Community into the European Union and redefinition of European identity in increasingly normative terms. During the 1990s, as EU actors challenged Turkey's 'Western' identity due to its failing democratic and human rights record, and successive US administrations proved unwilling to offer backing on purely geopolitical grounds, Turkey's 'ontological insecurity' reached a high point.[79] During this period, actors for and against remaining with the EU option have invoked geopolitical notions in making their arguments – hence the quantitative revival. The reason why the revival was not also qualitative is to do with the pre-existence of 'the geopolitics dogma' and its centrality to the security imaginary. Such centrality was reproduced in response to the post-Cold War crisis in Turkey's (foreign policy) identity. The following section will seek to illustrate this point with reference to debates on Turkey's accession to European integration.

Multiple actors, different agendas, tapping geopolitics

Increasingly since the 1999 decision of the EU to recognise its candidacy, Turkey has been making headway towards meeting EU conditionality. Around the same time Turkey's Eurosceptics began to increasingly invoke geopolitics

---

[77] Sidaway *et al.*, 2004.
[78] Bilgin, 2009.
[79] Bilgin, 2004.

in articulating their concerns regarding the potential implications of EU con-ditionality.[80] However, given Turkey's Republican founders' commitment to a westward orientation, making a case for Turkey turning away from the West/ Europe is not a politically correct argument to make. That said Turkey's Eurosceptics seems to have found a creative solution in propounding the so-called 'Eurasian option' (see below). Their very use of the term 'Eurasia' does half of the job. The word 'Eurasia' gives the impression of retaining the Republic's 'European' orientation and embracing the 'Asian' dimension while doing away with EU conditionality. The centrality of EU conditionality to the notion of 'Europeanness' seems to escape the proponents of Eurasianism. What has allowed Turkey's Eurosceptics to revive Eurasianism, which would have been considered unthinkable during the Cold War for fear of pan-Turkism at home and abroad, is post-Cold War re-inscription of Turkey's security imaginary with the geopolitics dogma enjoying central place. As will be shown below, increasingly since 1999, Turkey's Eurosceptics have tapped geopolitics to de-legitimise Turkey's accession to European integration while present-ing 'Eurasia' as the *geo*politically correct alternative.[81] That said Eurasianism's pre-existence as a resource in the security imaginary has its roots in pan-Turkist thought which suffered a devastating blow in World War I and was marginal-ised in Republican Turkey save the ultra-nationalist elements in the society (see the above discussion on Colonel Özdağ).

As early as 1989, General İlhan had begun calling for reviving the Eurasian dimension of Turkey's foreign policy.[82] The eastward dimension, which General İlhan called a 'mission', comprised leading the 'dispossessed nations of the East'. Although İlhan did not consider the context to be opportune at the time for Turkey fulfilling its 'mission', he was nevertheless convinced that Turks would one day 'find the strength that is needed to fulfil this mission bestowed upon them by geography and culture'.[83] More recently, General İlhan tapped geopol-itics to de-legitimise the EU option while justifying the appropriateness of his preferred alternative. Consider the following quote where General İlhan lays out the EU's 'geopolitical gains' from Turkey's membership:

> it enhances its horizons and sphere of influence to include the Caucasus, Middle East, Central Asia; attains the opportunity to enhance and reinforce the advantages created by the Customs Union treaty ... prepares the ground for the resolution of the Turco-Greek dispute in favour of Greece ... paves

---

[80] See Bilgin, 2005.
[81] It is a telling example that the lead article of the EU–Turkey relations special issue of *Avrasya Dosyası* (Eurasian Dossier) is an article entitled 'Türkiye'nin AB Sürecinde Avrasya Politikası: Niçin ve Nasıl Bir İşbirliği?' (Turkey's Eurasian Policy in the Process of the EU: Why and What Kind of a Cooperation?) (Erol, 2004).
[82] Also see İlhan, 1997 and 2005.
[83] İlhan, 1989, xii and 58.

the way for carving out Turkish territories via endeavours in 'minority rights'; and generates hope for the resolution of the 'Eastern Question' by way of side-tracking Turkey.[84]

The implication of all this for Turkey, according to İlhan, is that what the EU gains Turkey loses. Since the stakes are so high, maintains İlhan, the decision cannot be left for the politicians alone to make. This is not merely a political choice, he writes, for it is geopolitics that 'decides' what Turkey should do: remain outside the EU. Neither of the two are mere political choices, according to İlhan, but faits accompli of Turkey's geographical position.[85] Professor Ümit Özdağ concurs: 'Neither returning to Asian geopolitics nor joining Europe could be the Turks' aim ... What could and should happen is following a strategy of consolidation in Eurasia. Turkey ... should take up the struggle to resuscitate the Eurasian civilisation'.[86]

This, according to Özdağ, is what geopolitics tells Turkey to do. Geopolitics also tells Turkey how to do it: by forming a coalition with Russia (and perhaps Iran). As articulated by then General Secretary of the National Security Council, General Tuncer Kılınç, the Eurasian option calls for Turkey to cease its efforts to accede to European integration and turn towards Iran and Russia in its search for new allies.[87]

Following General Kılınç's intervention into the debates on Turkey–EU relations, Turkey's Eurosceptics became even more vocal in propounding Eurasianism as the option more in tune with Turkey's 'geopolitical realities'. There is very little agreement as to where 'Eurasia' is, let alone a coherent political project. What seems to allow Turkey's Eurasianists to act in concert is their scepticism towards Turkey's accession to European integration.[88] Accordingly, the proliferation in publishing outlets and think-tanks that specialise on geopolitics should be understood not merely as a condition that has allowed increasing appeals to geopolitics in Turkey but also as a consequence of Turkey's Eurosceptics seeking to make use of the epistemological certainty offered by geopolitics dogma at a time of 'ontological insecurity'. It is through resort to arguments warranted by the geopolitics dogma that the politics of

---

[84] İlhan, 2000, 22.
[85] İlhan, 2000, 40–42.   [86] U. Özdağ, 2003, 8.   [87] See Torbakov, 2005.
[88] In the past decade, coalitions have been formed between various actors in pursuit of the Eurasian agenda. For example, Küre publishing house that translated the Russian Eurasianist Alexander Dugin (2003) into Turkish has also published Davutoğlu's book. Ötüken publishing, which reprinted İlhan's books, is well-known for its ultra-nationalist leanings. Avrasya TV's (Eurasian TV) owner has been sponsoring the centre-left daily *Cumhuriyet*'s supplement, *Strateji*. Lastly, many of the publications identified carry articles that are heavily critical of Turkey's accession to European integration and favourable towards 'Eurasianism' which is presented as an alternative project more in tune with Turkey's geopolitics (Davutoğlu, 2001) if not 'necessitated' by it (see, for example: İlhan, 2000 and 2002; U. Özdağ, 2003).

foreign and security policy making gets suppressed and policy practices are portrayed as mere responses to *geo*politics of Turkey. The point being, post-Cold War pervasiveness of geopolitical discourse in Turkey is not merely a product of the structure of cultural resources that is the geopolitics dogma but has also helped to re-produce the dogma and entrenched its centrality to Turkey's security imaginary.

Conclusion

The pervasiveness of geopolitical images and notions in the practical, formal and popular discourses of myriad actors in present-day Turkey (as encapsulated in the cartoon in Figure 7.1) cannot be overemphasised. With the dissolution of the Eastern bloc, in defence against which Turkey had reaffirmed its 'Westernness', a significant marker of Turkey's 'Western' identity had also disappeared. Coupled with the ups and downs of Turkey–EU relations, the post-1989 period was characterised by a feeling of 'ontological insecurity' and seemingly incessant conversations on Turkey's identity, location, role and policies. Participants to these conversations have invariably made their case through deploying geopolitical images and notions. Indeed, given Turkey's current divide between the so-called 'secularists' and 'Islamists', it is difficult to overlook the dogma's appeal to and authority over those favouring ostensibly 'scientific' and/or 'god-given'/'natural' quality of Classical Geopolitics.

Pointing to the impact of 'external' dynamics as such should not be taken as establishing straightforward cause and effect relationships between the aforementioned developments and various actors' recourse to geopolitics. Not least because such an explanation would leave unanswered the question: 'Why geopolitics but not another set of notions and theories as to how the world works?' This, the chapter submitted, was because geopolitics was ready and available as a resource in Turkey's 'security imaginary'. In Turkey as in some other contexts considered in this volume, geopolitical thought seems to have offered myriad actors a degree of 'epistemological certainty' in their post-Cold War predicament of 'ontological anxiety'. Yet, Turkey's case shows that the very presence of a materialist tradition in foreign policy thinking, actors fluent in geopolitics-speak and their vigour in shaping policy debates can be taken as *both* a starting point for analysing the (re-)production of geopolitical thought *and* its consequence. For it is through the (re-)production of geopolitical thought that actors fluent in geopolitics have been socialised into using geopolitics-speak in justifying their (at times conflicting) positions in foreign policy debates.

As such, the chapter proposed a qualifier to the hypothesis of this volume regarding the use of geopolitical discourse mostly by conservative actors. In Turkey, the uses of geopolitics defy simply being classified as conservative vs.

radical, or pro- vs. anti-status quo. For myriad political actors, appeals to the 'facts' of geopolitics have helped in the struggle for political power and legitimacy needed to shape political processes at home and abroad. For example, in 2001, then Prime Minister and head of the DSP (Demokratik Sol Parti – Democratic Left Party) Bülent Ecevit appealed to geopolitics when seeking to justify Turkey's limited compliance with the EU accession criteria in the 'National Programme' (which was prepared to lay out the reformist steps the coalition government headed by Ecevit was going to take). What the 'National Programme' promised was already far too 'bold' for a country occupying Turkey's geographical location, argued Ecevit; given its geopolitical 'sensitivity', Turkey could only so much comply with EU calls for further democratisation and the reinstitution of civilian authority over military.[89] For policy practitioners and the bureaucracy, geopolitics helps to de-politicise what are essentially political processes. Through invoking assumptions about 'what geography tells Turkey to do', it becomes possible to remove issues from the realm of political debate and present existing policies as faits accomplis of geography – as with the criminalisation of both conscientious objection and citizens' objection to such criminalisation.[90] For the military in Turkey, geopolitics helps to portray as 'normal' the centrality of the role it plays in shaping political processes thereby (re-)producing a culture of militarism. Indeed, it is partly its self-proclaimed command over geopolitics that allows the military to enjoy a 'privileged perspective' on statecraft. When military actors intervene in current debates, they frequently tap geopolitics as a 'view from nowhere' that 'shows the way'. The connotation being: civilians 'fail' because of their 'ideals and ideologies' whereas the military is guided by the precepts of the 'science of geopolitics'. For 'journalists keen to be read as serious and worldly'[91] and 'intellectuals of statecraft' who present ostensibly scientific accounts of Turkey's international relations, references to geopolitical images and notions are helpful in enhancing the authority of what they 'say'. The point being, Turkey's case bears out how the implications of the uses of geopolitics defy neat categorisation.

In response to the question, 'Why geopolitics?' then, the chapter offered an answer in accord with Turkey's international relations (understood as a search for affirming its 'Westernness'), intra-national relations (i.e. domestic power struggles) and International Relations (the academic field). In supporting this conclusion, the chapter highlighted how practical, popular and

---

[89] Ecevit, 2001.
[90] In 2005–2006 a famous Turkish novelist was tried for criticising the criminalisation of conscientious objection in her weekly magazine article. The novelist, Perihan Mağden, was found 'not guilty'. But the laws that allow for individuals to be taken to court for committing such 'crimes' remain.
[91] Ó Tuathail, 1996, 260.

formal geopolitics makes use of the legitimacy driven from the 'Westernness' of Classical Geopolitics in justifying arguments regarding suspected 'Western' plots against Turkey – arguments that often contradict the very essence of the works cited by the author/speaker. The irony in Turkey's actors' reliance on warrant by 'Western' authors in establishing the timelessness of 'Western' conspiracies against Turkey and the impossibility of trusting the latter's intentions (as with the Sèvres metaphor) seems to escape many.

8

Banal Huntingtonianism: civilisational geopolitics in Estonia

MERJE KUUS

Introduction: the small map

In August 2003, leading up to the popular referendum on European Union (EU) accession the following month, six widely respected Estonian artists and intellectuals published a joint article in the country's largest newspaper urging the voters to say 'Yes' in the referendum. Their argument starts as follows:

> When one of the world's best-known political scientists Samuel Huntington published his 'clash of civilizations' theory in the early 1990s, it touched Estonians' soul. According to Huntington, the border of the European civilization runs exactly along the Narva river [between Estonia and Russia]. Estonians had assured each other of the existence of that border for 50 years, and stood for maintaining it for 5000 years ... For many, that small black-and-white map [in Huntington's book] was a symbolic confirmation that Narva river is the border between western Christianity and Orthodoxy, Latin and Cyrillic alphabet, Roman law and Russian lawlessness, democracy and autocracy, not just for us but for the whole humankind. And this is how it will always be.[1]

The proclamation is instructive of the civilisational and geopolitical narrative that has pervaded political debates in Estonia for much of the post-Cold War period, especially in the long decade between independence (in 1991) and EU accession (in 2004). The influence of that narrative on the political struggles of that period is difficult to overestimate; it is among the key conceptual bases of political speeches, policy analyses and academic research on foreign as well as domestic affairs. It bundles up geopolitics and culture, casting geopolitics in terms of essential identities and framing culture as a geopolitical matter.

A longer and more detailed analysis of the Estonian case and its broader international context appeared as Chapter 3, 'Civilizational Geopolitics' in Merje Kuus, 2007. The argument is reworked here with permission from Palgrave. The research was funded by a Standard Research Grant from the Humanities and Social Sciences Research Council of Canada. I thank Stefano Guzzini for constructive feedback and Michelle Drenker for editorial assistance.

[1] Luik *et al.*, 2003.

This chapter uses Estonia as an example to illuminate the mechanisms and effects of the civilisational narrative of geopolitics. It traces how Huntington's thesis of civilisational clash became influential in Estonia and how it functions within political debates there. I will first pick apart the civilisational framing of Estonia's foreign and security policies, and then detail a similar framing of citizenship and minority rights. Through this case study, I illuminate the production of a particular kind of geopolitics – one that operates primarily with cultural claims rather than the traditional arguments about inter-state power politics. Such culturalist geopolitics is quite different from the classical *Realpolitik* that constituted the dominant understanding of geopolitics in the twentieth century. It indeed seems to have little to do with geopolitics, understood traditionally as the 'geographic factors that lie behind political decisions'.[2] Quite the contrary, it appears as liberation from inter-state geopolitics of territory and resources. Within it, foreign policy is no longer about the crude geopolitics of material interests; it is about cultural identities and universal values. Yet, as I will show in the Estonian case, civilisational geopolitics relies heavily on geographical and geopolitical claims about the country's geopolitical location on a putative civilisational faultline.[3] Although mainstream political rhetoric does not necessarily cite a direct foreign threat, it evokes an insecurity that arguably results from Estonia's location in a 'geotectonically active' region. We are left with a predictable narrative of 'historical legacies', 'existential insecurities' and the necessity of urgent actions to which there is no alternative. This narrative offers a generic reiteration of 'security threats', or 'geopolitical memory' with little explication of how these terms are invested with particular meanings in everyday political practice. In counterpoint, this chapter focuses precisely on the question of how concepts work in political debates: how they channel discussion and bring about specific effects.

Although empirically concerned with Estonia, the chapter is not about Estonia per se. In the 1990s at least, the civilisational discourse of geopolitics is operational throughout the new member states of the EU and NATO. Insofar as these states still need to solidify their European credentials, a culturalist reframing of geopolitics is still attractive to them. It is ultimately that reframing, the processes by which geopolitics is bundled up with culture, that

---

[2] McColl, 1983, 33; see also Dodds and Atkinson, 2000.

[3] The West here refers to the core states of North America and Western Europe; East-Central Europe refers to the post-socialist countries of the former Soviet bloc; and Eastern Europe refers to the discourse of Eastern Europe. I capitalise all words because the terms refer at once to places (in the eastern or western part of Europe, for example) as well as to discourses about these places. Eastern or Central Europe here refer not to clearly located places but to political and intellectual projects. To differentiate between Eastern, Western and Central Europe in this manner is not to essentialise the differences between different parts of Europe, but to acknowledge their different power positions in European security discourses.

is my focus here.[4] That process was perhaps at its highest pitch in the 1990s, but its enabling assumptions are well entrenched in the present decade too. Even though the findings from Estonia are not directly transferable to other states, they illuminate a political climate in which geopolitics acquires peculiarly culturalist meanings. At the same time, although my claims transcend the specific Estonian context, that context is central to my argument. By showing how the civilisational thesis functions in context-specific political debates, the chapter offers an in-depth empirical investigation of the resilience and the appeal of Huntington's thesis. By taking seriously the everyday utility of the civilisational thesis, the chapter contributes to the voluminous critique of that thesis.[5]

Conceptually, the chapter investigates geopolitics as a contested political process. It draws from a substantial body of work, often labelled critical geopolitics, that focuses on the spatial scripting of world politics. That work starts from the position that geographical knowledge is a technology of power that does not simply describe but also produces political space.[6] Geographical claims inscribe places as particular types of places to be dealt with in a particular manner. Conversely, all politics is also geopolitics as it necessarily involves geographical assumptions about territories and borders, inside and outside, centre and margin, core and periphery. Even claims about 'escaping' geography and geopolitics are geopolitical as they assume a particular geographical configuration of power that is to be escaped.

Estonia offers particularly interesting examples of the geographical scripting of politics because that country, unlike the large European states like Germany, Russia or Great Britain, does not have a strong geopolitical tradition. Although geopolitics was a topic of scholarly concern in the interwar years,[7] there was no geopolitical writing to speak of between the 1940s and 1990s, when Estonia was occupied by the Soviet Union. Estonia was not a sovereign state – the traditional subject of geopolitics – and the field of geopolitics was tainted by its association with the Nazi regime. However, at the same time, and perhaps in part because of the Soviet occupation, geopolitical claims about Estonia's 'true' cultural position in the West remained central to popular narratives of Estonian identity.[8] These claims served as the intellectual bases from which to challenge Soviet rule. Partly as a result of such popular un-statist use, geopolitics in Estonia had a particularly folksy common-sense flavour throughout the 1990s. Even today it does not operate with the language of state interest; it rather evokes cultural identity. The borders it is concerned with are not the borders of states but those of cultures. This, I will argue, makes civilisational geopolitics more, not less, effective. It

---

[4] See Kuus, 2007, for an analysis of Central Europe as a whole.
[5] See Gusterson, 2004.   [6] Ó Tuathail, 1996, 7.
[7] Cf. Kant, 1931 and 1936/1937.   [8] Berg and Oras, 2000.

creates a frame of everyday, even banal, assumptions that usually remain in the background but can be activated and made politically operational very quickly. Like Michael Billig's banal nationalism, this banal Huntingtonianism functions as a set of ideological habits that enable to get things done while remaining analytically invisible.[9]

Methodologically, the chapter concentrates on public political discourse in Estonia. I focus on arguments that prevail in mainstream public debates: arguments advanced by national newspapers, major academics, as well as high-level elected and appointed officials. My concern is not with the full spectrum of geopolitical statements – from ultra-nationalists to (the rare) dissident intellectuals – but with those claims that have become common sense, unremarkable and banal.[10] Although I bring examples from speeches, academic analyses and newspaper articles, my object of analysis is not what is said. The object of analysis rather is the set of assumptions that enable specific statements and make them legible and legitimate. The aim of the many direct quotes used throughout the chapter is not to reveal the thoughts of the speaker – I cannot infer and I am not interested in private thoughts. The quotes are used rather to illustrate the unremarkable assumptions underpinning them. I show that the civilisational narrative of geopolitics has not – contra the opening quote – emerged naturally from the Estonians' soul. Rather, it has been *made* into a common-sense story by a regulated process of repetition in public debates.

Cultural borders

The notion that Estonia is culturally a 'Kidnapped West' – to invoke Kundera's famous characterisation of Central Europe – pre-dates the re-establishment of the country's independence in 1991.[11] Throughout the Soviet occupation, Estonia and the other Baltic states were considered 'the Soviet West' on both sides of the Iron Curtain. In the words of Peeter Vihalemm, a prominent philosopher and sociologist, Estonia was for nearly fifty years 'incorporated into the Eastern world, into the Soviet Empire influenced by Byzantine culture'.[12] However, the argument was not articulated in foreign policy terms as Estonia was not an independent country that could pursue such a policy. Civilisational arguments consequently remained in the realm of culture and identity, articulated by cultural elites rather than intellectuals of statecraft. Upon independence in 1991, the theme of returning to Europe and the West

[9] Billig, 1995.
[10] In keeping with my focus on the everyday rather than the spectacular, I exclude the early 1990s from the analysis. Political debates of the early 1990s were virulently anti-Russian, in part because of the right-wing coalition in power at the time, and are not representative of the more moderate claims that have dominated the public sphere since the mid 1990s.
[11] Kundera, 1984.   [12] Vihalemm, 1997.

immediately became the central key theme in the Estonian political discourse. This return is conceived largely in terms of culture, as a process propelled by collective identity.[13] As Marju Lauristin and Peeter Vihalemm put it, the 'wish to be accepted again by the West and to be recognized as an integral part of the Western cultural realm is a more substantial driving force in [Estonia's] development than mere economic or political motivation could ever be'.[14]

The concept of geopolitics plays a complicated role in the 'return to the West' narrative. On the one hand, 'geopolitics' is seen in terms of traditional power-politics of big states. The tragedies of the twentieth century are attributed to 'geopolitical' thinking, and Estonia's return to the West is to finally put an end to such power games. Estonia is in this line of thought not acting geopolitically but escaping geopolitics. On the other hand, the return to Europe is couched in geopolitical terms to give it an air of inevitability. Geopolitics is supremely useful as a rhetorical and conceptual tool precisely because of its connotations of permanence, stability and rationality. Geography, as Nicholas Spykman famously said, 'does not argue, it just is'.

The return to the West narrative is to some extent necessarily civilisational since it implies that Estonia returns to Europe from a place that is not 'Western'. The degree of an explicit civilisational overtone has varied over time, however. Indeed, it was not until the second half of the 1990s that this overtone became dominant in political debates. Up to the mid 1990s, the conception of Estonia as a gateway between Europe and Russia was also noticeable. Several prominent analysts stressed Estonia's potential to profit from Russia-bound transit, both by virtue of the country's location and transportation infrastructure as well as Estonians' knowledge of Russia.[15] Although military neutrality akin to Finland or Sweden was never a dominant vision, it was discussed as an option.[16] The future scenarios developed in the mid 1990s by an interdisciplinary group of experts likewise emphasised the gateway aspect. Of the four scenarios – labeled 'Big Bang', 'Southern Finland', 'Gateway' and 'Cordon Sanitaire', only the last one posited an exclusive Western orientation. However, that scenario was premised on the worsening of relations between the West and Russia. It does not even consider Estonia's identity. In academic and humanist circles, interwar notions of Baltoscandia were seen as a useful spatial framework for Estonia. The concept of Baltoscandia posits that Estonia's proper cultural place is the space of the Baltic Sea with Finland and Sweden. Baltoscandia is not a concept about great power politics; it is a concept that synthesises geo-economic, cultural and even ecological factors into a regional framework.

In this relatively fluid conceptual space and geopolitical vertigo of the early to mid 1990s, in which Estonia's identity and geopolitical location was being

---

[13] Lauristin *et al.*, 1997.   [14] Lauristin, 1997, 29.
[15] Eesti Tulevikuuuringute Instituut, 1997.
[16] Haab, 1998; Vares, 1999.

rethought and rewritten, Huntington's thesis offered clarity. Put forth as a *Foreign Affairs* article in 1993 and as a book in 1996, it supplied an unequivocally articulated prescription from the heights of the Western academy.[17] It cast the sphere of identity in terms of science and thereby crystallised it into a powerful tool in geopolitical arguments.

Huntington's thesis became prominent especially after the publication of an edited volume on Estonia's post-socialist transformations edited by the county's most prominent social scientists. The book, tellingly titled *Return to the Western World*, conceptualises these transformations primarily in terms of culture and identity. It received favourable publicity and established Huntington's civilisational thesis as a canonical text in Estonia. In 1999, Huntington's *The Clash of Civilizations and the Remaking of the World Order* was translated into Estonian. The translation features a foreword by Estonia's Minister of Foreign Affairs Toomas Hendrik Ilves. On this occasion, Huntington visited Estonia and spoke at a conference together with Estonia's Prime Minister Mart Laar and Foreign Minister Ilves. Major newspapers provided extensive publicity for his thesis. *Sirp*, the weekly newspaper of the country's intellectual elite, published Huntington's presentation at that conference. *Eesti Päevaleht*,[18] one of Estonia's two principal dailies, devoted two full pages to Huntington's argument. These included a map of civilisations and a conversation between Huntington and Foreign Minister Ilves. Commentary was provided by Märt Kivine, advisor to the Foreign Minister.

By the turn of the decade, the civilisational thesis had become an accepted postulate in academic and policy circles. It was hailed both as common sense and self-evident as well as rigorously scientific.[19] Marika Kirch, a prominent sociologist, discusses civilisational clash as clearly visible to the naked eye (albeit in 1994 already):

> If one supposes hesitatingly that the civilizational border between Estonia and Russia is anachronistic or negligible, one need only stand on the bridge over Narva river … and witness carefully the 'overt civilizational confrontation' of two cultures: On the Estonian side there is an historic fortress built by the Swedes, Danes and Germans in accordance with the cultural traditions of Western Europe; on the other [in Ivangorod] a primeval fortress as an exponent of Slavic-Orthodox cultural traditions.[20]

Recognising that Huntington is less popular in the West than in Estonia, Kirch emphasises the common-sense character of the civilisational thesis (ten years later, in 2003).

---

[17] See Gusterson, 2005, for a recent critique.
[18] *Eesti Päevaleht*, 1999.   [19] Saar, 1998.
[20] Kirch, 1994, 12.

> At Harvard, Huntington is understandably considered a bit strange
> because in the multicultural society of the United States, his thesis sounds
> quite uncompelling. In the Estonian context, the opposite is true. The
> re-establishment of Estonia's independence further underscored the exist-
> ence and significance of a civilizational border at the Narva-Piirissaare line
> [in Eastern Estonia].[21]

By the late 1990s, Huntingtonianism – to borrow a term from Timothy Garton
Ash[22] – had become virtually unquestioned in Estonia. Even beyond explicitly
geopolitical arguments, political issues were routinely discussed in geopolitical
terms as a choice between the West and Russia.[23] For example, when urging
voters to support centre-right political forces in the 1999 general election,
Estonia's President Meri said that Estonia's options were as unambiguous as 'a
mathematical equation'. 'On one side Europe, on the other Russia', he continued. 'We are on the border, and therefore only a small push is needed to make
us fall into one side or rise into the other.'[24] The pro-EU proclamation that starts
this chapter – mentioning Huntington by name – indicates his popular name
recognition. By the early 2000s the thesis was taught as a part of the middle
school history curriculum and the site described by Kirch – a view of the river
with fortresses on each side – is used as an illustration.[25] Hvostov, a prominent
columnist, aptly notes that the clash of civilisations is not really discussed in
Estonia. 'These days', Hvostov says, 'the topic of brainstorming is how to get out
from between the clashing civilizations.'[26]

   An important nuance to this story is that the popularity of Huntington in
the 1990s in Estonia (and beyond) was crafted by local intellectuals of statecraft. His thesis would not be as influential in Estonia (and in Central Europe
more generally) if it was not actively promoted by influential individuals in
the region. Conversely, being cited at the putative civilisational faultlines has
greatly enhanced the standing of Huntington's thesis in the West itself. It is
Havel's observation, that 'cultural conflicts are increasing and are more dangerous today than at any time in history', that Huntington quotes to substantiate his claims.[27] Huntington situates his argument explicitly in the context of
European proclamations. The civilisational thesis, Huntington claims, offers
the answer about the borders of Europe various European intellectuals and
political leaders have explicitly endorsed.[28] Conversely, Estonian (and, more
broadly, Central European) arguments about civilisational borders have been
greatly strengthened and legitimised by Huntington's position at the centre
of the Western security establishment. Huntington offered an easy package

---

[21] Kirch, 2003, 156.   [22] Garton Ash, 1999.
[23] See Katus, 1999.   [24] Feldman, 2001.   [25] Berg, 2002b.
[26] Hvostov, 1999. He is among the more critical voices in analyses of Estonian foreign policy,
   yet he too explicitly endorses Huntington's theory.
[27] Huntington, 1996, 160.   [28] Huntington, 1996, 158.

of explanations to Estonian foreign policy intellectuals: they no longer had
to convince their Western counterparts of civilisational conflict, they could
instead simply refer to Huntington.[29] In the West, arguments about Central
Europeans' 'natural' fears of Russia are often accepted as authentic in part
because Central European politicians, intellectuals, journalists and pollsters
tell so to Westerners, time and again. In order to grasp the prominence of the
concept of civilisational clash in Central Europe, one must therefore consider
its influence in Western governmental, academic and intelligence circles *as well
as* its high-level promotion in Central Europe. It is through the combined clout
and mutually lent legitimacy of the Western and local intellectuals of statecraft
that the notion of civilisational clash has been given mythical proportions in
the post-Cold War Estonia.

Cultural threats

Within the civilisational narrative, cultural difference is both irreducible and
inherently threatening. According to Huntington,[30] 'It is human to hate', and
hatred increasingly takes place along cultural lines. In his formulation: 'In
class and ideological conflicts, the key question was "Which side are you on?"
and people could and did choose sides and change sides. In conflicts between
civilizations, the question is "What are you?" That is a given that cannot be
changed.'[31] What is threatening in this framework is not action but identity.
Threat emanates not from what people do but from who they are.

In Estonia, then, the civilisational narrative articulates not only what Estonia
is but also what it is not. Just as it locates Estonia unequivocally in the West, it
also defines the country as fundamentally different from Russia, on the 'other'
side of the putative civilisational faultline. It functions not only to reaffirm
Estonia's Western identity, but also to deny any possibility of ambiguity or
hybridity. Rein Ruutsoo, a prominent academic and public intellectual, emphasised in his 1995 introduction to a *Nationalities Papers* special issue on Estonia
that despite the country's border location, Estonia is not 'a borderland in the
classical meaning of the term'. This is because it 'belongs historically and inte-
grally to the sphere of the so-called Lutheran-German civilization'.[32] Estonia is
constructed as a 'purely' Western country with no indigenously 'Eastern' characteristics. Ambiguity is exorcised. As President Lennart Meri put it in his 1994
Independence Day address: 'Our border is the border of European values.'[33]

---

[29] See Kuus, 2007, chapter 6.   [30] Huntington, 1996, 130.
[31] Huntington, 1993a, 25.   [32] Ruutsoo, 1995, 13–15.
[33] Lagerspetz, 1999, 19. In the mainstream narrative of Estonian identity, it is the ethnic nation
rather than simply the state that is the principal subject of geopolitics. The re-independent
Estonian state draws its legitimacy from the Estonian nation, which pre-dates the state
and continued existing during the Soviet occupation of the state as well. Huntington's

The civilisational narrative furthermore frames different – anything 'Orthodox', 'Byzantine', 'Russian', 'Eastern' or 'Asian' – as threatening. Cultural differences between Estonia and Russia thereby become a security problem. Especially in the early 1990s, security constituted the meta-narrative of political debates.[34] Jüri Luik, Estonia's Foreign Minister at the time, said in 1994 that:

> We find ourselves located on the front line ... of the growing crisis in the East. At the same time, we are at the frontier of democratic and free-market thinking prevalent amongst our closest neighbours, with whom we share a coastline. Some would characterize our position as being between the devil and the deep Blue Sea.[35]

Russia is ominously present in these claims, not by virtue of the policies of the Russian state but by Russian identity and culture – Russianness as such. It is treated as essentially unchanging: a power that can pretend a certain Westernness, and even fool Westerners with it, but to whom Western values are ultimately alien. Rein Taagepera, a well-known and well-respected academic, explicitly contrasts Estonia's European character with the non-European ways of Russia: 'Whenever Russia or Serbia consider adopting western ways they must go outside and give up parts of themselves. In contrast, when Estonia or its Baltic neighbours (Latvia and Lithuania) adopt western ways, they only have to reach deeper and actually recover parts of themselves.'[36] Enn Soosaar, a prominent columnist, posited in 2003 simply that: 'Russia is Russia is Russia'.[37] Foreign policy commentators frequently caution against 'emotionalism' (heldida) in relations with Russia because 'seemingly intelligent and democratic [Russian] politicians or analysts can unexpectedly express positions that are oddly reminiscent of old thinking'.[38] Estonia's policies must therefore be based on a 'crystal clear understanding that the Russian threat is not a matter of diplomatic talk but a true fact of the ruthless world'.[39] Even after EU and NATO accession, the country's politicians as well as commentators argued that Estonia should attempt to 'correct' EU policy toward Russia, to make it more 'realistic', based on a better understanding of Russia's tendencies.

In this framework of an omnipresent Russian threat, EU and especially NATO memberships are seen as the only guarantees of security against the Russian threat. Throughout the EU accession process, pro-EU commentators argued that the undesirable aspects of the Union's membership, such as

---

civilisational thesis allows to argue not on the basis of contemporary political borders but to evoke putatively much older cultural borders.

[34] Ruutsoo, 2002, 38.   [35] Smith, 2001, 147.
[36] Taagepera, 1999.   [37] Soosaar, 2003.
[38] Kaldre, 2001. The numerous articles by Marko Mihkelson and Mart Helme, both prominent commentators, offer similar examples.
[39] Gräzin, 1996.

bureaucratic decision-making and the loss of national sovereignty must be put aside in the face of the Russian threat. The proclamation that starts this chapter puts it as follows: 'If Estonians want to be worthy of their history, we have to believe and say as firmly as Martin Luther: We stand on this side of the border of Europe and we cannot be in any other way.'[40] NATO accession is within this argument more desirable than EU membership because NATO offers the main reason for integration – security – without posing any constraints to Estonia's sovereignty.[41] As Russia is constructed as a threat not only to Estonia but to the whole of Europe, Estonia is presented as a guardian of European identity and security as much as its own.[42]

The figure of the Russian threat is not monolithic. Over the 1990s, it changed considerably, as the category of national security was reframed from exclusive terms of confrontation with Russia into inclusive terms of alignment with the West. Statements on an immediate Russian military threat that were the staple of governmental rhetoric in the early to mid 1990s, when Russian troops were still stationed on Estonian territory, had all but disappeared from mainstream political debates by the late 1990s. Estonia is not pushed to the West by a threat of invasion but pulled by common values. The Minister of Foreign Affairs declared to a European Parliament committee in 1997 that 'Estonia does not want to join the NATO of the Cold War. In both location and spirit Estonia is a part of the new Europe and we feel entitled to be constructively involved in the formation of the new European defence arrangement'.[43] Estonia's pursuit of NATO membership is likewise cast not in military but in cultural terms. In the words of the (former) Foreign Minister Ilves, NATO membership would codify 'common values – peace, freedom, democracy and welfare – which Estonia values above all'.[44] While the National Defense Policy Framework states in 1996 that the main sources of threats to Estonia are 'aggressive imperial ambitions and political and/or military instability', the Minister of Foreign Affairs Toomas Hendrik Ilves (2000) stressed a year later that 'Estonia sees no specific threats to regional security'. The National Security Concept from 2000 indeed posits that Estonia perceived no military threat to itself from any state. The document articulates Estonia's security concerns in terms of risks not threats, listing 'possible instability and politically uncontrollable developments in the international arena as well as international crises' as Estonia's prime security risks.[45] With regard to Estonian–Russian relations, government officials allude to a steady improvement.

---

[40] Luik *et al.*, 2003.   [41] See Kuus, 2007, for further discussion.
[42] Luik, 1995.
[43] Ilves, 1997. This cultural framing of security corresponds to the re-conceptualisation of NATO in cultural and civilisational terms. See Williams and Neumann, 2000 and Kuus, 2009.
[44] Ilves, 1996.   [45] Estonian Ministry of Foreign Affairs, 2001.

Governmental security rhetoric changed so much as to fuel popular concern that the government was simply mimicking Western countries and neglecting Estonia's existential insecurities. At Parliamentary debates of the National Security Concept in early 2000, several Members of Parliament (MPs) from both the coalition and the opposition prodded Foreign Minister Ilves on the vague 'soft' definition of security. The Concept and the Ministry received back-handed compliments for having done an excellent job at producing a document that pleases the West. In 2003, the National Security Concept was revised again, and the notion of territorial defence based on mobilisation was taken out (in favour of a smaller and more mobile armed force). The change sparked criticism from several defence experts, and resulted in a broader and at times acrimonious debate about whether Estonia's security policy adequately considers the country's insecure geopolitical situation.[46] The argument revolved around the question of whether or not Estonia could afford to depart from the concept of territorial defence. The official government position was that, given the absence of direct threat and the obligations of NATO membership, territorial defence was no longer primary. The counter-arguments stressed that given Estonia's 'unpredictable neighbour', the country should maintain the principle of territorial defence.

These examples illustrate how security has become articulated not through images of an invading army but through the more opaque notions of 'the grey zone', 'unpredictable neighbour' or 'geopolitics'. Yet this has not dissolved or even diminished the figure of threat. Whereas references to a military threat declined over the second half of the 1990s, references to 'security' actually increased during the same time period.[47] Parallel with this softening of security rhetoric, the goal of NATO accession became more entrenched in political debates. By the mid to late 1990s, neutrality came to be evaluated as a dangerous policy that would make these countries more vulnerable (presumably to aggression).[48] The refrain of the pro-EU arguments was that 'a no to the EU is a yes to Russia'. In the words of Jüri Luik, a prominent politician and Estonia's ambassador to Washington at the time: 'If we reject the EU, we'll quietly but surely sink toward Russia.'[49]

---

[46] NATO recommended that Estonia develop more mobile and professional armed forces. In Estonia, this was seen as pressure to give up the principle of total defence. For the present argument, the important nuance here is that territorial defence is so important in Estonia, despite the rhetorical emphasis on no outside threats. This indicates ambivalence about what security is and how it ought to be achieved.

[47] Noreen, 2002.

[48] Haab, 1998, 118. Haab makes this comment in the context of all Baltic states. Such shifts are not endogenous to Estonia of course. In the mid 1990s, the Clinton administration also started advocating Baltic membership in NATO. The issue for me is not what 'caused' NATO membership pursuits, but how these pursuits are justified and legitimised in public debates.

[49] City Paper, 2003.

The category of foreign threat has therefore not lost its political expediency. Leading up to the referendum on EU accession, Prime Minister Siim Kallas used foreign threat as a key argument. If the referendum were to fail, Kallas[50] maintained, Estonia would slide 'dangerously close' to Russia, with its discernible 'wish to restore the Stalin-era empire'. Later that year, Minister of Justice Ken-Marti Vaher stressed that 'the much-feared threat from the East has not disappeared'.[51] Thus, the rationale for supporting US action in Iraq, action which over half of the population did not support, was the Russian threat. Prime Minister Kallas raised the spectre of 'Stalin junior' coming to power in Russia, and implied that opposition to the Iraq War was equal to 'bowing to' Russia or the Soviet Union.[52] Mart Helme, a former ambassador to Russia and a prominent foreign affairs commentator at the time, maintained that Estonia should support the United States because 'exaltedly flag-waving Americans' offer Estonia better protection than '[European] bureaucrats soaked in Brussels-style cleverness'.[53]

Do these examples illustrate only elite views or do they illuminate a broader popular mood? Yes and no. Opinion polls indicate that the majority of ethnic Estonians consider Russia a potential threat to Estonia and about one half think that about Russian-speakers in Estonia. At the same time, most Estonians do not consider Estonia under an imminent threat and many harbour what Anatol Lieven[54] calls (in the Latvian context) a 'relaxed attitude' towards Russian-speakers. Russophobia has been criticised in national newspapers both by ethnic Estonians and non-Estonians and there is a small counter-culture of mocking the official Russophobic rhetoric: for example the humour sections of the weekly *Eesti Ekspress*.[55] Business circles have been active behind the scenes to improve bilateral relations with Russia. This is not surprising considering that an estimated 10 per cent of Estonia's GDP was related to Russia-bound transit (in the early 2000s).[56] As one anonymous businessman put it when criticising Estonia's inflexible attitude in relations with Russia: 'If one wants a muscular leg, he does not have to cut off the other leg to accomplish this.'[57] Poor relations with Russia were one of the most consistent criticisms of Foreign Minister Ilves. When Kristiina Ojuland from the pro-business Reform Party became Foreign Minister in early 2003, there was considerable talk about more positive relations. The move towards a revised Russian policy as highly controversial, however. Ojuland was depicted as naive and inconsistent and her foreign policy was accused of lacking stamina.

These calls for a more flexible Russian policy did not result in any consistent questioning of the civilisational framing of public policy. The public

---

[50] Kallas, 2003b.   [51] *Eesti Päevaleht*, 2003.
[52] Kallas, 2003a.   [53] Helme, 2002.
[54] Lieven, 1993.   [55] E.g. *Eesti Ekspress*, 1999.
[56] Neivelt, 2002.   [57] Bronstein, 2002.

sphere – including national media, academic writing and public political proclamations – is dominated by Huntingtonian arguments. There is criticism of
particular statements or particular policies but not of the taken-for-granted
assumptions on which these statements and actions rest. Threat is not always
present but it is always available for activation. It is not publicly challenged. Tiit
Vähi, who served as Prime Minister twice in the 1990s, commented in 2001
that the Russian threat is a key source of progress in Estonia. That fear, he predicted, will take Estonia to the EU. 'But there are better reasons for joining the
eurounion than fear.'[58] Jaan Kaplinski, a pre-eminent poet and public intellectual has been virtually alone in his critical reflections on the Estonian security
and identity discourses. Estonian political debate, Kaplinski said in 1998, had
become a 'monomania' where all politics is reduced to security – defined in
cultural terms – and all security is reduced to getting into the EU and NATO.
In this monomania, culture has become 'a slogan for security policy', 'the work-
horse that should pull [Estonia's] wagon into the EU and NATO'.[59] Responding
to the claim that Estonians have held Europe's intellectual or spiritual border
on one place for 500 years, Kaplinski notes that 5,000 years ago, 'there were
no Estonians, Slavs, or European spirit. There was no Christianity or orthodox faith, Latin or Cyrillic alphabet or Russian lawlessness'.[60] Public reaction to
Kaplinski's scepticism on the civilisational framing of politics has been mostly
negative. Mihkel Mutt, a prominent writer, explicitly invokes geopolitics, calling such articles invitations to the grey zone.[61]

Civilisational ethnicity?

Defining security in terms of identity casts individuals as carriers of geopolitics. Within this definition, Estonia's Westernness is determined by the identity
and behaviour of individual (ethnic) Estonians. Lauristin and Vihalemm, for
example, use individualism as indicators of ethnic Estonians' Westernness.[62]
Among ethnic Estonians, they argue, it is difficult to find non-Western characteristics.[63] Among Russians, however, Western credentials are not as strong.

The civilisational narrative therefore operates on scales other than the state
and the nation. It takes geopolitics to the level of individuals and pervades political debates in a host of domestic issues too, including immigration, citizenship, minority rights and education. Kaido Jaanson,[64] a prominent academic,

---

[58] Vähi, 2001.   [59] Kaplinski, 1998.
[60] Kaplinski, 2003.   [61] Mutt, 2002.
[62] They compare the attitudes and behavioural patterns of Swedes, Estonians and Russians
living in Estonia. By the same criteria, they concede that Estonians are less 'Western' than
Swedes.
[63] Vihalemm and Lauristin, 1997.
[64] Jaanson, 1998.

stresses in his presentation to the President's Academic Council that it is ludicrous to define national security in terms of inter-state relations without considering demography and education.

The domestic effects of the civilisational narrative are discernible especially in discussions of minority rights and citizenship.[65] About one-third of Estonia's population is ethnically not Estonian, mostly Russian, Ukrainian and Belorussian. In everyday parlance, they are commonly labelled as non-Estonians or Russian-speakers as most have adopted Russian as their first language. Within the identity-based framing of security, they are bearers of a non-Western culture who inevitably dilute the European and Western character of Estonia.

The lines of the alleged civilisational conflict go not only between Estonia and Russia but also within Estonia, between the country's Estonian and Russian-speaking populations. Speaking of Estonian identity, Jaanson[66] argues that the Soviet era left in Estonia 'a community whose members originate from an alien civilization or even civilizations. In this sense, Estonia has become more distant from Europe as a civilization than at any time since the 13th century'. Jüri Saar, Professor of Psychology at the Academy of State Defence links this presence directly to threat, positing that:

> civilizational conflict exists as a reality in all of these persons here who still have to adapt to new values and norms. I think that it would be extremely short-sighted and silly to speak of Estonia as a territory with two peoples who speak different languages, but whose civilizational background is both unnecessary and impossible to distinguish.[67]

Individual behaviour that is deemed as not sufficiently Western becomes potentially threatening. Especially in the early 1990s, Estonia's non-Estonian population was frequently represented as a fifth column whom Russia could use to destabilise Estonia.[68] In his 'mid-way report' of Estonia's return to the West from 1997, Enn Soosaar,[69] a prominent intellectual, writes that:

> We should not forget that there are undoubtedly individuals and interest groups in today's Estonia who would support integration with the East, and even though they are in a clear minority, they may become active (possibly as a result of foreign inspiration). They do not have to play with open cards. It suffices, for example, to mask as ones looking for a 'third way'. If Estonia's

---

[65] The situation of the Russian-speaking population in Estonia (as well as Latvia) has received extensive media and academic coverage. For comprehensive overviews of the minority rights situation in 1990s Estonia, see Feldman, 2005; Jurado, 2003 and Kolstø, 2002. In legal terms, most Russian-speakers were not members of the national minority since they were not Estonian citizens. I use the term minority because Russian-speakers constitute a de facto ethnic minority in Estonia.

[66] Jaanson, 2003, 134.   [67] Saar, 1998.

[68] Raudsepp, 1998.   [69] Soosaar, 2003a, 37.

integration with the West is hampered, we will be sucked sooner or later ...
into the CIS or another similar association.

Ethnic integration thus becomes a potential threat to Estonia as it would
increase the role of Russia-friendly individuals in the Estonian society. The fifth
column metaphor comes up easily whenever Russian-speakers' opinions differ
from Estonians – on issues such as NATO accession or NATO's 1999 action
in Kosovo. Those differences are explained not in terms of political opinion
but cultural identity.[70] Klara Hallik's analysis of party platforms in the 1990s
Estonia shows a strong ethnic self-defence orientation among all Estonian parties. The presence of Russian speakers in Estonia is seen as a major existential
threat to the Estonian nation. Invoking Huntington, Mart Nutt, an MP and one
of the principal authors of Estonia's aliens and citizenship legislation, calls it
'a ruthless fact' that a Russian considers a Serb as a brother while an Estonian
will remain an alien. 'Blood is thicker than water', Nutt continues, 'And this
holds true also for the Russian who, according to some sociologists, has been
integrated'.[71]

Within this framework, ethnicity and ethnic identity become integral parts
of security policy. The 'Integration in Estonian Society 2000–2007' document,
the principal policy framework of ethnic integration, indeed starts from the
premise that there are two distinct societies in Estonia – the Estonian and the
non-Estonian one – and that this 'may become dangerous both socially and
from the point of view of security policy'.[72] Crucially, the issue is not the politics
of the Russian state but the given identity of individual Russians.[73] Similarly to
inter-state relations, the civilisational narrative presents a picture of immutable
identities that have been in place for a thousand years 'and will always be' to
quote the letter by Estonian intellectuals that started this chapter.

---

[70] Haab, 1998, points out that in 1995, the Ministry of Defence drew up a plan to establish an alternative service to non-citizen permanent residents – most of whom are
Russian-speakers – to train them for rescue operations and to provide them with Estonian
language courses. The proposal was stalled in the parliament because several MPs assessed
it as potentially leading to the formation of a trained fifth column. See also Taagepera,
1998.

[71] Nutt, 1999.

[72] Estonian Ministry of Ethnic Affairs, 2000, 17.

[73] The references to blood hark back to biological conceptions of identity. Kiin, a prominent
journalist and a press secretary of the Pro Patria faction in the Parliament, implies that
Estonians are European among other things because Germans and other landlords fathered
children with Estonian women for centuries (Kiin, 1999). As a mirror of that argument,
another prominent Estonian politician argued in 1989 that because Russian women had
been raped by Mongol men for centuries, the Russian people were untamed and wild and
tended to spread like a blob over all the territory they could find (Neumann, 1999, 107).
Utterances such as Made's had become rare in the mainstream politics by the second half of
the 1990s, but Neumann reports a Lithuanian diplomat calling it 'common folk wisdom' in
the Baltic states (Neumann, 1999).

As in foreign policy, the civilisational framing of ethnicity is not static. Over the 1990s, the keywords of minority rights debates changed from decolonisation and purification in the early 1990s to integration and multiculturalism late in the decade.[74] During Estonia's accession negotiations with the EU, successive governments made a number of policy changes to ease the integration of Russian-speakers, about two-thirds of whom were not Estonian citizens at the time, into the Estonian society. Estonia fully complies with European legal norms on citizenship and minority rights protection, since the late 1990s. Various monitoring missions, as well as EC reports throughout the accession negotiations, have found no systematic infringement on minority rights in Estonia.

This is not to imply that most Estonians are Russophobes. Indeed, explicit Russophobia no longer has the political cache it enjoyed in the early 1990s. Even many ethnic Estonians are getting increasingly tired of the 'stuffy ethnic state' and its archaic self-conceptions.[75] However, alongside a certain opening of Estonian identity narratives towards more inclusive conceptions of Estonianness, the territorial imaginary of a cultural homeland that is the eastern outpost of the Western civilisation has become normalised and further entrenched in Estonian political life. This inscription of civilisational difference and otherness has normalised ethnocentrism in Estonia. Maaris Raudsepp[76] notes that by the second half of the 1990s, formerly legitimate (although often disliked) members of the society were transformed into inferior states subjects. While the most negative characterisations of Russian-speakers decreased over the 1990s, terms such as alien became more mainstream and accepted.[77] While early in the decade Russian-speakers reacted angrily to such characterisations, by the mid to late 1990s these had become a part of common terminology. In the atmosphere where those 'properly' Western – that is, ethnic Estonians – have more legitimacy to speak, public debates are structured against non-Estonians before anything is said. The state project of ethnic integration does not undermine the concept of civilisational differences but is premised on such presumed differences. It seeks to manage putative civilisational antagonism while leaving the concept itself intact.

Conclusion

Above and beyond the specific political issues discussed above, the chapter foregrounds the ways in which geopolitics has been reframed from a political to a cultural enterprise in post-Soviet Estonia. To foreground the Huntingtonian premises of political debates in Estonia is not to imply vehement anti-Russian

[74] Lauristin and Heidmets, 2002.   [75] Lieven, 1993, 304.
[76] Raudsepp, 1998.   [77] Noreen, 2002.

sentiment among the elites or the population. Estonian–Russian relations have improved since the early 1990s. Ethnic relations are peaceful, and, according to opinion polls, most people characterise them as positive.[78] Multiculturalism is now the official vision of the Estonian society.[79] Many of the individuals quoted here are respected liberals who wish to see the Russian-speaking minority integrated into a multicultural society. Their effort is not to marginalise Russian-speakers but to describe Estonia's political and cultural situation so as to improve it. Many of the statements quoted in the chapter are not meant to conjure geopolitical maps or inscribe threats. They are intended as descriptions of the 'real' situation and they function as such within Estonian political debates.

My concern in this chapter was not with what is said (about geopolitics) but what makes this possible. The examples cited qualify not because everyone necessarily agrees with them but because they are widely held and common sense; they elucidate no reaction and can be uttered thoughtlessly. Huntington is important not only because his theory matches historical conceptions of Russia and the West in Estonia – although this dynamic is important. Hungtington has been *made* a key figure because his theory is supremely useful for multiple political projects. It resonates in domestic debates and, even more importantly, it resonates in the West. It is an effective marketing tool. A wide range of people from different political persuasions use the civilisational narrative because it works for their specific political goals. It takes geopolitics from the realm of explicit intellectual and political debate to the level of the common sense. It masks the theoretical framework and intellectual trajectory of the arguments. We are left with a common-sense narrative that 'wallows in the evident', as Roland Barthes[80] would put it. That narrative does not appear to be geopolitical, theoretical, even intellectual; it appears to only describe something as deeply personal and also fundamental as cultural identity. It brings a seeming clarity and a closure of people, places and events. Geopolitics appears as a harmonious display of essences.

The effect of civilisational geopolitics has been to make the figure of threat more flexible. Although threat is conceived in rather vague cultural terms, the lines of threatened us and threatening them are maintained and have in some cases become even more entrenched. The bundling up of security and identity has made security policy undisputable. Geopolitics is simultaneously banalised – taken to the level of 'mere' culture and fundamentalised – and cast in terms of essences 'that cannot be changed', to quote Huntington. Politics is shifted to a binary framework in which being not sufficiently Estonian or pro-Estonian equals supporting Russia.

---

[78] See Heidmets, 1998.
[79] Lauristin and Heidmets, 2002.
[80] Barthes, 1980, 150.

More broadly, the civilisational narrative works because is satisfies the requirements of enmity: the ways in which otherness is still a necessary part of identity construction. It does not simply rehearse negative images of what 'we' fear and what 'we' are not; it also produces identity and interest. It produces a domestic society, which the state can claim to protect. As much of Estonian, and Central European, politics has revolved around efforts of nation- and state-building, external threat has played an important if not essential part in it. Its productive functions are still in place. Civilisational geopolitics serves to consolidate the European and national identities to be secured, to reify Russia as essentially un-European, and to frame complex political issues in terms of emergency measures that should be above or beyond normal political debate.

The key change in the 1990s, then, was not the quantity of geopolitical reasoning but the specific political functions of such reasoning. Geopolitical claims were normalised and banalised. Arguments that still carried connotations of interest or belief in the mid 1990s were presented as truisms by the end of the decade. The circular reasoning in which geopolitics and identity are explained in terms of each other is so well-rehearsed and common sense as to no longer require evidence or elicit reaction. Historical and political complexities are rendered as essences that spring unproblematically from history. At the same time, civilisational geopolitics is not a cast-iron framework but a flexible enabling tool. Within it, a conception of Russians as others and as security risks emerges *logically*. If Estonian security is conceived in terms of a civilisational faultline, then any manifestation of orthodox civilisation can *only* be conceived as a problem. That conception is seen as common sense and unremarkable. It is, after all, taught even to schoolchildren. The significance of the civilisational narrative lies not in what it explicitly prescribes, but in what it implicitly enables.

9

Russia: geopolitics from the heartland

ALEXANDER ASTROV AND NATALIA MOROZOVA

In 2005, in his annual address to the Federal Assembly, the then Russian President Vladimir Putin defined the dissolution of the Soviet Union as 'the biggest geopolitical catastrophe of the century'. What better evidence can be provided for the revival of geopolitics in post-Soviet Russia?

Whereas hardly any reference to the geopolitical tradition could be found in the Russian or Soviet security imaginary prior to 1991, the 1990s witnessed an astonishing turn in both politics and academia. The leader of the embattled Russian Communists referred to Mackinder in his attempt to reorganise the party along national-patriotic lines.[1] On the other side of the political spectrum, the Chairman of the Duma Committee on Geopolitics, a Liberal Democrat, representing the Communists' bitter rivals, chose Haushofer as his reference.[2] An Academy of Geopolitical Problems was established, mainly by the former military, and actively proliferated its vision.[3] University courses devoted to the subject mushroomed across the country; the first Russian-language translations of key geopolitical texts were made available to the public, and a number of textbooks and more specialised monographs and articles were published.[4] And now even the President entered the fray.

Yet there is some counter-evidence as well. The rest of Putin's 2005 address had very little, if anything, to do with geopolitics or foreign policy, for that matter. Nor are there any references to geopolitics in his later Munich speech, presented in a more straightforwardly realist manner. By then, the Geopolitics Committee had long been disbanded. Still popular in academia, geopolitics nevertheless no longer enjoys the privileged position it seemed to hold throughout the 1990s. Historical analogies used in the discussion of the 2008 war in Georgia, for example, were centred on ideological and bureaucratic factors rather than environmental determinist ones.[5] Perhaps, more significantly, whereas in the 2005 address the geopolitical reading is presented as an antidote

---

[1] Bassin and Aksenov, 2006, 102–105.
[2] Mitrofanov, 1997, 220–222.
[3] Ivashov, 2002 and Nartov, 2003.
[4] Bassin and Aksenov, 2006, 100.
[5] Zatulin, 2008.

to the heated ideological debates, since then meaningful ideological debates of any kind are hard to come by, save for the discussions of history.

All in all, there is an impression that the 2005 address, with its bold geopolitical reference, marked a certain watershed in Russia's post-1991 history. Even the way the geopolitical reference was situated in the text brought the preceding period to a close, while the rest of the address, and Putin's second term in office generally, was more oriented towards the future, a future in which geopolitics was not to play a significant role, at least as far as the Russian security imaginary is concerned.

How are we to understand this, in view of the volume's main thesis that a geopolitical revival is best understood in the context of an 'ontological crisis' for which the environmental determinism intrinsic to geopolitics would provide a quick and easy fix? This chapter introduces a qualification of the main hypothesis. Although it seems fair to argue that geopolitics was mobilised to counter an identity crisis (and not only in foreign policy) in the 1990s, ultimately the security imaginary was recomposed without much geopolitical determinism. Instead, other identity lineages have been mobilised, and other political understandings fixed.[6]

Hence, a geopolitical revival did happen, but one which did not significantly affect Russia's redefined security imaginary. Although triggered as an easy fix, it eventually failed to turn the security imaginary geopolitical. How is this possible? The answer may be found in one of Jutta Weldes'[7] takes on the Cuban Missile Crisis, in which she supplements her main thesis – the way states experience certain events as crises is conditioned by their security imaginary – with the argument that the way states imagine their security is conditioned by their experience of crises: 'The construction of crises ... occurs in tandem with the construction and reconstruction of state identity.' Or, to paraphrase a well-known aphorism, states construct crises and crises construct states.

The importance of this claim consists in the supposition that states' security imaginaries predispose state officials to represent unsettling events as crises because crises, in turn, reinforce not only security imaginary but state identity as such by triggering the logic of difference/otherness constitutive of any identity.[8] The mutually constitutive relation between crises and state identity does not have to result in the reinforcement of the existing security imaginary. As long as security imaginaries are not fixed but selective, the foreign-policy-expert community can always emphasise one set of factors already present in 'their' security imaginary at the expense of others. Thus, if a geopolitical tradition

---

[6] Morozov, 2009b and Prozorov, 2010.

[7] Weldes, 1999b, 57.

[8] In this sense, representing Europe's past as Europe's Other, for example, is no less a social construction of crisis than a hypothetical transformation of the current 'security culture' of the EU into a Hobbesian one.

is already present in a given state's security imaginary, even if in dormant or ostracised form, its reawakening or rehabilitation is not impossible in principle, and would certainly signify a change in the security imaginary.

Still, whereas the mutually constitutive relation between state identity and crises does not exclude the possibility of change in the security imaginary, it does pose problems for the explanation of change when that happens, as it were, *ex nihilo*. And this seems to be the case in Russia, where most of the adherents of the geopolitical tradition never grew tired of emphasising both its timeless truths and its *novelty* for Russian foreign-policy making.

There are, of course, other, more sensitive proponents of geopolitics, who attempt to resolve the problem of origin by (re-)presenting the geopolitical tradition as Russia's own, usually linking it to some marginal, abortive or repressed tradition in the 'native' past.[9] These past traditions do not have to identify themselves directly with geopolitics. The task of constructing all necessary links and affinities lies with later representations. Yet these links and affinities still have to be constructed from available discursive resources, since ideas indeed, as stated in Part I to this volume, do not float freely. But where are these resources to be found if not in the security imaginary?

Again, Weldes' argument provides a possible answer. Before any analysis of the social construction of a crisis begins for real, certain discursive themes central to the identity of a given community have to be identified. In Weldes, such themes are already present in the security imaginary, but this does not necessarily have to be the case.[10]

Since security imaginaries are stable structures of meaning, the same themes may also exist outside of the security imaginary, since what matters, to use Waltzian language, is not only the identity of the units (themes) but also a possible difference in the principle of their organisation (the way these themes are woven into a coherent story). Yet, on occasion, it is possible that the mere similarity of the themes may trigger a process through which the circle of the mutual constitution of state identity and crises is broken. One tradition (as a specific arrangement of a given set of themes) located outside of a security imaginary is employed solely for the purpose of representing a set of events as a crisis, while the task of fixing this crisis is taken over by another tradition, already included into the security imaginary.

Think of George Kennan's life-long indignation with the appropriation of his analysis of the 'sources of Soviet conduct' by American policy makers. While

---

[9] Morozova, 2009.

[10] For example, people were always dying, giving birth or struggling with physical and mental diseases. These practices have always shaped the identity of a given community. Yet, until the rise of biopolitics, however one dates or defines this historic occurrence, they were of little interest to the state. So with certain discursive themes that may well exist (all or some of them) outside of the security imaginary, in so far as security imaginary is defined in relation to state-security, as it is defined in this volume.

accepting his conclusions ('containment'), they disregarded some of his analytical premises, most notably the idea that 'Soviet conduct', rather than being reducible to a single characteristic (ideology) had diverse 'sources' and thus required diversified modes of containment. In the long run, the difference in representation of the other did matter, but crises are rarely about the long run: they require urgent action, which often has to be content with less than making full sense of the situation. And so 'containment' it was, with Kennan named as its 'father'.

In a similar way, in our analysis, a geopolitical revival in Russia did happen and succeeded as far as the construction of the crisis was concerned. However, geopolitics was no longer needed for the purposes of fixing the crisis thus construed. Not least because the specific differentiation/othering built into the geopolitical construction of the crisis allowed for the reactivation of a more familiar security imaginary. Hence, the 'geopolitical catastrophe' worked as a diagnosis of the preceding situation, but geopolitical thinking did not provide any future remedy.[11]

This chapter retraces the different attempts to turn geopolitics from an inspiration which framed the understanding of the crisis of Russian foreign-policy identity into an actual solution to this crisis, an undertaking which eventually failed. We begin by identifying four themes in the post-1991 Russian debates: ideology, modernisation, Russia's distinctiveness, and possible objective grounds for the assertion of this distinctiveness. Geopolitics, initially brought in to address the first and the last of these themes, failed to provide a stable structure of meaning capable of addressing all four. As a result, the tradition of Eurasianism was invoked, which addressed the same four themes in a different manner. However, it was marked with tensions and incoherencies of its own. To address these, various interpretations of geopolitics were grafted onto the original Eurasianism.

Of these interpretations we focus on two, Aleksandr Dugin's and Vadim Tsymburskii's. This choice is justified by the following considerations. First, one of these versions, that of Dugin, is by far the most influential and the one most analysed by outside observers. Dugin stands out as probably the only representative of the 'patriotic' opposition in Russia whose vocabulary has made successful inroads into the official discourse and elicited support from political and military elites. Thus Dugin proceeded from attempting to create a united front of several extremist groups in Moscow in 1994 to being appointed official adviser to the then speaker of the State Duma in 1998. By 2000 his *Foundations of Geopolitics* had been reissued four times. He was invited to teach at the Academy of the General Staff and at the Institute for Strategic Research. Dugin is widely regarded in Western scholarship as the 'voice' of contemporary

---

[11] This is what they used to say about Metternich: 'Many in Europe admired his diagnoses, few would agree with his remedies.'

Russian geopolitics. He is also often defined as a 'conservative revolutionary' or a 'fascist', an exponent of the European New Right or a self-styled evangelist of Haushofer.

The second consideration is that the radical difference between Dugin's geopolitical treatment of Eurasianism and Tsymburskii's highlights the distinction between the two kinds of 'crises' constructed through such treatments. Unlike numerous other critics of Dugin, both in Russia and abroad, Tsymburskii invariably took his opponent seriously, never attempting to accuse him of crimes by association (with German Nazism or Russia's own nationalistic far-right), trying instead to analyse suggested associations theoretically. This analytical work was never merely reactive but remained grounded in Tsymburskii's own original version of geopolitics. The latter enjoyed far less support of policy makers in comparison to that of Dugin, yet continued to attract academic attention and appreciation.

Finally, speaking of the endorsement of Dugin's geopolitical construction of the crisis by Russian policy makers, this construction displays very little dependence on the materialist environmental factors and still, as we would argue, does contain within itself the element of determinism which allows for its substantive identification with neoclassical geopolitics. This mainly cultural determinism, or essentialism, provides the link between the explicitly geopolitical construction of the ontological crisis of the 1990s and the actual policies, no longer geopolitical in any meaningful sense, which were later deployed for the fixing of this crisis.

The ontological crisis of the 1990s

It is hardly surprising that as one of the principal protagonists of the Cold War story, Russia was affected by its abrupt ending. The extent of the resulting crisis is perhaps best appreciated when viewed in the light of the subsequent failure of Russian foreign-policy elites to fall back on any readily available security imaginary. In fact, the crisis entailed the radical questioning of the validity of both Soviet and Russian traditional views of the world and the country's place in it. This is not, of course, to say that no security imaginary was available in principle. That would have been tantamount to the lack of any foreign-policy identity. No crisis is so severe. Still, in a manner characteristic of the early 1990s in Russia generally, most of the available structures of meaning were fiercely contested.

Initially, geopolitics was invoked as a potential solution, particularly appealing precisely due to its alleged neutrality and thus 'objectivity' amidst the heated ideological debate. It soon became clear, however, that both sides, liberals and 'patriots', were keen to appeal to geopolitics in this objectivist manner. Yet, precisely because of the ideological thinness of such objectivist geopolitics, it could not possibly perform the function assigned to it. Both camps then came up with additional fixers to buttress their versions of geopolitics. In the case of the 'patriots', this took the form of Eurasianism. However, this intellectual tradition historically had important tensions of its own which had to be addressed before it could be placed in the service of geopolitics.

A cold war within: liberals vs. 'patriots'

To start with the most obvious reaction of Russian foreign-policy elites to the dissolution of the Soviet Union, it is certainly true, as many have argued, that they consistently sought recourse to what has always appeared as a preferred identity-fixer, namely Russia's 'great power' status.[12] There were, however, specifically post-Cold War problems associated with this strategy. To be sure, Russia's great-power ambitions have had their opponents throughout history; but, as Joseph Conrad's famous objection to Russia's membership in the great-powers club demonstrates, up until World War II, it was Russia's membership and not the legitimacy of the club itself that had been thus questioned. Later, the Cold War had its share of the debate on polarity, with the very notion of the 'pole' presupposing some ranking among states formally equal in status. Now, one of the important parts of the rapidly unfolding post-Cold War script was challenging any such ranking and leading to a much starker and overtly normative polarisation of the international society into 'normal' and 'rogue' states.[13]

Sensitive to this pressure, Russia's new, liberal foreign-policy elites attempted to come up with an array of variations on the 'normal great power' theme.[14] The problematic combination of the two adjectives, however, revealed the ambiguity of the liberal position within Russian foreign-policy elites generally. Whereas the demand for 'greatness' clearly came from within the domestic discourse, the specific liberal understanding of 'normalcy' was perceived as originating in the West. It was far from being universally shared domestically, and – most importantly – by associating 'normalcy' with democracy and economic modernisation, it subordinated foreign policy to domestic, the latter in turn conceived in overtly ideological terms.[15] This was nothing new to the old Soviet foreign-policy cadre, accustomed to taking Politburo orders, but for the various newcomers it served as an indication that, far from coming to an end, the Cold War was projected into Russian domestic politics.

Not surprisingly, despite the bewildering diversity (and often incoherence) of Russia's oppositional discourse of the early 1990s, one of its leading themes became that of the primacy of foreign policy. Democratisation, modernisation

---

[12] Hopf, 2002.   [13] Simpson, 2004.
[14] Crow, 1993; Kozyrev, 1992, 85 and Valdez, 1995, 94.
[15] Malcolm et al., 1996, 4 and Tuminez, 1996, 49.

and all other possible understandings of the post-communist transition were presented as ideologies legitimising the policy of diminishing Russia's global importance by forcing it to play by someone else's rules. Accordingly, Russia's freedom to set its own rules and to decide for itself was seen as a necessary alternative and a primary task of all politics; a view pitched against both post-Soviet liberals and the Soviet leadership they replaced. Both were presented as subordinating Russia's vital national interests to ideological dogmas. And this is where geopolitics first seems to enter the oppositional discourse as holding the key to these vital national interests.

The problem with this initial appropriation of geopolitics by the opposition was that it hardly differed from the version already adopted by the liberals in power. Thus, when Andrei Kozyrev, for example, invoked geopolitics, he also did so to signal Russia's new foreign policy's aversion to ideology and messianism and its preference for the pragmatic pursuit of national interests.[16] This 'difficulty' reveals the full extent of Russia's post-1991 'ontological crisis', which consisted not simply in the existence of two opposing positions on the nature of Russia's national interests and foreign policy, but rather in the absence of any set of criteria external to the debate itself to which the proponents of these positions could appeal in their confrontation.

Neither the traditional Russian nor the Soviet security imaginary provided any ready-made solutions for any of the camps. For instance, when, in 1992, one of the 'patriotic' groups central to the revival of geopolitics issued a statement on the Bosnian conflict, it appealed both to pan-Slavic solidarity and the idea of a renewed Holy Alliance between Russia and Central Europe (mostly, Germany). For pre-revolutionary Russia, however, these two alliances were contradictory rather than complementary. And when, as the most perceptive observers noticed, Russia had tried to play both Slavic and Germanic cards at once, 'keeping wolves not quite fed and sheep not quite safe', this had resulted in the Crimean War[17] – not the kind of security imaginary one can rely upon unproblematically. This is not to mention the fact that both pan-Slavism and the Holy Alliance, as code-names for Russian foreign policy, were based on elaborate ideological foundations, something post-1991 Russia not only lacked but actively sought to do without, not least with the help of geopolitics.

This aversion to ideology alone rendered problematic any straightforward recourse to the Soviet security imaginary. Hardly anyone in the Russia of the 1990s sought any renewal of the ideology-driven confrontation with the West modelled either on the immediate post-World War II 'containment' or the Reagan-inspired 'second Cold War'. Yet nor were there any discursive practices of the détente era that could be easily reactivated under the new conditions either. In so far as détente was understood as a trade-off between Western

---

[16] Valdez, 1995.   [17] Tsymburskii, 2007, 471.

assistance for Soviet modernisation and ideological decontamination of world politics, post-Soviet Russia, it seemed, wanted both of these things at once, expected both of them to be delivered by the West, and had very little to offer in exchange by way of a pragmatic 'linkage'. Throughout the 1990s, the only lever Russia more-or-less consistently attempted to use was a not-so-plausible threat of abandoning its democratic transition; and it was only in Putin's Munich speech of 2007 that détente-like rhetoric was used in its conceptually clear form.[18] However, even Putin's most loyal supporters could not fail to notice that the weakness of the Munich speech consisted not so much in 'the radicalism of its rhetoric, but in the underdevelopment of the standards for politics of the new, post-American world'.[19]

This criticism can also be applied to the initial Russian recourse to geopolitics. Rather than offering any solutions, the rhetorics of geopolitics invited instead at least two further debates: a (meta-)theoretical one, on the possible grounds for geopolitical objectivity, and a (meta-)practical one, on the character of Russian identity as a justification of Russia's civilisational distinctiveness and therefore its claims to 'freedom' the way the latter was understood by the advocates of the primacy of foreign-policy doctrine. Put differently, to serve as a fixer in the ongoing liberal/'patriotic' contestation, geopolitics itself required some fixing that, by explicitly moving away from the initial neutrality and objectivity, would buttress geopolitical claims with something distinctively 'Russian'. Liberals had already articulated such an addition as their case for 'normalcy', understood as Russia's long-standing need for further modernisation. The opposition was offered one in the form of Eurasianism.

Appealing as it was, because of its 'native' origins and similarity of the problem it was meant to address, namely Russia's place in a rapidly changing world, Eurasianism in its original form had theoretical difficulties of its own, again, rather similar to the ones it was now summoned to resolve. These we outline by drawing mostly on Nikolai Trubetzkoy's *Europe and Mankind*, the first explicitly Eurasian text written as a response to the crisis of the dissolution of the Russian Empire.[20]

Eurasian impasse: ideocracy and politics

If the 'ontological anxiety' experienced by Russian policy makers and the opposition after 1991 revolved around four major themes – modernisation,

---

[18] Putin's 'Munich speech' has often been presented as a declaration of a new 'Cold War'. This, however, overlooks one of its central points, clearly stressed by Putin: 'As is well-known, this organisation [OSCE] was created to examine all – I shall emphasise this – all aspects of security: military, political, economic, humanitarian *and, especially, the relations between these spheres*' (emphasis added). It is only after this allusion to 'linkage' that Putin launches his attack on Western unipolarity for disrupting the balance between the various spheres.

[19] Pavlovsky, 2010.   [20] Trubetzkoy, 1991, 1–64.

universalist ideological pressure coming from the West, the necessity to oppose or at least to neutralise this pressure through an appeal to some objective criteria and, last but not least, the question of Russia's civilisational distinctiveness – then Trubetzkoy's intervention provides the best starting point for tracing the process through which these four themes came to form the backbone of a fully-fledged geopolitical discourse. It is the best starting point because, although the themes themselves may be endemic to Russian political discourse at least since the first reactions to the reforms of Peter the Great, Trubetzkoy rearranges them in a genuinely original way. In this sense, his work is indeed the origin of the distinctive line of Russian political thought known as Eurasianism.

Perhaps, the most radical feature of *Europe and Mankind*, written when Russia had been abandoned by its former European allies, is that Trubetzkoy, in his turn, 'abandons' Europe. To begin with, he denies any meaningful political substance to the relations between European states. However subdivided legally, they form a single political entity driven by 'pan-European chauvinism': a combination of self-interest and civilising mission. The only viable alternative to both 'Europe' and Eurocentric, universalist 'mankind' would be an intermediate entity, similar to Europe in its intrinsic cultural diversity, but different in what makes it hang together politically. Whereas conventional Western middle-grounds were usually sought on the terrain of international law and customary diplomatic practices, Trubetzkoy's alternative, pan-Eurasian nationalism was rooted in two different levels, territorial and metaphysical, deliberately bypassing any legalistic structures. In fact, it was much closer to Mackinder's geopolitics read under the strong influence of Hegel.[21]

Read in this manner, Mackinder may be understood as claiming that a certain kind of history had come to an end. This history was driven by the tension between two closely linked processes: geographical exploration and imperial colonisation. Once these two processes encompassed the whole of the globe, history ended. However, a new tension, and therefore a new history and a new politics, come to the fore. Empires turn out to be different in kind. The first distinction is geographical, between maritime and continental powers, the second ideological, rooted in the various religious traditions. Geopolitics, as a new conflict that drives this new kind of history, is irreducible either to geography or ideology, but consists in the interplay between the two, with major lines of conflict located at the edges of the continental empires.

The Eurasian response to the geographical dimension of Mackinder's thesis was spearheaded by geographer-economist Petr Savitskii, who coined an oxymoronic label, 'continent-ocean', to describe Russia's distinctive place in the

---

[21] For Trubetzkoy's Hegelianism, see Anatoly Liberman, 'N.S. Trubetzkoy and His Works on History and Politics' (Trubetzkoy, 1991, 295–390).

global economy.[22] The general attack on Western theology and metaphysics was led by Georgii Florovskii, who attempted to lay bare what he believed to be the Judaic, and thus profoundly legalistic, core of Western philosophy and politics.[23] Neither of these two themes was genuinely new. Throughout the second half of the nineteenth century, the Slavophiles criticised Western rationalism on spiritual grounds, while scientists like Danilevskii attempted to provide a naturalistic response to the universalist aspirations of the West.[24] The distinctiveness of Eurasianism consisted not only in its attempt to bring together these two, previously unconnected, lines of critique but mostly – and this is where Trubetzkoy's contribution lies – in its radical revision of the history of Russian statehood.

All previous conceptualisations of Russian state identity revolved around the chain of principalities stretching from the Baltic to the Black Sea. The question, which the Slavophiles and the Westernisers chose to answer differently, was whether the future of this nucleus of the Russian state lay in the East or in the West. However, in both accounts, at least until the Russo-Japanese War of 1905, the East was perceived as a politically passive object of Russian expansion. Accordingly, even the Slavophiles attributed to Russia's political encounters with the West some special significance, often dramatised into a kind of love–hate relationship.

In Trubetzkoy's account, the so-called Kievan Rus' constituted a politically non-viable trading entity which in due course became an easy prey for the most ruthless conqueror around, Genghis Khan, who brought with him a new kind of political order, based on the nomadic code of honour, duty and absolute authority. However, this authority was thoroughly practical, not supported by any ideology capable of transcending the power of the ruler's personality. Although fascinated with the political virtues of the Tatars, Christian Russian elites could not accept the Yoke. Religious revival formed the backbone of their resistance, while the lasting authority conveyed by Orthodoxy onto sovereign power appealed to the Tatar nobility seeking more stable institutional arrangements. As a result, a new entity gradually took shape around two pillars: the Russian Church and the political legacy of Genghis Khan. This ideally autarkic polity was thoroughly multicultural, but required no elaborate legal or bureaucratic structures. The Church looked after the people's mores and represented them in the ongoing dialogue with the absolutist state, which, in turn, provided the people with benign power, mainly over the shared natural environment and the 'non-Orthodox element'.

Unfortunately, this power was also urgently needed elsewhere. To be able to respond to increasing pressure from the West, the Russian state had to learn its

---

[22] Vinkovetsky, 1996, 95–113.
[23] Vinkovetsky, 1996, 30–40.
[24] Vinkovetsky, 1996, 116–155.

new rival's technological trickery. Fatally, according to Trubetzkoy, technology went to its head and became an end in itself. The nomadic virtues of Genghis Khan were abandoned, giving way to non-creative bureaucratic servility. The Church was reformed and subjugated by the state as well. Thus, contrary to the Eurocentric myth according to which the servility of the Russian Church was the legacy of Byzantium, the later encounter with the Latin West was to blame for the destruction of the perfect synthesis of Orthodoxy and the legacy of Genghis Khan. The shocks of World War I and the Revolution duly followed.

Subsequent Soviet advances to the East, together with reforms that led to a stronger presence of Asian national minorities in Soviet political and cultural life, created a new situation: 'It seems that once again, as if it were seven hundred years ago, one can smell everywhere in Russia the odors of burning dung, horse sweat, camel hair – the smells of the nomad camp. And hovering over Russia is the shade of the great Genghis Khan, unifier of Eurasia.'[25]

So, here we have all the four themes identified in the post-1991 debates woven into a single story. Modernisation (now read as technological/bureau-cratic prowess) and ideology (as 'pan-European chauvinism') are presented as corrupting Western influences, so that no meaningful trade-offs or 'linkages' between the two can be found, or ought to be sought to begin with. Instead, his-torically, Russian civilisational distinctiveness, as well as the true source of its political power, lies in the 'Turanian' synthesis: a combination of Asian polit-ical virtues and Orthodox ideocracy, quite literally understood as a set of ideas capable of imbuing traditional conduct with lasting political power. Finally, the Stalinist rebuilding of the original site of the Turanian synthesis in the form of the Soviet Union suggested that there was more to this site than mere historical contingency. Now the task was to uncover the underlying regularities behind the continuity of Russian politico-territorial identity; and this is where original Eurasianism ran into an impasse.

Already at the level of geography, Eurasianism remained undecided about the exact delineation of Eurasia. Both Savitskii and Trubetzkoy equated Eurasia with Russia in a programmatic formula Russia-Eurasia. However, Russia-Eurasia, defined as 'neither Europe nor Asia' or 'both Europe and Asia', referred to two different entities at once. On the one hand, it designated an imaginary continent, to be found not on any map but only in the Russian pol-itical imagination. This continent was envisaged as a still centre amidst the turmoil of the anti-colonial movement that Eurasians clearly foresaw. On the other, it referred to the whole of the Old World. Trubetzkoy's theoretical com-mitment to constructing Russian political identity 'from the East', along with Stalin's de facto construction of Soviet identity through opposition to the West and incorporation of Eastern territories, clearly privileged the first option. However, even Trubetzkoy had to admit that any genuine Orthodox project

---

[25] Trubetzkoy, 1991, 224–225.

would be out of place as an ideocratic foundation of the newly emerging political entity. Consequently, instead of celebrating the new Turanian synthesis, Eurasianism was forced to choose between Orthodox ideocracy, as the unifying and legitimising power of ideas, and the sheer force of the Stalinist regime.

Again, it is tempting to see this choice as endemic to Russian political history; and again, it is important to stress the originality of the Eurasian formulation of it. Thus, when, in the wake of the European upheavals of 1848, the Russian diplomat and poet, Fyodor Tjutchev, proclaimed that there were only two forces left in Europe, traditionalist Russia and the Revolution, one of the foremost Russian Westernisers, Petr Chaadaev, was quick to point out that lamenting Russian traditional virtues demolished by Peter the Great and at the same time positing Russia as a pillar of the European order involved either naive self-contradiction or hypocrisy.[26] For Russia's position in Europe was due to the power violently invested in it by Peter. Tjutchev was indeed open to such criticism, as were Slavophiles generally, because he never questioned Russia's place in the European order, preferring to question specific configurations of that order instead. Eurasians considered themselves immune to this line of critique because they did not count Petrine/European power as power proper. For them, Peter was a dabbler, the emperor of the handicraftsmen, who in his fascination with numerous engineering projects neglected his only duty – to rule. Scientific man vs. power politics indeed.[27]

Yet faced with the necessity (and the impossibility) of establishing the continuity between the Turanian synthesis and Stalinist state-building practices, Eurasianism split along a number of different lines. Pragmatists, interested mainly in the viability of the new Russian political entity, abandoned any ideocratic pretences and allied themselves with the new Soviet rulers. Ideocratic fundamentalists accused Savitskii and Trubetzkoy of compromising the Orthodox core of Eurasianism for the sake of their fascination with the East. Geopoliticians of the continental persuasion saw any attempts to graft Orthodoxy onto geopolitics as unwarranted theoretical frivolity. Finally, Trubetzkoy himself, unwilling to embrace either communist or Nazi ideology, seemed to have come to the conclusion that the question of Russia's geopolitical identity required a prior rethinking of Russia's identity *tout court*. In 1925, he wrote to Savitskii:

> I am simply terrified by what is happening to us. I feel that we have got ourselves into a swamp that, with every new step of ours, consumes us deeper and deeper. What are we writing about to each other? What are we talking about? What are we thinking about? – Only politics. We have to call things by their real name – we are politicking, living under the sign of the primacy

[26] Chaadaev, 1991, 212–214.
[27] Such reading of Petrine experiment is forcefully stated by Marina Tsvetaeva (1980, 135), for example, who at some point was close to the Eurasian movement.

of politics. This is death. Let us recall what We are. We – is a peculiar way of perceiving the world. And out of this peculiar perception a peculiar way of contemplating the world may grow. And from this mode of contemplation, incidentally, some political statements may be derived. But only incidentally![28]

For one of the most attentive post-1991 commentators, Vadim Tsymburskii, this statement signified not merely the failure of the specifically Eurasian political project, but the problematic character of the very foundation of Eurasianism as an attempt to synthesise the political and ideocratic dimensions of Russia's identity through a detour via geography. After all, the Eurasian emphasis on geography was meant to explain and to justify the synthesis of politics and ideocracy, yet it ended up in an opposition between the two. Since then, the rest of the Eurasian story, including its post-1991 revival, unfolded in the shadow of power, all the talk about the 'common Orthodox-Moslem-Buddhist good' notwithstanding, and at the same time signalled 'the civilisational failure of Russia, the outcome of its slide towards a lowered spiritual and stylistic distinctiveness'.[29]

Geography and the ideocracy/politics nexus

For Tsymburskii himself, this 'civilisational failure' is what defines Russia's post-1991 situation as 'crisis'. Thus, for him, as for Trubetzkoy, this situation has to be discussed, and if possible resolved, on the level of Russia's civilisational identity. On this level, Russia cannot abandon its search for a 'good' common to the various peoples inhabiting it, yet this common good can no longer be associated with Orthodoxy. Therefore, the two questions defining Russia's (or any other state's) security imaginary – 'What to do with Russia? What to do with the world?' – are necessarily joined with the third, 'perhaps, just as important: What to do about Christianity?'.[30] Tsymburskii's answer is a 'secular geopolitical project' in which the two poles of the original Eurasian impasse – state-power and Orthodox ideocracy – are redefined as 'geostrategy' and 'geopolitics' respectively.

Russia-Eurasia vs. Island-Russia

If original Eurasian theorising revolves around the identity of Russian pre-Petrine territory and that of the Soviet Union as it emerged in the inter-war period, Tsymburskii begins with the almost perfect congruity between the

[28] Urkhanova, 1995, 28–29.
[29] Tsymburskii, 1998, 28.
[30] Tsymburskii, 2002.

borders of the Russian state on the eve of Peter's accession to power and the borders of the state which emerged after the dissolution of the Soviet Union. Eurasianism ambiguously defined this space as Russia-Eurasia, and attempted, but ultimately failed, to account for its recurrence by discovering geographic and economic regularities. Tsymburskii, by contrast, from the outset grounds this recurrence in the contingent and violent experience of conquering and inhabiting a particular space, akin to Schmittian *Landnahme*, land-appropriation.[31]

Here, the seventeenth-century 'discovery of Siberia' stands out as a momentous identity-constitutive event. The incorporation of this region into a single 'ethno-civilisational' plain turned Russia into a gigantic, internally homogenous 'island' inside the continent. Protected by vast uninhibited lands from any invasion from the East and shielded from direct political or economic dependence on the West by a belt of marginalised East European 'stream-territories', Russia asserted itself as a politically consolidated bulwark against the hegemonic upheavals that were sweeping revolutions and wars throughout the rest of the continent, turning it into a patchwork of distinctively modern states-system. This 'splendid isolation', which preceded Peter the Great's attempts to integrate Russia into Europe, assumes for Tsymburskii the form of 'Island Russia' that survived all the vicissitudes of the imperial phase(s) of Russian history and forms the stable core of Russia's civilisational identity.

Thus, rather than being a 'geopolitical catastrophe', the dissolution of the Soviet Union signifies Russia's 'return' to its island-identity. Now Russia has to abandon any attempts to incorporate the Caucasus and Central Asia into its geopolitical body. Historically, these attempts were not an expression of Russia's unifying mission, as Eurasians would have it, but followed instead from Russia's desire to 'kidnap' Europe and its inability to do so. By emulating European imperial practices in Central Asia, by incorporating into its political body parts of Eastern Europe or, finally, by trying to Westernise itself, Russia was persistently trying, in this way or another, to make Europe 'its own'. And it invariably failed to do so. Now it had a chance to resume its genuine, authentic political existence, grounded in a contingent and yet truly foundational historical event.

Such grounding clearly echoes Carl Schmitt's understanding of political order as constituted by an historical event of land-taking which, although located outside of formal law or any regularity, gives meaning to legality and regularity as such.[32] Yet, in a number of interviews, Tsymburskii repeatedly distances himself from Schmitt, arguing that as a civilisation Russia cannot, as Schmittian nation-states do, construe its relations with the world on the basis of the explicitly political friend/enemy distinction alone, without some conception of the common good. However, neither this common good, nor analytical

---

[31] Tsymburskii, 1993, 6–23.   [32] Schmitt, 2003, 73.

regularities sought by Eurasians in their study of geography, can be derived from the constitutive event itself. This is where geopolitics, in its mainstream variety, fails, appearing as a 'pathos of vast spaces', offering perhaps utopian consolations, but neither real guidance for action nor grounds for meaningful analysis.[33] Thus Tsymburskii dismisses Ratzel, for example, 'with his schemes of territorial control and power', as a mere 'geostrategist'.[34]

In this manner, Tsymburskii rejects not merely the initial objectivist versions of the geopolitical revival in Russia, but the very possibility of having any objective grounds for either political debates or political enquiry. Perhaps, allegedly neutral, objectivist geopolitics can be put to meaningful rhetorical work, but only if supported by the 'schemes of control and power'. Yet such schemes are not enough to address what Tsymburskii, here indeed following the Eurasians, sees as the real crisis faced by Russia: the crisis of its civilisational distinctiveness. To articulate, let alone fix, this kind of crisis, one has to fix the meaning of geopolitics first.

Geopolitics and geostrategy

To perform the tasks understood by Tsymburskii as central for post-1991 Russia, geopolitics has to provide answers to two questions: how to articulate a common good after the collapse of Soviet ideology and without recourse to the Orthodox one? How to link this common good to the constitutive historical event of land-taking which brought Island Russia into existence? Answering both of these questions will redefine the dissolution of the Soviet Union as an opportunity rather than a crisis. And, provided the answers leave enough room for Russia's civilisational distinctiveness by not equating Russia's common good with the globalised liberal 'normalcy', they will transcend the ideological confrontation of the 1990s.

Tsymburskii begins with the idea of common good, relating it to the then heated debates on 'national interests'. He immediately discards any equation of 'national interests' with the aspirations of any particular ethnic group. Since Tsymburskii's prerequisites for a community's very existence are its distinctiveness and freedom of global action, 'national interest' is nothing less than an interest in the security and further enrichment of this distinctiveness and freedom. In practice, 'national interests' are articulated through sovereign decisions which are never perfectly rational or subject to objectivist analysis. Such sovereign decisionism, however, always contains a threat of totalitarianism and has to be kept in check. The traditional Western solution to this is a domestic division of powers or, more generally, a distinction between state and society. However, while Western states and 'their' civil societies, as associations

---

[33] Tsymburskii, 2002.   [34] Tsymburskii, 2004.

of private property-owners, have learnt to keep their respective interests more or less in sync, in post-communist Russia reforms were driven by the representatives of an 'anti-national civil society', identifying their interests not with the Russian state or some compact between the state and society, but with the global economy and thus seeking a 'private political existence' outside of any specific community.[35]

This is where geopolitics proper should come in, so as to arrest the irresolvable conflict between a potentially absolutist state and 'anti-national civil society' through 'the art of superimposing short- and medium-term societal needs onto thousand-year old physical-geographical landscapes'.[36] A perfect example of such an art can be found in Mackinder, whom Tsymburskii explicitly compares with Homer: 'The First Geopolitician stands before us as a creator of epic projects "packed" into geography and leaving their mark on the imagination of several generations of politicians and experts, not to mention the Pleiades of later story-tellers, up to the contemporary epigones of the rank of Brzezinski.'[37] Approached in this manner, a genuine geopolitical mode of thinking can be rediscovered in Russian pre-revolutionary treatises and policy-documents which, although they never mention the word 'geopolitics', permit the imagining of a distinctively Russian tradition of geopolitical thought in no way limited to or centred on Eurasianism.

Such geopolitics is ridden with the same duality as the state-society complex. Its genuinely political component calls for bold expansive thinking whose sole purpose is imagining a community. Thus Mackinder, for example, not merely failed to predict any of the cataclysms of the twentieth century, but, according to Tsymburskii, often cunningly refused to pay heed to the strategic developments unfolding right in front of his eyes. This was not because of his strategic short-sightedness, but due to his ability to sustain an unusually long view of history focused exclusively on British identity. Yet precisely because such grand visions, while essential for the existence of a given community, cannot be traded between states, they have to be 'packed' into geography and the material resources attached to it, so that geostrategists can take over from politicians and speak the language of territorial control and power, the language in which Westphalian Leviathans speak to each other.

Put differently, the common good can only be articulated in the ongoing domestic political debates. These debates keep in check the potentially absolutist power of the state. At the same time, the potentially universalist aspirations of some influential participants in these debates must in turn be checked by almost literally earthing them down to 'thousand-year old physical-geographical landscapes'. The latter move links the publicly articulated common good to

---

[35] Tsymburskii, 1995.   [36] Tsymburskii, 1999, 20.   [37] Tsymburskii, 2004.

the constitutive event of land-taking and thus to the foundations of a given community's identity.

So politics cannot be read off the map in any direct manner, nor can different geopolitical readings be directly compared with each other. Politics can only be superimposed onto geography through a sovereign gesture. This is where classical Eurasianism falters, running into an impasse, unable either to reconcile the naked power of the Stalinist Soviet Union and the universalism of Russian Orthodoxy or to choose between the two. Rather than offering any once-and-for-all solutions to this problem, Tsymburskii insists on the distinction between geostrategy and geopolitics, as reflecting the basic duality of political life. When speaking the language of geostrategy, he is mostly pragmatic, cautious, commonsensical and even 'scientific'. His geopolitics, however, offers no solid props for political decisions, urging instead political decisions as a prerequisite for having a strategy of any kind. The interplay of geopolitics and geostrategy, freedom and necessity, can never be resolved once and for all, let alone eliminated, without abandoning the terrain of politics altogether.

In a way, such an abandonment of politics is described in Trubetzkoy's story as an outcome of Russia's power-centred encounter with the technologically advanced West which disrupted the historically achieved Orthodox/Turanian synthesis. In Tsymburskii's analysis, the story repeats itself at an even deeper level when the state, instead of arresting the global aspirations of local property-holders, itself joins in the globalised spectacle of ongoing modernisation. If during Yeltsin's rule any articulation of Russia's 'national interests' in the public sphere was hampered by the 'anti-national' disposition of Russia's nascent civil society, Putin's tenure was marked by the annihilation of any genuine public sphere for the sake of effective oligarchic utilisation of Russia's resources, the idea of 'Great Russia' and Russian population itself being utilised in the same technocratic manner as gas or oil.[38]

So Tsymburskii's (re-)definition of the crisis, articulated already during Putin's presidency, sounds as desperate as Trubetzkoy's:

> Russia, temporarily or forever, has lost the ability to choose its own future. Now our geocultural destiny is no longer defined by ourselves … This woeful condition was far from being inevitable. [Until recently] we had our own Future which we could build ourselves. We abandoned this future in hope of edging our way to the 'table of the rich and powerful'. Our only hope now is a fortunate turn of events, so that in five or six years 'Island Russia' at least preserves its internal sovereignty, not to mention a prospect of recapturing its geocultural subjectivity.[39]

What matters, however, is that this construal of the crisis is clearly different from both Trubetzkoy's and the liberal/patriotic one of the 1990s, even though it is constructed out of the same discursive themes: ideology, objectivity,

[38] Tsymburskii, 2002.   [39] Tsymburskii, 2001.

civilisational distinctiveness and modernisation. By rearranging these themes differently, Tsymburskii arrives at a view in which the crisis is associated not so much with any of these four themes but with the disruption of the balance between them; a balance that can only be achieved 'geopolitically'. This reading, in turn, could only be made possible through a prior construal of 'geopolitics' proper so that it can serve here both as an ideal fixer to the crisis thus construed and a theoretical tool for its construction in the first place.

Ultimately, Tsymburskii urges aestheticised sovereign decision: first as acceptance of the 'civilisational' character of the ontological crisis of the 1990s, and then as a resolve to overcome this crisis by restoring Russia's civilisational identity. Distinctly 'geopolitical' colouring is given to this decision, again, in a twofold manner: first, by linking civilisational distinctiveness with land-taking, and second, by positing geographical landscapes as a fixer to the potentially destructive public debates which, paradoxically, are the only means for reaching the decision.

Still, even these landscapes, let alone the continuity between them and the event of land-taking, have to be imagined, thus deliberately leaving Tsymburskii's overall construction highly indeterminate, which perhaps accounts for the lack of interest it attracted from Russian policy makers, who, it seems, were looking for more solid fixers and, in a way, found them in Dugin.

Metaphysics and the ideocracy/politics nexus

It is reasonable to expect then that a different kind of geopolitics would produce a different understanding of crisis; and this is what happens with Dugin's 'neo-Eurasianism'. Unlike Tsymburskii's, Dugin's version of geopolitics supplied exactly what 'patriots' in Russia demanded: an essentialist, foundational, self-enclosed cultural identity for Russia and thus an escape from ontological anxiety as 'patriots' experienced it.[40] Yet Dugin's underlying essentialism is far from being immediately obvious, while the idiosyncratic synthesis through which he constructs Russia's identity is anything but straightforward. Importantly, as far as the geopolitical revival is concerned, Dugin's Russia is no longer opposed to the rest of the Old World as in original Eurasianism, but rather constitutes a privileged part of the Eurasian whole. This whole, in turn, is constructed both with and contra 'neoclassical geopolitics' that 'dares to speak its name'.

Politics and metaphysics

In a way, Dugin starts with a reading of the Eurasian impasse that is rather similar to Tsymburskii's. He too recognises the ambiguity of Russia-Eurasia's position within the whole of the Eurasian continent and the unresolved tension

[40] Laruelle, 2008.

between Orthodox ideocracy and state power. Judging by the chronology of his publications, he also accepts Trubetzkoy's and Tsymburskii's position that the question of Russia's identity *tout court* has to be addressed prior to the articulation of its geopolitical identity. However, whereas Tsymburskii proceeds by secularising the original Eurasian project, Dugin radicalises its religious component by moving the overall discussion to the level of metaphysics, while retaining the initial Eurasian ambition to tell the story of Russia 'from the East'. The task now is to tell this story in such a way as to remove all previously identified oppositions and incoherencies.

So if in Trubetzkoy the political virtues of Genghis Khan are brought from the East but then clash with the transcendental ideals of Orthodoxy, to be synthesised later, Dugin presents Genghis Khan as already a possessor of divine authority which is also perfectly consonant with Orthodoxy. The two origins are complementary, rather than conflictual, throughout. However, this complementarity is visible only from a metaphysical level. Dugin borrows his view of the latter from René Guénon, 'correcting' it in one important respect. Whereas Guénon discards Christianity altogether in favour of the more metaphysically mature religions of the East, Dugin asserts the uniqueness of Orthodoxy within Christianity by arguing that Orthodoxy contains within itself all the metaphysical insights of Guénon's 'traditionalism'.[41]

Metaphysics here represents the higher, original and all-encompassing mode of reasoning and being. All the vicissitudes of becoming are always already present in metaphysics and can of necessity be traced to a single source. Although purporting to dispose of metaphysics, science inevitably resorts to the ethical foundations expressed in metaphysics to make sure that all the ontological bits 'hang' together. Thus, metaphysics establishes a universal source of ethics by way of denouncing the temporal dimension of events and ethical significance of linear, progressive development. Instead, 'within the metaphysical perspective the history of humankind acquires logic, a point of reference, a sense of direction when a transcendental value transforms the chaos of life and alone becomes the measure of ordering humans and objects alike'.[42] In other words, metaphysics by default supplies the common good required by Eurasianism. This common good, however, is not equally visible from within all earthly traditions; and this brings in the theme of Russia's distinctiveness grounded in its Orthodox experience.

The much needed transcendental dimension, reflected on the plane of religion, makes Orthodox Christianity unique. If, in contradistinction to the Judaic 'hopelessly mechanical' non-divinity of the creation and to the Hellenic 'optimistically natural' divinity of the world of matter, Christianity postulates the divinity of the non-divine, man's transformation in the light of God's grace

---

[41] Dugin, 1999.   [42] Dugin, 1999, 15.

and his unification with the absolute, Orthodoxy makes this experience immediately political.[43] According to the Eastern Church, humans can overcome
their inferior status and participate in the transcendental only through complete immersion in the political sphere, through collective political existence,
so that the realisation of God's kingdom requires an act of will on the part of the
whole people, a collective undertaking, an all-nation movement spearheaded
by the authority of the Emperor, who alone acts as a mediator between the
secular and the divine, ensuring what Dugin calls 'the collective reality of salvation'.[44] Politics now is far from being a sideshow in the process of contemplating Russia's distinctiveness, as in Trubetzkoy, but rather an experience to which
Russia owes its distinct place in the world.

Finally, the origin of Russia's political identity no longer has to be grounded
in a contingent historical event, as in Tsymburskii, and thus to remain in constant need of geopolitical reimagining. Having analysed semantic associations,
mythologies and legends of the Indo-European peoples of the present-day
Russia, Dugin presents 'Continent Russia' as a value-laden concept that signifies nothing less than a centre of the universe, a birthplace of humankind,
a projection of heaven on earth, a Holy Land of the forefathers. Siberia and
Northern Urals were a hearth of an ancient proto-civilisation created by the
forefathers of the historically more prominent Sumers, who, apart from distinctive migration dynamics, possessed a common cultural legacy. It is this
combination of allegedly common cultural and ethnic features and unique
historical development that finds its outmost political expression in the Great
Eurasian Empire under the rule of Genghis Khan.[45] Subsequently, the Tartars,
Bashkirs, Yakuts and Buryats perceived Russians not as colonisers but as suc-
cessors of Genghis Khan, accomplishing his sacred empire-building mission.
And vice versa, their inflow after the formation of the Soviet Union is no longer
seen as undermining the Orthodox foundations of Eurasianism.

In this manner, by telling the story of Russia from the (metaphysical) East,
Dugin addresses the themes of ideology, Russia's distinctiveness and the
objective grounds for the latter's assertion, and at the same time removes two
of the oppositions that plagued the original Eurasianism: between Orthodox
ideocracy and state power and between Orthodoxy and Russia's non-Orthodox
peoples. Yet, at this stage, there is nothing specifically geopolitical in his project. Geopolitics comes in with the fourth theme, modernisation, and the last
Eurasian tension: between Russia-Eurasia and the rest of the Old World. And it
is not just any geopolitics but the *Geopolitik* of Haushofer. Why?

Haushofer was prepared to see in Russia a non-confrontational other, even
an ally, provided it cleansed itself from those very nomads of the steppe whom
Trubetzkoy ambiguously portrayed as at once constitutive of and threatening

---

[43] Dugin, 1999, 266.   [44] Dugin, 1999, 498–500.   [45] Dugin, 1999, 638–639.

to Russian-Eurasian identity. While conceding to Haushofer the original meaning of Eurasia as denoting the whole of the continent, Dugin presents the Russia of Turanian myth as a true – spiritual and metaphysical – heartland of that very continent, thus removing the remaining Eurasian tension. Whereas the whole of Eurasia is constructed on Haushofer's terms, Russia, now as an integral part of this Eurasia, is constructed contra Haushofer on Trubetzkoy's terms.[46] The synthesis of Eurasianism and *Geopolitik* is thus promised on both initially opposing levels: ideocracy (now metaphysics) and politics (now geo-politics). It synthesises Russia's annunciation of the spiritual message common to the whole of Eurasia and Russian strategic resources needed by Haushofer's anti-Atlantist project for it to restore Eurasia to its annunciated position in the world. Modernisation no longer poses a problem for Russia's distinctiveness, as long as it is performed for the right reason, that of expunging from Europe the demon of Atlantism.

Neo-Eurasianism and the production of the crisis

This, obviously, redefines yet again the crisis experienced by the Russian 'pat-riotic' opposition throughout the 1990s. Now it has nothing to do with either modernisation as such, as in Trubetzkoy, or with the problematic character of the relations between the Russian state and 'its' civil society which, under the conditions of globalisation, leads to the loss of Russia's civilisational distinct-iveness, as in Tsymburskii. In fact, it has very little to do with Russia. The crisis is externalised in the form of a familiar threat, Atlantism, which now can be identified as such without recourse to either Marxist ideology or nuclear con-frontation. Consequently, the familiar security imaginary of the Cold War can be reactivated under these new conditions; including Russia's vision of itself not as a recipient of someone else's rules in the passive process of transition, but as an active promoter of a message with global validity; that is, a Great Power again, whose greatness no longer depends on the nature or quality of its domestic regime.[47]

Interestingly, this pattern was registered by Viatcheslav Morozov in his com-prehensive study of Russian post-1991 foreign-policy discourse, where it is labelled 'reactionary modernisation'.[48] Here as well, Russia is eager to ally itself with Europe, not least for the purposes of modernisation, but insists on the dis-tinction between the 'true Europe' of, say, the Holy Alliance, and the 'false' one, often identified with 'Americanism'. This discursive practice, stable enough to be defined as part of Russia's security imaginary, falls into the long-standing pat-tern identified by Tsymburskii as the 'kidnapping of Europe'. Tsymburskii him-self reads Dugin's construction as yet another instance of the familiar strategy

---

[46] Tsymburskii, 2007, 464–474.   [47] Neumann, 2008, 128–151.
[48] Morozov, 2009b, 449–577.

of Russian 'patriotic' opposition throughout history: 'to find in Euro-Atlantic history itself some shadowy, marginalised tradition and to associate with it the destiny of Russia, insisting that through the reconstruction of this tradition the Russia of Big Spaces will arise again, united with "its" Europe'.[49]

However, geopolitics hardly plays any role in Morozov's account. In fact, he argues, borders are the least stable part of Russian discursive constructions. Russian foreign-policy elites' near-obsession with a stable, self-contained identity continuously results in discursive dislocations, 'simply' because no such identity can ever be constructed. These dislocations are then securitised into external threats, of which Americanism is indeed the most common. Yet precisely because the borders between inside and outside have to be continuously redrawn, tiny Estonia or Georgia, Islamic terrorism or a Russian liberal 'fifth column', may, and on occasion do, easily displace the United States from the constitutive position of 'false Europe'.

So, if Dugin's Eurasianism falls into the pattern of the 'kidnapping of Europe', then how 'geopolitical' is his project really? After all, if the sole task of Haushofer's *Geopolitik* within Dugin's project is to remove the opposition between Russia and the rest of Eurasia introduced by Trubetzkoy, then surely this could be done by other means as well. Or, more specifically in the context of this volume, what elements of 'neoclassical geopolitics' identified in Chapter 2 are essential for Dugin's neo-Eurasianism, so that in his case we can speak of a genuine revival of geopolitics?

If anything, geopolitics is distinguished from other similar traditions, above all realism, by its determinism, which, in the case of Ratzel, is supplied by explicitly scientific procedures. Procedures may in principle differ, but as Andreas Behnke nicely puts it in his analysis of Haushofer, '*Geopolitik* is not about where a country finds itself on the map, but where it puts itself on the map'.[50] That is, before a scientific or any other analytical study of a fit between population, geography and natural resource endowment can even begin, a discursive 'putting' of the state onto the map has to happen, always through some form of differentiation of the self from the other, as in Weldes, often in the form of the friend/enemy distinction, as in Schmitt.

Dugin is clearly aware of this and moves his enquiry onto the plane of metaphysics not least because it is there that he seeks to overcome the limitations of science. Yet he also does so to eschew the Schmittian constitutive contingency adopted by Tsymburskii, and thus to essentialise the fit in question. Are these two moves really compatible?

This depends on the metaphysics employed. One way of examining Dugin's metaphysics is by looking at his discussion of symbols. Phenomena serving as symbols point towards a desired unity, similar to the Eurasian common

---

[49] Tsymburskii, 2007, 472.   [50] Behnke, 2006.

good, which is the origin/essence of these phenomena.[51] They also confer the idea of transcendence, similar to Dugin's 'collective reality of salvation', which, given the multilayered topography of Dugin's metaphysics, requires continuous eschatological movement.[52] But these are the characteristics of a metaphysical tradition in which symbols, often mythologised into the stories of origins, 'point to an ontological origin of the things: they are, so to speak, the translucid, thinned out, spots in the fabric of the world through which its invisible cause shines forth as for the Stoics the cosmic fire shone forth through the holes in the sky which we call stars'.[53] Similarly, in Dugin's version of Eurasianism, the various images of Russia serve precisely as symbols of this kind: symbols of the continent's true essence originating, or preserved, in the political body of Russia. Not the Russia as it appears to the practitioners and confused theorists, but the real Russia of the Eurasian myth.

Yet, what this tradition of metaphysics also presupposes, contrary to Dugin's construal of the opposition between metaphysics and science, is a view of 'genuine' reality, reality of 'essences', as causing or producing the realm of appearances, thus positing the relation of (scientific) causation and/or (technocratic) production from the outset and at the very heart of all enquiry and practice:

> This idea of making, or production, can be seen as permeating all levels of metaphysics: the Good, in Plato, is said to 'make' the universe; the intellect in Aristotle, 'makes' all things knowable, it produces intelligibles; Christian philosophy stands and falls with the idea of creation; Kant's transcendental critique begins with the wonderment at how reason can 'produce' a priori syntheses; Hegel's World Spirit is the very notion of fecundity.[54]

To this the various critics of this metaphysical tradition often oppose a view which construes the relation between theory and practice, appearance and reality, language and Being as that of 'symbolic' joining together; stressing that, unlike in statements purporting to be purely descriptive, in symbols there is always a second layer of meaning requiring interpretation. Interpretation, in turn, requires not an exercise of pure reason but participation in practice: 'Unless one plunges into the waters, jumps through the flames etc., the rejuvenating, purifying, initiatory effects attached to these symbols will not be comprehended.'[55] A metaphor for this mode of relating the part and the whole may be found in the ancient Greek understanding of 'symbol', not as a noun but a verb – *symballein*. It is indeed always ordered towards oneness. This oneness, however, is not produced teleologically but re-enacted by joining together, which is what *symballein* stands for. Thus two halves of the clay broken at the

---

[51] Dugin, 1999, 75–85.   [52] Dugin, 1999, 135–151.
[53] Schürmann, 1979, 106.   [54] Schürmann, 1979, 110–111.
[55] Schürmann, 1979, 99.

moment of a business transaction, once joined together, served as a proof of an honoured agreement.

Tsymburskii's vision of a Eurasian, and Euro-Atlantic, whole, and Russia's relation with it, is closer to the latter view. The whole is neither given a priori nor practically secured once and for all. It is a dynamic, polarised set of relations in which distinct civilisations support each other through their interaction even when this interaction is conflictual. The pulsating rhythm of this interaction is what gives shape not only to the shared space, but also to the shared time – that is, the history – of global order. In fact, Tsymburskii contemplates the possibility of abandoning geopolitics altogether for the study of 'chronopolitics', in which the distinctiveness of Russia's identity would be established not through its territoriality but rather its temporality, unthinkable outside of Euro-Atlantic history.[56]

Compared to Tsymburskii's, Dugin's version of geopolitics, grounded in his version of metaphysics, is much more deterministic, even though its determinism is hardly materialist and is located more on the level of 'putting' Russia on the map, through metaphysics, rather than 'finding' it there. This determinism, in turn, gives more substance to Dugin's self-identification with the tradition of geopolitics, even if the identity in question is shifted to the level of metaphysics. So, in this sense, no matter how idiosyncratic Dugin's construction may be, no matter how tenuously it is related to material environmental factors, it is possible to read in it an attempted revival of neoclassical geopolitics.

Conclusion

There was, then, an ontological anxiety in Russia after the breakup of the Soviet Union and there was a revival of neoclassical thought in Russia, as represented by Dugin. But that revival not only failed to actually fix the ontological security, it also made only limited inroads into the Russian security imaginary.

Dugin's geopolitics clearly succeeded in putting Russia back onto the map when the map itself was being redrawn. It did so by defining the post-1991 situation as a crisis to begin with, and then by offering a definition of the crisis which fit the experiences not only of Russia's 'patriotic' opposition but also of its foreign-policy makers, hence the 'geopolitical catastrophe'. This fit was due to the use of discursive material available for the construction, namely, the four themes present on all sides of the post-1991 debate: ideology, modernisation, Russia's distinctiveness and possible objective criteria for its assertion. These were rearranged by Dugin in ways conditioned by their prior introduction into the discourse by the inter-war Eurasians. Historically, that introduction required a move away from specific policy making towards thicker

---

[56] Tsymburskii, 2007, 472.

explorations of Russia's identity *tout court*. Hence the emphasis on 'putting', rather than 'finding', on the construction of identity by means of crisis, rather than fixing of the crisis by means of a security imaginary.

Partly as a result of such emphasis, the record of Dugin's geopolitics on the level of the security imaginary remains mixed at best. Recent studies of Russian politics assign little significance to geopolitics, thus confirming Tsymburskii's assessment, voiced back in 1995 when Dugin still had important patrons within Russian foreign-policy elites: 'For most of his admirers, Dugin, by and large, remains a DJ at the postmodern carnival'[57] where various notable figures from Russian and Soviet past can again and again be reshuffled as either Atlantists or Eurasians.

It seems then that Dugin's geopolitics succeeded in *producing* the crisis – the way such production of crises is discussed by Weldes – but was not necessarily needed for its *fixing*, not least because the way the crisis was produced, did not call, as in Tsymburskii, for a radical and continuous rethinking and remaking of Russian political space, but allowed instead for a relatively unproblematic reactivation of the familiar security imaginary. Indeed it hardly matters whom exactly we count as 'essential' Atlantists or Eurasians, much less on what metaphysical grounds, as long as the old enemy is in sight

[57] Tsymburskii, 2007, 465.

PART III

Empirical and theoretical conclusions

10

The mixed revival of geopolitics in Europe

STEFANO GUZZINI

At the end of the Cold War, when Europe was poised to reap the fruits of a new security environment, when the very nature of the de-escalation in Europe prompted such grandiose common security statements as the OSCE Paris Charter, when realism was facing its perhaps biggest theoretical challenge, many European countries would experience a revival not just of some version of realism, but of its more materialist and militarist wing: geopolitics. This project started by deriving a series of hypotheses for this puzzling revival. The initial setup specified four hypotheses: from the history of ideas, one might hypothesise the ideational path dependence of a materialist tradition; in terms of a sociology of knowledge, the revival of geopolitics might correspond to the reaction of a 'dissatisfied power'; from the perspective of constructivist foreign policy analysis, geopolitics might help to establish a new foreign policy identity following the disappearance of the previously existing roles with the events of 1989; finally, from a political economy or institutionalist perspective, the revival of geopolitics might be viewed within the context of the various epistemic communities, and differences in funding strategies, within the foreign policy expert field of individual countries, where the absence of political and theoretical distance of the expert system from politics – and particularly the military – would enhance the chances of a geopolitical revival.[1]

After a first cut of empirical studies (2004–2006), a common workshop took stock of those four hypotheses and introduced a series of amendments and extensions that have come to define the setup of the present volume. First, as the introductory chapters showed, the initial puzzle needed to be reframed and the meaning of 'geopolitics' specified for the purpose of the research project. Political geographers, and particularly researchers working within critical geopolitics, did not find much puzzling in the revival, because previous shifts in the international system had also almost inevitably spurred the 'geographical imagination' before becoming taken for granted, as a new shared vision of the world took hold. Yet, here we met the revival of something more substantial,

---

[1] Guzzini, 2003.

which, following Mark Bassin, could be called 'neoclassical geopolitics'. For the purposes of this volume, neoclassical geopolitics was defined as

> a policy-oriented analysis, generally conservative and with nationalist over-tones, that gives explanatory primacy, but not exclusivity, to certain physical and human geographic factors (whether the analyst is open about it or not), and gives precedence to a strategic view, realism with a military and nation-alist gaze, for analysing the 'objective necessities' within which states com-pete for power and rank. (p. 43)

Second, again taking our clue from political geographers, we noted that the revival of neoclassical geopolitics seemed linked not just to generic shifts in world politics, but also to the existence of an 'ontological anxiety' (Agnew). As David Atkinson remarks while discussing the revival of geopolitics in Italy in the 1930s and the 1990s, where each instance was characterised by inter-national instability, 'Italians developed forms of "geopolitical reasoning" to help themselves understand these contexts, and it is perhaps just such periods of flux and anxiety that tend to catalyse geopolitical reasoning'.[2] This important pointer, however, ends up begging the question: not all shifts and instabilities produce 'anxieties'. Geopolitical reasoning did not resurface in all countries exposed to the allegedly same international instabilities.

As a result, we decided to reconfigure the relation between the four pro-cess factors. Instead of thinking of them in additive terms, we opted to treat the factor of identity politics – or, indeed, the idea of a foreign policy identity crisis – as the fundamental one. Subsequently, we examined how some of the other factors influenced the process whereby certain identity crises prompted a return of geopolitical thought, while others did not. The occurrence of such an identity crisis within the foreign policy discourse would hence correspond to a situation in which (internal) self-understandings and/or (external) role con-ceptions were interpreted as being in jeopardy with the end of the Cold War, or at least in need of substantial redefinition.

Interpreting identity is done with reference to foreign policy discourses, which consist of a stock of common wisdom and collective memories, of shared lessons of the past and a series of *idées-forces*[3] with which to make sense of the world. Knowing the content of such discourses makes it possible to understand how they might predispose the interpretation of international events – indeed, of how these events interact with the self-conceptions embedded therein. For this type of analysis, we found Jutta Weldes' concept of a 'security imaginary' particularly useful.

The underlying hypothesis of the present volume accordingly became two-fold: first, the revival of geopolitical thought after 1989 can be best understood as the eventual effect of a foreign policy identity crisis triggered by a dissonance

---

[2] Atkinson, 2000, 112.   [3] Bourdieu, 2000, 63, 68.

in the way security imaginaries were able to relate to the events of 1989. Second, an identity crisis does not directly effect a geopolitical revival. This depends on a series of process factors. Also here, the workshop introduced some changes by insisting more on the agential level in which geopolitical claims are used to political profit. In sum, a revival of geopolitical thinking can be expected when at least some of the following factors apply: there is a materialist tradition of thinking foreign policy; this tradition is institutionalised within the foreign policy expert culture; and there exists a political game in which such thinking is rhetorically used for political gain (usually on the conservative side).

The first chapter of this concluding section will summarise the findings of the empirical chapters of the present volume. As set out in Chapter 3, these chapters had to analyse:

(1) whether or not a geopolitical revival had taken place in the country under study;
(2) whether a foreign policy identity crisis existed and, if so, of which kind; and
(3) which process factors intervened in the revival (or not) of geopolitical thought.

Each chapter should also analyse in depth the content of the geopolitical thought concerned. This was important for answering the specification of the puzzle in terms of 'neoclassical geopolitics'.

However, in a further step, this concluding section will also elaborate in more detail the second aim of the present volume, namely, theory development. This will be done in the final chapter, which develops the role of social mechanisms in constructivist analysis by presenting two social mechanisms that dynamically connect international events with changes in the cultures of international anarchy. The first mechanism appears in the interaction between international events and foreign policy/security imaginaries: the just-mentioned identity crisis that triggers discursive practices to reduce the new dissonance in self-understandings and external role conceptions. A second mechanism appears when a series of revivals affect the self-understanding of international society itself – that is, the cultures of anarchy. In the case in which several security imaginaries revive geopolitical thought, they trigger a realist view of the world with a militarist gaze, and this in turn will affect the self-understanding of European international society.

In relation to this latter mechanism, it is crucial to know the actual content of the geopolitical revival that formed the core of the individual country chapters. For the overall empirical thesis is that precisely when international events seemed to herald a further move from a Lockean to a Kantian culture of anarchy ('the common European home', pan-Europe as a security community), these same events also triggered a series of identity crises that, in turn, if they led to a revival of geopolitical thought in the security imaginaries of individual countries, brought Hobbesian understandings to the fore. The exact impact of these mechanisms may be difficult to judge. But, as with all mechanism analysis, focusing on them makes it possible to understand the present Lockean culture not necessarily as a stable one, but as one in which contradicting mechanisms may have been cancelling each other out. In short, knowing the geopolitical content of security imaginaries helps us to understand the actual working of the micro-mechanisms that underpin a constructivist theory at the systemic level.

The case selection for the research project included countries in which no geopolitical revival took place and also varied in terms of the different types of identity crisis that occurred and the hypothesised process factors. Countries were chosen for which some 'anxiety' was to be expected at the end of the Cold War either because they were new countries, or at least countries in new borders, or because their existing identities were closely connected to roles played in the Cold War. In this chapter, I will present the findings from the country studies and from there develop case-generated qualifications of the overall framework.

1   No identity crisis – no revival: the Czech Republic and Germany

The fundamental hypothesis of the present volume is that the geopolitical revival after 1989 is ultimately the qualified effect of an identity crisis. In cases where countries experienced no substantial geopolitical revival, the process tracing would allow three possible reasons for this. All of these concern the specification of the social mechanism reducing identity dissonance. First, a country might have been spared an identity crisis to start with because its foreign policy/security imaginary was disposed to interpret the events of 1989 in a manner in which its self-understanding and role conception were not challenged. Or, such a mechanism may have been triggered, but it was possible to answer it through means other than geopolitical reasoning. Or, finally, such a mechanism did trigger geopolitical reasoning, but the latter did not develop due to the opposite effect of the hypothesised process factors. In this context, the analysis of the two outlier cases may offer valuable insight into the functioning of the identity-crisis mechanism and its scope conditions.

The *Czech Republic* has not seen a revival of geopolitical thought since 1989. Even though Petr Drulák looks for occurrences of such a revival as widely as possible, both in formal and practical geopolitics, and although he employs a definition of geopolitics that is less restrictive than the neoclassical one used for the rest of the volume, he finds only instances of rhetorical but eventually inconsequential musings with geopolitical ideas. Drulák notes that there were two moments in which geopolitical ideas did appear: at the time of the breakup of Czechoslovakia and, much later, during the discussions around the installation of a missile defence system. In each instance, the small flare-up occurred when the right came to power. However, the use of geopolitics was mainly rhetorical and almost indistinguishable from realism. Also, the use of geopolitics had no equivalent or anchoring in formal geopolitics.[4] The Czech Republic's foreign policy expert system was not close to the military; and its research institutions could keep the political sector at arm's length.

Drulák gives one main reason for this non-event: political discourse in the Czech Republic is based on an anti-geopolitical tradition. Whereas geopolitics suggests inevitability and determinism, Czech political actors rely on a tradition that stresses the possibility of change. Such a stress on change and malleability is more consonant both with the communist dissidents' political tradition that Drulák traces back through history, as well as with the basically modernist setup of neoliberalism – views exemplified respectively by Václav Havel and Václav Klaus, the two most important politicians in the post-1989 period. In addition, this continuity in historical vision was somewhat Czech-centric, and hence not fundamentally affected by the breakup with Slovakia.

More fundamentally, the Czech foreign policy discourse seemed not to have displayed a foreign policy identity crisis in the first place. It was not self-evident that no such crisis would occur, however, since not only did the country emerge from the Cold War with a new foreign policy independence, a practical and strategic 'void' that 'needed' to be filled, but it also endured a further dramatic event: the separation from Slovakia – dramatic, that is, if the usual IR standards are applied. But the political elite felt no need for a reassessment; instead, it was as though they had just returned home from a temporary 'kidnap', to use Kundera's famous phrase.[5] The events of 1989 did not produce a dissonance with a given (foreign policy) identity: they put an end to it.

Still, in other countries of Central and Eastern Europe, not to speak of the former Soviet Union, such claims about simply restoring a previous identity – with the communist times being reduced to a hiccup of national history – did not have such a soothing effect and instead produced anxiety, as we will see in the case of Estonia.

To sum up the Czech case: the self-understanding that underlies the Czech foreign policy/security imaginary did not interpret the events of 1989 or the breakup of Czechoslovakia as threatening Czech foreign policy identity; quite the opposite. Therefore, the first mechanism of identity-dissonance reduction did not verify. In addition, the process factors would not have been conducive to such a development. With regard to ideational path dependency, the Czech case is characterised by the existence of a strong anti-geopolitical tradition. Its foreign policy expert system maintains a certain degree of independence from the military, whose own role is less significant than that of the militaries

[4] For further analysis of IR in the Czech Republic, see Drulák and Druláková, 2000 and 2006.
[5] Kundera, 1983.

of many other countries, and academic production is far from being primarily materialist. Finally, although political games did use geopolitical rhetoric, both on the right and on the left, and although such use was connected to the rise of right-wing governments or to military issues (as the example of the missile defence system shows), the use of such rhetoric seems so far to have been too weak to counterbalance the other factors and to initiate a reversal of the country's anti-geopolitical tradition.

Meanwhile, the analysis also highlights a complication for the setup of our process tracing. The anti-geopolitical tradition can be read both as underlying the foreign policy/security imaginary and as a process factor of ideational path dependence. Indeed, the latter two seem to interact with each other in the ongoing foreign policy identity process (and hence cannot be considered two truly independent factors or variables). Although it seemed a good idea to isolate identity crises as the main trigger, the Czech case leads us to infer that the absence of such a crisis may not be independent of at least one of the process factors. And, in principle, this problem of interaction would apply also to other cases and other factors. This is a point to which I will return later.

The *German* case appears to be more complicated. For one thing, that country has seen a rise in the use of geopolitical argument, indeed of the very word 'geopolitics', which had been shunned for a long time on account of its association with the Nazi regime. Many observers, be it in history or geography, have registered this rise.[6] Yet, on the basis of evidence from both the formal and the practical level, Andreas Behnke eventually argues that no *significant* rise in the use of geopolitical thought took place in Germany. Indeed, there was no identity crisis to start with, just as in the Czech case, although for different reasons. Whereas other chapters look at the mechanism and process through which geopolitics came to the fore in the countries concerned, the non-occurrence of such a development in the German case again calls for a different type of chapter. Behnke needs to substantiate his claim regarding the limited significance of the rise in the first place. And so he stacks the deck against himself by including both the practical level where many have located the rise and events from the period beyond the 1990s. Let us take his two main claims in turn.

All agree that 1989 and the subsequent reunification of Germany prompted a huge sense of satisfaction in that country, finally lifting the Sword of Damocles that had been hanging over it. But, these developments also provoked a certain degree of trepidation regarding the role of this new/old Germany in Europe and the rest of the world. Of this, there is perhaps no other more telling indicator than the two high-profile political assassination attempts that occurred in the context of reunification. Such assassination attempts are extremely rare in

---

[6] See Bach and Peters, 2002; Bassin, 2003; Dijkink, 1996, 32–36; Reuber and Wolkersdorfer, 2002; Sur, 1995 and van der Wusten and Dijkink, 2002.

Germany and seem to occur only in times of high political polarisation. Aside from these two attempts, the most well-known case is that of Rudi Dutschke, a Marxist student leader who survived a shot in the head during the 1968 revolts.[7] In the context of German reunification, the left-wing candidate for the chancellorship, Oscar Lafontaine, and the right-wing chief negotiator of the reunification treaty, Wolfgang Schäuble, were victims of assassination attempts during political campaign trips. Both survived. The two men were central personalities in the public debate over the procedure for reunification: Lafontaine standing for a more confederate position in which the German Democratic Republic (GDR) would be given time; Schäuble pushing for a swift unification where the GDR was not to be considered on a par with the Federal Republic of Germany (FRG), but would access the FRG and its constitutional setting.

Consequently, when offering reasons for the revival of geopolitics in Germany, observers seem also to agree that 1989 was crucial. In a passage that perfectly corresponds to the basic thesis of the present book, Etienne Sur writes:

> It seems to me … that the reference to geographic arguments … by many German intellectuals is the sign (precisely) of a certain disorientation, if not a certain discouragement, in front of a new geopolitical reality that … puts into question the established (*acquises*) representations of the idea of the nation … It is as though, for some people, 'the hard soil' of [geographic realities] became the preferred orientation point (*point de repère privilégié*) in their attempt to come to grips with a national sentiment in full reconstruction and the painfully experienced identity reconstruction.[8]

Accordingly, the main question is not whether some form of revival has taken place, but what was its exact content and significance. Again, most commentators on the geopolitical revival immediately stress that their analysis deals with a series of writings that are at the margin of German debate, whether academic or political. These writings 'should not be equated with public opinion or with tangible influences on the perception of the foreign policy elite',[9] or, in Bassin's words, 'much or most of the new *Geopolitik* remains on the political margins, well away from the mainstream'.[10] And, yet, looking at the protagonists of the revival is important for Behnke's second point, namely, that there was no major identity crisis in Germany. For who was it that did push for a revival?

There are basically three groups in this revival. A first group consists of members of the German military, such as Heinz Brill, an academic working within

---

[7] To indicate the deep rift of that time: in the subsequent German national elections in 1969, the NPD, the follow-up party to the Nazis in Germany, achieved its highest level of support ever: 4.3 per cent, 1,422,000 votes (in 1972, they were back to normal levels with 0.6 per cent). Rudi Dutschke survived but eventually died in 1979 from an epileptic seizure while bathing, a delayed effect of the earlier injury.

[8] Sur, 1995, 33.   [9] Dijkink, 1996, 34.   [10] Bassin, 2003, 351.

the Research Unit of the Bundeswehr, or Joachim F. Weber, press officer for the army and former editor of the *Ostpreußenblatt*, who spoke of a 'renaissance of geopolitics and Germany in a crisis of orientation'.[11] A second group consists of various writers, most of them analysed by Bassin, who are journalists and whose background is not what Bassin calls the 'new German geopolitics', but pretty much the old German *Geopolitik*. This would apply to Felix Buck, born in 1912, who was Vice-President of the NPD between 1970 and 1977 (leaving the party in 1979)[12] and whose work is full of praise for Haushofer.[13] And it would apply to Heinrich Lordis von Lohausen (1907–2002), an Austrian general who served in the Wehrmacht and whose writings represented a direct continuation of the tradition of *Geopolitik*. Finally, the third group consists of various intellectuals from the 'New Right' in Germany, mainly historians such as Karlheinz Weißmann, whose publication on the years 1933–1945 in a (formerly) prestigious series on German history provoked such a level of scandal (he was accused of revisionism for the history of the Nazi regime) that his contract was rescinded and the responsible commissioning editor fired. That commissioning editor was Rainer Zitelmann, together with whom Weißmann had published a reference book related to the revival of geopolitics.[14] Zitelmann moved to the conservative daily *Die Welt*, before finally deciding to get out of academia and public debate altogether. Since 2000 he has worked in, and publishes only on, real-estate management.

Now, if one were ever to wish for a group of challengers that would help to *solidify* established German national identity discourse, this would be it. For *Geopolitik* was not so much a taboo in German debates as it was the pre-established contender, easily defeated, in the national identity discourse. To paraphrase Ole Wæver's felicitous word about Europe: 'Germany's Other is Germany's Past.' Hence, when a heterogeneous group of marginal military thinkers and historical revisionists tried to use the moment of 1989 to find a place for geopolitical thought, they perfectly interpellated the pre-established 'Other' of German discourse. Trying to launch a redirection of German foreign policy thought by revisiting and rehabilitating parts of the (Nazi) German past, or simply sounding irredentist (as when Buck speaks of the Northeast Prussian territories under Russian command), does not exploit a disorientation within German national identity discourse; rather, it provides the 'Other' upon which such a discourse can be fixed, as Behnke writes. Moreover, as he shows, by the 1990s the German debate had just gone through a rehearsal in the *Historikerstreit*. With no new arguments, but only the hope of a different *Zeitgeist*, the revisionist onslaught failed to materialise.

In addition to these developments, and in order to conduct as wide an analysis of the potential revival as possible, Behnke also addresses practical

---

[11] Brill, 1994 and Weber, 1992.   [12] Virchow, 2006, 92.
[13] Buck, 1996.   [14] Zitelmann *et al.*, 1993.

geopolitics. Here, the Left–Green coalition's more assertive German foreign policy, in particular its military role, was seen as part of such a revival. Again, Behnke's analysis confirms the first argument: there was no identity crisis and no geopolitical revival. Indeed, the role expectation of the outsiders coincided with the self-perception mentioned above in terms of seeing Germany as a stabilising factor exactly because it did not play according to some 'old-fashioned' power political script, but would hold fast to its European German identity. Only when expectations regarding whether the German army should be able to intervene externally came to the fore did Germany's potentially different international role become a matter for discussion. Accordingly, if anything, it was not 1989 or the reunification that affected the discussion of German foreign policy identity, but outside expectations (which were undoubtedly also shared by some within the German government) that Germany would again become a military power. Again, Behnke's careful analysis shows that geopolitical references are at most superficial in the redirection of German foreign and security policy, which maintains a strong degree of continuity with that of the *Bonner Republik*.

All in all, neither formal nor practical geopolitics experienced a significant revival in Germany, the main reason being that the role and self-identification of Germany in its foreign policy/security imaginary were seen as being confirmed by the peaceful way in which the Cold War came to an end. The few attempts by German conservatives to use the profound political changes for a more nationalist definition of the national interest mobilised the past and hence the 'Other' of the existing self-understanding. Those geopolitical voices only reconfirmed the post-1945 (and mainly post-1966/1969) identity and prompted a quick and overwhelming response within academia, the expert field and politics for its continuation in the *Berliner Republic*.[15]

As with the Czech case, the analysis of the German case also has some implications for the general framework of analysis of the present book. In both country studies, the analysis of an ideational path dependence clearly interacted with the analysis of a security imaginary. Moreover, the German case shows that a foreign-policy identity crisis is nothing mechanical. All security imaginaries involve contending visions of the self, although one is (usually) predominant. As Chapter 3 of this volume insists, a foreign policy tradition provides interpretative material for diverging positions, although the range of the acceptable or discursively authorised positions is limited. As the German case shows, agency enters into the very definition of foreign-policy identity

---

[15] Perhaps it will strike many as bizarre, this non-occurrence of an identity crisis, indeed the perseverance of the post- or even anti-nationalist national identity underlying German foreign policy discourses. Does not (or, must not) Germany have an 'identity problem'? But, the German identity concerned would strike many Germans as being quite self-evident: only German nationalists and some non-Germans seem to have a problem with that allegedly 'unnatural', 'abnormal' German identity, not many or most Germans themselves.

crisis: neither in materialist terms (unification and the change of the international structure requires policy redefinition) nor in idealist ones (unification
means a new identity hence identity crisis) is such a crisis simply the effect of
external changes. Whether or not the interpretation of an event finally triggers
a crisis is itself the effect of symbolic battles. In this case, there were attempts to
challenge the post-1969 German identity of *Vergangenheitsbewältigung* (coming to terms with one's past), but these attempts mobilised the discursive Other
and were thus quickly delegitimised. Hence, agency is part and parcel of the
beginning of an identity crisis, not just its unfolding, while existing security
imaginaries empower certain positions rather than others.

Finally, the hypothesised relation between the existence of an identity crisis and the revival of geopolitical thought does not so far seem to have been
disconfirmed. In a sense, it would have been nicer for the framework of this
book if at least in one case the process factors would have made the difference.
But, in both of the cases discussed above, it was the initial trigger that did not
work. This could imply, however, that process factors and the identity crisis are
closely connected in a kind of common configuration, rather than lined up in a
process. This is a point to which I will return in the final chapter.

2   Different types of identity crises and geopolitical revivals

Italy: geopolitics after 1989 and 'Tangentopoli'

In Italy, there was a clear revival of 'geopolitics', as exemplified by the success of
Carlo Jean's writings and the establishment of *Limes: rivista di geopolitica*, which
had a distribution of up to 100,000 copies at the time of the Kosovo War.[16] And,
according to Brighi and Petito, Italy did indeed experience a sense of ontological
anxiety after 1989. To some extent, this may seem puzzling. Looking from the
outside, not much had changed, at least relative to the other countries examined
in this volume. No new borders, no reunification, no central Cold War role lost,
no new enemy or threats. So, why would such an anxiety be felt in Italy?

The analysis suggests that Italy has experienced a latent identity crisis for
some considerable time, one that the Cold War could only temporarily quell.
There is sensitivity within Italy's collective memory about the allegedly unfair
treatment that the country experienced after World War I, which gave rise to
'irredentism' and a sense that the international community does not take Italy
as seriously as it deserves. While outsiders barely took notice, Italian public
opinion was reminded again and again of the 'sorpasso' (overtaking), the nick-
name given to the developments in 1987 whereby Italy's economy grew larger
than that of Britain in absolute GDP terms (though not in terms of GDP per

---

[16] Atkinson, 2000, 111.

capita or PPP).[17] Whenever the G-7 is discussed, or the possible reform of the UN Security Council, there tends to be an insistence within Italian foreign policy discourse that 'objectively' Italy should be treated as being on a par with all of the major European powers (hence Italy's resistance to a permanent seat for Germany). What is remarkable is the continuous sense of being treated as inferior, of having to prove one's worth. Thus, an important theme within the Italian foreign policy imaginary turns on the idea of Italy as a country that other countries do not respect as fully they should, a country that is not given its due.[18]

During the Cold War, Italy's position as one of the founding members of the EU and its unflinching support of US policies could ensure a foreign policy that was both passive and yet – through the United States, NATO and the EU – 'importantly' connected to world events. In exchange for its support, external powers refrained from scrutinising Italy's domestic politics, which were riddled with various problems related to the unfinished nature of the country's democratic system, and much was excused (if not funded) on account of the Italian authorities' central role in the anti-communist front that went right through the middle of Italian society.[19]

With the end of the Cold War, several events could be seen as shaking this deal, however. First, what was to be the role of NATO in Europe after 1989? How far would the EU go? And what was to be Italy's place in this context? What would it get from being a passive supporter? In addition, the anti-communist bulwark had become less important. Indeed, communism in Italy went quickly on the defensive. Instead, with the opening to the East, 'democratic standards' had become the main way of assessing countries in Europe's core. Such expectations began to be formulated at the exact same time that Italy's clientelistic system was running into a major financial crisis in the early 1990s, leading to

---

[17] Never mind that this 'sorpasso' was financed by a huge debt that would come back to haunt the political system in its major crisis in the early 1990s and facilitated by a change in statistical accounting, through which a larger part of the black economy was included within GDP (causing GDP to increase by 18 per cent in a year).

[18] Dinger, 2011. In general, Italy's political self-understanding tends to oscillate between highly self-critical assessments of the country's political system and international importance, a position most often found in internal debates and on the political left, and a self-representation, used abroad and predominantly on the political right, as a cultural and economic powerhouse, an old nation whose importance has been systematically marginalised by (jealous or arrogant) foreign powers or international society at large.

[19] Italy was also the staging ground for the largest contingent in NATO's secret 'Stay Behind' paramilitary organisation (which had recruited many former Nazi and fascist soldiers and officers), known as 'Gladio'. These troops were responsible for reconnaissance and sabotage in the event of a Soviet invasion, but have also been linked to strategies of terror and subversion against 'internal enemies' – communist, social democratic and/or pacifist – when that invasion never came about. For a short presentation of Gladio, see Ferraresi, 1992.

its implosion.[20] The exit of old political protectors laid bare the systematic corruption and fiscal crime, a complex system of 'parallel government' and the role of organised crime in Italian society. The legal uncovering of 'Tangentopoli' ('Bribesville') and the prosecution of high-level politicians and managers was surely seen by many Italians as a moment of long-awaited national pride. Finally, it was possible to identify with a country that had, on its own, started to cast off the rotten parts of the system. However, this 'purification' ('*mani pulite*', or 'clean hands') also led to the delegitimation of major parts of the existing elite. The breakdown of a system that had kept the Christian Democratic Party in power since the beginning of the post-1945 Republic – Giulio Andreotti had been longer in a government position (1947–1992) than Enver Hoxha in Albania, critics wryly remarked – left a void. The definition of what Italy was to be was up for discussion. Old answers would no longer suffice. The positions within which Italian identity were to be discussed were also less defined than in the German case. There was a sense that Italy had to look for new bearings. At the same time, the debate (mainly on the right) reflected an increasing concern over the possibility of being moved back down to second class within the European powers.

The vigorous revival of geopolitics falls into this context of Italy's redefinition and reassertion of status, with a right-wing political spectrum on the defensive following the *Democrazia Christiana*'s demise. The rhetorically strong references to 'geopolitics' – an idea that was almost as *non grata* in political and academic debates in Italy as in Germany – seemed to respond to the created void in two ways. First, the revival mobilised the materialism and determinacy in geopolitical thought to argue for a new necessity in Italian foreign policy. Building on a desire to leave the passivity of the Cold War period behind, 'geopolitics' would be the wake-up call for a self-conscious definition of Italy's national interest and foreign policy. Such a view is clearly one of the rationales behind Carlo Jean's writings (and success).

Second, the establishment of *Limes* corresponded to the need for a new forum in which Italian foreign policy could be debated. This is probably part of the explanation for the fact that, as Brighi and Petito show, the geopolitical revival also came from the left, not just the right, to the extent that *Limes* is published by a centre-left publishing house. The success of *Limes*, whose launch was supported by government funds in 1993, initially lay in its creation of a forum where 'security intellectuals' could attempt to address the post-1989 void in a language that seemed to hold out the promise of answers. In its appeal to allegedly natural 'facts', geopolitics suggested to provide a good way of establishing a 'neutral' – because more ideology-independent – ground for overcoming the Cold War divides that characterised Italian political discourse. However, along with ideology, *Limes* also kept 'academic' theoretical distance

---

[20] Guzzini, 1995.

at bay, remaining almost entirely untouched by theoretical findings within the field of international relations. This was done to ensure a wider audience, but not solely for that reason. Accordingly, *Limes* often reproduces the common-sense language of diplomacy (realism) and military strategy (geopolitics). This was to be the common 'bipartisan' ground. Furthermore, the editor(s) of *Limes* was (were) not looking for such common ground: he (they) wanted to create it. So, the publication was open to both the right and the left, but only within a certain predefined realm. According to its statement of purpose, *Limes* was

> founded on the open and opposing (*contrastivo*) confrontation of diverse geopolitical projects and representations. The essential point is that they refer to conflicts of power in space (land, sea, air), and that they can be put on maps (*cartografabili*) ... with no wink (*ammiccamento*) to the geographic determinism *en vogue* in the political geography of the 19th century or in some geopolitical schools of the 20th century.[21]

Yet, it should be added that, besides the presence of a rather clear Italian self-assertion in its editorial work[22] and an editor who tends to see the world strongly through geopolitical eyes,[23] in *Limes* geopolitics can also be defined rather widely – for example, in relation to the 'geopolitics of taxis'.[24]

Hence, to sum up, there was both anxiety and a foreign policy identity crisis in Italy; geopolitics appeared a promising way of handling these developments; and actors within the political, military and media establishment picked up on this potential. Why geopolitics? Here, the different process factors play a role. Indeed, as Brighi and Petito show, almost all of the factors specified for this study favoured a revival. There is a strong materialist tradition in Italian political culture (ideational path dependence); the foreign-policy expert system is close to the political and military establishment; and independent academic or parallel expertise is rare, underdeveloped and non-theoretical.[25] Things have started to change during the last decade – albeit in a patchy manner – with an increasing professionalisation of IR in academia and increased openness towards foreign literature that goes beyond the limited theoretical inspiration of the early 'Huntington–Kissinger–Brzezinski' triad of the 1990s. Indeed, theoretical work itself has made a new and modest inroad in this period, while geopolitics has receded.

---

[21] See the homepage at http://temi.repubblica.it/limes/chi-siamo.
[22] Caracciolo *et al.*, 1997.
[23] Indeed, at a talk in Copenhagen, he based his vision for Russia's foreign and security policy on Russian geopolitical writings. See Lucio Caracciolo, 'Eurussia: is Pan-European Security Possible?', presentation at a conference at the Danish Institute for International Studies, 22 April 2009. See www.diis.dk/sw76035.asp.
[24] http://temi.repubblica.it/limes/geopolitica-dei-taxi-guidatrici-velate-alla-ribalta/12321.
[25] See the courses and programmes assembled by Bonanate, 1990.

*Turkey: geopolitics left and right and the problem
of an endemic identity crisis*

If Germany was a country where almost all of the relevant factors seemed to
pre-empt the possibility of a revival of geopolitical thought, in Turkey the situation was almost the opposite. As with other countries where military regimes
continued to exist after the period of European fascism, as on the Iberian
Peninsula or in South America, geopolitics did not need a revival: it was always
there.[26] True, there was a considerable upsurge in publications and open references, as evidenced by Pinar Bilgin in Chapter 7, but there was little novel in
these developments.

Yet, such an upsurge was made possible by the existence of a Turkish security
imaginary characterised by what Bilgin calls 'geopolitics dogma'. Such dogma
is characterised by:

(1) the assumption that geographic elements are natural and constant facts,
    which establishes geopolitics as a scientific and objective view of the world;
(2) an axiomatic belief in the primacy, if not determinacy, of geography as a fac-
    tor shaping world politics;
(3) the assumption that Turkey's geographical location is special in a way that
    makes such factors extra-determinist for the Turkish case; and
(4) the presentation of Turkey as occupying a place envied by friends and foes
    alike.

This dogma plays an important role for Turkey's security imaginary, since
it relates closely to two of the latter's main features. First, it is connected to the
perennial question of Turkey's identity, which, with the arrival of the Turkish
Republic, has been decided as 'Western'. And in this context, whatever differences there may be in relation to other Western countries (in terms of religion,
culture and so on), common security interests – the 'geopolitics' so to speak –
placed Turkey on safe Western terrain during the Cold War. Besides helping
to interpellate a safe Western identity, the geopolitics dogma also serves to
negotiate Turkey's Westernness with a conflicting but equally foundational collective memory, namely the Treaties of Sèvres in which the Ottoman Empire
was divided up by Western powers. The Sèvres metaphor stands for a West
that cannot be trusted and that was ready to undermine the very integrity of
the Turkish Republic's precursor. Here, the geopolitics dogma mediates, since
its emphasis on geographic necessities means that there was nothing intrinsic
about the behaviour of the 'Western' nations at that time: they were basically
compelled to act as they did.

[26] See respectively, for example, Dodds, 1997 and 2000; Gangas-Geisse, 2001; Hepple, 1992;
      Kacowicz, 2000; Santis-Arenas, 2001 and Sidaway, 2000. For earlier assessments, see Child,
      1979; Hepple, 1986a; Kelly, 1984 and Reboratti, 1983. Note that Chile's General Augusto
      Pinochet has himself published a book with the title *Geopolitics* (in 1968).

Given the central role of the underlying materialist logic of the security imaginary in general, and the fixation on the 'Western' identity in particular, the events of 1989 did, according to Bilgin, produce an 'ontological anxiety' (Agnew). When, during the 1990s, the EU proved less than forthcoming in terms of granting Turkey membership, despite enlarging to include countries of Central and Eastern Europe, when even the United States had shown some signs of impatience with regard to Turkey's democratisation process and human rights record, whatever the self-understanding of Turkish foreign policy identity, the resulting external role ascription was one of a marginal Western, perhaps not entirely European, state with a Mediterranean or even Middle Eastern identity. In this context of perceived betrayal, Turkey experienced the large expansion of geopolitical writings that Bilgin documents, which stretches from a series of new journals to academics and politicians, including the present Foreign Minister (Prof.) Ahmet Davutoğlu.

But why retrieve geopolitics? Although, in this case, the geopolitics dogma seems to suggest that looking for geopolitical arguments will be the 'natural' response, according to Bilgin, two of the process factors did play a further role by limiting the search for answers to the vocabulary of geopolitics: the central role of the military and the state of academic IR (whose professionalisation and independence has however improved over the last years). The ubiquity of the military and the mainly materialist teaching with little theory to provide observational distance to common-sense understandings or even critique of the geopolitical 'view from nowhere', amplify the pull of geopolitical argument and the promptness with which the resort to it is made.

Bilgin's chapter also highlights the importance of the agential process factor hypothesised in the framework, since geopolitics featured prominently in Turkey's daily political battles. This, however, did not pitch conservative forces using geopolitical arguments against a left wing that shunned them. Rather, both sides used geopolitical argumentation freely. Bilgin notes that the basic vacuity of much geopolitical argument – being twistable for any environmental determinacy that would come in handy in political debates – readily facilitates such a situation.

For the general framework of analysis, the Turkish case therefore leads to two follow-up questions, one concerning the process by which geopolitics is mobilised, the other related to its role in appeasing identity crises. For the first issue, Bilgin's analysis questions the role of conservatism for geopolitical argument. We have already experienced in earlier chapters that geopolitical rhetoric was not alien to non-conservative forces, be they Havel in the Czech Republic, various politicians from the Green–Red coalition in Germany, the editor of *Limes* (although his belonging to the left is debatable) in Italy, and here Ecevit and others in Turkey. It is clear that even though conservative nationalists seemed to have used geopolitical arguments with more ease or naturalness, geopolitics is not their exclusive domain.

Is this 'bipartisan' use of geopolitics due to a merely rhetoric strategy? A purely rhetorical use is indeed more easily explained: every political actor tries to mobilise and tap into a security imaginary in order to enhance the resonance of his or her argument. When symbols become a conscious tool and not only a cultural disposition, actors will engage in symbolic battles in which any 'authorised' argument may be used if it serves to increase the legitimacy of one's point. Only in contexts where actors are aware and critical of the implications that a reproduction of geopolitical ideas might have (militarising international politics) will they be hesitant about such use, and may either not resort to geopolitical argument or seek to limit its use (as in the case of Germany). In fact, in such countries, one might expect that the arguments will not resonate as 'naturally' as elsewhere.

But, what about neoclassical geopolitical thought? There are two ways in which the left or reformists may become attracted not only by the rhetoric but also by (some of) the content of geopolitics. In a cogent discussion of Social Darwinism, Mike Hawkins has shown how this worldview has been appropriated by racists, reactionaries and reformists alike.[27] Darwin's theory of evolution includes both a sense of natural inexorability and a sense of the possibility of change if external conditions are altered – it is both nature and evolution. Consequently, much depended on which side of the tension the theorist came down on. The more conservative side would construct a line from some Malthusian shortage to a perennial struggle for land or primacy, whereas the more pacifist would insist on Darwin's analysis of a selective process of increasing social complexity, in which physical violence has become replaced by economic and ideational competition. Being fundamentally about an agnostic process, ideological contenders could decide either to stress the unchangeable nature of human selection or the evolutionary effects of such selection. Applied to our geopolitical argument, this would mean that, at least in principle, there could be ways of arguing for the primacy of geographic factors that nevertheless, by sufficiently stressing the historical character of such factors, allow for a reformist vision.

The Turkish case, however, seems rather different and leads to a second way of understanding the presence of the left in the geopolitical revival: nationalism. If, as the present book argues, geopolitical revival occurs as a response to a foreign policy identity crisis, then discussions around the nature of such identity, the 'national interest' and the very 'nation' itself are bound to flare up. In many countries, the issue of nationalism is almost exclusively reserved for the right, but not in all. There is, for instance, a republican (sometimes even Jacobin) tradition on the French left, and a liberal republican patriotic tradition in the United States (which makes nationalism a very broadly shared value within political discourse in that country). In Turkey, the main established party on

<hr />

[27] Hawkins, 1997.

the left (the Republican People's Party, or CHP) regards itself as the heir to the Kemalist tradition. That tradition may appear leftist, since it is the Westernising tradition within Turkey, and hence reformist in comparison with more traditionalist understandings of Turkish society. At the same time, however, it also tends to defend the exceptionalist role of the military in Turkish society, which, seeing itself as the guarantee for Turkey's territorial integrity and secular society, has kept Turkey in a state of limbo between a regime that is democratic and one that is constantly in a (cold) civil war (with all the 'necessary' consequences for human rights that this entails). In other words, it is not the conservative but the nationalist component that seems to be crucial for understanding the role of our process factor, at least in relation to Turkey.

But, the Turkish case is also instructive for a second facet of our framework of analysis. So far, the first mechanism was understood as occuring at the meeting between the foreign policy/security imaginary and an outside event (the end of the Cold War), where the interpretation of this event triggers a dissonance within the foreign policy identity contained within the imaginary. The theoretical framework clearly indicated that this had to be seen in an interpretivist way, in the sense that there was no automatism involved: a certain event did not necessarily have to trigger an identity crisis (as we have also seen in the German and Czech cases). The Turkish case, however, does point to a particular qualification: the possibility of an endemic identity crisis in which no stable self–other understanding exists. Obviously, all identity is a process, not some fixed entity. And, yet, to be 'identical' requires a sense of continuity (in the making). The nature of the geopolitical revival in Turkey seems to suggest that identity is more precarious within some security imaginaries than in others, and hence a Turkish identity crisis may be endemic. Inversely, if the main hypothesis is correct – that is, that identity crises may trigger the rise of geopolitical thought – the repeated inability of geopolitics to provide a stable fix to this may indicate the existence of a vicious circle – an idea that I will now develop in a bit more detail.

The events of 1989 only exposed an ongoing and permanent identity crisis that was exacerbated by the fact that Turkey's strategic importance (the geopolitical fix) could no longer outweigh the increasing distance between expectations concerning what it means to be part of the West (the EU) and what Turkey is willing to deliver as of now. It is basically the crisis of Kemalism when being Western is no longer measured by the 'right' alphabet, the secularisation (and militarisation) of the state, not even by the market economy (ever since Prime Minister Turgut Özal in the 1980s), but by the democratic and human rights record. This is partly the result of the positioning of the EU in its *acquis communautaire* – or, indeed, in its attempt to project itself as a normative power (at least at times). But, it also results from the Cold War and its termination, since human rights records were a key argument in the ideological struggle against the USSR.

Second, it seems that identity processes in the Turkish case may be taking the form of a vicious circle. On the one hand, geopolitical arguments are readily resorted to in times of crisis. But, if the foreign policy identity crisis is latent, since the Western anchoring has never been secured, it needs little to surface time and time again, continuously mobilising the geopolitical dogma. On the other hand, according to a hypothesis derived from the Turkish case, exactly for the apparent determinacy of such thought, which tends however to be useable for all possible positions, geopolitics does not ultimately stabilise identity discourses. Its suggested determinacy makes it attractive; its actual indeterminacy means that the fix it provides is always precarious. Hence, although geopolitical thought is an easy and quick fixer, it is not sufficient in itself, and indeed may become part of the problem: if it crowds out any other forms of discourse, the latent identity crisis is bound to return. In these circumstances, one could expect social mechanisms similar to those available for the reduction of individual cognitive dissonance. One of these, *wishful thinking*, adapts the perception of reality (or beliefs); here, this would involve assuming that Turkey's Westernness is acknowledged after all. The other, '*sour grapes*', will tend to adapt the desires; hence, as Bilgin shows, some alternative vision like 'Eurasianism' will surface in a way that enables Turkey's self-identification and role perception to coincide better.[28] Nevertheless, despite the lure of geopolitics, the latent identity crisis will not be resolved by a geopolitical approach and the debate on the issue will tend to oscillate like a pendulum without coming to a halt, even an imagined one (see the comparison with the Russian case, below). This is a point to which I will return in the next chapter.

Estonia: civilisational geopolitics

The background for the Estonian case is different again. Here, 1989 cannot be seen as an event that was interpreted in such a way as to produce a crisis for a given security imaginary (as in Italy or Turkey), nor as an event that would put an end to such an imaginary (as in the Czech Republic). Estonia was not just kidnapped: it ceased to exist as an independent state for several decades. Hence, the return to independence in 1991 meant not a crisis in the identity processes within a given foreign policy tradition, but rather the latter's very creation. Indeed, the fact that Estonia had not been an independent country for quite some time, argues Merje Kuus, meant that identity was initially articulated not in foreign policy terms, but in civilisational ones – and by cultural elites rather

---

[28] This idea is obviously inspired by Jon Elster's discussion on social mechanisms within a widely conceived rationalist analysis (see, for example, Elster, 1998 and 2007). Whether or not, or how, such ideas may be used for an analysis of mechanisms of discursive practices will be discussed in the next chapter.

than intellectuals of statecraft. Not physical, but human and cultural geography would lead the geopolitical revival.

Therefore, as Kuus shows, Estonian identity discourse focuses on, and actively constructs, the cultural entity of a nation rather than a state and its interests.[29] The Estonian nation and its legitimacy hark back to times immemorial, well before the Soviet hiatus. The discourse locates Estonia – including its religion and its culture – in the West, and not with Russia (automatically cast as the East). Estonia is the front state at the faultline. This produces a strong sense of 'othering', because the discourse functions on what people are, and not on what they do. And this has implications for Estonian society to the extent that the civilisational Other can be individuals 'among us'. Individuals become, writes Kuus, 'carriers of geopolitics'. The civilisational concept of identity thus pervades political debates, from those on foreign and security policies to those surrounding a host of domestic issues that include immigration, citizenship, minority rights and education. Its vision of threat is as much the power of the Russian Empire, as it is the fifth column inside.

It is in this context that Kuus analyses how Huntington's mappings and cultural identifiers were eagerly and prominently appropriated in the Estonian public sphere, so much so that they became part of and legitimated 'common sense'. Huntington's theses bundle up geopolitics and culture, 'casting geopolitics in terms of essential identities and framing culture as a geopolitical matter'. And, since the security imaginary is not formed in terms of the language of state interest, but that of cultural identity and civilisational faultlines, its embedded identity does not allow any vision of hybridity or mixture. As with every essentialist ethnic argument, it leads to tropes of 'purity', where mixing is never a compromise or the natural evolution of an identity in process, but merely a witness to decline or defeat.

Kuus' account prompts three reconsiderations for the initial framework of analysis. One has to do with the very definition of geopolitics, since some may consider Huntington's 'clash of civilisations' as not being 'geopolitical'. The second has to do with the interaction of domestic and international discourses – or, indeed, the question of to what extent foreign influences can impact on the process under investigation. Finally, her analysis shows how nationalism is not only reserved for great or dissatisfied powers, but also for a 'geopolitics of the weak'.

How can Huntington be a part of geopolitics? Does he not speak all about culture, not nature? There is little doubt that Huntington's thesis about a clash of civilisations falls squarely into the geopolitical tradition. Classical geopoliticians have always insisted in the national/ethnic component as a fundamental principle of the geography and politics of the state. This could be seen in the

---

[29] For a related discussion that examines various levels of Estonian discourses, including visual ones, see Berg, 2003.

early Ratzel, where he discusses how soil (*Boden*) and humans together form a state, and how the nature of that state depends on ideas and a common consciousness: the borders of the state reach as far as do the '*leitende Gedanken*' (guiding thoughts) about it. Ratzel mentions religious and national ideas, as well as historical memories, insisting on the role of national consciousness.[30] For his part, Kjellén has his chapter on geopolitics immediately followed by one on ethnopolitics, showing how both are part of the personality of a state and how loyalty (to the regime) and nationality (to the nation) feed into each other.[31] The national principle appears in Mackinder's defence of population exchanges as they occurred after World War I between Greece and Turkey,[32] or in the various visions of the civilisational primacy of Europe/the West/the White Race, in which versions of Social Darwinism would make *nations* struggle for survival.[33] And, of course, German *Geopolitik* was closely connected to a 'virulent ethnic German nationalism'.[34] Classical geopolitics has always included ethnopolitics, physical and human/cultural geography. Once the link between geopolitical discourse and nationalism is identified (see the discussion of the Turkish case, above), this should come as no surprise.

However, the problem for geopolitical analysis is that when it includes cultural and ideational factors (national awareness), we can no longer be sure what exactly the 'necessities' of nature are. In fact, in this context, it does not seem intellectually bizarre to search for biological continuities or roots that could serve as a way of reducing culture to nature once again. Such a move would obviously be shunned today if it came in a 'racial guise', but not necessarily if it were based on psychology or cognitive sciences, as with social identity theory, for instance.[35]

Hence, including civilisational and cultural factors does not cause an argument to step out of geopolitical logics. Material and cultural factors are tied to each other by the underlying concern of nationalism. But by using cultural factors, geopolitics does something to them. By adding more and more indeterminate (and socially constructed) items to the list of crucial factors, while keeping an argumentative logic based on a 'natural determinacy', geopolitics tends to objectify culture and to essentialise nations. It is not fortuitous that Huntington's last book eventually led him from the clashes of (homogeneous) civilisations to the national threats that, according to him, Hispanic immigrants pose to an ultimately essentialised Anglo-Protestant core of the United States.[36] This reproduces

---

[30] Ratzel, 1897, respectively 13–14, 32.
[31] Kjellén, 1924 [1916], 123. These are the only two chapters that are thoroughly developed.
[32] Mackinder, 1944 [1919].   [33] E.g. Kjellén, 1924 [1916], 122.
[34] Herb, 2002, 179.
[35] For ways in which such a take can be used to defend realist critiques of constructivism, see Mercer, 1995 and Snyder, 2002.
[36] Huntington, 2004. For a thoughtful critique of these political and conceptual walls, see Katzenstein, 2010.

the dilemma mentioned in Chapter 2 of this volume: the moment geopolitical writers acknowledge that such non-material factors are both necessary and not reducible to nature or necessity, the civilisational turn loses its alleged determinacy, one of the very reasons of its appeal.

The second point raised by Kuus' chapter concerns the interrelationship between domestic identity discourses and the outside world. In fact, here we not only meet the internal logic of geopolitical argument, the disposition to fix foreign policy identity by allegedly natural or necessitous constraints, but the fact that the argument comes from an external and authorised centre of knowledge. As Kuus writes, Huntington's theses were regarded as external proof of Estonian common sense; in return, Huntington himself used the way in which some Eastern European countries were able to identify with his thesis as a confirmation. Still, the reason why Huntington – and not some other legitimate Western voice – would be received with such esteem has to do with the predisposition of the foreign-policy common sense, i.e. with the action made by local intellectuals, and is hence not reducible to some foreign 'imposition'.

Finally, we can see in the Estonian case how geopolitics can be informed by a sociology of knowledge, whereby it is not meant to aggrandise the claims of actual or aspiring great powers, but rather defends – or indeed brings into being – the independent existence of a nation. Then it stands for a 'geopolitics of the weak', the defensive nationalism of the small country.[37] References to a greater (protective) community to which one belongs hark back to the same defensive sense of nationalism, however offensive its implications might be for Estonian citizens of Soviet/Russian descent.

Russia: geopolitical revival unable to fix the security imaginary

The end of the Cold War and the demise of the Soviet Union led to much rethinking of what 'Russia' stands for, its role and self-identification in the 1990s. Indeed, as one insightful observer has noted, both politics and international studies have been 'obsessed with identity'.[38] This obsession was accompanied by a flurry of geopolitical arguments mobilising different historical lineages of the Russian nation in an attempt to fix a new foreign policy/ security imaginary. So far, the hypothesis of this volume seems to hold. But, as Astrov and Morozova argue, for all the ubiquity of geopolitical argument within Russian political and public discourse, ultimately the recomposition of the security imaginary relied on inspirations that were not strictly geopolitical. Geopolitics was a quick response to a crisis – in fact part of the very definition of the crisis – but it provided no long-term fix.

---

[37] Thanks to Eiki Berg for having insisted on this in a private communication.
[38] Morozov, 2009a.

The Russian case offers interesting comparisons with Estonia and Turkey. As in Estonia, the revival was to a considerable degree civilisational, since what was at stake was the redefinition not just of the state, but of the nation. In both Russia and Estonia, the geopolitical revival would at first prompt essentialised understandings. But, whereas Estonia used civilisational arguments in a defensive way in order to bolster its position within the West and against another civilisation further East, Russia, perceiving itself as being at the core of such a civilisation, was looking for a more self-assured way of defining itself. This enabled Russia to make a more substantial recourse to its own symbolic resources. And those proved more multifaceted, open to diverse historical lineages.

Like Turkey, Russia seems to have been caught in a kind of perennial identity crisis. Both countries have been considered part of Europe – but not really (cf. the idea of the Ottoman Empire as 'the sick man of Europe'). More specifically, the role assignment of a 'great power' by international society has usually been half-hearted for both countries. Whereas Russia (and later the Soviet Union) had seen itself as a central player, subsequent international societies have not necessarily been forthcoming in granting that status. Hence, the discussion of whether or not Turkey or Russia were part of Europe and/or the West was always paired with a discussion of whether they were 'acceptable' members of international society. And, with every turn whereby international society became more demanding – increasingly in terms of the criteria domestic regimes needed to fulfil, not just the power a country was able to project – both Russia and Turkey were facing exclusion.[39] Indeed, often the two sides constructed each other as the (significant) other.[40] Astrov and Morozova show that, as in Turkey, geopolitics did not provide a stabilisation of the identity in Russia's foreign-policy imaginary.

The authors identify four themes that have dominated post-1991 Russian debates, namely, ideology, modernisation, Russia's distinctiveness and possible objective grounds for Russia's (re-)assertion following the demise of communism and the Soviet Union.[41] They argue that the 1990s posed a major problem for the rearticulation of the relevant foreign-policy imaginary. To the outside observer, often prone to confuse Russia with the Soviet Union, it may appear a quick step to simply refer back to the long history of Russian identity and foreign policy, breaking with the immediate Soviet past while reaching out to the rich reservoir of lessons and lineages from before. However, this would not prove easy. The first 'liberal' years, in which Russia's identity and foreign policy was grafted onto an existing 'Western' model, failed in the economic

---

[39] For the more recent Turkish case, see Rumelili, 2003 and 2004; for an analysis of Russia's repeated attempts to achieve great-power status, see Neumann, 2008.

[40] For Russia, see, for example, Neumann, 1995 and 1999; for the Ottoman Empire, see, among others, Said, 1979.

[41] Note that the first themes are compatible with the ones that Hopf has found prominent in the identity debate in the Soviet Union and Russia; see Hopf, 2002.

crisis and provoked turmoil by the end of the decade. Hence, the break with the Soviet past was not successful. But, nor was a return to it possible: the role of communist ideology in the self-understanding within Russia's foreign-policy imaginary was gone. Accordingly, argue Astrov and Morozova, there was no ready imaginary to fall back upon. More precisely, the crisis was not just a new debate about which historical memories should become dominant within a given foreign-policy imaginary; it also involved a decision regarding which type of imaginary would be chosen as the baseline in the first place – a result of the multiple subjectivities of the Russian/Soviet past. Hence, the Russian case is one of a foreign-policy identity crisis in which there is no longer an identity. As analysed in the opening chapters of the book, crises arise when the security imaginary predisposes for the understanding of events in such a way as to unsettle an established or dominant self-understanding or the relationship between that self-understanding and outside role attribution. Russia is not only a case of the second, but also of the first.

In this disorientation, geopolitical thought did flare up and did mobilise previous geopolitical thought. Indeed, what would be more appropriate than to reflect upon the last time in which the Russian foreign policy/security imaginary had faced some similar problems, namely, when Russia became the Soviet Union? Both Vadim Tsymburskii and Aleksandr Dugin would rely on that past for their Eurasian recomposition of a more geopolitically informed identity and, potentially, security imaginary. Astrov and Morozova show the different ways in which the two seek to recompose this identity, arguing that, with some qualifications, Dugin can be considered a 'neoclassical geopolitical thinker'.

However, the authors' main point is that although we have an identity crisis and a geopolitical revival, including a neoclassical one (Dugin), and although there is a clear redefinition of foreign-policy identity happening, the foreign-policy tradition is ultimately rearranged in a way that does not strongly rely on geopolitics. Instead, and this move is accomplished with the second Putin presidency, some version of technocratic realism informs it, which externalises the reasons for the crisis and ends up mobilising a Cold War identity, removed of its communist components and the risk of nuclear confrontation, but with the same threat – 'Atlantism' or 'Americanism' (the 'false Europe'). Stabilising at first, this externalisation epitomises an endemic identity crisis.

Accordingly, the Russian case also has some wider implications for the present volume. A revival of geopolitical thought has taken place in that country, and it has been plausibly triggered by the identity crisis that leading thinkers and politicians tried to address. The chapter does not dwell much on the other process factors, since we know that they all lead in the same direction. In fact, Russia was an 'obvious' case of a state where a revival of geopolitical thought could be expected to occur as a way of addressing a crisis. What is less obvious is the relationship between that first trigger and the security imaginary. As we have seen in several cases now, even if geopolitical thought is mobilised for an easy fixing in times of identity crisis, it may not necessarily succeed. In the Turkish case, and to some extent also in the Italian case, a reason for this failure is that, despite its alleged determinism, geopolitical thinking can be rearranged to fit several stories (which all lay claim to determinism). Or, put differently, there is a determinism for each geopolitical story, but no determinism as to which determinism will be chosen. In the Russian case, this has produced a situation in which geopolitical debate, so important in the definition of the identity crisis, did not significantly affect the security imaginary, since other political actors were able to mobilise other historical lineages. Hence, the revival has had a more limited effect, at least so far.

This provides an important reminder that the link between the main social mechanism of this study (see next chapter) – that of dissonance reduction in an identity crisis – and the potential second one – the self-fulfilling prophecy of remilitarising security imaginaries – is far from direct. Russia witnessed an open debate about the reconstitution of its foreign policy identity (and political subjectivity more generally) within which geopolitical argument was highly visible. Hence, the geopolitical revival was indeed part of the mechanism that was sought to reduce the dissonance or indeed to reconstitute the country's foreign policy identity. But, although it affected the acuteness of the identity crisis, this revival of geopolitical discourse did not eventually become a major part in the reconstitution of the security imaginary, occurring in the guise of a technocratic great power realism (a kind of internal balancing, as realists would put it). It is not impossible that also this realism mobilises a version of a more militarised security imaginary that would feed back into a more Hobbesian European order, the second mechanism. However, its link to the geopolitical revival could, at best, be indirect and outside of the reach of the present volume's analysis.

It is in any case probably too early to tell. For rhetoric can inform behaviour that is subsequently rationalised/made sense of in such a way as to affect the security imaginary, to make it 'coherent'.[42] In a public debate in which geopolitical references have become self-evident and legitimate, their rhetorical power can be called upon in later crises. Talk is not cheap, and identities and imaginaries are ongoing processes.

3   Conclusion

The present chapter's survey of the findings of the six cases can be summarised as follows (see Table 10.1).

---

[42] This echoes Deborah Larson's argument that Cold War behaviour was not an effect of a pre-existing frame and ideology; rather, the Cold War ideology was an *ex-post* rationalisation that sought to make sense of improvised practices. See Larson, 1985.

Table 10.1. *A synthesis of the country studies*

	Foreign policy identity crisis?	Which crisis?	Which geopolitics (formal, popular, practical)?	Which process factors? (+ for positive effect on revival)
Czech Republic	No crisis and no geopolitical revival	Potential crisis for 'no longer' identity since new borders, indeed new country. Finding: no crisis	Marginally formal and practical (and hence no significant revival)	(-) satisfied power for achieving political and national sovereignty (-) ideational path dependence: anti-geopolitical tradition (+/-) new institutionalisation of academia and expert system allowing a certain autonomy, but not yet much influence, and no military role in knowledge production (-) political debate not in terms of nationalist escalation
Germany	No crisis and no geopolitical revival	Potential crisis for 'no longer' identity since new borders, indeed new country. Finding: no crisis	Marginally formal and practical (and hence no significant revival)	(-) satisfied power for achieving national sovereignty (unification) (-) ideational path dependence: geopolitics – taboo through its past (-) peace research tradition, academia in role of observer (theory), military no special role in knowledge production[a] (-) political debate not in terms of nationalist escalation

Table 10.1. (*cont.*)

	Foreign policy identity crisis?	Which crisis?	Which geopolitics (formal, popular, practical)?	Which process factors? (+ for positive effect on revival)
Italy	Yes and geopolitical revival	Potential crisis for 'no longer' identity, since the established one closely connected to the Cold War. Finding: crisis for perceived status decline	Mainly formal and at the interstices between formal, popular and political (LiMes)	(+) dissatisfied power for lacking status recognition (+) ideational path dependence: materialist tradition (+) no peace research tradition and military role in knowledge production (+/-) role of academia increasingly observer oriented, but isolated (+/-) political debate sometimes in terms of nationalist escalation (government dependent)
Turkey	Yes and geopolitical revival	Potential crisis for 'no longer' identity, since the established one closely connected to the Cold War. Finding: crisis for perceived status decline	All	(+) dissatisfied power for lacking status recognition (+) ideational path dependence: geopolitical dogma (+) no peace research tradition; military role in knowledge production; increasing academic autonomy but isolated (+) political debate in terms of nationalist escalation

Estonia	Yes and geopolitical revival	Potential crisis for 'not yet' identity, since newly established country and elite. Finding: crisis in status recognition and very definition of the 'essential' self	All, but mainly practical	(+) insecure power (+/-) no clear ideational path dependence (+/-) new institutionalisation of academia and expert system allowing a certain autonomy, but not yet much influence; no military role in knowledge production (+) political debate in terms of nationalist escalation
Russian Federation	Yes and geopolitical revival	Potential crisis for 'no' identity, since both self-understanding and role recognition in jeopardy. Finding: crisis for perceived status decline and insecure subjectivity	Mainly formal and practical	(+) dissatisfied power for lacking status recognition (+) ideational path dependence: materialist, but not strictly in geopolitical way (+) marginalised peace research tradition; a direct role of politics and military in knowledge production (+) political debate in terms of nationalist escalation

Note:

[a] Moreover, even if it were, the military tradition in post-1945 Germany ('Staatsbürger in Uniform') is not specifically geared towards geopolitics either.

1   Was there a foreign policy identity crisis?

A foreign policy identity crisis was identified in four of the six cases. Where such a crisis occurred, it followed a clear sense of disorientation regarding how to cope with the new role and/or self-identification the (sometimes new) country had to face. The two countries that experienced no foreign policy identity crisis also experienced no significant revival of geopolitical thought. In the Czech Republic and Germany, the events of 1989 (which here include the subsequent German reunification and the breakup of Czechoslovakia) seemed rather to reconfirm the prevailing identity within the security imaginary. Yet, the process factors stipulated by this comparative study (see below) seemed to work parallel with the underlying security imaginary. In other words, most if not all of the process factors that would facilitate a revival of geopolitical thinking were absent or weak in these two cases. Both countries had experienced a non-materialist political culture (for a longer period of time in the Czech Republic than in Germany), a clear separation of the military from the political and academic elite, and an expert system that was relatively independent – in terms of observer status and finance – and only partly co-opted by the political system.

2   What kind of crisis?

The study had selected six cases that varied in terms of the kind of potential crisis situation – that is, instances in which previously established self-understandings and external role conceptions could be reasonably expected to be challenged. We distinguished between three types of potential foreign policy identity crisis: no identity, no longer the previously established identity, and no identity as yet.

The first type – 'no identity' – can be seen in the case of Russia, where both the country's previously established role as a superpower in the world and its self-understanding (neither Soviet Union nor Tsarist Russia) were in jeopardy. In addition, both of these aspects were intertwined in the geopolitical revival that has since been temporarily resolved through the revival of a technocratic great-power identity that incorporates a known adversary.

The second type – 'no longer the previously established identity' – covered different subtypes. The external roles of Italy and Turkey, for example, were so closely connected to the Cold War that the latter's end ushered in some anxious self-reflection. In both cases, this resulted in an attempt to stem the perceived decline of status that clashed with the established self-understanding in which the country was either a pillar of the Western alliance (Turkey) or of the European project (Italy). Interestingly, this seems to have provoked more anxiety – indeed crisis – than the subtype of states that found themselves in new borders, such as the Czech Republic and Germany. Although the fact of having a new state seemed to lay the ground for a potential identity crisis, in these two cases at least it did not result in one. In both states, there was a major debate about the 'new' state that had now come into being and had never existed within the current borders. But, internally, the changes met pre-existing aspirations rather than challenging them. And externally all was fine as long as the two countries would abide to the status expectations in the world, which for Germany meant in particular that it would largely maintain its Bonner Republic identity – which it did. Hence, to repeat the basic interpretivist point, the important trigger does not lie in the shifting of borders or indeed the production of new states; rather, it lies in the way in which the foreign policy imaginary, with its embedded identity discourses and international role attribution, makes sense of the historical changes. By implication, in other cases within the same subtype of 'new' old countries, an identity crisis might well have developed.

The last type – 'not yet an identity' – was represented by Estonia, where it was mostly the country's internal self-understanding that was at stake, while the very fact of access to the sovereign status of a state had established Estonia's international role to a large extent. There remained, however, an element of status recognition about which the new country's elite was quite anxious. Here, the role of Huntington's maps proved crucial, since they allowed a clear and 'objective' anchoring in the West (together with the status that comes with that).

3   Which geopolitics?

Did a revival take place within formal, practical or popular geopolitics – that is, within academic, political or public debate – during the 1990s? In this context, the authors of the case studies were asked to concentrate primarily on the expert system within the countries studied – that is, on both the academic and the political level, within which we also include parts of the public (when journals are analysed). Regarding the two countries in which no identity crisis occurred, it was shown that the openings that did take place in Germany occurred solely within the political sphere, while academic involvement was marginal; and, in the Czech Republic, it was again only within the political sphere that some temporarily significant borrowing of geopolitical wording could be found. In Italy and Russia, the revival took place within both practical and formal geopolitics. And, although the term 'revival' may not be the most appropriate expression in relation to the Turkish case, since geopolitics never really left the scene in that country, Turkey has seen the presence of geopolitical thinking across the spectrum, including at the popular level. In Estonia, geopolitics was also present in all three domains, although it has definitely receded within academia over the last decade.

4   Which process factors were present?

As noted earlier, identity crises and process factors were more closely tied to each other (see Chapter 3). Accordingly, these are probably best understood not as factors that kick in only after a crisis has occurred, but as accompanying factors all the way along. Still, our process factors were not equally present in all of the cases under study:

- We hypothesised that the ideology of a great or dissatisfied power would enhance the chances for a geopolitical revival in response to a foreign policy identity crisis. The existence of such an ideology clearly contributed to such a revival in the cases of Italy, Russia and Turkey, but not the others.
- Ideational path dependence (the existence of a materialist political culture) was clearly present in Italy, Russia and Turkey; difficult to assess in relation to a new country like Estonia; and not (or no longer) present in the Czech Republic and Germany.
- In the field of foreign policy expertise, we suggested a series of hypotheses, namely, that (1) the existence of peace research institutes or, more widely, an academia in which IR is taught at the observer level that provides distance to the language of world politics and its practitioners, (2) the existence of institutional guarantees for the independence of expertise from politics and the military, and (3) the checked influence of foreign military or strategic experts would reduce the probability that the response to the foreign policy identity crisis would involve an attempt to fix it with the help of geopolitical thinking. This element could not be systematically covered in the chapters of the present volume (an adequate treatment would have required almost a book for each case study), since their primary focus was on the analysis of the revival and its content.[43] That said, some general trends are known. With the exception of Germany, none of the countries has any strong tradition of peace research. With the exception of Turkey, and to some extent Russia, the military is not particularly present within the foreign policy expert system. The issue of the independence of academia and the domination of non- or anti-geopolitical traditions is more tricky, however. For even if a country's academia is independent, it may well be insignificant within the foreign policy expert culture. Hence, one needs both to have an observer status and to be taken seriously by the field, which includes the political and/or military elite and the general media – which remains a challenge in many countries.[44]

---

[43] The initial research project had even envisaged conducting Bourdieu-inspired foreign expert field studies in the particular countries. See Guzzini, 2003. However, this had to be dropped due to missing financial means. Nevertheless, some authors have set off down that road on an individual basis. See Kuus, 2010 and 2011.

[44] For an analysis of the Baltic states in this regard, see Berg and Chillaud, 2009.

Also, in some countries the political elite is actually able to provide some of the self-observing distance itself. Hence, the foreign policy expert system is best understood in terms of a configurational analysis of actors and institutions that only more detailed studies would be able to provide. Table 10.1, however, does include general trends for the countries examined.

- Finally, we included agency in the political debate as one factor that may contribute to the rise of a particularly geopolitical answer to a foreign policy identity crisis. There, so the expectation, the rhetorical power of 'geopolitics' can show when used for dealing with territorial issues, when being mobilised in a threat rhetoric, controlling domestic dissent and strengthening conservatism, as well as when establishing the primacy of foreign policy and the need for long-term strategy. This initial hypothesis had to be amended: although it was predominantly conservative forces that pushed for a revival, this was only the case in countries in which the use of nationalist arguments was limited to the conservative side. As it turns out, nationalism is the more fundamental category here. And that also means that if the debate turns on the definition of the state or the nation, geopolitics may not just provide arguments, but may become the frame of the argument. Here, among the four countries that have seen a geopolitical revival, all had experienced this circle of resonance at least during the 1990s.

5   Did geopolitics provide a fix?

Have the security imaginaries of the countries studied been affected in such a way that the now-dominant identity discourses rely predominantly on geopolitical determinism? This question is crucial for understanding the second social mechanism ('self-fulfilling geopolitics'), which will be discussed in more detail in the next chapter. The country studies cannot give a final answer on this, but with the added hindsight of two decades after the 1990s, it could well be that the structural effects of the geopolitical revivals under study have been less pronounced than perhaps anticipated. Here, the Turkish case stands out, since 'geopolitical dogma' was already part and parcel of that country's security imaginary. And, yet, since geopolitics does not provide a clear determinate fix, the country is still searching for an enduring foreign policy identity, its absence repeatedly but each time only temporarily fixed by the geopolitical dogma: Turkey remains in a latent continuous identity crisis. And this limbo could potentially affect the geopolitical dogma and its force. The jury is still out on Estonia, Italy and Russia, the other countries that experienced a geopolitical revival, but where the security imaginary was not already geopolitical. The Russian chapter argues that, ultimately, strictly geopolitical ideas have not become dominant within the Russian security imaginary. For both Estonia and Italy, it is possible to observe an increasingly critical academia and a more general decline of (neoclassical) geopolitical ideas, although geopolitical thinking is still very present within Estonia's defensive nationalist discourses. In all of the cases concerned, the appeal to geopolitics seems to have been limited in time, and hence – or so the hypothesis would go – perhaps also in depth.

11

Social mechanisms as micro-dynamics in constructivist analysis

STEFANO GUZZINI

In a first step, the case studies in the study presented here have proved crucial in specifying the occurrence of a foreign policy identity crisis as the major explanatory factor in the revival of geopolitical thinking in certain countries following the events of 1989. The other factors – ideational path dependence, institutional factors/political economy of a country's foreign policy expert system, and political struggles – were considered to be process factors that helped explain why geopolitical discourse was chosen as a way of responding to such a crisis. This suggested an analysis in terms of process tracing, since (1) we had a common starting point, the end of the Cold War, and were attempting to explain/understand a given (variable) end, the revival or not of geopolitical thought, and (2) it was impossible to rule out equifinality or to assume unit homogeneity. The process tracing would be both comparative and interpretivist. The comparison would make it possible to cross-check the different explanatory factors within their particular contexts. The interpretivist part was necessary since the starting point of the process was not a given outside event (i.e. the end of the Cold War), but rather the way in which that event was interpreted within different countries. More precisely, to start off the process leading to a potential revival of geopolitics, the interpretation of this event unsettled previous identity roles within a country's security.

After the second round of empirical analysis, further specifications about the relationship between the hypothesised factors became necessary, since it was found that these factors did not simply 'line up' in the analysis of the process. In the first section of this chapter, I will therefore present a way of thinking about process tracing not in terms of a linear scheme, but as the intermeshing of several parallel processes. A second section will then specify and qualify how causal/social mechanisms can be fruitfully applied in such process tracing and coherently used in an intersubjective and non-positivist social theory. The third section of the chapter will establish the two basic mechanisms underpinning the empirics of this study: a social mechanism of identity crisis reduction and a self-fulfilling prophecy mechanism (which I term a 'vicious circle of essentialisation'). Both of these mechanisms function as micro-dynamics for the analysis of structural change in constructivist theorising and provide the theory development of this book.

1   Interpretivist process tracing and parallel historical dynamics

This section will further develop the idea of interpretivist process tracing by adding a crucial component identified during the empirical analysis in Part II: the need to look for parallel processes and their interaction, rather than for a single timeline from a critical juncture to the outcome.

Initially, the process-tracing design of the comparative study involved an Input–Mechanism/Process–Output model, with a qualification at the input side. That qualification concerned the inside-out vision of the input: rather than assuming that the end of the Cold War ('the events of 1989') had a direct impact on ideas, it would be the interpretation of those events on the basis of the pre-existing security imaginary – the reservoir of shared experiences and meanings, national lessons of history and embedded identity discourses – that would form the initial input into the process. Then, the study privileged one factor – the potential occurrence of a foreign policy identity crisis – as the starting point for the actual process, adding further dis/enabling factors later. This approach would correspond to an almost classical I(nput)–M(echanism)–O(utput) scheme (see Figure 11.1)

Though the process-tracing design was initially interpretivist, factors would be used both within a linear timeline and in a cumulative sense, whereby they were regarded as simply adding significance for the understanding of the outcome: the revival. It was thus possible to carry out the process tracing in a manner not too different from that of a more positivistic approach, in which the various factors would count as simple intervening variables (and, given the empirical record, probably also having interactive effects).

The empirical case studies, however, added several complications to the initial framework. First, the initial trigger and the process factors were internally linked. In the analysis of the Czech case, the historical lineage of an anti-geopolitical tradition certainly predisposed the public and academic debate for anti-determinist and even progressivist assumptions regarding the nature of politics. But, it most probably interacted with the foreign policy imaginary itself: it is difficult to imagine a collective memory of scripts and lessons of the past (and 'Munich' surely rings a bell within the Czech foreign policy tradition) that could remain unconnected from such wider ideational traditions. Furthermore, such a link would go both ways. Hence, we cannot simply say that an identity crisis occurred and then ideational path dependence sets in: the respective ideational structures were already part of the understanding of the security imaginary, and hence of the development of the crisis in the first place. By implication, rather than seeing one factor prompting another,

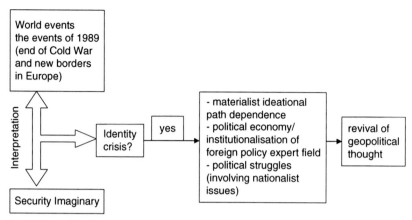

Figure 11.1. The return of geopolitics (I): a simple interpretivist process model

their relationship should be seen as an *ongoing process*, in which the events of the decade after 1989 represent just a temporary external shock.

Similarly, second, the German case indicated the existence of a link between one of the study's process factors and the initial trigger of a foreign policy identity crisis. For attempts have been made to use 1989 and the 'mitteleuropäische Lage' to redefine Germany's 'national interest', in which geopolitical arguments were used to support the 'necessity' of such a move. Hence, there has been an ongoing symbolic struggle, one that could have provoked a crisis. For one thing, this means that a foreign policy identity crisis is not simply some kind of mechanical event in which a certain world history (that of 1989) encounters identities embedded in security imaginaries. Agency is present from the start, not just in the mobilisation of geopolitical thought after a crisis has occurred. Indeed, this very geopolitical thinking may be part of the symbolic struggle for a different dominant identity discourse in the first place, a struggle in which academic, popular and political voices will be heard. In a Bourdieu-inspired way, that agency is best understood within the specific rules of the game in their respective fields. Agency and the general dynamics of those fields, in turn, are also best seen as *ongoing processes* that are both parallel to and interact with the different ideational structures.

Third, the analysis of the Turkish case (and to some extent the Italian and Russian cases) points to the phenomenon of an 'endemic' identity crisis – a crisis, moreover, for which geopolitical thinking may be both a solution and a contributing factor. Geopolitical thought has been always a central feature of Turkish foreign policy expert culture, partly because of the importance of the military's (Kemalist) role in defining and defending the nation, and partly because of the existence of a more general materialist lineage within the foreign policy field.

And, yet, exactly because geography provides no unambiguous point of reference, it offers no lasting fix: the decision about Turkey's role in or in relation to the West cannot be read from the maps. Hence, the strategic crisis brought about by the end of the Cold War brings Turkey's endemic identity crisis to the fore, prompting a geopolitical response; but, the very response in terms of geopolitics is part of a later crisis foretold. For we have here a vicious circle: when in crisis, a geopolitically framed security imaginary with a precarious identity construction makes recourse to a remedy that provides only short-term solace and so nurtures the next outbreak of crisis, for which it finds no other interpretive means than to return to geopolitics, and so returns in a circle.

Finally, the cases of both Estonia and Russia forcefully reminded us that geopolitics does not necessarily or mainly refer to the physical components of geography that are so important for the military or strategic thinker, but also to cultural aspects and the nation. Geopolitics' reference back to cultural geographies and imaginaries, its mobilisation of content and symbolics of nationalism, although part of the reference definition of neoclassical geopolitics, was insufficiently stressed in Part I. Furthermore, the cultural component might qualify the second mechanism discussed later in this study, which so far was assumed to be the 'militarism as self-fulfilling prophecy' of peace research. Although it starts from the 'essentialisation' of geography – here, human and cultural rather than physical (although obviously connected to a space!) – its dynamics are probably different, a point to which I will later return in my discussion of the second mechanism.

These four findings from the empirical analysis have implications for the type of process tracing most congenial to this problematique. Clearly, the use of an input–output scheme that took as its starting point a foreign policy identity crisis and as its output a geopolitical revival would only beg the question. The input itself needs to be explained, and such explanation is partly provided by factors that the input generates during the process: geopolitical thought is both effect and cause of the identity crisis. At the same time, process factors are not 'variables' whose explanatory power 'add up' in a linear explanation;[1] rather, they are interlinked in a way that is not co-variational but relational – or, as Charles Ragin put it, 'combinatorial'.[2]

In my understanding, this requires a specific understanding of process tracing: one that is interpretivist, historical and multilayered. Process tracing needs to be *interpretivist* for reasons already outlined in Chapter 3. The outside 'shock' event of the end of the Cold War is only a shock for some. Its meaning and effect depend on the way in which it is seen and interpreted. At the same time, the interpretation of such an event is not something that is carried out

---

[1] For an early statement, see, for example, Abbott, 1988. See also the collection of essays in Abbott, 2001.
[2] Ragin, 1987, for instance at 13–15.

on the individual level alone, for example by individual politicians, academics or journalists. Meaning is given within a particular context. An individualist focus on 'beliefs' (propositions about the world that particular actors hold to be true) is not sufficient to account for 'meanings', since it underplays the symbolic component of ideas and the background knowledge necessary for forming such beliefs in the first place.[3] To understand meaning requires placing particular beliefs/ideas within their wider cultural context or more specific discourses.

In this volume, the central cultural structure is that of the security imaginary, a depository of meaningful collective memory, with its battles and defining positions, its scripts and metaphors that inform and, in turn, provide legitimacy when used in political and other discourses. Agency and individual interpretation enter into the process in which the security imaginary develops and evolves, but the latter cannot be reduced to it. Like any language, the security imaginary has a grammar of its own. Furthermore, given that the explanandum of this volume is itself an ideational fact (the revival of geopolitical thought), the process tracing conducted for this study has to account for how different ideational structures relate to each other. And this is done within an interpretivist understanding of ideas. For ideas are not conceptualised as objects that externally cause behaviour, but are constitutive of interests and identity (and hence provide reasons for behaviour).[4]

Process tracing also has to be *historical*: time/timing and sequence matter for any attempt to understand the unfolding of a given process. It did make a difference that there had been a previous geopolitical revival in Germany during the 1980s that mobilised the 'Other' in German identity discourses and hence eventually helped to 'vaccinate' (if such a metaphor is taken very loosely) German debates during the 1990s, when geopolitics no longer only appeared in its right-wing nationalist guise. As in all identity related processes, also memory and the representation of history and sequence needs to be endogenised into the analysis. And, as the interdependency of the relationship between geopolitical thought and identity processes in the Turkish case shows, the critical juncture in the present study relates to some of the process factors in both ways: it prompts them and is prompted by them. Here, sequence is crucial.[5]

---

[3] Gross, 2009, 369.

[4] This is an old discussion within all of the social sciences. For IR, it was held in the 1980s–1990s. See in particular Goldstein and Keohane, 1993; Kratochwil and Ruggie, 1986; Laffey and Weldes, 1997 and Yee, 1996.

[5] This is one of the points stressed by historical institutionalists. See Pierson, 2000a and 2000b; Thelen, 1999 and 2000. When, unlike in the present volume, comparative historical studies stretch over long periods of time, the analysis needs also to include 'demonstration effects': when Barrington Moore notes that although the three types of revolutions he analyses could be seen as alternative routes, they correspond also to 'successive historical stages', where one revolution sets the stage for the next. See Moore, 1987 [1966], 413–414.

Finally, process tracing would gain from being *multilayered* – that is, by showing how autonomous processes evolve and interact with each other during the period an analyst has decided to study. Rather than assuming one single process line that various factors punctuate, we might look for a series of layers that can each be considered as having a path-dependent – that is, autonomous – process line of its own. Thus, 'the focus is not … on the trajectory of a single process. It is on the temporal intersection of distinctive trajectories of different, but connected, long-term processes'.[6] As Falleti and Lynch show, such processes can be conceptualised within (horizontal) layers in an analysis that cuts a certain (vertical) time period out of them for the sake of studying a theory-informed puzzle.[7] In her empirical case on welfare-state development, and on the basis of previous theoretical discussion, Lynch identified three such layers: the political arena, the institutional arena for social policy programmes, and slow-moving background processes such as population aging and the development of the private–public insurance market. Each such layer moves at its own logic and rhythm (or speed). Yet the analysis can investigate intersections at particular points in time which can provoke changes in the processes. Consequently, such an approach can lead to an understanding of change, if not creativity, by the way otherwise habitual practices interact[8] (see Figure 11.2. for the ensuing reconceptualisation of process tracing).

2   Making sense of social mechanisms in interpretivist process tracing

How exactly can social mechanisms be used in an interpretivist context? As with process tracing, the literature on social or causal mechanisms has known considerable success in recent decades.[9] Mechanisms seem to offer a way of

---

[6] Aminzade, 1992, 467.

[7] Falleti and Lynch, 2009, 1156–1158. For my own application of a similar approach (although I was not aware of this at the time), see Guzzini, 1995.

[8] This is not the place to make a longer argument on this issue, but it can be derived from a post-Bourdieusian analysis. For the idea that changes in a field of practice can be induced by interference and transfer of practices from another field, see Guzzini, 1994. For an argument that habit can induce change, see Barnes, 1982. For a related and good discussion on how to combine habit with creativity, see Dalton, 2004.

[9] The wording is not coherent in the literature. Since individualist approaches were prominent early on in the discussion, there is a certain tendency for non-individualist approaches to refer to 'social mechanisms'. Also, some authors seem to prefer the latter term as a way of avoiding the risk of giving any impression that their theories might rely on an understanding of 'causality' as stringent as that contained in the idea of universal laws: interpretivists have traditionally been cautious with regard to causality. That said, with the necessary qualifications and provisos that are part and parcel of the mechanism literature, even constructivists can refer to 'causal' mechanisms. For some scholars, the whole point of the mechanism debate is to redefine causality in a different manner, not to deny it. For an early

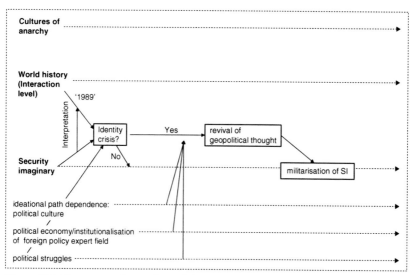

Figure 11.2. The return of geopolitics (II): a time-layered interpretivist process model

theorising below the level of general laws and yet above that of mere description. They make it possible to overcome the limitations of correlational analysis, where causality is reduced to the constant conjunction of variables without it being possible to check how we get from one to the other. When connected to the idea of process tracing – and the two are often, and for some observers even necessarily, linked – mechanisms have become the standard focus for rationalist analysts and basically all classical versions of institutionalism, whether rationalist, historical or sociological.[10] More recently, constructivist versions of institutionalism have entered the fray and refer to theoretically informed process tracing and discourse analysis as their preferred methods, whether within political science or in IR,[11] while asking for the need to use mechanistic explanations.[12]

This section, then, will try to advance an understanding of social mechanisms that is congenial with constructivist assumptions.[13] All central parts of an explanatory theory, hence also mechanisms, need to be conceptualised

statement, see Patomäki, 1996. Here, I will use both terms interchangeably, with the understanding that, as Hedström and Ylikovski (2010, 53) write, this excludes approaches that define 'causality in terms of regularities (such as Hume's constant conjunction theory or many probabilistic theories of causation)'.

[10] The *locus classicus*: Hall and Taylor, 1996.

[11] See, respectively, Hay, 2006, 58 and Checkel, 2005 and 2008.

[12] Wendt, 1999 and 2000.

[13] For my attempt to understand the Copenhagen School of Security Studies through causal mechanisms, see Guzzini, 2011.

within the meta-theoretical setting in which they are used. Despite the need to conform to meta-theoretical coherence, and the resulting pluralism of conceptualisations of mechanisms, there is no necessary, let alone total, incommensurability between them. But understanding their difference requires some translation. For this reason, I will try to rely as much as possible on research on mechanisms as it has been carried out by others; but I will sometimes need to translate their theories and mechanisms into the theoretical framework that informs the present study.[14]

Let me start again with the main finding of this volume: the end of the Cold War provoked a revival of geopolitical thinking only in those countries that experienced a foreign policy identity crisis. And let us assume, therefore, that there is a link between crisis and revival. However, the crisis in itself does not 'explain' the revival, nor does it cause it in any kind of necessary or even probabilistic manner. Such an assertion would indeed beg the very question that induced much of the empirical analysis in the second round: *how* could the foreign policy identity crisis *cause* the revival? The wording in this sentence is deliberate.[15] For, apparently, we are dealing with an analysis that seeks to understand the process involved (how). Yet, that process seems to have in itself some causal implications, since we can trace the event backwards as being the effect of some initial phenomenon. Although not causal in any strong sense, the analysis is surely a 'causal' one of sorts, albeit similar to the type conducted by historians. Process tracing appears to be about the causal 'how' of mechanisms, not the causal 'what' of correlational analysis.[16] It is about how effects have been brought about ('causes of effects'), not what a cause effects ('effects of causes').[17] This point leads naturally into a discussion of the status of an explanation, and how process tracing and causal or social mechanisms are linked. Let me derive my own use of mechanisms by making a short detour through the usual mechanism literature.

In recent methodological writings, there has been a tendency to see process tracing as the addition of intermediate steps to move from an independent to a dependent variable, or from input to output with a mechanism in between.[18] This is often represented in terms of I(nput)–M(echanism)–O(utput). In one such reading, we would basically reduce the analysis of mechanisms to the specification of intervening variables and then apply the same type of correlational

---

[14] Translation makes incommensurability less of a problem. At the same time, it does not necessarily allow all types of eclecticism, since it does require coherence with the meta-theoretical context. For a different take on a discussion that is otherwise very congenial to my own, see Sil and Katzenstein, 2010.

[15] This is Elster's formulation in his discussion of mechanisms; see Elster, 2007, 35.

[16] For the wording of causal 'how' and 'what', see Vennesson, 2008, 232.

[17] Bennett and Elman, 2006, 456–458.

[18] See the discussion of George and Bennett, 2005 in Chapter 3.

analysis, but now to the distinct steps.[19] De facto, this means that correlations are 'explained' by more micro correlations.[20] With such an approach, the only thing process tracing or mechanisms change for an analysis is the number of causal links involved; they do nothing to the very idea of causality implied. Indeed, for the positivist, mechanism or process tracing add little to an explanation, since there is nothing to exclude an ever-increasing chain of links, and hence an infinite regress, making the mechanisms involved ultimately descriptive, not causal.[21] Consequently, in this vein, even authors defending mechanisms have insisted that it may be going too far, if not simply wrong, to pit correlational against mechanistic analysis. For them, bivariate correlations can and may need to serve as a first step of an analysis, or may even be combined with positivist (Hempel–Oppenheim) covering-law explanations.[22]

However, reducing mechanisms to variables in this way does away with their very specificity. First, an intervening variable 'is added to increase the total variance explained in a multivariate analysis', but that is different from providing and specifying the links in a process.[23] Such an approach starts from an assumption of static and additive causes, which are moreover understood as constant conjunctions, not in terms of sequence and the relational configuration of factors. Second, reducing mechanisms to variables implies that they are 'not just observable but observed', which not all mechanisms are.[24] Here, the positivist commitment to observation primes and effectively excludes that which is the specificity of at least some mechanisms. Third, at least in some approaches, mechanisms are not attributes of the unit of analysis, as they would be as variables. Instead, 'mechanisms describe the relationships or the actions among the units of analysis or in the cases of study'.[25] Assuming otherwise denies again the possibility of a combinatorial causality.

To avoid this reduction of mechanisms to variables, most early defenders of mechanistic analysis phrased it in a soft rationalist manner. They openly repudiated the covering-law model and simple correlational analysis. In these readings, a correlation does not explain; at best, it summarises an explanation. Hence, it is important to open the 'black box' of how the event was actually reached. In Elster's prominent approach to the matter, mechanisms are the intermediate level of generalisation available between universal laws, which are unattainable in the social sciences, and descriptions, which are too unambitious. Not being general laws, mechanisms can explain (*ex post*) why something happened, but cannot be used for predictions, since we cannot know whether a mechanism will be activated or not and/or whether it will always have the same effects.[26]

---

[19] Gerring, 2007, 172.   [20] Mahoney, 2001, 578.
[21] King *et al.*, 1994, 86.   [22] Opp, 2005.
[23] Mayntz, 2004, 245.   [24] Johnson, 2006, 248.   [25] Falleti and Lynch, 2009, 1147.
[26] These formulations are taken from Elster 1998, 45. For an earlier argument making the same point, but in a different language, see Grosser, 1972.

It is quite understandable that rationalist scholars have insisted on mechanisms. Such an approach squarely meets the demands of methodological individualism, which says that all events, micro or macro, need eventually to be connected to the effects of intended or unintended agency. It is therefore quite normal to double-check which micro-behaviour has resulted in which macro-states. Applying a straightforward macro–micro–macro scheme, there would be three mechanisms: one relating the macro to the micro level, one on the micro level, and one from the micro to the macro level.[27] In the most extreme version of this understanding of mechanisms, an analysis that short-circuits individual action avoids the analysis of mechanisms altogether.[28] But, also more relaxed versions tend to define mechanism analysis in terms of a rationalist action theory alone. Diego Gambetta, for instance, defines mechanisms as 'those minimal assumptions about agents' make-up that we require to deduce how they both interact with one another and respond to external conditions'.[29] Consequently, different versions of rationality or cognitive processes (including emotions) become all that there is to mechanisms.

Still, it needs to be stressed that most rationalists using mechanisms are sociologists who base their analyses on a not exclusively utilitarian understanding of rationality. Here, *Werterationalität* plays an equal if not more important role than instrumental rationality.[30] Alternatively, the analysis is conducted in terms of *reasons*, widely defined, drawing on the classical rationalist desire–belief–(opportunities)–behaviour triangle.[31] In this wider post-Weberian lineage, interpretation is part and parcel of the approach and methodology.

Yet, even this thicker rationalism falls short of the interpretivist process tracing advocated here. The problems are now less about the philosophy of science (as in the discussion about variables): the issue becomes one of social ontologies. That means, first, that we need to move beyond methodological individualism. Arguing from an institutionalist position, Renate Mayntz stresses that once we try to understand relational mechanisms (see below), we may find that the latter may not involve motivated individual behaviour to start with. Institutional and structural components are decisive parts of the micro–macro link: 'If the *explanandum* is a macro-phenomenon, or the connection between two macro phenomena ... the main cognitive challenge is therefore to identify the structural and institutional features, that organize ... the actions of different actors so as to produce their macro effect'.[32] Yet,

---

[27] Hedström and Swedberg, 1998a.
[28] For conflating (rational) action with mechanisms, see Hedström and Swedberg, 1998a, 11–12.
[29] Gambetta, 1998, 103.   [30] Boudon, 1998.
[31] Elster, 1998 and 2007.   [32] Mayntz, 2004, 252.

as Mayntz writes, we have, as yet, 'no similarly filled tool box of mechanisms where specific types of corporate actor constellations and relational structures play the crucial role'.[33]

Furthermore, second, it is essential to be aware of the risk of a naturalist or materialist reductionism. There is nothing in the analysis of mechanisms that per se calls for a materialist conception of institutions and structures. True, looking for mechanisms that might explain particular effects, and opening up box after box may produce a tendency towards naturalist reductionism. Individualist approaches (and perhaps not only them), for instance, can easily end up in the realm of cognitive psychology. Elster in particular has used findings from psychology to exemplify the working of mechanisms, such as the pair of 'forbidden fruit' and 'sour grapes'. Unable to reach the fruits growing in a neighbour's garden, some people start to think that those particular fruits are the very best, whereas others convince themselves of the opposite. Thus, deprivation may cause some people to desire an object more, others less. Although we might be hard-pressed to predict the behaviour, we can retroactively explain the psychological mechanism behind whatever happened. And, so, Elster rightly notes that, for a methodological individualist position, the recourse to 'psychology and perhaps biology' are of 'fundamental importance in explaining social phenomena'.[34]

This can be pushed too far, however. When Mario Bunge, who has done much to introduce mechanistic explanations, writes that 'learning is explained by the formation of new neuronal systems that emerge when they fire jointly in response to certain (external and internal) stimuli'.[35] This explanation does not touch what is significant for social scientists. In an excellent response to Bunge, Colin Wight exposes Bunge's physicalist reductionism and demonstrates the need to include what he calls conceptual and/or semiotic mechanisms in social analysis:

> All social activity presupposes the prior existence of social forms. Speech requires language; making, materials; actions, conditions; agency, resources; activity, rules. Equally, these prior social forms are concept dependent ... the concepts possessed by agents 'matter'; they make a difference. And in complex social settings they are part of the causal complex and, hence, may be mechanisms.[36]

To sum up: thinking in mechanisms is different from correlational analysis *and* perfectly feasible within a non-individualist and interpretivist framework. There is no necessary connection between mechanisms and methodological individualism or versions of materialism.

---

[33] Mayntz, 2004, 255.
[34] Elster, 2007, 36. This reliance on psychology can however also lead to the critique of (utilitarian) rationality. See, in particular, Mercer, 2005 and 2010.
[35] Bunge, 2004, 202.   [36] Wight, 2004b, 296.

Defining mechanisms

Not a big fan of new definitions, I follow Jon Elster's (standard) definition of mechanisms as 'frequently occurring and easily recognizable causal patterns that are triggered under generally unknown conditions or with indeterminate consequences'.[37] Such mechanisms are 'portable', in the sense that they are small, perhaps often trivial, components of an explanation that can be moved to other contexts and cases, although that new context may affect their working. They travel. And, although this does not necessarily herald a general theory with wide applicability, it makes it possible to connect cases and to transfer knowledge from one to another. Several components need to be clarified, however. First, the level of determinacy of such mechanisms is not clear. Second, also the exact level of theorisation (or empirical abstraction) is contested. I will argue that it is fruitful not to think of mechanisms in terms of determinacy and would make a plea to locate them at not too general a level.

Let me start with the last, the level of generality on which mechanisms are to be found. This can be quite high. According to some rationalists, it is basically 'rationality' itself that is to be seen as a mechanism. Such a view may seem strange, but it is coherent with the general rationalist outlook. Once one argues that general laws are impossible and that correlations are not real explanations, any real explanation comes through human action and the fundamental behavioural assumption about it (for rationalists): rationality. Rationality is crucial since it also provides an expectation of coherence against which 'non-rational' action can be judged. More importantly for the analysis of mechanisms, the assumption of rationality travels almost seamlessly between the level of action and the level of observation. Accordingly, the coherence it seems to promise applies also to the actors themselves: an actor becoming aware of some irrationality can therefore be expected to attempt to remedy this incoherence. Thus, the coherence requisite of rationality prompts corrective behaviour, and so rationality can well be seen as a trigger, a mechanism. Still, even within rationalism, rather than locating a mechanism within rationality itself, it makes more sense to refer to mechanisms as the different pathways through which attempts are made to reduce incoherence. Rationality may be the basic theoretical assumption for those mechanisms, but it is not the mechanisms themselves.

Consequently, if one thinks in terms of trigger and incoherence reductions, it requires no long stretch to think about all equilibria dynamics as possible mechanisms. The underlying theory that informs the latter posits a tendency towards an equilibrium. Accordingly, any event that puts the system out of equilibrium, or any actor out of a balanced (satisfied) mental state, may trigger mechanisms that seek to enable a return to the stable state or equilibrium. It comes therefore as no surprise that utilitarian rationalists (rational-choice

---

[37] Elster, 1998, 45 and, 2007, 36.

analysts) would see in models of economic equilibrium a starting point for social mechanisms.[38] And it takes little imagination to rephrase balance-of-power 'theory' into a series of social mechanisms: (internal or external) balancing, chain-ganging, buck-passing, and band-waggoning. Indeed, it may be a research programme to confront one of the major criticisms levelled against realism. With behavioural output so diverse as to cover all possible reactions, realism is non-falsifiable.[39] As a result, realists may be tempted to define *ex ante* all the possible conditions for which one mechanism rather than another would be triggered. If that were possible, it would save (neo-)realism as a behaviouralist theory. Colin Elman's work on typological theorising seems to be inspired by such an aspiration.[40] Nevertheless, it seems useful not to confound mechanisms with theory/theoretical assumptions, although the two are obviously linked.

Nor should they be equated with the process proper, as sometimes appears to be the case in Charles Tilly's stimulating work on mechanisms. Tilly worked on the *longue durée*. Accordingly, whereas methodological individualists tend to cut down a process until they find the core in rational action, giving rise to a process with many smaller mechanisms, Tilly's approach maintains a holistic view of the process and therefore tends to see fewer but much larger mechanisms (or, indeed: processes). He distinguishes between three forms of mechanism: environmental, relational and cognitive. Cognitive processes are the ones already seen in rationalist approaches; environmental processes refer to 'externally generated influences on conditions affecting social life'; while relational mechanisms 'alter connections among people, groups and interpersonal networks'. And, 'processes are frequently occurring combinations or sequences of mechanisms'.[41]

When it comes to the specification of mechanisms, however, the distinction between processes and mechanisms starts to blur (and not only because Tilly constructs a table in which they are added up and not distinguished). In principle, mechanisms 'have uniform immediate effects, their aggregate, cumulative and longer-term effects vary considerably depending on the initial conditions and combinations with other mechanisms'.[42] But, what would be, to take some of his mechanisms promoting democratisation, the uniform immediate effect of 'bureaucratic containment of previously autonomous military forces' or 'disintegration of existing trust networks' or 'visible governmental meeting of commitments to the advantage of substantial new segments of the population' (or 'elite defection', for that matter)?[43] It is not clear there is an

[38] Cowen, 1998, 129.
[39] Vasquez, 1997. Making the same case but on the basis of a conceptual analysis of power in realist theories, see Guzzini, 2004b.
[40] Bennett and Elman, 2006 and Elman, 2005.
[41] Tilly, 2001, 24, 26.   [42] Tilly, 2001, 25.   [43] McAdam *et al.*, 2008, 319.

immediate *effect* which has been explained, but one which has been announced or described. Indeed, Tilly admits that those mechanisms and processes are in some sense tautological. He defends himself by suggesting that such tautologies point to mechanisms as 'proximate causes' for democratisation. It seems, then, that rather than having uniform immediate effects, some of the mentioned mechanisms stand for wider processes whose relational and combinatorial effects are stipulated by an underlying framework of analysis. For the sake of the present volume, this kind of conceiving mechanism may be useable for thinking long-term self-fulfilling prophecies, but not for the main mechanism under analysis: the identity crisis reduction mechanism.

This leads to the second important issue: the determinacy of mechanisms. There are three main ways of dealing with (in)determinacy in mechanism studies. First, the conditions under which mechanisms come into place is left open. In other words, mechanisms are conceived as latent or emerging capacities that need to be triggered by some initial conditions. Those conditions can be varied, and their triggring effect on a mechanism may be contingent. But, once the mechanism is triggered, some 'uniform immediate effect' or sufficient causality (Mahoney) is assumed. Thus, indeterminacy is not in the mechanism, but in its triggering conditions. A second way consists in saying that certain conditions do trigger mechanisms, but they can trigger more than one; hence, the actual mechanism that is triggered in a specific case cannot be predicted. Here, indeterminacy derives from the alternative mechanisms that could respond to a certain input: the environment is underdetermining the response. Finally, a third way sees indeterminacy in the mechanism itself, which is said not to have determinate effects, since all depends on its interaction with other mechanisms and/or the process in which it unfolds.

Obviously, if we had a process tracing in which all three indeterminacies applied, the mechanism would carry no explanatory power at all. For this is a real conundrum. On the one hand, mechanisms are attractive to scholars who wish to explain in the absence of general laws, and who hence look for causalities as combinatorial, relational, conjunctural elements whose working is left open by the importance of conditions and changing contexts, or indeed the mechanisms themselves. On the other hand, leaving such working very open means that a given mechanism may no longer be able to explain anything at all. Opening up the black box of explanation beyond correlation would end up in mechanisms that would equally not explain but simply summarise or – worse – just presume an explanation.

Perhaps, therefore, Elster's definition is such not to accumulate those indeterminate moments. His analysis always stresses the indeterminacy due to the existence of several mechanisms which can be triggered at the time. But with regard to the other two indeterminacies, he posits that it is either the conditions under which a trigger works that are unknown or its effects. That would make for two different types of mechanisms and their analysis.

3 Two social mechanisms as (micro-)dynamics in constructivist theory

Having established how mechanisms are best understood within an interpretivist process-tracing framework,[44] we can now try to conceptualise a first mechanism identified in the process that stretches from the end of the Cold War to the revival of geopolitical thought and then one in the effect such a revival could have on the culture of anarchy. The first mechanism will need to be established first and discussed more generally, since it is one that can be expected more generally to play an important role in constructivist theorising. At the same time, I will also touch on a second mechanism that links the revival of geopolitical thought to a change in the culture of anarchy, the mechanism of a self-fulfilling prophecy. The existence of such a type of mechanism has been established within the sociological literature for some considerable time, and I will therefore focus more on its potential role in constructivist theorising.

Before discussing these mechanisms, let me shortly specify the type of social theory of action that is consistent with this use of mechanisms in constructivism. Undoubtedly, the study has been informed by Bourdieu's theorising, which provides the reference for understanding the context within which agents 'play out' their struggles within their field.[45] This includes also the fundamentally political definitional struggles for imposing a certain 'vision and division of the world' as the correct one.[46] The basic move consists probably in a theory of action that focuses less on rationality and primarily on social recognition which happens in a certain context or spheres or fields, usually more than one at the same time. And so: how do identity processes unfold which establish a coherence in one's relation to time (e.g. past/history), space and social context in what Alessandro Pizzorno calls 'circles of recognition'?[47] Many parts of Pizzorno's analysis could be easily transferred to the present project in order to further specify the mechanisms under study here. Pizzorno shows that having several circles of recognition to which one belongs reduces the power of each individual circle in terms of defining status and constraining action, a point that has been also made in the 'shaming' literature within IR.[48] It also implies

---

[44] See also Piki Ish-Shalom's (2006) analysis of 'discourse-tracing' and hermeneutical mechanisms.

[45] Bourdieu, 1994.

[46] For an analysis of Bourdieu stressing its non-structuralist features, see Leander, 2011.

[47] Pizzorno, 2007, 146ff. For a (too) short statement in English, see Pizzorno, 2008. For further developments by some of his students/disciples, see in social theory Davide Sparti, 1996 and 2000, and in IR Erik Ringmar, 1996. See also Alexander Wendt's attempt to provide dynamics to his theory by referring to 'struggles for recognition' in Wendt, 2003.

[48] Pizzorno, 2007, 139. For the literature on shaming strategies, which obviously imply a social recognition–status–identity nexus, see, for example, Risse et al., 1999. This is also

that the identity crisis reduction mechanism is therefore not to be conceived in terms of a given equilibrium, but as a dynamic process with no fixed point of return. In the present study, this process is also played out with two circles of recognition, both domestically and abroad. Having a collective actor is therefore in principle no problem, precisely because the collectivity is opened up as a circle of recognition within the analysis.

To this must be added the performative components of Ian Hacking's 'looping effect', which can become a kind of mechanism in terms of dynamic circles.[49] For instance, Pizzorno refers to the virtuous circle of reputation.[50] Having a good reputation has self-fulfilling effects: people believing the good reputation will tend to inform their interpretations of acts and events to see it confirmed; and the actor to whom the reputation is ascribed will tend to conform to the expectation shared in their circle(s). Shared ideas and social practices of naming interact with and can affect other social realities.

A mechanism of foreign policy identity crisis reduction

The most fundamental factor for understanding the geopolitical revival that took place in several of the countries studied here was the occurrence of a foreign policy identity crisis within a country's national security imaginary. In combination with – and prompted by – ideational path dependence, institutional factors and political struggles (now understood as processes themselves), the occurrence of such a crisis made the revival of geopolitical thought possible. The actual content of the revival that took place in each country was defined by the symbolic struggles of the agents involved, whether these were in the sphere of politics, academia or public opinion. Precisely because the main process is about collective identity, strategic action becomes symbolic action, which, in a conscious fashion or otherwise, intervenes to define identity. Framed in and by the processes in the three layers, agents engage in a struggle over the definition of the nation's and/or state's self-understanding.[51] And, in some of our cases, geopolitical argument appeared 'natural' within the terms of such a struggle and/or came in strategically handy, which led eventually to the revival of this type of thinking.

This process can now be analysed in more detail through a look at its central mechanism: identity crisis reduction. In Tilly's terminology, such a mechanism is intersubjective. Prompted by the occurrence of an identity crisis, whose

compatible with assumptions about human motives that feature the motive of honour or self-esteem. See Lebow, 2003 and 2008.

49 Hacking, 1999.
50 Pizzorno, 2007, 231.
51 Johnson, for example, insists on this non-rational component in symbolic action as a way of connecting cultural approaches to a theory of action; see Johnson, 2002.

origin is contingent, the mechanism has effects which, in turn, are only partly contingent. When an identity crisis occurs in foreign policy discourses, it will trigger symbolic actions to reduce that dissonance. However, the content of any such attempts will be dependent on the context within which the mechanism operates. It was only where many of the process factors identified for the present study accompanied the occurrence of a foreign policy identity crisis that geopolitics could appear as a possible solution and be revived. If the mechanism as such seems transferable to other environments, its exact content is context-dependent.

The underlying idea for conceiving this mechanism is that identity processes can be linked to dynamics of coherence or congruence. In a (loose) analogy to the cognitive dissonance-reducing mechanisms analysed by (soft) rationalists,[52] one might view such processes as identity incongruence/dissonance-reducing mechanisms. A foreign policy identity crisis appears when there is either a tension or a contradiction in the self-understanding of a collective actor or a mismatch between that understanding and the dominant external role perception. Such a dissonance would then trigger more concrete responses, which include: (1) *denial* that there is any dissonance to start with; (2) *negotiation*, that is, attempts to dissuade the other from the faulty identity vision (i.e. there is a perceived dissonance, but this is based on a misunderstanding); and (3–4) the acceptance of a real dissonance, which then spurs either attempts to change the international culture in such a way as to enable one's own identity to fit (*imposition*) or efforts to redefine the identity as a way of adapting to external expectations or projections (*adaptation*). I posit these responses as components of the overall analysis of this discursive mechanism.

To illustrate the first of these responses, we can draw on Jutta Weldes' initial analysis of the 1962 Cuban Missile Crisis. Her puzzle was a non-event: why was it almost inconceivable for US decision-makers to view the presence of Soviet missiles on Cuban soil as being primarily aimed at defending Cuba from another attack, when such an interpretation seemed almost natural to the Cubans? Weldes peels away a series of possible explanations (such as the non-proportionality of the weapon systems for such a goal) to show that such a vision would have flatly contradicted the self-understanding of the United States in its foreign relations. Despite the United States' own colonialist past, which could have enabled a degree of empathy, and despite its involvement in an earlier attempted invasion of post-revolutionary Cuba, the US security imaginary predominantly mobilised an identity of anti-imperialism: the United States as the defender of the free world. Empathising with the Cuban version of the event would prompt a major dissonance, since it would portray the United States as the originator of the crisis, expansionist and aggressive. When the interpretation of a purely defensive missile installation contradicted

---

[52] Besides Elster, see in particular Kuran, 1998.

US foreign policy identity, something had to give way. The Cuban vision was seen as pure propaganda. This example thus illustrates a first response: the denial of any dissonance.

A related response consists in keeping the identity within the foreign policy discourse unchanged yet adapting one's behaviour. Here, Janice Bially Mattern's analysis of US–UK relations during the Suez crisis provides a good illustration.[53] Bially Mattern analyses the way in which US foreign policy was able to change the British government's behaviour through the application of not only strategic but also symbolic force. Besides financial pressure, US foreign policy put its UK counterpart before a mirror which portrayed a picture of the UK as neocolonial and aggressive, no longer a friend and close to Western civilisation. This created a form of blackmail whose operation is understandable once we see the identity mechanism involved: either the UK abandoned the actions in which it was engaged and thus demonstrated to have kept its valued identity and the social recognition by the United States, its most significant other; or it continued its actions at the risk of being ostracised, of seeing its status, indeed its very membership in the exclusive Anglo-American Atlantic club, denied. In this case, under conditions of amity, the UK opted to keep the better image, the one that was in tune with its own self-understanding, and thus changed its behaviour. Whereas in the first kind of response, the discourse writes on the existing self-understanding, by not empathising with a different mirror-image, in the second it does so by accepting the vision of the Other (but then adapting its own behaviour). It is perhaps not accidental that both examples are from foreign policy crisis situations in which the mechanism, if triggered, needs a quick response.

The second type of response would be more typical for non-crisis situations where negotiation is given more time, and is hence closer to the conditions of the present study. Here, the logic is that though there appears to be a dissonance, it is not real, and better communication and diplomacy will resolve any misunderstanding. Now, in order to count as a response to a real crisis, such misunderstanding must be interpreted as being significant, as something that touches upon an important component of the identity embedded in the foreign policy imaginary. Not just any identity mismatch will automatically produce a crisis. Still, a crisis can occur, if, for instance, an external actor systematically emphasises components of a country's identity discourses that its own foreign policy elite wishes to regard as secondary – for example, Italy as an ambiguous political culture exemplified by widespread corruption and organised crime. Here, the mismatch is threatening because it might lead to an opening up of 'old wounds' or a reopening of identity clashes that it was hoped had been left behind. It may also touch a weak spot within the self-understanding, a point where national discourses can be ambivalent, if not contradictory. The

---

[53] Bially Mattern, 2005.

response can consist in public diplomacy alone, but more probably in particular deeds meant to impress on international society the country's preferred vision of its identity. US President Jimmy Carter's human rights initiatives after the Vietnam War can be read in this manner, aiming to deflect attention from a vision of the United States as a neocolonial or imperialist power, and to instead focus on the country's intended status as the universal defender of rights.

The third and fourth types of response are similar to each other in that in each case dissonance is first accepted and then faced. However, the two responses differ in terms of the locus of adaptation: at home or in the circle of recognition within international society. The policies of South Africa's former apartheid regime surely fit the first case of 'adaptation'. Besides economic pressure, the pariah status involved in being a country in which racism was legally condoned placed immense pressure on efforts to maintain a self-understanding as respectable, fomenting opposition from within (also among the white parts of the population) and eventually leading to a complete redefinition of state and national identity. In a weaker version, the same argument applies to all successful 'shaming' strategies where the response and adaptation lies primarily with the ostracised country. In a different version, as with the late Soviet Union, there can also be an active self-redefinition aimed at making one's identity more congenial to international society. Both *glasnost* and *perestroika*, along with a series of actions that ranged from allowing foreign inspectors to access nuclear bases (the Stockholm Treaty) to the acceptance of the independence of countries in the former Eastern bloc, not only undermined the rules of the Cold War game, but also provided a new self-identification of the Soviet Union that could be acceptable to international society. Note that the point here is not to engage in discussion on whether military competition, economic or other 'hard' sanctions were more important than shaming strategies in terms of bringing about such a change. The significant point is that the change is not just behavioural, but relational, since it also demands the recognition of a new identity beyond the previous pariah status. It hence affects the self-understanding of the country involved, a more long-term effect. For, if there is the exertion of pressure in the absence of an identity crisis – as is arguably happening with some so-called rogue states today (e.g. North Korea, Iran) – it prompts reactions of pride and efforts to maintain one's own status, not adaptation.

A last response, which I have dubbed 'imposition', consists in trying to make self-understanding and outside recognition coincide by changing the underlying rules for successful recognition. This strategy is clearly not open to actors whose status is low or insignificant in the self-understanding of international society. Moulding the culture of international society upon one's own image is surely one of the most ambitious diplomatic games there is. Arguably, this has been the US strategy since 1945, one to which it has resorted with particular force more recently, during the administrations of President George W.

Bush.[54] But, it also fits all the attempts to portray the EU's 'normative power' as an alternative for running international affairs and hence for establishing the values that define status in world society. Finally, and despite the impression that today's Russia is simply lagging behind in relation to the new rules for defining status in world affairs, the last Putin and Medvedev governments can be often seen as trying to steer the international environment in such a way as to return to the older, more *Realpolitik*-oriented norms.

In summary, the mechanism of identity crisis reduction consists of a complex including the trigger provided by the foreign policy identity crisis and the reactions it prompts. Although a response aimed at recomposing the coherence of the foreign policy identity is generally to be expected, its content will vary. I established four different types of reaction, which are derived from logical ways in which identity crises can be resolved. Hence, the mechanism of identity crisis reduction has some determinacy and seems to be transferable to different contexts. But, whereas the general mechanism is comparable across contexts, the content is context-specific, as is the process in which the mechanism unfolds. In that process, symbolic agency plays a major role, though this may be unintentional. Seen this way, the revival of geopolitics stands for the revival of a particular conduit or medium within which a foreign policy identity crisis is created and an attempt is made to resolve it.

Mechanisms of self-fulfilling prophecies: the vicious circle of essentialisation

A first purpose of the study set out in this volume was to explain the puzzle of a revival of geopolitical thought in Europe after it had just experienced the end of the Cold War. The first mechanism is central for this explanation. For the second specific purpose of the study, the possible self-fulfilling effects of a revival in geopolitical thought, a further mechanism would need to come into play. Although a systematic analysis of this mechanism lies outside the empirical part of our study, it can be now more precisely theorised with the knowledge we have at hand.[55]

For the chain in that mechanism is quite long. Whereas the identity crisis reduction is a relatively short- or mid-term mechanism, self-fulfilling prophecies that affect deep structures are almost by necessity closer to the Tilly type of social mechanisms that stretch over a long time. They may not even realise, or, rather, given the long historical context, they may be neutralised by other

---

[54] See, for example, Buzan, 2004 and Guzzini, 2002.

[55] Self-fulfilling prophecies are some of the classical mechanisms recognised in the literature. See the repeated reference to Merton's initial formulation in Hedström and Swedberg, 1998b.

events and dynamics, other mechanisms. Nevertheless, their working can be assessed.

In the present case, the chain would start with the link from a revival in geopolitical thought and its effects on the security imaginary. Only in those cases where neoclassical geopolitics would have impacted on the foreign policy imaginary and hence imported realism's military gaze, as defined in Chapter 2, or where it would have reconfirmed such a gaze (as in the Turkish case) would we expect a militarisation of that security imaginary.[56] As a short-hand, such militarisation leads to the reversal of Clausewitz's famous dictum, namely, that politics becomes the continuation of war by other means. Priority is given to worst-case thinking. Within its logic, a pre-emptive strategy, uni-laterally decided, is admissible, if not necessary. Politics has to follow the primacy not just of foreign policy but also of military strategy. This corresponds to the classical peace research-cum-constructivist critique of the Cold War as a self-fulfilling prophecy.[57]

However, the close analysis of the actual geopolitical argument in the cases contained in this volume shows that this is not the whole story. If a militarisa-tion results from an essentialisation of physical geography typical for a certain type of strategic thinking, the mechanism can also start from the essentiali-sation of human or cultural geography. As the Estonian case, among others, indicates, this type of essentialisation can even be the main effect. Identity is essentialised by locating it back in time – as linked to a specific space. By sug-gesting immutable and unchangeable human geographies, it easily translates into a vision not just of 'us' versus 'them', but of friends and foes, be these out-side or inside the community. As Morozov notes while discussing the Russian case, geopolitics' 'very basic theoretical premises produce a predisposition to view global politics in Manichean terms'.[58]

In other words, the self-fulfilling geopolitics mechanism would start with any one of the two types of essentialisation typical for geopolitical discourse: that of physical geography, which informs and mobilises the military gaze of realism, or that of human/cultural geography, which prompts a homogenisa-tion of ego and alter and a clean division between a (cultural) inside and out-side, with the potential to make culture and spatial size coincide (nationalism, anti-immigration, in some cases also ethnic cleansing) and the conviction of an unalterable friend–foe vision of the world. Obviously, a combination of both would have the strongest effect in terms of triggering the mechanism, since nothing less than the ultimate military defence of a threatened nation/culture/ethnic group would then be at stake.

---

[56] This does not imply that the revival of geopolitical thought and its impact on the security imaginary is the sole way of militarising the latter.

[57] For an analysis of that link, see Guzzini, 2004a.

[58] Morozov, 2009a, 202.

A next step in the chain is the level of social – here, international – interaction. Once the essentialisation of the security imaginary begins to affect foreign policy behaviour, it will also affect foreign policy interaction, both directly and indirectly. For that interaction will increasingly be interpreted in a certain light. Hence, the essentialisation affects not only the action–reaction chain, but also the agents' understanding of that chain. That, in turn, will affect behaviour again. When Germany first stalled in the discussions regarding a possible bail-out for the Greek government as it faced financial crisis in 2010, France's Minister for European Affairs Pierre Lellouche (who has a background as a scholar in strategic studies), said that this was to be expected: 'Twenty years after reunification, there is a new generation, there is globalisation, there is demographic pressure, you have a Germany that like everyone claims its national interests.'[59] 'Demographic pressure' – nothing less than Haushofer's 'Volksdruck'. Never mind that Germany has for decades had a birth-rate too low for its demographic reproduction, which would imply a 'deflation' of that so-called 'pressure'. Moreover, since 2008, Germany has also a negative migration balance and is actually becoming less populous (by 13,000 people in 2009 – whatever change in 'pressure' that may possibly imply).[60] Also, regardless of this, with every new German generation, there seems to be a reason to say that the Germans are no longer kept in check by their past. In other words, it is not whatever event that prompts a need for geopolitical thought in explaining German policy, it is a geopolitical conviction read backwards into the political event and policy.

This leads then to the third step of the mechanism, the one crucial for linking it up with a self-fulfilling prophecy. Should several security imaginaries be essentialised at the same time and/or be diffused through interaction,[61] a vicious circle of distrust takes hold in formerly friendly relations or is reconfirmed in inimical ones. Geopolitics becomes self-fulfilling by affecting the culture of anarchy, confirming its pre-existing Hobbesian culture or moving towards it.

This mechanism is hence similar to the mechanism of identity crisis reduction in that it concerns an intersubjective and (deep?) structural level, but it

[59] Hall, 2010.
[60] See the figures published by the *Statistisches Bundesamt*. For the birth–mortality balance, which has been negative since 1972, see www.destatis.de/jetspeed/portal/cms/ Sites/destatis/Internet/DE/Navigation/Statistiken/Bevoelkerung/GeburtenSterbefaelle/ GeburtenSterbefaelle.psml. For the migration balance, see www.destatis.de/jetspeed/portal/cms/Sites/destatis/Internet/DE/Navigation/Statistiken/Bevoelkerung/Wanderungen/ Wanderungen.psml.
[61] The research design of this study can fall prey to a type of 'methodological nationalism', if it is read merely through the individual country studies and their aggregation. The international context (cultures of anarchy), and transnational factors are immediately more prominent in this second mechanism.

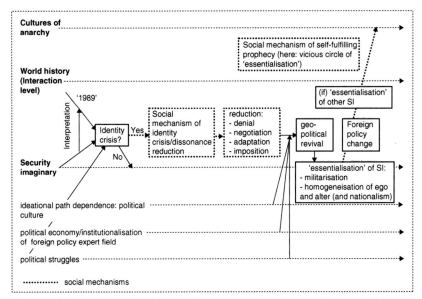

Figure 11.3. The return of geopolitics (III): social mechanisms in a time-layered interpretivist process model

functions in a different manner. And it is the 'concatenation'[62] of the two that connects the end of the Cold War with a potential move towards not a more Kantian collective identity, but a more Hobbesian one. Here lies the paradox: it is via the mechanisms of identity crisis reduction and the 'vicious circle of essentialisation' that peaceful change could trigger practices that are less conducive to peace.

This volume cannot comprehensively answer the question to what extent that second mechanism has been triggered in the Europe of the 1990s, nor assess how many countervailing processes have occurred.[63] However, it can specify some findings for the different links in the chain. For one thing, geopolitics did not experience a revival in two of the countries studied, and in some countries it is not yet clear whether the revival that did occur has affected the identity discourses embedded in the security imaginary (Italy, Russia), all the more since its effects are now receding (see also in Estonia). Hence, the essentialisation of security imaginaries did not take place in a comprehensive fashion during the 1990s for all of the countries under analysis. It seemed at one point as though international interaction could further militarise the self-understanding of

---

[62] Tilly, 2004.

[63] In a personal communication, Emanuel Adler rightly insists on the possible presence of other parallel mechanisms, belonging to European practices and institutions, which can tame or even cancel out the effect of the 'vicious circle of essentialisation'.

international society – namely, in the run-up to the Iraq War, where the administration of George W. Bush pushed for such a change. Its effects are too early
to tell.

As for the essentialisation of human geography and its potential mobilisation of established and inflexible friend–foe schemes, such dynamics are visible. This said, the one scheme that would be connected to the end of the Cold
War (the anti-Russian or – seen from the other side – anti-Atlantist European
scheme) only appeared later, in the aftermath of the Russian–Georgian war,
clearly mobilising a sense of 'them there' and 'us here'. The most important
identity divide, though, would pitch these two sides against 'Islamism'. Here,
the securitisation of religious identity has reached the interaction level, where
it is – often because of a reflexive awareness of the self-fulfilling effects of such
an approach – also opposed (i.e. it also triggers a de-securitising response). It is
here that Huntington's theses, rightly or wrongly, are often mobilised to legitimate an essentialised Europe (if not a Christian Europe, or, more politically
correct, a Judeo-Christian Europe). But, although such essentialisation would
stand for the same type of trigger and mechanism, it is only indirectly part of
the concatenation of mechanisms that starts with the end of the Cold War. In
cases where an identity crisis was answered with a revival of geopolitics, this
was never with the Islamist as the 'Other'. Yet, having prepared the terrain for
such essentialised thinking, as it were, such a revival would make it possible
for the essentialising logic of geopolitical argument to be transferred (and even
further essentialised) to 'Islamism'.

This leads to the final point that I wish to stress. We have analysed how the
revival of geopolitical thought took place in a varied fashion within the respective national contexts. But, of course, it also occurred not only within a certain
period of world history, but within a certain state of the culture of international
anarchy.

Accordingly, it is necessary to ask how that culture relates to the ongoing
processes within the sphere of political interactions and within security imaginaries. Just as the revival of geopolitical thought in individual countries needs
to be seen in the context of the respective (national) security imaginaries, its
aggregative effect needs to be embedded within the existing international culture. As we have seen on the national level, the path dependency of certain
security imaginaries, as well as particular ideational traditions, institutional
structures and political constellations, are more conducive to the revival's having a structural effect. The same applies internationally. Here, the ongoing
processes of Europe's Lockean culture,[64] the institutional settings of a security

---

[64] If the Cold War can count as a Lockean environment, and the EU itself as an almost Kantian
      environment (at least a solidarist Grotian one), then the pan-European order of the 1990s
      is quite surely within the Lockean category. I do not wish to further dwell on the point
      that these categories appear rather crude. For if both the Cold War and the post-Cold War

community in the process of enlargement (via the EU), and the effects of the dense multilateralism within which diplomatic engagements take place within Europe ensure that the possible effects of a militarisation of security imaginaries have been mainly checked, although partly encouraged (via NATO). The existence of such an institutional web makes Lockean cultures of anarchy quite 'sticky'.[65]

But, at the same time, the essentialisation of identities has been progressing. It is as though it fell into an institutional void with fewer buffers. Constantly fed by domestic populist nationalist debates, it is in this context that the second mechanism may indeed still be playing out its influence. Geopolitics is part of a more ethnic/cultural definition of the nation, as opposed to a civic/political one. The latter has been weakened in many corners of Europe where it used to be strong (e.g. France). And although this circle of essentialisation has not ushered in a complete reversal towards a more Hobbesian culture of anarchy, it has arguably pre-empted the move towards a more Kantian one. The stalling of European integration – or, more precisely, its federal component – is ample testimony to this. This is a counterfactual statement, for sure. But it is not arbitrary: it is based on the finding of such a mechanism.[66] It is in this context that social mechanisms may play one of their most important explanatory roles.

4   Conclusion

The present volume has sought to shed light on the paradoxical revival of geopolitical thought in Europe just as the end of the Cold War seemed to herald a new era. It argues that when a foreign policy identity crisis occurred, the alleged ease and determinacy of geopolitical thought came in handy to provide orientation, although such orientation was not necessarily long-lasting. Yet, such a crisis was not necessary, nor was it present in all of our cases. In the event of a

period count as Lockean, then the category is surely too wide. In fact, it seems to encompass almost all known international (not national) cultures of anarchy. It is almost as though it were the residual category, once situations of civil war (Hobbes before the Leviathan) and functioning democracies (or Kantian Republics) are excluded. Since neither a system of continuous civil war nor a comprehensive Republic have ever existed on the international level, all international societies were by definition Lockean. It may be one of the ironies of the English School that it argued in favour of conceptualising an international society qualitatively different from domestic ones (contra the domestic analogy) and made a plea for the Grotian or middle category, when, perhaps, this is the only category world history has ever experienced in international society in the first place – once the domestic analogies of civil wars and democracies excluded the others. For the purpose of this book, the main important point, however, is that we have to think about structural change of that culture of anarchy, however we label it, and then find words to categorise significant differences. It is about the dynamics of this culture, not its static definitions.

[65]   Wendt, 1999 and 2003.

[66]   This links the analysis of mechanisms to counterfactual reasoning. See also Lebow, 2010.

crisis, a response aimed at re-establishing internal coherence is to be expected, but, again, the content of such a response is not necessarily preordained. The content of geopolitical argument was contingent on a series of other ongoing processes, such as ideational path dependency, the institutional framework and political economy of national foreign policy expertise, and political struggles around the definition of the 'national' interest. The volume hence sought to understand the revival of geopolitical thought through an analysis of open parallel historical processes, within which it conceptualised a social mechanism of identity crisis reduction that, given a certain context, would trigger a response that mobilised or introduced geopolitical ideas.

The volume also suggested a second mechanism in the possible functioning of a self-fulfilling prophecy. If geopolitical thought affected security imaginaries, it would 'essentialise' either physical geography or human/cultural geography, or both. Such a development could set off a mechanism that, via foreign policy interactions, security-imaginary diffusion and the autonomous development of imaginaries, could mobilise a militarised vision of politics and essentialised identities (ego and alter) that, in combination, would make nationalist foreign policy and a rigid friend–foe scheme possible and likely. And, although militarisation in the classical sense was found to have been limited, the process of homogenising identities is going strong, albeit not without opposition. I called this second mechanism a vicious circle of essentialisation. Only the concatenation of these two mechanisms would produce the initial normative concern of a 'self-fulfilling geopolitics'.

These links are causal in the sense of 'how' causality. They are embedded in a process that, despite its focus on structures (security imaginaries, identity discourses, cultures of anarchy), institutional processes and their path dependencies, is basically open, since it is contingent on a series of contexts and factors.[67] In some cases, the concatenation of mechanisms did not get much beyond the start; in others it was halted elsewhere.

The analysis also shows that a pure focus on the interactive level of world events does not do justice to the simultaneous processes going on for which such events may have very different implications. Conceived in this way, the analysis is informed by a non-linear type of history and tracing of the historical process. In fact, the problem for the analysis then becomes to justify the necessarily few arrows that connect the ongoing processes. Looking at Figures 11.2 and 11.3, we see that the mutual effects of these processes are continuous and would, in principle, need to be represented by arrows all over. This, however, is a problem not only for this analysis, but for all analysis. Explanation isolates certain arrows as significant in terms of their role in making sense of the cacophony of events, actions, practices and processes. Of course, the focus on

---

[67] The need to incorporate that openness of process within historical institutionalism is a point repeatedly stressed by Kathleen Thelen, 1999 and 2000.

certain links can turn out wrong. But this is akin to the usual risk of misjudging the significance of certain links, not for the fact of having to isolate some. Hence, it is a problem generally shared by all explanations.

And, so, we now reach the end of the actual analysis. By conceptualising mechanisms in a manner consistent with constructivism, and by and showing their empirical import, these last two chapters can finally shed light on the initial puzzles of the study. With the specified process and concatenation of mechanisms, it becomes possible to understand how both the revival of geopolitical thought and the move away from a Kantian culture of anarchy appeared not *despite* the end of the Cold War but paradoxically *because of* it. And by having identified two different types of mechanisms, the study provides theory development of the micro-dynamics of (macro-)structural change within a constructivist analysis.

BIBLIOGRAPHY

Aalto, Pami, 2000. Beyond Restoration: The Construction of Post-Soviet Geopolitics in Estonia. *Cooperation and Conflict* 35 (1): 65–88.

2001. *Constructing Post-Soviet Geopolitics in Estonia: A Study in Security, Identity and Subjectivity*. University of Helsinki, Acta Politica No. 19.

Aalto, Pami and Eiki Berg, 2002. Spatial Practices and Time in Estonia: From Post-Soviet Geopolitics to European Governance. *Space & Polity* 6 (3): 253–270.

Abbott, Andrew, 1988. Transcending General Linear Reality. *Sociological Theory* 6 (2): 169–186.

2001. *Time Matters: On Theory and Method*. University of Chicago Press.

Agnew, John, 1998. *Geopolitics: Re-visioning World Politics*. London: Routledge.

2003. *Geopolitics: Re-visioning World Politics*, 2nd edn. London and New York: Routledge.

Akyol, Taha, 2003. Stratejik Derinlik [Strategic Depth]. *Milliyet*, 17 February.

Allan, Pierre and Kjell Goldmann, eds., 1992. *The End of the Cold War: Evaluating Theories of International Relations*. Dordrecht: Martinus Nijhoff.

Altınay, Ayşe Gül, 2003. Militarizm, İnsan Hakları ve Milli Güvenlik Dersi [Militarism, Human Rights and the National Security Course]. Available at: www.bianet.org (accessed 11 April 2005).

2005. *The Myth of the Military-Nation: Militarism, Gender, and Education in Turkey*. London: Palgrave.

Aminzade, Ronald, 1992. Historical Sociology and Time. *Sociological Methods & Research* 20 (4): 456–480.

Ancel, Jacques, 1936. *Géopolitique*. Paris: Delagrave.

Andreatta, Filippo and Christopher Hill, 2000. Struggling to Change: The Italian State and the New Order. In *Rethinking the European Order: West European Responses 1989–1997*, edited by William Wallace and Robert Niblett, 242–267. Oxford: St Martin's Press.

Andreescu, Gabriel, 1998. The Transylvanian Issue and the Issue of Europe. *The Hungarian Quarterly* 39 (152): 56–64.

Antonsich, Marco, 1996. *Geopolitica e geografia politica in Italia dal 1945 ad oggi*. Università di Trieste: Quaderni del Dottorato di Ricerca in Geografia Politica, n. 2, special monographical issue.

1997a. Santoro, i nomi e i numi della geopolitica. *Limes: rivista italiana di geopolitica* 1 (1997): 289–291.

1997b. *Geopolitica e Geografia Politica in Italia dal 1945 ad oggi.* Trieste: Quaderni del dottorato in geografia.

Antonsich, Marco, Alessandro Colombo, Aldo Ferrari, Riccardo Redaelli, Alessandro Vitale and Fulvio Zanoni, 2001. *Geopolitica della crisi: Balcani, Caucaso e Asia centrale nel nuovo scenario internazionale.* Milan: ISPI-EGEA.

Anzera, Giuseppe and Barbara Marniga, 2003. *Geopolitica dell'acqua: gli scenari internazionali e il caso del Medio Oriente.* Milan: Guerini studio.

Aron, Raymond, 1962. *Paix et guerre entre les nations,* 8th edn. Paris: Calmann-Lévy.

1967. Max Weber et la politique de puissance. In *Les étapes de la pensée sociologique,* 642–656. Paris: Gallimard.

1976. *Penser la guerre, Clausewitz. II: L'âge planétaire.* Paris: Gallimard.

Ashley, Richard K., 1987. The Geopolitics of Geopolitical Space: Toward a Critical Social Theory of International Politics. *Alternatives* XII (4): 403–434.

1988. Untying the Sovereign State: A Double Reading of the Anarchy Problematique. *Millennium: Journal of International Studies* 17 (2): 227–262.

1989. Imposing International Purpose: Notes on a Problematique of Governance. In *Global Changes and Theoretical Challenges: Approaches to World Politics for the 1990s,* edited by Ernst-Otto Czempiel and James Rosenau, 251–290. Lexington Books.

Ataöv, Türkkaya, 1961. Symposium on the Teaching of International Politics in Turkey. *Milletlerarası Münasebetler Türk Yıllığı* 2: 188–196.

Atkinson, David, 2000. Geopolitical Imaginations in Modern Italy. In *Geopolitical Traditions: A Century of Geopolitical Thought,* edited by Klaus Dodds and David Atkinson, 93–117. London: Routledge.

Auswärtiges Amt [AA], 1995. *Außenpolitik der Bundesrepublik Deutschland. Dokumente von 1949 bis 1994. Herausgegeben aus Anlaß des 125. Jubiläums des Auswärtigen Amts.* Cologne: Verlag Wissenschaft und Politik.

Axelrod, Robert and Robert O. Keohane, 1986. Achieving Cooperation under Anarchy: Strategies and Institutions. In *Cooperation under Anarchy,* edited by Kenneth Oye, 226–254. Princeton University Press.

Aytürk, İlker, 2004. Turkish Linguists against the West: The Origins of Linguistic Nationalism in Atatürk's Turkey. *Middle Eastern Studies* 40 (6): 1–25.

Bach, Jonathan and Susanne Peters, 2002. The New Spirit of German Geopolitics. *Geopolitics* 7 (3): 1–18.

Banchoff, Thomas, 1999. German Identity and European Integration. *European Journal of International Relations* 5 (3): 259–289.

Barnes, Barry, 1982. *T.S. Kuhn and Social Science.* London: Macmillan.

Barthes, Ronald, 1980. *Mythologies.* London: Vintage Classics.

Bassin, Mark, 1987a. Imperialism and the Nation State in Friedrich Ratzel's Political Geography. *Progress in Human Geography* 11 (4): 473–495.

1987b. Race contra Space: The Conflict between German *Geopolitik* and National Socialism. *Political Geography Quarterly* 6 (2): 115–134.

2003. Between Realism and the 'New Right': Geopolitics in Germany in the 1990s. *Transactions of the Institute of British Geographers* 28 (3): 350–366.

2004. The Two Faces of Contemporary Geopolitics. *Progress in Human Geography* 28 (5): 620–626.

Bassin, Mark and Konstantin E. Aksenov, 2006. Mackinder and the Heartland Theory in Post-Soviet Geopolitical Discourse. *Geopolitics* 11 (1): 99–118.

Bednář, Miloslav, 1999. Význam Palackého filosofické obnovy české státní ideje. In *František Palacký 1798/1998, dějiny a dnešek*, edited by František Šmahel and Eva Doležalová, 63–72. Prague: Historický ústav AV ČR.

Beer, Francis A. and Robert Harriman, 1996. Realism and Rhetoric in International Relations. In *Post-Realism: the Rhetorical Turn in International Relations*, edited by Francis A. Beer and Robert Harriman, 1–34. East Lansing: Michigan State University Press.

Behnke, Andreas, 2006. The Politics of Geopolitik in Post-Cold War Germany. *Geopolitics* 11 (3): 396–419.

Bennett, Andrew and Colin Elman, 2006. Qualitative Research: Recent Developments in Case Study Methods. *Annual Review of Political Science* 9: 455–476.

Berg, Eiki, 2002a. *Eesti tähendused, piirid ja kontekstid* [Estonian Meanings, Contexts and Boundaries]. Tartu: Tartu Ülikooli Kirjastus.

2002b. Local Resistance, National Identity and Global Swings in Post-Soviet Estonia. *Europe-Asia Studies* 54 (1): 109–122.

2003. Some Unintended Consequences of Geopolitical Reasoning in Post-Soviet Estonia: Texts and Policy Streams, Maps, and Cartoons. *Geopolitics* 8 (1): 101–120.

Berg, Eiki and Matthieu Chillaud, 2009. An IR Community in the Baltic States: Is there a Genuine One? *Journal of International Relations and Development* 12 (2): 193–199.

Berg, Eiki and Saima Oras, 2000. Writing Post-Soviet Estonia on to the World Map. *Political Geography* 19 (5): 601–625.

Berger, Peter L. and Thomas Luckmann, 1966. *The Social Construction of Reality: a Treatise in the Sociology of Knowledge*. New York: Anchor Books.

Bially Mattern, Janice, 2005. *Ordering International Politics: Identity, Crisis, and Representational Force*. London and New York: Routledge.

Bilge, Suat, 1959. Jeopolitik [Geopolitics]. *Kara Kuvvetleri Dergisi* 2 (5): 1–30.

Bilgin, Pinar, 2001. Turkey and the EU: Yesterday's Answers to Tomorrow's Security Problems? In *EU Civilian Crisis Management*, edited by Graeme P. Herd and Jouko Huru, 38–51. Surrey: Conflict Studies Research Centre, Royal Military Academy Sandhurst.

2003a. The 'Peculiarity' of Turkey's Position on EU-NATO Security Cooperation: A Rejoinder to Missiroli. *Security Dialogue* 34 (3): 343–347.

2003b. Türkiye-AB İlişkilerinde Güvenlik Kültürünün Rolü [The Role of Security Culture in Turkey-EU Relations]. In *Turkey and Europe in the Post-Cold War Era*, edited by Cem Karadeli, 192–220. Ankara: Ayraç.

2004. A Return to 'Civilisational Geopolitics' in the Mediterranean? Changing Geopolitical Images of the European Union and Turkey in the post-Cold War Era. *Geopolitics* 9 (2): 269–291.

2005. Turkey's Changing Security Discourses: The Challenge of Globalization. *European Journal of Political Research* 44: 1–27.

2007. 'Only Strong States Can Survive in Turkey's Geography': The Uses of 'Geopolitical Truths' in Turkey. *Political Geography* 26: 740–756.

2008a. Thinking Past 'Western' IR? *Third World Quarterly* 29 (1): 5–23.

2008b. The State of IR in Turkey, *BISA News* (The Newsletter of the British International Studies Association).

2009. Securing Turkey through 'Western-oriented' Foreign Policy. *New Perspectives on Turkey* (special issue on Turkish foreign policy) 40: 105–125.

Bilgin, Pinar and Oktay Tanrısever, 2009. A Telling Story of IR in the Periphery: Telling Turkey about the World, Telling the World About Turkey. *Journal of International Relations and Development* 12 (2): 174–179.

Billig, Michael, 1995. *Banal Nationalism*. Thousand Oaks: Sage.

Bir, Çevik, 1998. Turkey's Role in the New World Order. *Strategic Forum* 135. Available at: www.ndu.edu/inss/strforum/forum135.html (accessed 19 November 2001).

Bittermann, Klaus and Thomas Deichmann, eds., 1999. *Wie Dr. Joseph Fischer lernte, die Bombe zu lieben*. Berlin: Verlag Klaus Bittermann.

Bobbio, Norberto, 1996 [1969]. *Saggi sulla scienza politica in Italia*, 2nd edn. Roma-Bari: Editori Laterza.

Boesler, Klaus-Achim, 1994/1995. Neue Ansätze der politischen Geographie und der Geopolitik zu Fragen der Sicherheit. In *Sicherheitspolitik an der Schwelle zum 21. Jahrhundert. Ausgewählte Themen – Strategien – Handlungsoptionen. Festschrift für Dieter Wellershoff*, edited by Wolf-Ulrich Jorke, 75–87. Berlin: Bundesakademie für Sicherheitspolitik.

Bonanate, Luigi, 1990. *Studi Internazionali*. Torino: Fondazione Giovanni Agnelli.

1997. Qualche argomento contro l'interesse nazionale. *Limes: rivista italiana di geopolitica* 2 (1997): 303–311.

Booth, Ken, 2005. Critical Explorations. In *Critical Security Studies and World Politics*, edited by Ken Booth, 1–18. Boulder: Lynne Rienner.

Bosworth, R.J.B., 1979. *Italy the Least of the Great Powers: Italian Foreign Policy before the First World War*. London: Cambridge University Press.

1996. *Italy and the Wider World, 1860–1960*. London: Routledge.

Boudon, Raymond, 1998. Social Mechanisms Without Black Boxes. In *Social Mechanisms: An Analytical Approach to Social Theory*, edited by Peter Hedström and Richard Swedberg, 172–203. Cambridge University Press.

Bourdieu, Pierre, 1994. *Raisons pratiques. Sur la théorie de l'action.* Paris: Éditions du Seuil.

2000. *Propos sur le champ politique.* Presses Universitaires de Lyon.

2001. *Language et pouvoir symbolique,* 2nd rev. and enlarged edn. Paris: Seuil.

Brighi, Elisabetta, 2006. One Man Alone? A Longue Durée Approach to Italy's Foreign Policy under Berlusconi. *Government and Opposition* 41 (2): 278–297.

Brill, Heinz, 1993. *Geopolitik und Geostrategie. Begründung–Degeneration–Neuansätze.* Bergisch Gladbach: Amt für Studien und Übungen der Bundeswehr.

1994. *Geopolitik heute. Deutschlands Chance?* Frankfurt/M.: Ullstein.

Bronstein, Mihhail, 2002. Idapoliiitika on tundeline teema [Eastern Policy is a Sensitive Topic]. *Postimees,* 5 July.

Brooks, Stephen G. and William C. Wohlforth, 2000/2001. Power, Globalization and the End of the Cold War: Reevaluating a Landmark Case for Ideas. *International Security* 25 (3): 5–53.

Brubaker, Rogers and Frederick Cooper, 2000. Beyond 'Identity'. *Theory and Society* 29 (1): 1–47.

Brunhes, Jean, 1920. *Géographie humaine de la France.* Paris: Société de l'histoire nationale.

Brzezinski, Zbigniew, 1997. *The Grand Chessboard: American Primacy and its Geostrategic Imperatives.* New York: Basic Books.

1998. *La grande scacchiera.* Milano: Longanesi.

Buck, Felix, 1996. *Geopolitik 2000: Weltordnung im Wandel – Deutschland in der Welt am Vorabend des 3. Jahrtausends.* Frankfurt/M.: Report Verlag.

Bull, Hedley, 1977. *The Anarchical Society: A Study of Order in World Politics.* London: Macmillan.

1982. Civilian Power Europe: A Contradiction in Terms? *Journal of Common Market Studies* 12 (2): 149–164.

Bunge, Mario, 2004. How Does It Work? The Search for Explanatory Mechanisms. *Philosophy of the Social Sciences* 34 (2): 182–210.

Buzan, Barry, 2004. *The United States and Great Powers: World Politics in the Twenty-First Century.* Cambridge: Polity Press.

Buzan, Barry, Ole Wæver and Jaap de Wilde, 1998. *Security: A New Framework for Analysis.* Boulder: Lynne Rienner.

Cagnetta, Mariella, 1994. Mare Nostrum, un mito geopolitica da Pompeo a Mussolini. *Limes: rivista italiana di geopolitica* 2 (1994): 251–257.

Caracciolo, Lucio. 2001. *Terra incognite: le radici geopolitiche della crisi italiana.* Roma-Bari: Laterza.

Caracciolo, Lucio and Michael Korinmann, 1993. Editoriale. *Limes: rivista italiana di geopolitica* 1 (1993): 1.

1998. *Italy and the Balkans.* Washington, DC: Center for Strategic & International Studies.

Caracciolo, Lucio and Giovanni Orfei, eds., 1993. Tavola rotonda: alla ricerca dell'interesse nazionale. *Limes: rivista italiana di geopolitica* 1.

Caracciolo, Lucio, Michel Korinmann and Empedocle Maffia, eds., 1997. *What Italy Stands for*. Washington, DC: Center for Strategic & International Studies.

Carr, Edward Heller, 1946. *The Twenty Years' Crisis: An Introduction to the Study of International Relations*, 2nd edn. London: Macmillan.

Castoriadis, Cornelius, 1987. *The Imaginary Institution of Society*. Cambridge, MA: MIT Press.

CeMiSS, 1997. *Il Sistema Italia: gli interessi nazionali nel nuovo scenario internazionale*. Milan: FrancoAngeli.

Cerreti, Claudio, 1997. San Giuliano e la non-geopolitica dei geografi. *Limes: rivista italiana di geopolitica* 3 (1997): 249–260.

Cesa, Marco, 1995. Geopolitica e realismo. *Quaderni di Scienza Politica* 4 (1995): 511–512.

Chaadaev, Petr, 1991. *Polnoe sobranie sochinenii*, vol. II. Moscow: Nauka.

Chabod, Federico, 1951. *Storia della politica estera italiana dal 1870 al 1896*. Bari: Laterza.

   1998. *Italian Foreign Policy: The Statecraft of the Founders*. Princeton University Press.

Checkel, Jeffrey T., 2005. International Institutions and Socialization in Europe: Introduction and Framework. *International Organization* 59 (4): 801–826.

   2008. Process Tracing. In *Qualitative Methods in International Relations: A Pluralist Guide*, edited by Audie Klotz and Deepa Prakash, 114–128. Houndmills: Palgrave Macmillan.

Child, John, 1979. Geopolitical Thinking in Latin America. *Latin American Research Review* 14 (2): 89–111.

Childs, Timothy, 1990. *Italo-Turkish Diplomacy and the War Over Libya, 1911–1912*. Leiden: Brill.

City Paper, 2003. EU Referendum News, September. Available at: www.balticsww.com/EU:BalticsSayYes.html (accessed 18 December 2003).

Claude, Inis L., Jr., 1962. *Power and International Relations*. New York: Random House.

Claval, Paul, 1996. *Geopolitica e geostrategia: pensiero politico, spazio, territorio*. Bologna: Zanichelli.

Cohen, Saul B., 1963. *Geography and Politics in a Divided World*. New York: Random House.

   1991. Global Geopolitical Change in the Post-Cold War Era. *Annals of the Association of American Geographers* 81 (4): 551–580.

   2003. Geopolitical Realities and United States Foreign Policy. *Political Geography* 22 (1): 1–33.

Colombo, Alessandro, 1996. *La componente sicurezza/rischio negli scacchieri geopolitici Sud ed Est. Le opzioni del Modello di Difesa italiano*. Roma: CeMiSS.

Copeland, Dale C., 2003. A Realist Critique of the English School. *Review of International Studies* 29 (3): 427–441.

Čornej, Petr, 1999. Ke genezi Palackého pojetí husitství. In *František Palacký 1798/1998, dějiny a dnešek*, edited by František Šmahel and Eva Doležalová, 123–138. Prague: Historický ústav AV ČR.

Corsico, Fabio, ed., 1998. *Interessi nazionali e identità italiana*. Milan: FrancoAngeli.

Cowen, Tylor, 1998. Do Economists use Social Mechanisms to Explain? In *Social Mechanisms: An Analytical Approach to Social Theory*, edited by Peter Hedström and Richard Swedberg, 125–146. Cambridge University Press.

Cox, Robert W., 1986 [1981]. Social Forces, States and World Orders: Beyond International Relations Theory (+Postscript 1985). In *Neorealism and its Critics*, edited by Robert O. Keohane, 204–254. New York: Columbia University Press.

Crow, Suzanne, 1993. Russia Asserts Its Strategic Agenda. *RFE/RL Research Report* 2 (17 December 1993): 1–8.

Dalby, Simon, 1990a. American Security Discourse: The Persistence of Geopolitics. *Political Geography Quarterly* 9 (2): 171–188.

1990b. *Creating the Second Cold War: The Discourse of Politics*. London: Pinter Publishers.

Dalton, Benjamin, 2004. Creativity, Habit, and the Social Products of Creative Action: Revising Joas, Incorporating Bourdieu. *Sociological Theory* 22 (4): 603–622.

Davutoğlu, Ahmet, 2001. *Stratejik Derinlik: Türkiye'nin Uluslararası Konumu* [Strategic Depth: Turkey's International Position]. İstanbul: Küre.

Demangeon, Albert, 1932.Géographie politique. *Annales de géographie* XLI: 22–31.

de Martonne, E., 1930. Europe Centrale I. *Géographie universelle*, vol. IV. Paris.

De Michelis, Gianni, 2003. *La lunga ombra di Yalta: la specificità della politica italiana, conversazione con Francesco Kostner*. Venice: Marsilio Editori.

Derrida, Jacques and Jürgen Habermas, 2003. Nach dem Krieg: Die Wiedergeburt Europas. *Frankfurter Allgemeine Zeitung*, 31 May.

Dessler, David, 1991. Beyond Correlations: Toward a Causal Theory of War. *International Studies Quarterly* 35 (3): 337–355.

Diez, Thomas, 2004. Europe's Others and the Return of Geopolitics. *Cambridge Review of International Affairs* 17 (2): 319–335.

Diez, Thomas and Ian Manners, 2007. Reflecting on Normative Power Europe. In *Power in World Politics*, edited by Felix Berenskoetter and M.J. Williams, 173–188. London: Routledge.

Dijkink, Gertjan, 1996. *National Identity and Geopolitical Visions: Maps of Pride and Pain*. London and New York: Routledge.

Diner, Dan, 1999. Knowledge of Expansion: On the Geopolitics of Karl Haushofer. *Geopolitics* 4 (3): 161–188.

Dinger, Dörte, 2011. From Friends to Collaborators: A Constructivist Analysis of Changes in Italo-German Relations with the End of the Cold War. University of Bremen, BIGSSS, PhD diss.

Dini, Lamberto, 2001. *Fra Casa Bianca e Botteghe Oscure. Fatti e retroscena di una stagione alla Farnesina*. Milan: Guerini Associati.

Dodds, Klaus, 1997. *Geopolitics in Antarctica: Views from the Southern Oceanic Rim.* Chichester: Wiley.

— 2000. Geopolitics and the Geographical Imagination of Argentina. In *Geopolitical Traditions: A Century of Geopolitical Thought,* edited by Klaus Dodds and David Atkinson, 150–184. London: Routledge.

Dodds, Klaus and David Atkinson, eds., 2000. *Geopolitical Traditions: A Century of Geopolitical Thought.* London: Routledge.

Doğanay, Hayati, 1989. Türkiye'nin Coğrafi Konumu ve Bundan Kaynaklanan Dış Tehditler [Turkey's Geopolitical Position and the External Threats it Causes]. *Türk Dünyası Araştırmaları* 10 (58): 9–69.

Dossena, Paolo, 2002. *Hitler & Churchill. Mackinder e la sua scuola. Alle radici della geopolitica.* Milan: Asefi Terziaria.

Doty, Roxanne Lynn, 1993. Foreign Policy as a Social Construction: A Post-positivist Analysis of U.S. Counterinsurgency Policy in the Philippines. *International Studies Quarterly* 37 (3): 297–320.

Drulák, Petr, 2006a. Probably a Problem-solving Regime, Perhaps a Rights-based Union: European Integration in the Czech and Slovak Political Discourse. In *Questioning EU Enlargement: Europe in Search of Identity,* edited by Helene Sjursen, 167–185. London and New York: Routledge.

— 2006b. Between Geopolitics and Anti-Geopolitics: Czech Political Thought. *Geopolitics* 11 (3): 420–438.

— 2006c. Qui décide la politique étrangere tchèque? Les internationalistes, les européanistes, les atlantistes ou les autonomistes? *La Revue internationale et stratégique* 61 (Printemps): 71–84.

— 2006d. Motion, Container and Equilibrium: Metaphors in the Discourse about European Integration. *European Journal of International Relations* 12 (4): 499–531.

— 2007. Wozu die Raketenabwehr gut ist. *Financial Times Deutschland,* 3 April. Available at: www.ftd.de/politik/international/gastkommentar-wozu-die-rak etenabwehr-gut-ist/182120.html (accessed 1 December 2011).

Drulák, Petr and Radka Druláková, 2000. International Relations in the Czech Republic: A Review of the Discipline. *Journal of International Relations and Development* 3 (3): 256–282.

— 2006. The Czech Republic. In *International Relations in Europe: Traditions, Perspectives and Destinations,* edited by Knud-Erik Jørgensen and Tonny Brems Knudsen, 172–196. London: Routledge.

Drulák, Petr and Lucie Königová, 2005. The Czech Republic – From Socialist Past to Socialized Future. In *Socializing Democratic Norms: The Role of International Organizations for the Construction of Europe,* edited by Trine Flockhart, 149–168. London: Palgrave.

Duchêne, François, 1973. Die Rolle Europas im Weltsystem: von der regionalen zur planetarischen Interdependenz. In *Zivilmacht Europa – Supermacht oder Partner?* edited by Max Kohnstamm and Wolfgang Hager, 11–35. Frankfurt/M.: Suhrkamp.

Dugin, Alexander, 1999. *Absoljutnaja Rodina* [Absolute Motherland]. Moscow: Arctogaia.

2003. *Rus Jeopolitiği: Avrasyacı Yaklaşım*, trans. Vügar İmanov [Russian Geopolitics: The Eurasianist Perspective]. İstanbul: Küre.

Dvorský, Viktor, 1918. *Území československého národa* [The Territory of the Czechoslovak Nation]. Praha: Český čtenář.

1919. Hranice Československé republiky [The Boundaries of the Czechoslovak Republic]. *Sborník Československé Společnosti Zeměpisné*, sv. 24, 37. Prague.

1923. *Základy politické geografie a československý stat* [The Basics of Political Geography and the Czechoslovak State]. Prague: Český čtenář.

Ebeling, Frank, 1994. *Geopolitik. Karl Haushofer und seine Raumwissenschaft 1919–1945*. Berlin: Akademie Verlag.

Ecevit, Bülent, 2001. Prime Minister Ecevit's Address to Republican Peoples' Party Group. Available at: www.belgenet.com/2001/be_210301.html (accessed 5 May 2005).

Eesti Ekspress, 1999. Eestimaa aastal 2050: õnnelik riik [Estonia in Year 2050: A Happy State]. 25 February. Available at: www.ekspress.ee (accessed 19 November 2000).

Eesti Päevaleht, 27 November 1999: 17–18. Available at: www.epl.ee (accessed 16 January 2001).

Eesti Tulevikuuuringute Instituut, 2003. Vaher: paljukardetud oht idast ei ole kadunud [Vaher: the Much-feared Threat from the East Has Not Disappeared]. 22 December. Available at: www.epl.ee (accessed 18 November 2004).

2004. Ilves loodab korrigerida euroliidu välispoliitikat [Ilves is Hoping to Adjust EU's Foreign Policy]. 23 July. Available at: www.epl.ee (accessed 18 November 2004).

1997. *Eesti Tulevikustsenaariumid* [Estonia's Future Scenarios]. Tallinn: Eesti Tulevikuuuringute Instituut.

Elman, Colin, 2005. Explanatory Typologies in Qualitative Studies of International Politics. *International Organization* 59 (2): 293–326.

Elsässer, Jürgen, 1999. *Nie wieder Krieg ohne uns. Das Kosovo und die neue deutsche Geopolitik*. Hamburg: Konkret Literatur Verlag.

Elster, Jon, 1998. A Plea for Mechanisms. In *Social Mechanisms: An Analytical Approach to Social Theory*, edited by Peter Hedström and Richard Swedberg, 45–73. Cambridge University Press.

2007. *Explaining Social Behavior: More Nuts and Bolts for the Social Sciences*. Cambridge University Press.

Eralp, Atila, 1996. Giriş [Introduction]. In *Devlet, Sistem Ve Kimlik: Uluslararası İlişkilerde Temel Yaklaşımlar* [State, System and Identity: Basic Approaches to International Relations], edited by Atila Eralp, 7–13. Ankara: İletişim.

Eren, Ahmet Cevat, 1964. *Jeopolitik Tarihine Toplu bir Bakış* [An Overview of the History of Geopolitics]. İstanbul: Nurgök Matbaası.

Eriksson, Johan, ed., 2002. *Threat Politics: New Perspectives on Security, Risk and Crisis Management*. Aldershot: Ashgate.

Erol, Mehmet Seyfettin, 2004. Türkiye'nin AB Sürecinde Avrasya Politikası: Niçin ve Nasıl Bir İşbirliği? [Turkey's Eurasian Policy in the Process of the EU: Why and what kind of a cooperation?]. *Avrasya Dosyası* 10 (2): 5–37.

Estonian Ministry of Ethnic Affairs, 2000. *State Programme Integration in Estonian Society 2000–2007*. Tallinn: Ministry of Ethnic Affairs. Available at: www.riik. ee/saks/ikomisjon.htm (accessed 16 January 2001).

Estonian Ministry of Foreign Affairs, 1996. *Guidelines of the National Defence Policy of Estonia*. Tallinn: Ministry of Foreign Affairs. Available at: www.vm.ee/eng/ nato/def.policy.html (accessed 14 March 2001).

    2001. *National Security Concept of the Republic of Estonia*. Tallinn: Ministry of Foreign Affairs.

Evangelista, Matthew, 1999. *Unarmed Forces: the Transnational Movement to End the Cold War*. Ithaca: Cornell University Press.

    2001. Norms, Heresthetics and the End of the Cold War. *Journal of Cold War Studies* 3 (1): 5–35.

Fahri [Fındıkoğlu], Ziyaeddin, 1946. Jeopolitik [Geopolitics]. In *Jeopolitik: İlmi Antoloji Denemesi* [Geopolitics: A Scientific Anthology], 81–93. İstanbul: Gençlik Kitabevi.

Falleti, Tulia G. and Julia F. Lynch, 2009. Context and Causal Mechanisms in Political Analysis. *Comparative Political Studies* 42 (9): 1143–1166.

FAZ, 1993a. Für ein Europa der Nationen und gegen den europäischen Bundestaat. *Frankfurter Allgemeine Zeitung*, 4 September. Available at: www.web. nexis-lexis.com. On file with author.

    1993b. Das Auswärtige Amt weist Stoibers Europa-Rüge zurück. *Frankfurter Allgemeine Zeitung*, 4 November. Available at: www.web.nexis-lexis.com. On file with author.

    1993c. Kohl gegen Stoiber. *Frankfurter Allgemeine Zeitung*, 12 November. Available at: www.web.nexis-lexis.com. On file with author.

    1994. Die CDU doch für Bundestaat Europa. *Frankfurter Allgemeine Zeitung*, 7 February. Available at: www.web.nexis-lexis.com. On file with author.

Feldman, Gregory, 2001. European Integration and the Discourse of National Identity in Estonia. *National Identities* 3 (1): 5–21.

    2005. Culture, State, and Security in Europe: The Case of Citizenship and Integration Policy in Estonia. *American Ethnologist* 32 (4): 676–694.

Feldmeyer, Karl, 1993. Die NATO und Deutschland nach dem Ende des Ost-West-Gegensatzes. In *Westbindung: Chancen und Risiken für Deutschland*, edited by Rainer Zitelmann, Karlheinz Weißmann and Michael Großheim, 459–476. Frankfurt/M.: Propyläen Verlag.

Ferraresi, F., 1992. A Secret Structure Codenamed Gladio. In *Italian Politics: A Review, vol. 7*, edited by Stephen Hellman and Gianfranco Pasquino, 29–48. London: Pinter Publishers.

Ferraris, Luigi Vittorio, 1993. Dal Tevere al Danubio: L'Italia riscopre la geopolitica a tavolino. *Limes: rivista italiana di geopolitica* 1–2 (1993): 213–225.

Fischer, Joschka, 1991. Kaum ist die Einheit da, schickt man deutsche Soldaten zur Front. Interview mit dem Fraktionssprecher der hessischen Grünen, Joschka Fischer, zum Golfkonflikt. *Frankfurter Rundschau*, 9 January: 6.

1999a. Rede des Außenministers zum Natoeinsatz im Kosovo. Available at: www. mediacultureonline.de/fileadmin/bibliothek/fischerjoschka_kosovorede/ fischer_kosovorede.pdf (accessed 1 December 2011).

1999b. Rede bei der Mitgliederversammlung der Deutschen Gesellschaft für Auswärtige Politik. 24. November 1999. Available at: www.glasnost.de/db/ DokZeit/99fischer.html (accessed 1 December 2011).

2000. Vom Staatenbund zur Föderation – Gedanken über die Finalität der europäischen Integration. Available at: www.auswaertiges-amt.de/diplo/de/ Infoservice/Presse/Reden/2000/000512-EuropaeischeIntegrationPDF.pdf (accessed: 3 November 2008).

2001. Rede des Bundesaußenministers Joschka Fischer zur Aktuellen Lage nach Beginn der Operation gegen den internationalen Terrorismus in Afghanistan. Available at: www.documentarchiv.de/brd/2001/rede_fischer_1011.html (accessed 1 December 2011).

2007. *Die rot-grünen Jahre. Deutsche Außenpolitik – vom Kosovo bis zum 11. September.* Cologne: Kiepenheuer & Witsch.

Flockhart, Trine, 2004. 'Masters and Novices': Socialization and Social Learning through the NATO Parliamentary Assembly. *International Relations* 18 (3): 361–380.

Forsberg, Tuomas, 1999. Power, Interest and Trust: Explaining Gorbachev's Choices at the End of the Cold War. *Review of International Studies* 25 (4): 603–621.

Fossati, Fabio, 1999. *Economia e politica estera in Italia: l'evoluzione negli anni Novanta.* Milan: Franco Angeli.

Frattini, Franco, 2004. *Cambiamo Rotta.* Milan: Piemme.

Frei, Daniel, 1985. *Feindbilder und Abrüstung: Die gegenseitige Einschätzung der UdSSR und der USA.* Munich: Beck.

Galli della Loggia, Ernesto, 1996. *La morte della patria.* Rome: Laterza.

1998. *L'identità nazionale.* Bologna: Il Mulino.

Gambetta, Diego, 1998. Concatenations of Mechanisms. In *Social Mechanisms: An Analytical Approach to Social Theory*, edited by Peter Hedström and Richard Swedberg, 102–124. Cambridge University Press.

Gangas-Geisse, Mónica, 2001. Ratzel's Thought in Chilean Geography. In *On the Centenary of Ratzel's Political Geography. Europe between Political Geography and Geopolitics*, edited by Marco Antonsich, Vladimir Kolossov and M. Paola Pagnini, 193–201. Rome: Società Geografica Italiana.

Garton Ash, Timothy, 1994. Germany's Choice. *Foreign Affairs* 73: 65–81.

1999. *History of the Present: Essays, Sketches and Dispatches from Europe in the 1990s.* London: Penguin Books.

Geis, Anna, 2005. Die Zivilmacht Deutschland und die Enttabuisierung des Militärischen. *HSFK Standpunkte* Nr. 2.

Gellner, Ernest, 1983. *Nations and Nationalism.* Oxford: Blackwell.

———. 1995. The Price of Velvet: Thomas Masaryk and Václav Havel. *Czech Sociological Review* 3 (1): 45–58.

Genscher, Hans-Dietrich, 1995. *Erinnerungen.* Berlin: Siedler Verlag.

George, Alexander, 1979. The Causal Nexus between Cognitive Beliefs and Decision-Making Behaviour: The 'Operational Code' Belief System. In *Psychological Models in International Politics*, edited by Laurence Falkowski, 95–124. Boulder: Westview Press.

George, Alexander and Andrew Bennett, 2005. *Case Studies and Theory Development in the Social Sciences.* Cambridge, MA: MIT Press.

Germain, Randall, 2000. E.H. Carr and the Historical Mode of Thought. In *E.H. Carr: A Critical Appraisal*, edited by Michael Cox, 322–336. Houndmills: Palgrave.

Gerring, John, 2007. Review Article: The Mechanistic Worldview: Thinking Inside the Box. *British Journal of Political Science* 38 (2): 161–179.

Gheciu, Alexandra, 2005. Security Institutions as Agents of Socialization? NATO and the 'New Europe'. *International Organization* 59 (4): 973–1012.

Gilpin, Robert, 1981. *War and Change in World Politics.* New York: Cambridge University Press.

Göksu-Özdoğan, Günay, 2001. *'Turan'dan 'Bozkurt'a Tek Parti Döneminde Türkçülük (1931–1946)*, 2nd edn [From 'Turan' to 'Greywolf', Turkism During the Single-party Era, 1931–1946]. İstanbul: İletişim.

Goldstein, Judith and Robert O. Keohane, 1993. Ideas and Foreign Policy: An Analytical Framework. In *Ideas and Foreign Policy: Beliefs, Institutions, and Political Change*, edited by Judith Goldstein and Robert O. Keohane, 3–30. Ithaca: Cornell University Press.

Gönlübol, Mehmet, Cem Sar, Ahmet Şükrü Esmer, Oral Sander, Haluk Ülman, Suat Bilge, Ömer Kürçüoğlu and Duygu Sezer, 1989 [1967]. *Olaylarla Türk Dış Politikası*, 7th edn. Ankara: Alkın.

Gray, Colin S., 1986. *Nuclear Strategy and National Style.* Lanham: Hamilton Press.

———. ed., 2003. *Jeopolitik, Strateji ve Coğrafya* [Geopolitics, Strategy and Geography]. Ankara: ASAM.

Gräzin, Igor, 1996. Julgeolek ja elujäämine kõigepealt [Security and Survival First]. *Postimees*, 23 March.

Gregory, Derek, 1998. *Explorations in Critical Human Geography. Hettner Lecture 1997.* Department of Geography, University of Heidelberg.

Gross, Neil, 2009. A Pragmatist Theory of Social Mechanisms. *American Sociological Review* 74 (3): 358–379.

Grosser, Alfred, 1972. *L'explication politique. Une introduction à l'analyse comparative.* Paris: Armand Colin.

Großheim, Michael; Karlheiz Weißmann and Rainer Zitelmann, 1993. Einleitung: 'Wir Deutschen und der Westen'. In *Westbindung: Chancen und Risiken für*

Deutschland, edited by Rainer Zitelmann, Karlheinz Weißmann and Michael Großheim, 9–17. Frankfurt/M.: Propyläen Verlag.

Gürkan, İhsan, 1987a. Türkiye'nin Jeopolitik Önemi ve Bundan Kaynaklanan Tehditlerin Genel Değerlendirilmesi [Turkey's Geopolitical Significance and an Examination of the Threats it Causes]. *İstanbul Üniversitesi Atatürk İlkeleri ve İnkılap Tarihi Enstitüsü Yıllığı* 2: 343–358.

1987b. Türkiye'nin Jeostratejik ve Jeopolitik Önemi [Turkey's Geostrategic and Geopolitical Significance]. In *Türkiye'nin Savunması* [Turkey's Defence] (n.a). Ankara: DPE: 10–31.

Gusterson, Hugh, 2004. *People of the Bomb: Portraits of America's Nuclear Complex*. Minneapolis: University of Minnesota Press.

2005. The Seven Deadly Sins of Samuel Huntington. In *Why America's Top Pundits Are Wrong: Anthropologists Talk Back*, edited by Catherine Besteman and Hugh Gusterson, 24–42. Berkeley: University of California Press.

Guzzini, Stefano, 1994. Power Analysis as a Critique of Power Politics: Understanding Power and Governance in the Second Gulf War. European University Institute, PhD diss.

1995. The 'Long Night of the First Republic': Years of Clientelistic Implosion in Italy. *Review of International Political Economy* 2 (1): 27–61.

1997 [1995]. Machtbegriffe am Ausklang (?) der meta-theoretischen Wende in den Internationalen Beziehungen (oder: Gebrauchsanweisung zur Rettung des Konstruktivismus vor seinen neuen Freunden). In *The Aarhus-Norsminde Papers: Constructivism, International Relations and European Studies*, edited by Knud-Erik Jørgensen, 69–82. Aarhus: Institut for Statskundskap.

1998. *Realism in International Relations and International Political Economy: The Continuing Story of a Death Foretold*. London and New York: Routledge.

2000a. A Reconstruction of Constructivism in International Relations. *European Journal of International Relations* 6 (2): 147–182.

2000b. Strange's Oscillating Realism: Opposing the Ideal – and the Apparent. In *Strange Power: Shaping the Parameters of International Relations and International Political Economy*, edited by Thomas C. Lawton, James N. Rosenau and Amy C. Verdun, 215–228. Aldershot: Ashgate.

2001a. Calling for a Less 'Brandish' and Less 'Grand' Reconvention. *Review of International Studies* 27 (3): 495–501.

2001b. The Different Worlds of Realism in International Relations. *Millennium: Journal of International Studies* 30 (1): 111–121.

2002. Foreign Policy without Diplomacy: The Bush Administration at a Crossroads. *International Relations* 16 (2): 291–297.

2003. 'Self-fulfilling Geopolitics?', or: The Social Production of Foreign Policy Expertise in Europe. Copenhagen: DIIS (Danish Institute for International Studies) *Working Paper* 2003/23.

2004a. 'The Cold War is what we Make of It': When Peace Research Meets Constructivism in International Relations. In *Contemporary Security Analysis and Copenhagen Peace Research*, edited by Stefano Guzzini and Dietrich Jung, 40–52. London and New York: Routledge.

2004b. The Enduring Dilemmas of Realism in International Relations. *European Journal of International Relations* 10 (4): 533–568.

2005. The Concept of Power: A Constructivist Analysis. *Millennium: Journal of International Studies* 33 (3): 495–522.

2006. From (Alleged) Unipolarity to the Decline of Multilateralism? A Power-Theoretical Critique. In *Multilateralism under Challenge? Power, International Order and Structural Change*, edited by Edward Newman, Ramesh Thakur and John Tirman, 119–138. Tokyo: United Nations University Press.

2007. Re-reading Weber, or: The Three Fields for the Analysis of Power in International Relations, Copenhagen: DIIS (Danish Institute for International Studies) *Working Paper* 2007/29.

2011. Securitization as a Causal Mechanism. *Security Dialogue* 42 (4–5): 329–341.

Haab, Mare, 1998. Estonia. In *Bordering Russia: Theory and Prospects for Europe's Baltic Rim*, edited by Hans Mouritzen, 109–129. Aldershot: Ashgate.

Hacisalihoğlu, I. Yaşar, 2003. Jeopolitik Doğarken [Geopolitics Born]. *Jeopolitik* 1 (1): 1.

Hacke, Christian, 1993. *Weltmacht wider Willen. Die Aussenpolitik der Bundesrepublik Deutschland*. Frankfurt am Main and Berlin: Ullstein Verlag.

Hacking, Ian, 1999. *The Social Construction of What?* Cambridge, MA: Harvard University Press.

Hahn, Karl-Eckhard, 1994. Westbindung und Interessenlage. Über die Renaissance der Geopolitik. In *Die Selbstbewusste Nation. 'Anschwellender Bocksgesang' und weitere Beiträge zu einer deutschen Debatte*, edited by Heimo Schwilk and Ulrich Schacht, 327–344. Berlin: Ullstein Verlag.

Hall, Ben, 2010. French Minister Says Bail-out Alters EU Treaty. *Financial Times*, 27 May. Available at: http://cachef.ft.com/cms/s/0/d6299cae-69b5-11df-8432-00144feab49a.html#axzz1FoWpU1LA (accessed 5 March 2011).

Hall, Peter A., 2003. Aligning Ontology and Methodology in Comparative Research. In *Comparative Historical Analysis in Social Sciences*, edited by James Mahoney and Dietrich Rueschmeyer, 373–404. Cambridge University Press.

Hall, Peter A. and Rosemary C.R. Taylor, 1996. Political Science and the Three New Institutionalisms. *Political Studies* 44 (5): 936–957.

Hallik, Klara, 1998. Rahvuspoliitilised seisukohad parteiprogrammides ja valim-isplatvormides [Ethnopolitical Positions in Party Programs and Election Platforms]. In *Vene küsimus ja Eesti valikud* [The Russian Question and Estonia's Choices], edited by Mart Heidmets, 77–100. Tallinn Pedagogical University.

Harp Akademileri Komutanlığı [Office of the Commander of the Military Academy], 1963. Türkiye'nin Jeopolitik Durumu üzerine bir inceleme [A Study on Turkey's Geopolitical Position]. *Silahlı Kuvvetler Dergisi* 83 (210): 3–17.

Haslam, Jonathan, 2002. *No Virtue like Necessity: Realist Thought in International Relations since Machiavelli*. New Haven and London: Yale University Press.

Haslingerová, Ivana, 2007. Samostatnou zarhaniční politiku musíme bránit zuby nehty. *Fragmenty*. Available at: www.fragmenty.cz/iz00014.htm (accessed 19 June 2008).

Haushofer, Karl, 1924. *Geopolitik des Pazifischen Ozeans. Studien über die Wechselbeziehungen zwischen Geographie und Geschichte*. Berlin: Kurt Vowinckel Verlag.

   1934. *Weltpolitik von heute*. Berlin: 'Zeitgeschichte' Verlag und Vertriebs-G.m.b.H.

Havel, Václav, 1978/1985. The Power of the Powerless. In *The Power of the Powerless: Citizens Against the State in Central-Eastern Europe*, edited by John Keane. London: Hutchinson.

   1999a. *Letní přemítání. Spisy VI*. Prague: Torst.

   1999b. *Projevy a jiné texty z let 1992–1999. Spisy VII*. Prague: Torst.

Hawkins, Mike, 1997. *Social Darwinism in European and American Thought, 1860–1945*. Cambridge University Press.

Hay, Colin, 2005. Ever-Diminishing Expectations? Or Why Politics Is Not All That It Was Once Cracked Up to Be. Paper presented at the Department of International Relations, London School of Economics and Political Science. London, 26 January.

   2006. Constructivist Institutionalism. In *The Oxford Handbook of Political Institutions*, edited by R. A. W. Rhodes, Sarah A. Binder and Bert A. Rockman, 56–74. Oxford University Press.

Hedström, Peter and Richard Swedberg, 1998a. Social Mechanisms: An Introductory Essay. In *Social Mechanisms: An Analytical Approach to Social Theory*, edited by Peter Hedström and Richard Swedberg, 1–31. Cambridge University Press.

   1998b eds. *Social Mechanisms: An Analytical Approach to Social Theory*. Cambridge University Press.

Hedström, Peter and Petri Ylikovski, 2010. Causal Mechanisms in the Social Sciences. *Annual Review of Sociology* 36: 49–67.

Heidmets, Mart, ed., 1998. *Vene küsimus ja Eesti valikud* [The Russian Question and Estonia's Choices]. Tallinn Pedagogical University.

Hellmann, Gunther, 2000. Rekonstruktion der 'Hegemonie des Machtstaates Deutschland unter modernen Bedingungen'? Zwischenbilanzen nach zehn Jahren neuer deutscher Außenpolitik. Johann Wolfgang Goethe-Universität Frankfurt. Mimeo available at: www.soz.uni-frankfurt.de/hellmann/mat/hellmann-halle.pdf (accessed 1 December 2011).

   2005. Der neue Zwang zur großen Politik und die Wiederentdeckung besserer Welten. *WeltTrends* 13: 117–125.

   2007. '… um diesen deutschen Weg zu Ende gehen zu können.' Die Renaissance machtpolitischer Selbstbehauptung in der zweiten Amtszeit der Regierung Schröder-Fischer. In *Ende des rot-grünen Projektes. Eine Bilanz der Regierung*

Schröder 2002-200, edited by Christoph Egle and Reimut Zohlnhöfer, 453–479. Wiesbaden: VS Verlag für Sozialwissenschaften.

Hellmann, Gunther, Rainer Baumann, Monika Bösche, Benjamin Herborth and Wolfgang Wagner, 2005. De-Europeanization by Default? Germany's EU Policy in Defense and Asylum. *Foreign Policy Analysis* 1 (1): 143–164.

Helme, Mart, 2002. Eesti teevalik Euroopa ja USA veskikivide vahel [Estonia's Path between the Millstones of Europe and USA]. *Eesti Päevaleht*, 28 September. Available at: www.epl.ee (accessed 12 October 2002).

Hepple, Leslie W., 1986a. Geopolitics, Generals and the State in Brazil. *Political Geography Quarterly* S5 (4): S79–S90.

1986b. The Revival of Geopolitics. *Political Geography Quarterly* 5 (4): S21–S36.

1992. Metaphor, Geopolitical Discourse and the Military in South America. In *Writing Words: Discourse, Text and Metaphor in the Representation of Landscape*, edited by Trevor J. Barnes and James S. Duncan, 136–154. London and New York: Routledge.

Herb, Guntram, 2002. A Journey into the Thicket of German *Geopolitik*. *Geopolitics* 7 (3): 175–182.

Hirschman, Alfred, 1991. *The Rhetoric of Reaction: Perversity, Futility, Jeopardy.* Cambridge, MA: Belknap Press of Harvard University Press.

Hnízdo, Bořek, 1994. Základní geopolitické teorie. *Mezinárodní vztahy* 4: 72–79.

1995. *Mezinárodní perspektivy politických regionů.* Prague: Institut pro středoevropskou kulturu a politiku.

Hofstadter, Richard, 1944. *Social Darwinism in American Thought.* Boston: Beacon Press.

Holsti, K.J., 1970. National Role Conceptions in the Study of Foreign Policy. *International Studies Quarterly* 14 (3): 233–309.

1992. International Theory and War in the Third World. In *The Insecurity Dilemma: National Security of Third World States*, edited by Brian Job, 37–60. Boulder: Lynne Rienner.

Hopf, Ted, 2002. *Social Construction of International Politics: Identities and Foreign Policies, Moscow, 1955 and 1999.* Ithaca: Cornell University Press.

Hrabová, Libuše, 1999. Palacký a kontinuita dějin. In *František Palacký 1798/1998, dějiny a dnešek*, edited by František Šmahel and Eva Doležalová, 87–92. Prague: Historický ústav AV ČR.

Hülsse, Rainer, 2003. Sprache ist mehr als Argumentation: Zur wirklichkeitskonstruierenden Rolle von Metaphern. *Zeitschrift für Internationale Beziehungen* 10 (2): 211–246.

Hunter, James H., 1986. Commentary on 'The Social Origins of Environmental Determinism'. *Annals of the Association of American Geographers* 76 (2): 277–281.

Huntington, Samuel P., 1993a. The Clash of Civilizations? *Foreign Affairs* 72 (3): 22–49.

1993b. Why International Primacy Matters. In *The Cold War and After: Prospects for Peace*, expanded edn, edited by Sean M. Lynn-Jones and Stephen E. Miller, 307–322. Cambridge, MA: The MIT Press.

1996. *The Clash of Civilizations and the Remaking of the World Order*. New York: Simon & Schuster.

1999. *Tsivilisatsioonide kokkupõrge ja maailmakorra ümberkujundamine*, trans. Mart Trummal [The Clash of Civilizations and the Remaking of the World Order]. Tartu: Fontese Kirjastus.

2004. *Who Are We? The Challenges to America's National Identity*. New York: Simon & Schuster.

Huysmans, Jef, 1998. Security! What do you mean? From Concept to Thick Signifier. *European Journal of International Relations* 4 (2): 226–255.

Hvostov, Andrei, 1999. Soometumise saladus. *EPL*, 30 November. Available at: www.epl.ee (accessed 19 January 2000).

Ilari, Vigilo, 1996. *Inventarsi una patria: esiste l'identità nazionale?* Rome: Ideazione.

İlhan, Suat, 1971. *Jeopolitikten Taktiğe* [From Geopolitics to Tactics]. Ankara: Harp Akademileri Komutanlığı.

1986. Jeopolitik ve Tarih İlişkileri [The Relationship Between Geopolitics and History]. *Belleten* XLIX (195): 607–624.

1989. *Jeopolitik Duyarlılık* [Geopolitical Sensitivity]. Ankara: Türk Tarih Kurumu.

1997. *Türkiye'nin ve Türk Dünyasının Jeopolitiği* [The Geopolitics of Turkey and the Turkic World]. Ankara: Türk Kültürünü Araştırma Enstitüsü.

1999. *Dünya Yeniden Kuruluyor: Jeopolitik ve Jeokültür Tartışmaları* [World Born Anew: Geopolitics and Geoculture Debates]. İstanbul: Ötüken.

2000. *Avrupa Birliğine Neden Hayır: Jeopolitik Yaklaşım* [Why No to the European Union: Gepolitical Perspective]. İstanbul: Ötüken.

2002. *Avrupa Birliğine Neden Hayır-2* [Why No to the European Union-2]. İstanbul: Ötüken.

2004. *Türkiye'nin Zorlaşan Konumu: Uygarlıklar Savaşı-Küreselleşme-Petrol* [Turkey's Deteriorating Position: Civilisational Warfare-Globalisation-Oil]. İstanbul: Ötüken.

2005. *Türklerin Jeopolitiği ve Avrasyacılık* [The Geopolitics of the Turks and Eurasianism]. Ankara: Bilgi.

Ilves, Toomas Hendrik, 1996. Address to Riigikogu, 5 December. Tallinn: Estonian Ministry of Foreign Affairs. Available at: www.vm.ee/eng/pressreleases/speeches/1996/9612min.html (accessed 2 June 1999).

1997. Estonia, Sweden, and the Post-Post-Cold War Era. Remarks by Toomas Hendrik Ilves, Minister of Foreign Affairs of the Republic of Estonia, at the Institute of International Affairs, Stockholm, 9 January. Tallinn: Estonian Ministry of Foreign Affairs. Available at: www.vm.ee/eng/pressreleases/speeches/1997/970109ilv.htm (accessed 4 May 1999).

Inacker, Michael J., 1994. Macht und Moralität. Über eine neue deutsche Sicherheitspolitik. In *Die Selbstbewusste Nation*. '*Anschwellender Bocksgesang*' *und weitere Beiträge zu einer deutschen Debatte*, edited by Heimo Schwilk and Ulrich Schacht, 346–389. Berlin: Ullstein Verlag.

Incisa di Camerana, Ludovico, 1996. *La vittoria dell'Italia nella terza guerra mondiale*. Roma-Bari: Laterza.

Ingram, Alan, 2001. Alexander Dugin: Geopolitics and Neo-Fascism in Post-Soviet Russia. *Political Geography* 20 (8): 1029–1051.

Ish-Shalom, Piki. 2006. Theory as Hermeneutical Mechanism: The Democratic-Peace Thesis and the Politics of Democratization. *European Journal of International Relations* 12 (4): 565–598.

Işık, Hüseyin, 1987. Stratejik Konumu Nedeniyle Türkiye Kuvvetli Olmak Zorundadır [Turkey has to be Strong Due to its Strategic Position]. *Güncel Konular* 8: 37–52.

Ivashov, Leonid, 2002. *Rossiia ili Moskoviia? Geopoliticheskoe Izmerenie Natsional'noi Bezopasnosti Rossii* [Russia or Muscovy? The Geopolitical Dimension of Russia's National Security]. Moscow: EKSMO.

Jaanson, Kaido, 1998. EL ja Eesti rahvuslik identiteet. Prof. Kaido Jaansoni peaettekande teesid akadeemilisel nõukogul [EU and Estonian National Identity. Thesis of the Keynote Speech by Professor Kaido Jaanson at the President's Academic Council]. Tallinn, Estonia: Office of the President, 19 February.

2003. Eestlase identititeet 20. sajandil [The Identity of an Estonian in the 20th Century]. In *Mõtteline Euroopa: valik esseid Euroopa Liidust* [Imagined Estonia: A Selection of Essays on the European Union], edited by Marek Tamm and Märt Väljataga, 127–137. Tallinn: Kirjastus Varrak.

Jackson, Patrick Thaddeus, 2004. Hegel's House, or 'People are States too'. *Review of International Studies* 30 (2): 281–287.

Jean, Carlo, 1993. Geopolitica, *Enciclopedia delle Scienze Sociali*, vol. II. Rome: Istituto dell'Enciclopedia Italiana, 275–285.

1995. *Geopolitica*. Roma-Bari: Laterza.

1997. *Guerra, strategia e sicurezza*. Roma-Bari: Editori Laterza.

2000. *Geopolitica dell'Europa centro-orientale*. Levico Terme: CSSEO.

2003. *Manuale di geopolitica* (revised edition of *Geopolitica* [1995]). Roma-Bari: Laterza.

2004. *Geopolitica del XXI secolo*. Roma-Bari: Laterza.

Jean, Carlo and Tito Favaretto, eds., 2004. *Geopolitica dei Balcani orientali e centralità delle reti infrastrutturali*. Milan: Franco Angeli.

Jepperson, Ronald L., Alexander Wendt and Peter J. Katzenstein, 1996. Norms, Identity and Culture in National Security. In *The Culture of National Security*, edited by Peter J. Katzenstein, 33–75. New York: Columbia University Press.

Jervis, Robert, 1976. *Perception and Misperception in International Politics*. Princeton University Press.

1993. International Primacy: Is the Game Worth the Candle? In *The Cold War and After: Prospects for Peace*, expanded edn, edited by Sean M. Lynn-Jones and Stephen E. Miller, 291–306. Cambridge, MA: The MIT Press.

Joenniemi, Pertti, 1988. Models of Neutrality: the Traditional and the Modern. *Cooperation and Conflict* 23 (1): 53–67.

1993. Neutrality beyond the Cold War. *Review of International Studies* 19 (3): 289–304.

Joffe, Josef, 1993. Kettenrasseln für Deutschland. Wie sich Bayerns Wahlkämpfer Stoiber eine europäische Friedensgemeinschaft vorstellt. *Süddeutsche Zeitung*, 4 November. Available at: www.web.nexis-lexis.com. On file with author.

Johnson, James, 2002. How Conceptual Problems Migrate: Rational Choice, Interpretation, and the Hazards of Pluralism. *Annual Review of Political Science* 5: 223–248.

2006. Consequences of Positivism: A Pragmatist Assessment. *Comparative Political Studies* 39 (2): 224–252.

Johnston, Alastair Iain, 1995. Thinking about Strategic Culture. *International Security* 19 (4): 32–64.

Jones, Charles, 1998. *E.H. Carr and International Relations*. Cambridge University Press.

Jurado, Elena, 2003. Complying with European Standards of Minority Rights Education: Estonia's Relations with the European Union OSCE and Council of Europe. *Journal of Baltic Studies* 34 (3): 399–431.

Kacowicz, Arie M., 2000. Geopolitics and Territorial Issues: Relevance for South America. *Geopolitics* 5 (1): 81–100.

Kagan, Robert, 1998. The Benevolent Empire. *Foreign Policy* 111: 24–35.

Kaldre, Peeter, 2001. Milline kolmas tee? [What Third Way?]. *Postimees*, 15 February.

Kallas, Siim, 2002. Vaata raevus kaugemale [Look Farther in Anger]. *Eesti Päevaleht*, 30 October. Available at: www.epl.ee (accessed 13 November 2002).

2003a. Kelle poolt on Eesti? [Whom does Estonia Support?]. *Postimees*, 11 February. Available at: www.postmees.ee (accessed 16 March 2003).

2003b. Peame mõtlema 85 aastat ette! [We Must Think 85 Years in Advance!]. *Postimees*, 25 February. Available at: www.postimees.ee (accessed 16 March 2003).

Kallis, Aristotle, 2000. *Fascist Ideology: Territory and Expansionism in Italy and Germany, 1922–1945*. London: Routledge.

Kant, Edgar R.K., 1931. *Eesti geopoliitilisest ja geoökonoomilisest asendist, eriti Venemaa suhtes* [Estonia's Geopolitical and Geoeconomic Location, especially in Relation to Russia]. Tartu: Postimehe trükk.

1936/1937. Baltoskandia: eriti Eesti majandusgeograafia. *Loeng* [Baltoscandia: especially Estonian Economic Geography]. Tartu: K/V A. Aasa Koduülikooli kirjastus.

Kaplinski, J., 1998. Kultuur ja kuldpuur. *Sõnumileht*, 5 September. Available at: www. sl.ee (accessed 3 January 1999).

2003. Euroopa piir ja piirivalvurid. *Eesti Ekspress*, 2 October. Available at: www. ekspress.ee (accessed 19 December 2003).

Katus, Kalev, 1999. Rahvastiku areng [Population Development]. In *Eesti 21. sajandil: arengustrateegiad, visioonid, valikud*, edied by Ahto Oja, 42–46. Tallinn: Estonian Academy of Sciences Press.

Katzenstein, Peter J., 2010. 'Walls' between 'those People'? Contrasting Perspectives on World Politics. *Perspectives on Politics* 8 (1): 11–25.

Kelly, Philip L., 1984. Geopolitical Themes in the Writings of General Carlos de Meira Mattos of Brazil. *Journal of Latin American Studies* 16 (2): 439–461.

Kennan, George F., 1951 [1947]. The Sources of Soviet Conduct. In *American Diplomacy 1900–1950*, 107–128. University of Chicago Press.

1967. *Memoiren eines Diplomaten*. München: dtv.

Kiin, Sirje, 1999. Eesti-pildist maailmas [On Estonia's Image in the World]. *Eesti Ekspress*, 15 January.

King, Gary, Robert O. Keohane and Sidney Verba, 1994. *Designing Social Inquiry: Scientific Inference in Qualitative Research*. Princeton University Press.

Kirch, Marika, 1994. *Changing Identities in Estonia: Sociological Facts and Commentaries*. Tallinn: Estonian Science Foundation.

2003. Eesti Identiteet ja Euroopa liit [Estonian Identity and the European Union]. In *Mõtteline Euroopa: valik esseid Euroopa Liidust* [Imagined Estonia: A Selection of Essays on the European Union], edited by Marek Tamm and Märt Väljataga, 150–166. Tallinn: Kirjastus Varrak.

Kirste, Knud and Hanns W. Maull, 1996. Zivilmacht und Rollentheorie. *Zeitschrift für Internationale Beziehungen* 3 (2): 283–312.

Kissinger, Henry A., 1957. *A World Restored: The Politics of Conservatism in a Revolutionary Era*. London: Victor Gollancz Ltd.

1979. *The White House Years*. Boston: Little Brown.

1983. *The Years of Upheaval*. Boston: Little Brown.

1996. *L'arte della diplomazia*. Milan: Sperling & Kupfer.

Kjellén, Rudolf, 1924 [1916]. *Der Staat als Lebensform*, trans. J. Sandmeier (neue berechtigte Übertragung). Berlin-Grunewald: Kurt Vowinckel Verlag.

Klaus, Václav, 1992. Z projevu ministerského předsedy Václava Klause v Budči (26 September). *Československá zahraniční politika – dokumenty* 39 (9). Prague: Federal Ministry of Foreign Affairs, 832–833.

2000. *Masaryk a jeho obraz v dnešní české společnosti*. Speech at the conference T.G. Masaryk, idea demokracie a současné evropanství. Prague, 2 March.

Kliot, Nurit and Sam Waterman, eds., 1983. *Pluralism and Political Geography*. London: Croom Helm.

Knox, MacGregor, 2002. Fascism, Ideology, Foreign Policy and War. In *Liberal and Fascist Italy*, edited by Adrian Lyttelton. Oxford University Press.

Knudsen, Olav, ed., 1999. *Stability and Security in the Baltic Sea Region. Russian, Nordic and European Aspects*. London and Portland: Frank Cass.

Kogan, Norman, 1963. *La politica estera italiana*. Milan: Lerici.

Kolstø, Pål, ed., 2002. *National Integration and Violent Conflict in post-Soviet Societies*. Lanham: Rowman & Littlefield.

Kömürcü, Güler, 2003. Bu İsme Dikkat; Ahmet Davutoğlu [Watch out for this Name: Ahmet Davutoğlu]. *Akşam*, 29 August.

Korčák, Jaromír, 1938. *Geopolitické základy Československa: Jeho kmenové oblasti*. Prague: Orbis.

Koslowski, Roy and Friedrich Kratochwil, 1994. Understanding Change in International Politics: The Soviet Empire's Demise and the International System. *International Organization* 48 (2): 215–247.

Kozyrev, Andrei, 1992. A Transformed Russia in a New World. *International Affairs (Moscow)* 38 (1992): 85–91.

Kramer, Mark, 1999. Ideology and the Cold War. *Review of International Studies* 25 (4): 539–576.

   2001. Realism, Ideology, and the End of the Cold War. *Review of International Studies* 27 (1): 119–130.

Krasner, Stephen D., 2000. Wars, Hotel Fires, and Plane Crashes. *Review of International Studies* 26: 131–136.

Kratochwil, Friedrich, 1993. The Embarassment of Changes: Neo-Realism and the Science of Realpolitik without Politics. *Review of International Studies* 19 (1): 63–80.

Kratochwil, Friedrich and John Gerard Ruggie, 1986. International Organization: A State of the Art on an Art of the State. *International Organization* 40 (4): 753–775.

Krauthammer, Charles, 1991. The Unipolar Moment. *Foreign Affairs* 70 (1): 23–33.

   2002–2003. The Unipolar Moment Revisited. *The National Interest* 70: 5–17.

Krejčí, Oskar, 1993. *Český národní zájem a geopolitika*. Prague: Universe.

Kruzel, Joseph and Michael H. Haltzel, eds., 1989. *Between the Blocs: Problems and Prospects for Europe's Neutral and non-Aligned States*. Cambridge University Press.

Kundera, Milan, 1983. Un occident kidnappé, ou la tragédie de l'Europe Centrale. *Le Débat* (n. 27): 2–24.

   1984. The Tragedy of Central Europe. *The New York Review of Books*, 26 April: 33–38.

Kuran, Timur, 1998. Social Mechanisms of Dissonance Reduction. In *Social Mechanisms: An Analytical Approach to Social Theory*, edited by Peter Hedström and Richard Swedberg, 147–171. Cambridge University Press.

Kurki, Milja, 2008. *Causation in International Relations: Reclaiming Causal Analysis*. Cambridge University Press.

Kuus, Merje, 2002. Toward Cooperative Security? International Integration and the Construction of Security in Estonia. *Millennium: Journal of International Studies* 31 (2): 297–317.

2007. *Geopolitics Reframed: Security and Identity in Europe's Eastern Enlargement.* New York: Palgrave Macmillan.

2009. Cosmopolitan Militarism? Spaces of NATO Expansion. *Environment and Planning A* 41: 545–562.

2010. EUrope and the Baroque. *Environment and Planning D: Society and Space* 28 (3): 381–387.

2011. Policy and Geopolitics: Bounding Europe in EUrope. *Annals of the Association of American Geographers* 101 (5): 1140–1155.

Lacoste, Yves, 1978. *La géographie, ça sert d'abord à faire la guerre.* Paris: Maspéro.

1993. Préambule. In *Dictionnaire de géopolitique*, edited by Yves Lacoste, 1–35. Paris: Flammarion.

Laffey, Mark and Jutta Weldes, 1997. Beyond Belief: From Ideas to Symbolic Technologies in the Study of International Relations. *European Journal of International Relations* 3 (2): 193–237.

Lagerspetz, Mikko, 1999. Postsocialism as a Return: Notes on a Discursive Strategy. *East European Politics and Societies* 13 (2): 377–390.

Laitin, David, 1996. National Revival and Competitive Assimilation in Estonia. *Post-Soviet Affairs* 12: 25–39.

Larson, Deborah Welch, 1985. *The Origins of Containment: A Psychological Explanation.* Princeton Univesity Press.

Laruelle, Marlène, 2008. *Russian Eurasianism: An Ideology of an Empire*, trans. Mischa Gabowitsch. Washington, DC: Woodrow Wilson Center Press.

Lauristin, Marju, 1997. Contexts of Transition. In *Return to the Western World: Cultural and Political Perspectives on the Estonian Post-Communist Transition*, edited by Marju Lauristin, Peeter Vihalemm, Karl Erik Rosengren and Lennart Weibull, 25–40. Tartu University Press.

Lauristin, Marju and Mart Heidmets, eds., 2002. *The Challenge of the Russian Minority. Emerging Multicultural Democracy in Estonia.* Tartu University Press.

Lauristin, Marju, Peeter Vihalemm, Karl Erik Rosengren and Lennart Weibull, eds., 1997. *Return to the Western World: Cultural and Political Perspectives on the Estonian Post-Communist Transition.* Tartu University Press.

Leander, Anna, 2001. The Globalisation Debate: Dead-Ends and Tensions to Explore. *Journal of International Relations and Development* 4 (3): 274–285.

2005. The Power to Construct International Security: On the Significance of Private Military Companies. *Millennium: Journal of International Studies* 33 (3): 803–826.

2008. Thinking Tools. In *Qualitative Methods in International Relations: A Pluralist Guide*, edited by Audie Klotz and Deepa Prakash, 11–27. Houndmills: Palgrave Macmillan.

2010. The Paradoxical Impunity of Private Military Companies: Authority and the Limits to Legal Accountability. *Security Dialogue* 41 (5): 467–490.

2011. The Promises, Problems, and Potentials of a Bourdieu-inspired Staging of International Relations. *International Political Sociology* 5 (3): 294–313.

Lebow, Richard Ned, 1994. The Long Peace, the End of the Cold War, and the Failure of Realism. *International Organization* 48 (2): 249–77.

2003. *The Tragic Vision of Politics: Ethics, Interests and Orders.* Cambridge University Press.

2008. *A Cultural Theory of International Relations.* Cambridge University Press.

2010. *Forbidden Fruit: Counterfactuals and International Relations.* Princeton University Press.

Lebow, Richard Ned and Thomas Risse-Kappen, eds., 1995. *International Relations Theory and the End of the Cold War.* New York: Columbia University Press.

Lebow, Richard Ned and Janice Gross Stein, 1994. *We All Lost the Cold War.* Princeton University Press.

Le Prestre, Philip G., ed., 1997. *Role Quests in the Post-Cold War Era: Foreign Policies in Transition.* Montreal: McGill-Queen's University Press.

Lévesque, Jacques, 1995. *1989: la fin d'un Empire, l'URSS et la libération de l'Europe de l'Est.* Paris: Presses de Sciences Po.

Lieven, Anatol, 1993. *The Baltic Revolution: Estonia, Latvia and Lithuania and the Path to Independence,* rev. edn. New Haven: Yale University Press.

Light, Margot, 1988. *The Soviet Theory of International Relations.* Brighton: Harvester Wheatsheaf.

Lindemann, Thomas, 2000. *Die Macht der Perzeptionen und die Perzeption von Mächten.* Berlin: Duncker & Humblot.

Lise Milli Güvenlik Bilgisi, 2004. [National Security Knowledge for High School Students], 7th edn. İstanbul: Devlet Kitapları.

Lorot, Pascal, 1997. *Storia della geopolitica.* Trieste: Asterios Editore.

Lowe, C. J. and Frank Marzari, 1975. *Italian Foreign Policy, 1870–1940.* London: Routledge and Kegan Paul.

Lowenthal, Abraham F., 2003. Geopolitical Realities and US Foreign Policy: Comments on a Paper by Professor Saul B. Cohen. *Political Geography* 22 (1): 35–38.

Lucarelli, Sonia and Roberto Menotti, 2002a. Le relazioni internazionali nella terra del 'Principe'. *Rivista Italiana di scienza Politica* 1: 31–82.

eds. 2002b. *Studi internazionali: i luoghi del sapere in Italia.* Rome: Edizioni Associate.

2002c. No-constructivists' Land: International Relations in Italy in the 1990s. *Journal of International Relations and Development* 5 (2): 114–142.

Luik, Jüri, 1995. Remarks by Mr Jüri Luik, Minister of Foreign Affairs of the Republic of Estonia, at the Final Conference for a Pact of Stability in Europe. 20 March, Paris. Tallinn: Ministry of Foreign Affairs. Available at: www.vm.ee/eng/pressreleases/speeches/1995/9503221sp.html (accessed 5 May 1999).

Luik, Viivi, Elmo Nüganen, Jüri Arrak, Jüri Englebrecht, Hirvo Surva and Andrus Kivirähk, 2003. Eestlaseks jääda saab vaid eurooplasena [Only as Europeans can we remain Estonians]. *Postimees,* 8 August.

Luke, Timothy W., 1991. The Discipline of Security Studies and the Codes of Containment: Learning From Kuwait. *Alternatives* 16: 315–344.

Luttwak, Edward, 1990. From Geopolitics to Geoeconomics: Logic of Conflict, Grammar of Commerce. *The National Interest* 20 (Summer): 17–23.

2001. *Strategia: la logica della guerra e della pace*, 2nd rev. edn. Milan: Rizzoli.

Lynch, Allen, 1989 [1987]. *The Soviet Study of International Relations*. Cambridge, MA: Cambridge University Press.

Mackinder, Halford John, 1904. The Geographical Pivot of History. *The Geographical Journal* 23 (4): 421–437.

1944 [1919]. *Democratic Ideals and Reality: A Study in the Politics of Reconstitution*. Harmondsworth: Penguin.

Mahoney, James, 2001. Beyond Correlational Analysis: Recent Innovations in Theory and Method. *Sociological Forum* 16 (3): 575–593.

Malcolm, Neil, Alex Pravda, Roy Allison and Margot Light, 1996. *Internal Factors in Russian Foreign Policy*. Oxford University Press.

Mälksoo, Maria, 2010. *The Politics of Becoming European: A Study of Polish and Baltic post-Cold War Security Imaginaries*. London, New York: Routledge.

Malmborg, Mikael af, 2001. *Neutrality and State-Building in Sweden*. Houndmills: Palgrave.

Mamadouh, Virginie and Gertjan Dijkink, 2006. Geopolitics, International Relations and Political Geography: Geopolitical Discourse. *Geopolitics* 11 (3): 349–366.

Manners, Ian, 2002. Normative Power Europe: a Contradiction in Terms? *Journal of Common Market Studies* 40 (2): 235–258.

Mannheim, Karl, 1936. *Ideology and Utopia*. New York: Harvest Books.

Masaryk, Tomáš G., 1925. *Světová revoluce*. Prague: Orbis.

Maull, Hanns W., 1990/1991. Germany and Japan: The New Civilian Powers. *Foreign Affairs* 69 (5): 91–106.

Mayntz, Renate, 2004. Mechanisms in the Analysis of Social Macro-Phenomena. *Philosophy of the Social Sciences* 34 (2): 237–259.

Mazzei, Franco, 2000. Invarianti e proiezioni geopolitiche della Cina. In *Conoscere la Cina*, edited by Lionello Lanciotti. Turin: Fondazione Giovanni Agnelli.

McAdam, Doug, Sidney Tarrow and Charles Tilly, 2008. Methods for Measuring Mechanisms of Contention. *Qualitative Sociology* 31 (4): 307–331.

McColl, Robert W., 1983. A Geographical Model for International Behaviour. In *Pluralism and Political Geography*, edited by Nurit Kliot and Sam Waterman, 284–294. London: Croom Helm.

MccGwire, Michael, 1991. *Perestroika and Soviet National Security*. Washington, DC: The Brookings Institution.

Mearsheimer, John, 1990. Back to the Future: Instability in Europe after the Cold War. *International Security* 15 (1): 5–56.

2001. *The Tragedy of Great Power Politics*. New York: W.W. Norton.

2003. *La logica di potenza: l'America, le guerre, il controllo del mondo*. Milan: Università Bocconi.

Meinecke, Friedrich, 1916. Einführung. In *Die großen Mächte*, by Leopold von Ranke, 3–10. Leipzig: Insel Verlag.

Mercer, Jonathan, 1995. Anarchy and Identity. *International Organization* 49 (2): 229–252.

2005. Rationality and Psychology in International Politics. *International Organization* 59 (1): 77–106.

2010. Emotional Beliefs. *International Organization* 64 (1): 1–31.

Merle, Marcel, 1982. *Sociologie des relations internationales*, 3rd edn. Paris: Dalloz.

Merseburger, Peter, 2002. *Willy Brandt. 1913–1992. Visionär und Realist*. Stuttgart and Munich: DVA.

Milliken, Jennifer, 1996. Metaphors of Prestige and Reputation in American Foreign Policy and American Realism. In *Post-Realism: The Rhetorical Turn in International Relations*, edited by Francis A. Beer and Robert Hariman, 217–238. East Lansing: Michigan State University Press.

1999. The Study of Discourse in International Relations: A Critique of Research and Methods. *European Journal of International Relations* 5 (2): 225–254.

Milner, Helen, 1991. The Assumption of Anarchy in International Relations Theory: A Critique. *Review of International Studies* 17 (1): 67–85.

Ministry of Defence of the Republic of Turkey, 2000. *White Paper*. Available at: www.msb.gov.tr (accessed 9 June 2005).

Mitrofanov, Alexei, 1997. *Shagi Novoi Geopolitiki* [The Advance of New Geopolitics]. Moscow: Russkii Vestnik.

Mitu, Sorin, 1998. Illusions and Facts about Transylvania. *The Hungarian Quarterly* 39 (152): 64–74.

Mitzen, Jennifer, 2006. Ontological Security in World Politics: State Identity and the Security Dilemma. *European Journal of International Relations* 12 (3): 341–370.

Molnár, Gusztáv, 1997. The Geopolitics of NATO-Enlargement. *The Hungarian Quarterly* 38 (146): 3–16.

1998. The Transylvanian Question. *The Hungarian Quarterly* 39 (149): 49–62.

Moore, Barrington Jr., 1987 [1966]. *Social Origins of Dictatorship and Democracy: Lord and Peasant in the Making of the Modern World*. Harmondsworth: Penguin.

Moravec, Emmanuel, 1939/2004. *V úloze mouřenína*. Pardubice: Filip Trend Publishing.

Moreau Defarges, Philippe, 1996. *Introduzione alla geopolitica*. Bologna: Il Mulino.

Morgenthau, Hans J., 1946. *Scientific Man vs. Power Politics*. University of Chicago Press.

1948. *Politics Among Nations: The Struggle for Power and Peace*. New York: Knopf.

Morozov, Viatcheslav, 2009a. Obsessed with Identity: IR in Post-Soviet Russia. *Journal of International Relations and Development* 12 (2): 200–205.

2009b. *Rossija i Drugie: Identichnost' i Granitsy Politicheskogo Soobschestva* [Russia and Its Others: Identity and the Boundaries of Political Community]. Moscow: Novoe Literaturnoe Obozrenie.

Morozova, Natalia, 2009. Geopolitics, Eurasianism and Russian Foreign Policy under Putin. *Geopolitics* 14 (2009): 667–686.

Moscati, Ruggero, 1963. Gli esordi della politica estera fascista, il periodo Contarini, Corfù. In *La politica estera italiana dal 1914 al 1943*, edited by Augusto Torre. Torino: Eri, Edizioni Rai Radiotelevisione italiana.

Murphy, Alexander B. and Corey M. Johnson, 2004. German Geopolitics in Transition. *Eurasian Geography and Economics* 45 (1): 1–17.

Murphy, Alexander B., Mark Bassin, David Newman, Paul Reuber and John Agnew, 2004. Forum: Is there a Politics to Geopolitics? *Progress in Human Geography* 28 (5): 619–640.

Mussolini, Benito, 1934. *Scritti e Discorsi di Benito Mussolini*. Milan: Ulrico Hoepli Editore.

Mutt, Mihkel, 2002. Repliik: kaks rumalat põrsakest väntavad filme. *Sirp*, 15 November.

Nartov, Nikolai, 2003. *Geopolitika* [Geopolitics]. Moscow: Unity.

Nau, Henry R., 2002. *At Home Abroad: Identity and Power in American Foreign Policy*. Ithaca: Cornell University Press.

Neivelt, Indrek, 2002. Unustatud Venemaa [Forgotten Russia]. *EPL*, 6 November. Available at: www.epl.ee/artikkel.php?ID=219467&P=1 (accessed 13 November 2002).

Nejedlý, Zdeněk, 1951. *Velké osobnosti*. Prague: Mladá fronta.

Neumann, Iver B., 1995. *Russia and the Idea of Europe: A Study in Identity and International Relations*. London and New York: Routledge.

1999. *Uses of the Other: The 'East' in European Identity Formation*. Minneapolis: University of Minnesota Press.

2004. Beware of Organicism: The Narrative Self of the State. *Review of International Studies* 30 (2): 259–267.

2008. Russia as a Great Power, 1815–2007. *Journal of International Relations and Development* 11 (2): 128–151.

Noreen, Erik, 2002. Verbal Politics of Estonian Policy-Makers: Reframing Security and Identity. In *Threat Politics: New Perspectives on Security, Risk and Crisis Management*, edited by Johan Eriksson, 84–99. Aldershot: Ashgate.

Nutt, Mart, 1999. Tsivilisatsioonide kokkupõrge? [The Clash of Civilizations?]. *Eesti Päevaleht*, 4 August. Available at: www.epl.ee (accessed 14 January 2000).

Ó Tuathail, Gearóid, 1996. *Critical Geopolitics: The Politics of Writing Global Space*. London: Routledge.

1998. Thinking Critically About Geopolitics. In *The Geopolitics Reader*, edited by Gearóid Ó Tuathail, Simon Dalby and Paul Routledge, 1–14. London and New York: Routledge.

2002. Theorizing Geopolitical Reasoning: The Case of the United States' Response to the War in Bosnia. *Political Geography* 21: 601–628.

2004. Geopolitical Structures and Cultures: Towards Conceptual Clarity in the Critical Study of Geopolitics. In *Geopolitics: Global Problems and Regional Concerns*, edited by Lasha Tchantouridze, 75–102. Bison Paper #4, Centre for Defence and Security Studies, Winnipeg, Manitoba: The Centre for Defence and Security Studies, University of Manitoba.

Ó Tuathail, Gearóid and John Agnew, 1992. Geopolitics and Discourse: Practical Geopolitical Reasoning in American Foreign Policy. *Political Geography* 11 (2): 190–204.

1992/1998. Geopolitics and Discourse: Practical Geopolitical Reasoning in American Foreign Policy. In *The Geopolitics Reader*, edited by Gearóid Ó Tuathail, Simon Dalby and Paul Routledge, 78–91. London and New York: Routledge.

Ó Tuathail, Gearóid and Simon Dalby, 1998. Introduction: Rethinking Geopolitics: Towards a Critical Geopolitics. In *Rethinking Geopolitics*, edited by Gearóid Ó Tuathail and Simon Dalby, 1–15. London and New York: Routledge.

Oja, Ahto, ed., 1999. *Eesti 21. sajandil: arengustrateegiad, visioonid, valikud.* Tallinn: Estonian Academy of Sciences Press.

Olcaytu, Turhan, 1996. Türkiye'nin Jeostratejisi [Turkey's Geostrategy]. *Atatürkçü Düşünce* 3 (25): 8–9.

O'Loughlin, John, 2001. Geopolitical Fantasies, National Strategies and Ordinary Russians in the Post-Communist Era. *Geopolitics* 6 (3): 17–48.

Öngör, Sami, 1963. Siyasi Coğrafya ve Jeopolitik [Political Geography and Geopolitics]. *Siyasal Bilgiler Fakültesi Dergisi* 18: 301–316.

Oolo, Antti, 2000. Venemaa-hirm tuleneb ajaloost [Fear of Russia Comes from the History]. *Eesti Päevaleht*, 20 March.

Opat, Jaroslav, 1999. TGM – pokračovatel v Palackého díle politickém. In *František Palacký 1798/1998, dějiny a dnešek*, edited by František Šmahel and Eva Doležalová, 349–360. Prague: Historický ústav AV ČR.

Opp, Karl-Dieter, 2005. Explanations by Mechanisms in the Social Sciences: Problems, Advantages, and Alternatives. *Mind & Society* 4 (2): 163–178.

Oran, Baskın, 2005. *Türk Dış Politikası: Kurtuluş Savaşından Bugüne Olgular, Belgeler, Yorumlar, Cilt I-II* [Turkish Foreign Policy: Phenomena, Documents and Commentray from the War of Independence to Contemporary Era], vols. I–II. Ankara: İletişim.

Orbie, Jan, 2006. Civilian Power Europe: Review of the Original and Current Debates. *Cooperation and Conflict* 41 (1): 123–128.

Osmanağaoğlu, Behçet, 1968. *Geopolitik: Devlet İdaresinde, Dış Siyasette Coğrafyanın Rolü* [Geopolitics: The Role of Geography in Statecraft and Foreign Policy]. İstanbul: İstanbul Ticaret Odası.

Østerud, Øyvind, 1988. The Uses and Abuses of Geopolitics. *Journal of Peace Research* 25 (2): 191–199.

Özdağ, Muzaffer, 2000. *Türk Dünyası ve Doğu Türkistan Jeopolitiği Üzerine* [On the Geopolitics of the Turkic World and Eastern Turkestan]. İstanbul: Doğu Türkistan Vakfı Yayınları.

——— 2001. *Türkiye ve Türk Dünyası Jeopolitiği Üzerine* [On the Geopolitics of Turkey and the Turkic World]. Ankara: ASAM.

——— 2003. *Türk Dünyası Jeopolitiği, Cilt I-IV* [The Geopolitics of the Turkic World, vols. I–IV]. Ankara: ASAM.

Özdağ, Ümit, 2003. *Türk Tarihinin ve Geleceğinin Jeopolitik Çerçevesi* [The Geopolitical Framework of Turkish History and Future]. Ankara: ASAM.

Pagnini, Maria Paola, 1987. La geografia politica. In *Aspetti e problemi dell geografia*, vol. 1, edited by G. Corna Pellegrini, 409–442. Milan: Marzorati Editore.

Palacký, František, 1907. *Dějiny národa českého v Čechách a v Moravě* [History of the Czech Nation in Bohemia and Moravia]. Prague: B. Kočího.

Palacký, Franz, 1868. Die Geschichte des Hussitenthums und Prof. Constantin Höfler. Kritische Studien. Prague: Verlag von Friedrich Tempsky.

Parker, Geoffrey, 1985. *Western Geopolitical Thought in the Twentieth Century.* London and Sydney: Croom Helm.

Patman, Robert, 1999. Reagan, Gorbachev and the Emergence of 'New Political Thinking'. *Review of International Studies* 25 (4): 577–601.

Patočka, Jan, 1991. *Tři studie o Masarykovi.* Prague: Mladá fronta.

Patomäki, Heikki, 1996. How to Tell Better Stories about World Politics. *European Journal of International Relations* 2 (1): 105–133.

Pavlovsky, Gleb, 2010. Konsensus Ischet Stolitsu [Consensus in Search of a Capital]. *Russkii Zhurnal*, 26 March.

Pernik, Piret, 2000. Eesti identiteet välispoliitilises diskursuses 1990–1999 [Estonian Identity in the Foreign Policy Discourse 1990–1999]. *Bakalaureusetöö.* Tallinn: Eesti Humanitaarinstituut.

Petrignani, Rinaldo, 1987. *Neutralità e alleanza: le scelte di politica estera dell'Italia dopo l'Unità.* Bologna: Il Mulino.

Petrova, Margarita H., 2003. The End of the Cold War: A Battle or Bridging Ground between Rationalist and Ideational Approaches to International Relations? *European Journal of International Relations* 9 (1): 115–163.

Pierson, Paul, 2000a. Increasing Returns, Path Dependence, and the Study of Politics. *American Political Science Review* 94 (2): 251–267.

——— 2000b. Not just what, but when: Timing and Sequence in Political Processes. *Studies in American Political Development* 14 (Spring): 72–92.

Pizzorno, Alessandro, 2007. *Il velo della diversità. Studi su razionalità e riconoscimento.* Milan: Feltrinelli.

——— 2008. Rationality and Recognition. In *Approaches and Methodologies in the Social Sciences: A Pluralist Perspective*, edited by Donatella della Porta and Michael Keating, 162–173. Cambridge University Press.

Polanski, David, 2005. *L'impero che non c'è. Geopolitica degli Statu Uniti d'America.* Milan: Guerini e Associati.

Portinaro, Pier Paolo, 1999. *Il realismo politico.* Roma-Bari: Editori Laterza.

Prozorov, Sergei, 2010. *The Ethics of Postcommunism: History and Social Praxis in Russia.* Basingstoke: Palgrave Macmillan.

Putnam, Robert D., 1988. Diplomacy and Domestic Politics: The Logic of Two-level Games. *International Organization* 42 (3): 427–460.

Ragin, Charles C., 1987. *The Comparative Method: Moving Beyond Qualitative and Quantitative Strategies.* Berkeley: University of California Press.

Ranke, Leopold von, 1916 [1833]. *Die großen Mächte.* Leipzig: Insel Verlag.

Ratzel, Friedrich, 1882. *Anthropo-Geographie oder Grundzüge der Anwendung der Erdkunde auf die Geschichte.* Stuttgart: Verlag von J. Engelhorn.

1896. Der Staat als Organismus. *Die Grenzboten* 55: 614–623.

1897. *Politische Geographie.* Munich and Leipzig: Oldenbourg.

1940. *Erdenmacht und Völkerschicksal. Eine Auswahl aus seinen Werken,* edited and introduced by Karl Haushofer. Stuttgart: Alfred Kröner Verlag.

Raudsepp, Maari, 1998. Rahvusküsimus ajakirjanduse peeglis. In *Relations Between Turkey and the European Union,* edited by Heidmets: 113–134. Available at: www.mfa.gov.tr/grupa/ad/adab/relations.html (accessed 26 March 2001).

Reboratti, Carlos E., 1983. El encanto de la oscuridad: notas acerca de la geopolitica en la Argentina. *Desarrollo Económico* 23 (89): 137–144.

Reuber, Paul and Günter Wolkersdorfer, 2002. The Transformation of Europe and the German Contribution – Critical Geopolitics and Geopolitical Representations. *Geopolitics* 7 (1): 39–60.

2003. Macht, Politik und Raum. Available at: www.politische-geographie.de/ Docs/PolGeoForschungsjournal.pdf (accessed 1 December 2011)

Rhodes, Edward, 2003. The Imperial Logic of Bush's Liberal Agenda. *Survival* 45 (1): 131–154.

Ringmar, Erik, 1996. *Identity, Interest and Action: A Cultural Explanation of Sweden's Intervention in the Thirty Years War.* Cambridge University Press.

Risse-Kappen, Thomas, 1991. Did 'Peace Through Strength' End the Cold War? Lessons from INF. *International Security* 16 (1): 162–188.

1994. Ideas do not Float Freely: Transnational Coalitions, Domestic Structures, and the End of the Cold War. *International Organization* 48 (2): 185–214.

2004. Kontinuität durch Wandel: Eine 'neue' deutsche Außenpolitik? *Aus Politik und Zeitgeschichte* B11, 8 March: 24–31.

Risse, Thomas, Stephen C. Ropp and Kathryn Sikkink, eds., 1999. *The Power of Human Rights: International Norms and Domestic Change.* Cambridge University Press.

Rochau, Ludwig August von, 1972 [1853/1869]. *Grundsätze der Realpolitik (angewendet auf die staatlichen Zustände Deutschlands).* Frankfurt/M.: Ullstein Verlag.

Roletto, Giorgio and Ernesto Massi, 1938. Per una Geopolitica Italiana, *Geopolitica* 1 (1): 5–11.

Romano, Sergio, 1996. Rinegoziamo le basi americane. *Limes: rivista italiana di geopolitica* 4 (1996): 249–253.

Rose, Gideon, 1998. Neoclassical Realism and Theories of Foreign Policy. *World Politics* 51 (1): 144–172.

Routledge, Paul, 1998. Anti-Geopolitics: Introduction. In *The Geopolitics Reader*, edited by Gearóid Ó Tuathail, Simon Dalby and Paul Routledge, 245–255. London and New York: Routledge.

Rumelili, Bahar, 2003. Liminality and the Perpetuation of Conflicts: Turkish-Greek Relations in the Context of the Community-Building by the EU. *European Journal of International Relations* 9 (2): 213–248.

——— 2004. Constructing Identity and Relating to Difference: Understanding EU's Mode of Differentiation. *Review of International Studies* 30 (1): 27–47.

Rumi, Giorgio, 1968. *Alle origini della politica estera fascista*. Bari: Laterza.

Ruutsoo, R., 1995. Introduction: Estonia on the Border of Two Civilizations. *Nationalities Papers*, 23 (1): 13–15.

——— 2002. Discursive Conflict and Estonian Post-Communist Nation-Building. In *The Challenge of the Russian Minority. Emerging Multicultural Democracy in Estonia*, edited by Marju Lauristin and Mart Heidmets, 31–54. Tartu University Press.

Saar, Jüri, 1998. Tsivilisatsioonide kokkupõrke teooria retseptsioonist Eestis. *Akadeemia* 10 (7): 1512–1518.

Said, Edward, 1979. *Orientalism*. New York: Vintage Books.

Salvatorelli, Luigi, 1923. *Nazionalfascismo*. Turin: Gobetti.

Sander, Oral, 1982. Türk Dış Politikasında Sürekliliğin Nedenleri [The Causes of Continuity in Turkish Foreign Policy]. *Siyasal Bilgiler Fakültesi Dergisi* XXXVII (3–4): 105–124.

Santis-Arenas, Hernán, 2001. Ratzel's Thought in Chilean Geopolitics. In *On the Centenary of Ratzel's Political Geography. Europe between Political Geography and Geopolitics*, edited by Marco Antonsich, Vladimir Kolossov and M. Paola Pagnini, 183–191. Rome: Società Geografica Italiana

Santoro, Carlo Maria, 1991. *La politica estera di una media potenza: l'Italia dall'Unità ad oggi*. Bologna: Il Mulino.

——— 1995. La geopolitica del Mediterraneo. *Affari Esteri* 109 (1995): 108–120.

——— 1996a. Relazioni Internazionali. *Enciclopedia delle Scienze Sociali* 7. Rome: Istituto dell'Enciclopedia Italiana, 342–355.

——— 1996b. L'ambiguità di Limes e la vera geopolitica: elogio della teoria. *Limes: rivista italiana di geopolitica* 4: 307–313

——— 1997. *Studi di geopolitica, 1992–1994*. Turin: UTET.

——— 1998. *Occidente: geoteoria dell'Europa*. Milan: Franco Angeli.

Sassoon, Daniel, 1978. The Making of Italian Foreign Policy. In *Foreign Policy-Making in Western Europe: A Comparative Approach*, edited by William Wallace and William E. Paterson. Hants: Saxon House.

Schäuble, Wolfgang and Karl Lamers, 1994. Überlegungen zur europäischen Politik. Available at: www.wolfgang-schaeuble.de/positionspapiere/schaeublelamers94.pdf.

Schimmelfennig, Frank and Uli Sedelmeier, eds., 2005. *The Europeanization of Central and Eastern Europe*. Ithaca: Cornell University Press.

Schlögel, Karl, 1993. Deutschland: Land der Mitte, Land ohne Mitte. In *Westbindung: Chancen und Risiken für Deutschland*, edited by Rainer Zitelmann, Karlheinz Weißmann and Michael Großheim, 441–458. Frankfurt/M.: Propyläen Verlag.

Schmierer, Joscha, 1996. *Mein Name sei Europa. Einigung ohne Mythos und Utopie*. Frankfurt/M.: Fischer Taschenbuch Verlag.

Schmitt, Carl, 2003. *The Nomos of the Earth in the International Law of Jus Publicum Europaeum*, trans. G. L. Ulmen. New York: Telos Press.

Schöllgen, Gregor, 1992. *Die Macht in der Mitte Europas*. Munich: Verlag C. H. Beck.

——— 1993. *Angst vor der Macht. Die Deutschen und ihre Außenpolitik*. Frankfurt am Main and Berlin: Ullstein.

Schröder, Gerhard, 1998. 'Weil wir Deutschlands Kraft vertrauen'. Regierungserklärung des Bundeskanzlers am 10. November 1998 vor dem Deutschen Bundestag in Berlin. Available at: www.mediacultureonline.de/fileadmin/bibliothek/schroeder_RE_1998/schroeder_RE_1998.pdf (accessed 1 December 2011).

——— 1999. Eine Außenpolitik des 'Dritten Weges?'. *Gewerkschaftliche Monatshefte* 50: 392–396.

——— 2001. Regierungserklärung des Bundeskanzlers Gerhard Schröder zur Aktuellen Lage nach Beginn der Operation gegen den internationalen Terrorismus. Available at: www.documentarchive.de/brd/2001/rede_schroeder__1011. html (accessed 3 November 2008).

——— 2002a. Rede von Bundeskanzler Schröder beim Weltwirtschaftsforum 2002 in New York. Available at: http://usa.embassy.de/gemeinsam/schroeder020102. htm (accessed 3 November 2008).

——— 2002b. Rede von Bundeskanzler Gerhard Schröder zum Wahlauftakt am Montag, 5. August 2002, in Hannover (Opernplatz). Available at: http://powi.uni-jena.de/wahlkampf2002/dokumente/SPD_Schroeder_Rede_WahlkampfauftaktHannover.pdf (accessed 1 December 2011).

Schumpeter, Joseph A., 1975 [1942]. *Capitalism, Socialism, and Democracy*. New York: Harper.

Schürmann, Reiner, 1979. The Ontological Difference and Political Philosophy. *Philosophy and Phenomenological Research* 40 (1979): 99–122.

Schwarz, Hans-Peter, 1994. *Die Zentralmacht Europas. Deutschlands Rückkehr auf die Weltbühne*. Berlin: Siedler Verlag.

Schwilk, Heimo and Ulrich Schacht, eds., 1994. *Die Selbstbewusste Nation. 'Anschwellender Bocksgesang' und weitere Beiträge zu einer deutschen Debatte*. Berlin: Ullstein Verlag.

Semjonov, Jurij N., 1951. *Fašistická geopolitika ve službách amerického imperialismu*. Prague: Naše vojsko. (Russian original: 'Fashistskaja geopolitika na sluzhbe amerikanskogo imperializma'. Moscow: Gospolitizdat, 1949.)

Senghaas, Dieter, 1992. *Friedensprojekt Europa*. Frankfurt/M.: Suhrkamp Verlag.

Sergounin, Alexander A., 2000. Russian Post-Communist Foreign Policy Thinking at the Cross-Roads: Changing Paradigms. *Journal of International Relations and Development* 3 (3): 216–255.

Serra, Enrico, 1984. *La diplomazia in Italia*. Milan: FrancoAngeli.

1999. *Professione: ambasciatore d'Italia*. Milan: FrancoAngeli.

Sezgin, Emin and Selahattin Yılmaz, 1965. *Jeopolitik* [Geopolitics]. Ankara: Harp Akademileri Yayınları.

Sidaway, James Derrick, 2000. Iberian Geopolitics. In *Geopolitical Traditions: A Century of Geopolitical Thought*, edited by Klaus Dodds and David Atkinson, 118–149. London and New York: Routledge.

Sidaway, James Derrick *et al.*, 2004. Translating Political Geographies. *Political Geography* 23 (8): 1037–1049.

Sil, Rudra and Peter J. Katzenstein, 2010. Analytic Eclecticism in the Study of World Politics: Reconfiguring Problems and Mechanisms across Research Traditions. *Perspectives on Politics* 8 (2): 411–431.

Simpson, Gerry J., 2004. *Great Powers and Outlaw States: Unequal Sovereigns in the International Legal Order*. Cambridge University Press.

Smith, David J., 2001. *Estonia: Independence and European Integration*. London and New York: Routledge.

Smith, Jean Edward, 1992. *George Bush's War*. New York: Henry Holt and Company.

Smith, Steve, 1988. Belief Systems and the Study of International Relations. In *Belief Systems and International Relations*, edited by Richard Little and Steve Smith, 11–36. Oxford: Basil Blackwell.

Smith, Woodruff D., 1980. Friedrich Ratzel and the Origins of Lebensraum. *German Studies Review* 3 (1): 51–68.

Snyder, Jack, 2002. Anarchy and Culture: Insights from the Anthropology of War. *International Organization* 56 (1): 7–45.

Šolle, Zdeněk, 1999. Palacký, Masaryk, habsburská monarchie a střední Evropa. In *František Palacký 1798/1998, dějiny a dnešek*, edited by František Šmahel and Eva Doležalová, 467–480. Prague: Historický ústav AV ČR.

Soosaar, Enn, 2003a. Eesti tee Euroopasse: vahekokkuvõte 1997 [Estonia's Road to the European Union: Mid-way Report 1997]. In *Mõtteline Euroopa: valik esseid Euroopa Liidust* [Imagined Estonia: A Selection of Essays on the European Union], edited by Marek Tamm and Märt Väljataga, 33–52. Tallinn: Kirjastus Varrak.

2003b. Venemaa on Venemaaa on Venemaa [Russia is Russia is Russia]. *Eesti Ekspress*, 5 August.

Sparti, Davide, 1996. *Soggetti al tempo. Identità personale tra analisi filosofica e costruzione sociale*. Milan: Feltrinelli.

2000. *Identità e coscienza*. Bologna: il Mulino.

Sprengel, Rainer, 2000. Geopolitik und Nationalsozialismus: Ende einer deutschen Fehlentwicklung oder fehlgeleiteter Diskurs? In *Geopolitik. Grenzgänge im*

Zeitgeist, Band 1.1: 1890 bis 1945, edited by Irene Diekmann, Peter Krüger and Julius H. Schops, 147–168. Potsdam: Verlag für Berlin-Brandenburg.

Spykman, Nicholas, 1938. Geography and Foreign Policy, I. *American Political Science Review* 32 (1): 28–50.

Stanzione, Luigi, 1995. Le parole o le cose? Adhuc sub iudice lis est. *Geotema: Organo Ufficiale dell'Associazione Geografi Italiani* 1 (1995): 115–120.

Steele, Brent J., 2005. Ontological Security and the Power of Self-Identity: British Neutrality in the American Civil War. *Review of International Studies* 31 (3): 519–540.

———. 2007. *Ontological Security in International Relations: Self-Identity and the IR State*. London and New York: Routledge.

Stein, Janice Gross, 2002. Psychological Explanations of International Conflict. In *Handbook of International Relations*, edited by Walter Carlsnaes, Thomas Risse and Beth A. Simmons, 292–308. London: Sage.

Steinbruner, John D., Jr., 1974. *The Cybernetic Theory of Decision: New Dimensions of Political Analysis*. Princeton University Press.

Sterling-Folker, Jennifer, 2006. Lamarckian with a Vengeance: Human Nature and American International Relations Theory. *Journal of International Relations and Development* 9 (3): 227–246.

Stoiber, Edmund, 1993. SZ Interview mit Edmund Stoiber. *Süddeutsche Zeitung*, 2 November. Available at: web.nexis-lexis.com. On file with author.

Stürmer, Michael, 1992. *Die Grenzen der Macht. Begegnung der Deutschen mit der Geschichte*. Berlin: Siedler.

Sur, Étienne, 1995. La référence à la *Geopolitik*, ou la tentation du déterminisme spatial. *Matériaux pour l'histoire de notre temps* (37–38): 31–37.

Taagepera, Rein, 1998. Endise tsiviilgarnisoni integratsioon. *Postimees*, 21 September. Available at: www.postimees.ee/leht/98/09/21/arvamus.htm (accessed 21 March 2000).

———. 1999. Europa into Estonia, Estonia into Europa. *Global Estonian*, Summer: 24–27.

Tamm, Marek and Märt Väljataga, eds., 2003. *Mötteline Euroopa: valik esseid Euroopa Liidust* [Imagined Estonia: A Selection of Essays on the European Union]. Tallinn: Kirjastus Varrak.

Taylor, Philip M., 1992. *War and the Media: Propaganda and Persuasion in the Gulf War*. Manchester and New York: Manchester University Press.

Thelen, Kathleen, 1999. Historical Institutionalism in Comparative Politics. *Annual Review of Political Science* 2: 369–404.

———. 2000. Timing and Temporality in the Analysis of Institutional Evolution and Change. *Studies in American Political Development* 14 (Spring): 101–108.

Thies, Jochen, 1993. Perspektiven deutscher Außenpolitik. In *Westbindung: Chancen und Risiken für Deutschland*, edited by Rainer Zitelmann, Karlheinz Weißmann and Michael Großheim, 523–536. Frankfurt/M.: Propyläen Verlag.

Thomas, Lewis V. and Norman Itzkowitz, 1972. *A Study of Naima*. New York University Press.

Tickner, Arlene B., 2003. Hearing Latin American Voices in International Relations Studies. *International Studies Perspectives* 4 (4): 325–350.

Tilly, Charles, 2001. Mechanisms in Political Process. *Annual Review of Political Science* 4: 21–41.

——— 2004. Observations of Social Processes and Their Formal Representation. *Sociological Theory* 22 (4): 595–602.

Torbakov, Igor, 2005. Eurasian Idea Could Bring Together Erstwhile Enemies Turkey and Russia. *Eurasia Insight*, 18 March 2002. Available at: www.eurasianet.org (accessed 5 May 2005).

Trubetzkoy, N. S., 1991. *The Legacy of Genghis Khan*. Ann Arbor: Michigan Slavic Publications.

Tsvetaeva, Marina, 1980. *The Demesne of the Swans*, trans. Robin Kemball. Ann Arbor: Ardis.

Tsymburskii, Vadim, 1993. Ostrov Rossiia (Perspektivy Rossiiskoi Geopolitiki) [Island Russia: Prospects of Russian Geopolitics]. *Polis* 5: 6–23.

——— 1995. Vtoroje Dyhanije Leviafanov [Leviathans' Second Wind]. *Polis* 1: 87–92.

——— 1998. Dve Evrasii: omonimia kak kljuch k ideologii rannego evrasiistva [Two Eurasias: Homonymy as a key to early Eurasianism]. *Acta Eurasica* 1–2: 28.

——— 1999. Geopolitika kak Mirovidenie i Rod Zanyatii [Geopolitics as a Worldview and Activity]. *Polis* 4: 7–28.

——— 2001. Eto Tvoi Poslednii Geokulturnyi Vybor, Rossija? [This is Your Last Geocultural Choice, Russia?]. *Polis*, November.

——— 2002. ZAO Rossija [Closed Joint Stock Company 'Russia']. *Russkii Zhurnal*, 8 May.

——— 2004. Halford Mackinder: Trilogiya Hartlenda i Prizvanie Geopolitika [Halford Mackinder: The Heartland Trilogy and the Calling of a Geopolitician]. *Russkii Arkhipelag*.

——— 2007. *Ostrov Rossija: Geopoliticheskie i Khronopiliticheskie Raboty, 1993–2006* [Island-Russia: Geopolitical and Chronopolitical Publications, 1993–2006]. Moscow: ROSSPEN.

Tucker, Robert W. and David C. Hendrickson, 1992. *The Imperial Temptation: The New World Order and America's Purpose*. New York: Council of Foreign Relations Press.

Tuminez, Astrid S., 1996. Russian Nationalism and the National Interest in Russian Foreign Policy. In *The Sources of Russian Foreign Policy After the Cold War*, edited by Celeste A. Wallander, 41–61. Boulder: Westview Press.

Turfan, Ruhi, 1962. *Geopolitik: Geopolitikle İlgili Ana Konular* [Geopolitics: Major Issues in Geopolitics]. İstanbul: İstanbul Matbaacılık Okulu.

'Turkey entry "would destroy EU"', 2002. BBC News, 8 November. Available at: http://news.bbc.co.uk/2/hi/europe/2420697.stm (accessed 15 May 2008).

Türk, Hikmet Sami, 1999. Turkish Defence Policy. Speech delivered at the Washington Institute for Near East Policy, 3 March 1999. Available at: www. washingtoninstitute.org (accessed 19 November 2001).

Türsan, Nurettin, 1971b. Jeopolitik ve Jeostratejinin Işığı Altında Türkiye'nin Stratejik Değeri-II [Turkey's Strategic Value in view of Geopolitics and Geostrategy-II]. *Belgelerle Türk Tarihi Dergisi* 41: 30–35.

Tyulin, Ivan, 1997. Between the Past and the Future: International Studies in Russia. *Zeitschrift für Internationale Beziehungen* 4 (1): 181–194.

Uçar, Orkun and Burak Turna, 2005. *Metal Fırtına* [Metal Storm]. İstanbul: Timaş.

Urkhanova, Rimma, 1995. Evrasiitsy i Vostok: Pragmatika Ljubvi? [Eurasians and the East: Pragmatism of Love?]. *Acta Eurasica* 1 (1995): 12–31.

Uzun, Hayrettin, 1981. Türkiye'nin Artan Jeopolitik Önemi [Turkey's Increasing Geopolitical Significance]. *Silahlı Kuvvetler Dergisi* 100 (279): 43–47.

Vähi, Tiit, 2001. Kaks suur hirmu, mis viivad Eesti elu edasi [The Two Big Fears that Advance Life in Estonia]. *Eesti Paevaleht*, 5 June.

Valdez, Jonathan, 1995. The Near Abroad, the West, and National Identity in Russian Foreign Policy. In *The Making of Foreign Policy in Russia and the States of Eurasia*, edited by Adeed Dawisha and Karen Daweesha, 84–110. Armonk: M. E. Sharpe.

Válka, Josef, 1999. Palacký a francouzští liberální historikové. In *František Palacký 1798/1998, dějiny a dnešek*, edited by František Šmahel and Eva Doležalová, 93–100. Prague: Historický ústav AV ČR.

van der Wusten, Herman and Gertjan Dijkink, 2002. German, British and French Geopolitics: The Enduring Differences. *Geopolitics* 7 (3): 19–38.

Van Evera, Stephen, 1991. Primed for Peace: Europe After the Cold War. In *The Cold War and After: Prospects for Peace*, edited by Sean M. Lynn-Jones, 193–243. Cambridge, MA: The MIT Press.

Vares, Peeter, 1999. Estonia and Russia: Interethnic Relations and Regional Security. In *Stability and Security in the Baltic Sea Region. Russian, Nordic and European Aspects*, edited by O. Knudsen. London and Portland: Frank Cass.

Vasquez, John A., 1997. The Realist Paradigm and Degenerative versus Progressive Research Programs: An Appraisal of Neotraditional Research on Waltz's Balancing Proposition. *American Political Science Review* 91 (4): 899–912.

Veber, Václav, 1939/2004. Úvod. In *V úloze mouřenína*. In Emmanuel Moravec, 5–12. Pardubice: Filip Trend Publishing.

Vennesson, Pascal, 2008. Case Studies and Process Tracing: Theories and Practices. In *Approaches and Methodologies in the Social Sciences: A Pluralist Perspective*, edited by Donatella della Porta and Michael Keating, 223–239. Cambridge University Press.

Vidal de la Blache, Paul, 1910. Régions francaises. *Revue de Paris* 6.

Vigezzi, Brunello, 1997. *L'Italia unita e le sfide della politica estera*. Milan: Unicopli.

Vihalemm, Peeter, 1997. Changing National Spaces in the Baltic Area. In *Return to the Western World: Cultural and Political Perspectives on the Estonian*

Post-Communist Transition, edited by Marju Lauristin, Peeter Vihalemm, Karl Erik Rosengren and Lennart Weibull, 129–162. Tartu University Press.

Vihalemm, Triin and Marju Lauristin, 1997. Cultural Adjustment to the Changing Societal Environment: The Case of Russians in Estonia. In *Return to the Western World: Cultural and Political Perspectives on the Estonian Post-Communist Transition*, edited by Marju Lauristin, Peeter Vihalemm, Karl Erik Rosengren and Lennart Weibull, 279–297. Tartu University Press.

Vinkovetsky, Ilya, ed. and trans., 1996. *Exodus to the East: Forebodings and Events. An Affirmation of the Eurasians*. Idyllwild: Charles Schlacks.

Virchow, Fabian, 2006. *Gegen den Zivilismus. Internationale Beziehungen und Militär in den politischen Konzeptionen der extremen Rechten*. Wiesbaden: VS Verlag für Sozialwissenschaften.

Voigt, Karsten, 2002. 'Die deutsch-französischen Beziehungen und die neue *Geopolitik*' – Rede von Karsten D. Voigt, Koordinator für die Deutsch-Amerikanische Zusammenarbeit im Auswärtigen Amt, im Rahmen des Deutsch-Französisches Seminars der Association Jean Monnet am 05.07.02. Available at: www.auswaertiges-amt.de/diplo/de/Infoservice/Presse/Reden/Archiv/2002/020705-DtFrBeziehungen.html (accessed: 12 January 2005).

Wæver, Ole, 1995. Securitization and Desecuritization. In *On Security*, edited by Ronnie Lipschutz, 46–86. New York: Columbia University Press.

1996. European Security Identities. *Journal of Common Market Studies* 34 (1): 103–132.

2002. Identity, Communities and Foreign Policy: Discourse Analysis as Foreign Policy Theory. In *European Integration and National Identity: The Challenge of the Nordic States*, edited by Lene Hansen and Ole Wæver, 20–49. London and New York: Routledge.

Wagener, Martin, 2004. Auf dem Weg zu einer 'normalen' Macht? Die Entsendung deutscher Streitkräft in der Ära Schröder. *Trierer Arbeitspapiere zur Internationalen Politik* 8.

Walker, Stephen G., ed., 1987. *Role Theory and Foreign Policy Analysis*. Durham, NC: Duke University Press.

Walt, Stephen M., 1987. *The Origins of Alliances*. Ithaca: Cornell University Press.

Waltz, Kenneth N., 1979. *Theory of International Politics*. Reading: Addison-Wesley.

Watzal, Ludwig, 1993. Der Irrweg von Maastricht. In *Westbindung: Chancen und Risiken für Deutschland*, edited by Rainer Zitelmann, Karlheinz Weißmann and Michael Großheim, 477–500. Frankfurt/M.: Propyläen Verlag.

Weber, Joachim F., 1992. Renaissance der Geopolitik. Deutschland in der Orientierungskrise. *Criticon* 129: 31–33.

Weldes, Jutta, 1996. Constructing National Interests. *European Journal of International Relations* 2 (3): 275–318.

1999a. *Constructing National Interests: The United States and the Cuban Missile Crisis*. Minneapolis: University of Minnesota Press.

1999b. The Cultural Production of Crises: U.S. Identity and Missiles in Cuba. In *Cultures of Insecurity: States, Communities and the Production of Danger*, edited by Jutta Weldes, Mark Laffey, Hugh Gusterson and Raymond Duvall, 35–62. University of Minneapolis Press.

Wendt, Alexander, 1992. Anarchy is what States Make of it: The Social Construction of Power Politics. *International Organization* 46 (2): 391–425.

1995. Constructing International Politics. *International Security* 20 (1): 71–81.

1999. *Social Theory of International Politics*. Cambridge University Press.

2000. On the Via Media: A Response to the Critics. *Review of International Studies* 26: 165–180.

2003. Why a World State is Inevitable: Teleology and the Logic of Anarchy. *European Journal of International Relations* 9 (4): 491–542.

2004. The State as Person in International Theory. *Review of International Studies* 30 (2): 289–316.

Wiberg, Håkan, 1992. Peace Research and Eastern Europe. In *The End of the Cold War: Evaluating Theories of International Relations*, edited by Pierre Allan and Kjell Goldmann, 147–178. Dordrecht: Martinus Nijhoff.

Wight, Colin, 2004a. State Agency: Social Action without Human Activity? *Review of International Studies* 30 (2): 269–280.

2004b. Theorizing the Mechanisms of Conceptual and Semiotic Space. *Philosophy of the Social Sciences* 34 (2): 283–299.

2006. *Agents, Structures and International Relations: Politics as Ontology*. Cambridge University Press.

Williams, Michael C., 2005. What is the National Interest? The Neoconservative Challenge in IR Theory. *European Journal of International Relations* 11 (3): 307–337.

Williams, Michael C. and Iver B. Neumann, 2000. From Alliance to Security Community: NATO, Russia, and the Power of Identity. *Millennium: Journal of International Studies* 29 (2): 357–387.

Wohlforth, William C., 1993. *The Elusive Balance: Power and Perceptions during the Cold War*. Ithaca: Cornell University Press.

1994/1995. Realism and the End of the Cold War. *International Security* 19 (3): 91–129.

Wolfers, Arnold, 1962. *Discord and Collaboration: Essays on International Politics*. Baltimore and London: The Johns Hopkins University Press.

Yanık, Lerna K., 2008. Those Crazy Turks that Got Caught in the 'Metal Storm': Nationalism in Turkey's Best Seller Lists. *RSCAS Working Paper*. Available at: http://hdl.handle.net/1814/8002 (accessed 22 May 2008).

2009. Valles of the Wolves-Iraq: Anti-geopolitics. *Alla Turca, Middle East Journal of Culture and Communication* 2 (1): 153–170.

Yee, Albert S., 1996. The Causal Effects of Ideas on Politics. *International Organization* 50 (1): 69–108.

Yılmaz, Eylem and Pinar Bilgin, 2005. Constructing Turkey's 'Western' Identity during the Cold War: Discourses of the 'Intellectuals of Statecraft'. *International Journal* 61 (1): 39–59.

Yılmaz, Mehmet, 2001. Derin bir Kitap (A Deep Book). *Zaman*, 4 June.

Zatulin, Konstantin, 2008. Pochemu nam nado segodnja priznat' nezavisimost' Abhazii i Juzhnoi Osetii [Why do We Need to Recognise the Independence of Abkhazia and South Ossetia Today]. *Izvestia*, 25 August.

Zehfuss, Maja, 2001. Constructivism and Identity: A Dangerous Liaison. *European Journal of International Relations* 7 (3): 315–348.

—— 2002. *Constructivism in International Relations: The Politics of Reality.* Cambridge University Press.

Zieleniec, Josef, 1992a. Rozhovor Národní obrody s ministrem mezinárodních vztahů ČR Josefem Zieleniecem – Aj po rozvode si ostaneme blízki (6 October 1992). *Československá zahraniční politika – dokumenty* 39 (10). Prague: Federal Ministry of Foreign Affairs, 885–888.

—— 1992b. Rozhovor ministra mezinárodních vztahů ČR Josefa Zieleniece v Práci (29 September 1992). *Československá zahraniční politika – dokumenty* 39 (9). Prague: Federal Ministry of Foreign Affairs, 836–839.

—— 1993. Rozhovor ministra zahraničí Josefa Zieleniece pro Hospodářské noviny – Dva státy, dvě diplomacie (19 January 1993). *Česká zahraniční politika – dokumenty* 40 (1). Prague: Czech Ministry of Foreign Affairs, 74–79.

Zitelmann, Rainer, Karlheinz Weißmann and Michael Großheim, eds., 1993. *Westbindung: Chancen und Risiken für Deutschland.* Frankfurt/M.: Propyläen Verlag.

INDEX

CAMBRIDGE STUDIES IN INTERNATIONAL RELATIONS

Lightning Source UK Ltd.
Milton Keynes UK
UKOW04f0615070115

244069UK00002B/181/P